Llewellyn's 1993 Sun Sign Book

Printed in the United States of America
Typography property of Llewellyn Worldwide, Ltd.

ISBN: 0-87542-901-7

Cover art from Images Colour Library

Forecasts: Gloria Star

**Contributing Writers: Sharon L. Harbeck &
Scott Hubanks, Jean A. Innis, Ninah Kessler,
Anthony Louis, Roxana Muise, Vince Ploscik,
Carolyn Reynolds, Louise Riotte, Bruce Scofield,
Philip Sedgwick**

Editor: Emily Nedell

Published by
LLEWELLYN WORLDWIDE, LTD.

Distributed by:
W. FOULSHAM & CO. LTD.,
EOVIL ROAD, SLOUGH, SL1 4JH ENGLAND

DECEMBER 1992	JANUARY 1993	FEBRUARY 1993
S M T W T F S	S M T W T F S	S M T W T F S
1 2 3 4 5	1 2	1 2 3 4 5 6
6 7 8 9 10 11 12	3 4 5 6 7 8 9	7 8 9 10 11 12 13
13 14 15 16 17 18 19	10 11 12 13 14 15 16	14 15 16 17 18 19 20
20 21 22 23 24 25 26	17 18 19 20 21 22 23	21 22 23 24 25 26 27
27 28 29 30 31	24 25 26 27 28 29 30	28
	31	

MARCH 1993	APRIL 1993	MAY 1993
S M T W T F S	S M T W T F S	S M T W T F S
1 2 3 4 5 6	1 2 3	1
7 8 9 10 11 12 13	4 5 6 7 8 9 10	2 3 4 5 6 7 8
14 15 16 17 18 19 20	11 12 13 14 15 16 17	9 10 11 12 13 14 15
21 22 23 24 25 26 27	18 19 20 21 22 23 24	16 17 18 19 20 21 22
28 29 30 31	25 26 27 28 29 30	23 24 25 26 27 28 29
		30 31

JUNE 1993	JULY 1993	AUGUST 1993
S M T W T F S	S M T W T F S	S M T W T F S
1 2 3 4 5	1 2 3	1 2 3 4 5 6 7
6 7 8 9 10 11 12	4 5 6 7 8 9 10	8 9 10 11 12 13 14
13 14 15 16 17 18 19	11 12 13 14 15 16 17	15 16 17 18 19 20 21
20 21 22 23 24 25 26	18 19 20 21 22 23 24	22 23 24 25 26 27 28
27 28 29 30	25 26 27 28 29 30 31	29 30 31

SEPTEMBER 1993	OCTOBER 1993	NOVEMBER 1993
S M T W T F S	S M T W T F S	S M T W T F S
1 2 3 4	1 2	1 2 3 4 5 6
5 6 7 8 9 10 11	3 4 5 6 7 8 9	7 8 9 10 11 12 13
12 13 14 15 16 17 18	10 11 12 13 14 15 16	14 15 16 17 18 19 20
19 20 21 22 23 24 25	17 18 19 20 21 22 23	21 22 23 24 25 26 27
26 27 28 29 30	24 25 26 27 28 29 30	28 29 30
	31	

DECEMBER 1993	JANUARY 1994	FEBRUARY 1994
S M T W T F S	S M T W T F S	S M T W T F S
1 2 3 4	1	1 2 3 4 5 6 7
5 6 7 8 9 10 11	2 3 4 5 6 7 8	8 9 10 11 12 13 14
12 13 14 15 16 17 18	9 10 11 12 13 14 15	15 16 17 18 19 20 21
19 20 21 22 23 24 25	16 17 18 19 20 21 22	22 23 24 25 26 27 28
26 27 28 29 30 31	23 24 25 26 27 28 29	
	30 31	

Contents

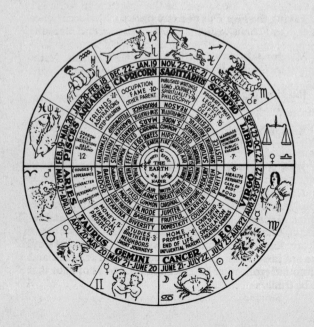

1993—
The Year of the Snake

Philip Sedgwick

1993, the highly touted year of enlightenment, is finally here. Not since 1989, when Saturn and Neptune had made three conjunctions, and before that 1988, when Saturn and Uranus had made three alignments, has there been such excitement in the astrological community. This time, with three of the aspects about to occur, the anticipation rises significantly higher.

When Uranus and Neptune occupy the same degrees in the zodiac in 1993 it will be the first time in some 171 years (171.40 years to be precise) since such an occurrence took place. The alignment in 1989 of Saturn and Neptune occurs once every 35.87 years, while 1988's Saturn to Uranus configurations repeat at 45.36 year intervals. Naturally, the astrological stakes are higher this year within this longer cycle.

It was last in 1821, and before that in 1650, when Uranus and Neptune aligned at the same zodiacal degrees. Everywhere you go in astrological circles this year, the topics will focus on how profound alignment of these two outer planets should be.

What makes this alignment so significant is not just the length of the cycle of the conjunctions. The fact that Uranus and Neptune will park right in front of a nearby (relatively speaking) unusual galactic entity adds to the importance. Think of the two planets like crystals, magnifying and reflecting the energy of this powerful point in space into a clearer focus for Earthlings to receive. In theory, anyway, we are in store for gobs of potential enlightenment and profound realization for Humankind. Let's hope for that to be true.

First the technical data on the conjunctions themselves. The first exact alignment of Uranus and Neptune begins on February 2, 1993 at 8:11 a.m., GMT (Greenwich Mean Time) at 19 Capricorn 34. The second conjunction involving both planets in retrograde motion results at 7:44 a.m., GMT, August 20th, 1993 at 18 Capricorn 48. The third act of this astrological production concludes at 8:18 p.m., GMT, October 24, 1993 at 18 Capricorn 32.

Yes, all of the above time frames will mark significant occurrences within the realm of human reaction, but when Uranus and Neptune emphasize the energy of Star System SS433, the fun should really begin! SS433 is a highly anomalistic binary star system consisting of a neutron star and a yellow star locked in some sort of gravitational do-si-do around each other. From the Earth's point of view, SS433 resides at the zodiacal placement of 19 Capricorn 56. Naturally this point will affect everyone born on the 19th through 21st days of each sign. Those more significantly affected are those born in Capricorn conjunct this point (January 10th ± 5 days), those in opposition through Cancer (July 12th ± 5 days), and the squares from Aries and Libra (April 10th ± 5 days; October 13th ± 5 days). Through the use of other astrological angles of importance, the semi-square (45°) and the sesquiquadrate (135°) the following dates of birth may also feel the importance of these alignments more personally: February 23rd ± 3 days, May 26th ± 3 days, August 28th ± 3 days and November 27th ± 3 days.

SS433 tilts at an unusual angle as seen from Earth. This angle provides the binary system with a periodic wobble—a precession—which half the time appears to be approaching us and half the time seems to be receding. Stated in astronomical terms, the object blue shifts (approach) and red shifts (retreat) in intervals of 82 days, half of an overall 164 day resonance. Aloha! It seems difficult to know if one is coming or going! Or in Sanskrit terms, "Namaste." Namaste means that one recognizes the Divinity of another and likewise, allowing for a bi-directional spiritual mirroring. Today in India the term loosely applies to hello and good-bye, a major attenuation of the spiritual implication.

When astronomers draw the patterns of light shifts seen from SS433, a spiraling pattern of alternating red and blue lines 180° degrees out of phase with one another emerges. This pattern, if oriented vertically, closely resembles the double helix structure of the DNA molecule, as well as the energy patterns prevailing in front of the Hindu god, Shiva. Shiva is the god who represents the basic essence of Kundalini, a term which means coiled, like a snake. A theory of Kundalini is that the snake-like coils represent the integrated spiritual energy of an individual's spirit in body. With this level of enlightenment one assumes full power, manifests total creativity and acts as a karmic magnet, drawing in all appropriate things for the evolution of the soul.

The essence of this potent inner power source is emphasized by SS433 at its most basic level. The alignments of Uranus and Neptune to this star system this year stand to provide incredible breakthroughs in our awarenesses of what the essence of life really is. Realizations about DNA, life extension (serious consideration given to the possibility for immortality), the integration of spirit in the body and appropriate use of sexual energy are all likely. It would be reasonable to assume that advances in genetic engineering, cracking the DNA/RNA codes, issues of birth (Roe v. Wade) and death (euthanasia) stand to occupy legislative, political, theological and philosophical channels.

On a personal level, each individual will be called to recognize his/her own inner energy for what it is and pull it up from the base of the spine, through all vital energy centers, and claim full birthright of creativity, understanding, and capability. It is important to recognize that pull up, not push up, is the correct term. The energy of Kundalini originates at the base of the spine, near the tail bone, rises along the vertebrae and extends out the top of the head. This inner magnet creates the core of one's aura, feeling, sensitivity, creativity—vibes, if you will.

This rush of energy can be recognized by a corkscrewing spiral of vitality accelerating up the backbone. This can be induced by a shudder of fear or a shiver of excitement, in either case, a clear proclamation of one's aliveness! When the Kundalini releases on a regular basis an individual feels more creative, more at peace, more powerful and more aware of life. Colors get brighter, smells become more intense and all sensory perceptions approach maximum levels.

To accentuate this energy, which should be easy to do with all of the galactic support this year, two things must take place. First, each person must decide to really dig into life and participate fully with unlimited vigor and make "passion" the keyword. Secondly, each individual must accept all inner talents, creative abilities and agree to utilize them in life in an innocent, non-cynical manner, assuming that the fruits of one's labors will be rewarded. Simple, right? Maybe in theory.

SS433 personifies the fear of accomplishment, the pressures of success and the performance pressure which accompanies doing something great once. Should any of these anxieties kick into high gear, odds are that one will back away from the desired goal. Overcoming these fears requires a re-programming of one's DNA; or, put into today's metaphysical jargon, clearing one's Karma. Regardless of where it comes from, the womb, a past life, childhood, many people hold resident fears in the memories of their cells. These memories periodically activate, ruining innocent approach to life and causing the negative driving force of the critic who lives in the heads of most people. "Who do you think you are?" "What makes you think you're special?" "Who said you could think up new ideas?" are examples of the psychological red marking pencil many use to defeat themselves in life even before getting started.

Several things can be done to assist the elimination of this negative process. First and foremost, breathe! Unlock the jaw, push the shoulders back and breathe fully from as deep inside the body as possible. Make sure that the exhales are not regulated like the thrust of a 747 on take off. Just let it out however it wants to come. Recall childhood fantasies of what ideal adult life was supposed to be like. Do things which are fun and for which you feel burning passion. Visualize each of your body parts rejuvenating on a daily basis. Discuss your creative fantasies with others who can understand those fantasies. Become sensitive to your body's rhythms.

SS433 maintains a long term cycle of 164 days to rotate about once in its precessionary evolution. For 82 days the relentless pursuit of something can be maintained, then it must be chilled for 82 days, then reactivated for 82 days. Individuals who have to be creative for a living are aware of the cycles of creativity. Some call it a flow, a *tao*, or many writers in Hollywood refer to it as "juice."

A second cycle resides within SS433 of 13.1 days in length. Individuals connected to this point in their birth chart tend to respond to this resonance physically. In 1993 all people will try to catch the wave of this rhythm and use it productively. This period subdivides into two 6.55 day intervals, roughly a week. Notice that when the SS433 cycles are active the best use of energy is a week on/a week off, with three times the activity in the "ON" week as the "OFF" week. Since most people tend to ride this cycle out of phase, inspiring that "always tired" mode in life, try for two consecutive low energy weeks prior to bringing personal output to full speed again. Any of the timing cycles of activity to SS433 in 1993 will serve as an appropriate trigger for this change in action.

It is most interesting to notice that the setup for this grand parade of energy events in 1993 started before the first of the year. In fact, Mars in October of 1992 began the most recent sequence of activity. That trigger was only a recall of decisions made on July 11, 1991, when the total solar eclipse at 18 Cancer 59 in opposition prepared us for these powerful connections. Incidentally, that eclipse (combined with a few other aspects) brought about the long overdue nuclear weapons reduction treaty signed in July, 1991.

So on October 22, 1992, Mars in Cancer opposed SS433, directly aligned with the 1991 eclipse. This represented some sort of obstruction so aggravating you gritted your teeth. That's right. Now breathe and remember what the big picture goal is as you ease into 1993. Good!

Mars reviews this point, retrograde, on January 2nd, making sure that your New Year's resolutions are consistent with your aspirations and fullness of potential. If not, well, not to worry, help is on the way! February loads it up in a big way as Uranus crosses in front of SS433 on the 8th, waking you up to the dream again. It's shocking to realize that you may not be "on your path" but the vision comes back again to be re-enforced on the 12th as Neptune embraces SS433. Notice how good it feels to be back in touch with what you really want to do!

Mars completes the oppositions to SS433 on April 4th, just in time for the tax season. Maybe those energies you thought were in opposition to your fulfillment aren't as taxing as it seems; maybe it just requires attracting support for your efforts instead of resistance to verify your strength. Mars is also the next trigger in 1993 as it forms a sesquiquadrate (135°) to SS433 on July 1st from its placement in Virgo. Despite the ominous sound of this, the implication is simplify, get rid of distractions and unneeded negativity and create clear, well developed priorities.

This organizational track is necessary at this point, as just four days later on July 5th, Neptune celebrates your personal independence by reviewing the dream and feeling the freedom which comes from locking on to your visions for life fully, with passion and powerful resilience. Uranus plays cosmic traffic cop and directs a few necessary changes in direction and momentum, mostly momentum, occurring on July 19th.

Now the really tricky track of all this swirling and shifting occurs in September. On September 11th, Mars forms a square to SS433 from Libra followed by a Jupiter square, also from Libra on September 24th. These somewhat tense configurations require the breaking away from all those who do not support your personal evolution—a sort of freedom from spiritual codependence, if you will. Some separation anxiety may be experienced but should be healed not later than November 15th, when Mars semi-squares (45°) SS433 from early Sagittarius. This energy stands to align you with those who think like you, who are similarly committed to being full of themselves, powerful and creative in spirit.

The last of the powerful connections of the trans-Saturnian planets to SS433 both come in December. Uranus brings forth a new awareness of the intended path on December 1st. This sounds like someone listening to a tape of an astrological reading done nine months before saying, "Oh WOW! That's what that meant!" It sure is, and isn't it great how the sequence has evolved?! As the final adjustments are made in reclaiming personal talent and daring to use it, the dream becomes even richer and more realized on December 17th as Neptune strolls past SS433 for the final inspiration injection.

By this time in 1993, even if things have only progressed at an all right rate, the wriggling excitement of feeling the results of full creativity energy should have you doing the dance of the Kundalini snake. A younger appearance, a more sustained level of vitality and an increase in your overall contentment stand to be the products of this path of progress. Not a bad investment for spending a year reconnecting to who you really are and finding out where you really want to go in life!

Some of you may not be born on the 20th day, plus or minus a few, of a sign, nor on the fifth day of a sign, nor have any major planets, angles, configurations, or other obscure astrological debris making contact with this potent point, SS433. Not to lament. These alignments are taking place. At some point or in some house in your natal horoscope this energy will be pumping up an aspect of your life. A summary of house placements for the SS433, 19 Capricorn 56 alignments follow. If you do not know the houses of your horoscope, you may wish to consult a professional astrologer or send away for one of the many fine, accurate computer horoscope analyses available.

THE SS433 ALIGNMENTS
BY HOUSE PLACEMENT

First House: Here the call is to be full of yourself. Breathe, relax the throat muscles and allow for others to know what you really desire to do. Then, as it has been stated in the Cosmic Doctrine of athletic shoes, Just Do It!! Remember that a journey of a thousand miles begins with one step. The fulfillment of a dream of a lifetime begins with a thought, a breath and a simple action.

Second House: How resourceful can you perceive yourself to be? You are not what you have, or have done. More you are what you desire to do. Your greatest asset in this time will be the uninhibited passion to produce the fullness of all your talents, backed by the belief that some of the best attributes are of spirit and intangible.

Third House: If it is true that as one thinketh, so one is, then you may have a little cobweb cleaning to do in your head. Don't hide those thoughts, express them. Implement the ideas. The ideas may be different, possibly confrontational, but that doesn't make them wrong. Insist on being heard. But in order to do that you must first express.

Fourth House: It is time to abandon the idea of a little fledgling and to ensure a hearty push out of the nest. Bounce your energies and passions off others who carry the same desires. Find yourself at home with those who understand the beat of your drum and create a powwow of support, not a drumming into the ground of your nature by those afraid to lose you.

Fifth House: Certainly, these are one of the strongest groups of people to need to do something with all the energy trying to burst through. Birth be given, not necessarily to a child, but to that thing which has been nurtured in your heart for so long. Stretch your shoulders, rub your heart and get over yourself.

Sixth House: Healing is important here before anything else. Get rid of toxins, bad habits, negative companions and daily routines which take up time and don't get anything done. Then there should be room for prioritizing what should be done first. Body work on the shoulders and feet is good. Take a stand and show others how to heal.

Seventh House: This is probably the only placement in which another individual can be successfully included in the process of evolution with one major contingency. The partner of choice must be completely aligned with the effort. It might be a good idea here not to discuss efforts or progress until YOU are content with the final results. Be all one (all-one = alone), whatever it takes.

Eighth House: This position is clearly one of the most critical of the sequence. Passion is the largest factor here, yet passion may be severely critiqued by the inner editor and discounted. Minimizing emotional reactions is extremely negative. Body work could focus on the hips and buttocks and chin. For these persons the physical sensations may be some of the strongest and scariest. Find a good teacher on mystical body energies such as Kundalini

Yoga, Tantra, chakras. Pick sexual activities which are regenerative only!

Ninth House: A strong, yet resilient, mindset is required to implement the nature of this configuration. Surely, at least ten times in 1993, it will be assumed, "Eureka!" Not yet. That was only a step in the awareness agenda. Listen to the views of others embarking on similar travels with different destinations. Seek the common denominator of truth.

Tenth House: This is the most intense of all of the SS433 placements. These individuals should feel the call of a specific, highly stylized destiny. These are not delusions of grandeur; these are the call to fulfillment of spirit and the acknowledgement of destiny. If the Whole Purpose of activity is understood, the accomplishments possible may exceed one's wildest expectation. Buttocks, mouth and chest work are essential.

Eleventh House: This crew of people also need to assemble a large supporting cast. The burden on these individuals is the one of being the first to proclaim the unusual, create a new idea or even greater in difficulty: to state the obvious. These are the people needed to get the ball, not rolling, but spiraling with a new slant on the same old perspectives. Allies will be essential.

Twelfth House: These are the souls requiring that feelings be fully felt, grounded, and made part of the nature, not apart from one's nature. A fear of overreacting may occur, but really the conflict would be based upon not reacting enough. Remember that the backbone spiral of energy may be partly based on fear, before it transforms into the thrill of aliveness. Ankle massage and rotation may help these spirits be less restless.

Well there you have it—A new slant on the same old repetitive pattern of Uranus and Neptune. This is a cataclysmic time. It is a time of empowerment, of fullness of one's fruits, reverence of all one's inner gifts and respectful of the inner gifts of others. If all these factors are kept in mind, then the rest will take care of itself.

Wriggle and shiver to the vibrating energies of your inner spirit, in this, a symbolic year of the Kundalini snake! Namaste.

Taking the Fear Out of Retrogrades

Roxana Muise

It's time to remove the fear associated with retrograde motion. Astrology is a symbolic language composed of tools for self understanding; and there is no need to be afraid of tools if they are correctly used. Retrograde motion, used properly as a tool, can provide much constructive information about the process of living. Contemporary astrologers use this information to help their clients to improve their lives, but retrogrades were not always regarded so favorably.

ASTROLOGY IN THE PAST

Astrologers of the past believed that a retrograde planet in a natal chart was ineffective—or worse, evil or cursed, and transiting retrograde planets were associated with difficulties, obstacles, and even death. Guido Bonatus (ca. 1220-1300) considered a retrograde planet to be at the top of his list of ways that planets could be debilitated, weakened, and afflicted.[1] William Lilly (1602-1681) said of retrogrades: "When any planet is decreasing in longitude ... It is a very great debility."[2]

Modern astrologers do not share this belief. Considerable study and observation have been done since the 17th century to show the positive potential of retrogrades, but the fear connected with retrograde planets lingers on.

Hundreds of years ago, when only kings and great leaders could afford to have their horoscopes drawn, astrologers were few, and had little time to observe more than the small number of charts that they could calculate by hand. Only the planets that could be seen with the naked eye could be used; and since that gave them only a small number of variables to use in a chart, each item took

14

on greater importance. These astrologers were primarily asked about life-or-death issues. Whatever befell the ruler of a country influenced everyone he ruled, and so his horoscope became the horoscope of the people. Compared to conditions today, life and astrology were less sophisticated, and fewer choices were available. The choices of a ruler were likely to bring about dramatic changes for the lives of all his people.

ASTROLOGY TODAY

Today's astrologers deal more with process than crisis. This is not, as some might think, because astrologers do not wish to upset their clients, but rather because new data based on improved understanding of the workings of the solar system (giving contemporary astrologers more data to use in their delineations) and repeated observations (computers make it possible for them to do a great number of accurate charts) has shown astrologers that retrogrades really do offer constructive options to life problems. Modern observations show that people do survive, and even thrive, with retrograde planets in their natal charts. It has been observed time and time again by many modern astrologers that transiting retrogrades offer unique perspectives that can help to avert a crisis.

RETROGRADE MOTION EXPLAINED

Modern science and technology enables us to record and understand the astronomical data upon which astrology relies. If we viewed the solar system from its center, the Sun, we would see all the planets moving in their orbits in one direction without interruption. Seen from the earth, planets often seem to slow down in their normal orbits, stop, and move in the opposite (retrograde) direction. We know that this retrograde motion is an illusion, a result of our perspective from the Earth.

Here's how the illusion works: Say that you (the Earth) and eight others (the other planets) are running in a counter-clockwise direction around a small circular track. Each of you has your own lane. You are about to catch up to and pass the other runners. Mercury and Venus are in their lanes on your left, and Mars, Jupiter, Saturn, Uranus, Neptune and Pluto are in their lanes on your right. From your perspective, as you move forward and pass the runners on your right and you left, it seems as if they are moving backward, although from someone (the Sun) standing in the center of the track, it looks like all the runners are still moving in the same direction.

Periodically, all of the planets except the Sun[3] and the Moon go retrograde. Pluto, Neptune and Uranus are retrograde about five months out of the year. Saturn and Jupiter are retrograde for more than four months each year; and Mars averages eleven weeks of retrograde motion every two years. Inside the Earth's orbit, Venus averages six weeks of retrograde motion each 19 months; and Mercury retrogrades three times a year for two to three weeks at a time. There are very few days during a year when there is not at least one planet in its retrograde path, and so you can see that retrograde motion is an important phenomenon that must be considered when interpreting a chart.

THE RETROGRADE PROCESS

From an astrological viewpoint, when a planet goes through the retrograde portion of its cycle, it travels through a portion of the zodiac three times—first forward—then backward—then forward again. The time planets spend moving through this area three times is called the Retrograde Period. You might think of that section of the zodiac as temporarily sensitized—as if it were symbolically marked with a retrograde flag, which casts a shadow over the entire area. In 1980, I first referred to this area of the zodiac as the Retrograde Shadow. As the planet moves through the Shadow for the first time, ideas and situations will emerge that will need to be re-examined during the rest of the retrograde cycle. While the planet is actually retrograde, a different perspective will be available. There may be a reversal of energies at this time. This is a time to gather information and review what has been happening. When the planet turns "direct" and moves through the Shadow for the last time, a new perspective may be viewed; and all that was learned during the first two passes may be absorbed and integrated. When the planet leaves the Shadow, that knowledge may be put into practice. This shadowed area of the zodiac is in every chart, and will have special meaning for each person.

An advantage of the retrograde cycle is that it allows you to look at a situation three times from different perspectives. Symbolically, we might say that an area of your life is highlighted, pointed out to you so that you may examine it more closely.

In addition, when a planet is retrograde, it is closer to the Earth than when it is moving forward in the zodiac. So, a retrograde planet can signal you to pay attention to a condition that is right under your nose. For example, imagine that you are close enough to see someone about to spill a cup of coffee on your new white couch. This is a signal for you to pay attention. You may be able to take action to avoid the incident, or move quickly to clean up a mess.

Another example shows that closeness may also have disadvantages. Stand with your nose touching a door. Now, try to observe any details about the texture of the door, the size of the door, or the frame around the door. Closeness makes perspective difficult.

RETROGRADE MESSAGES

What can we learn from retrograde planets and what can we do during retrograde periods?

1. Know that there is an area of your life that needs more of your attention than usual.

2. Be aware of concepts and principles and avoid getting lost in details.

3. Avoid rushing into making decisions—there may be information that you are not yet aware of, or have missed.

4. Expect to feel more intensity than usual—and know that the intensity will pass.

5. Reexamine situations for new perspectives and to correct possible errors.

6. Plan some time to be by yourself to work on internal processes.

PLANETARY STATIONS

The day upon which a planet turns retrograde or direct (forward motion) is very powerful and intense—even more so if there is a contact to one of your natal planets. Figure 1 shows the positions in the zodiac of the retrograde shadows for 1993. You may want to write your natal planets into the wheel to see if they contact any of the retrograde paths. If you don't know the positions of your planets, Llewellyn Personal Services will calculate your chart for you.

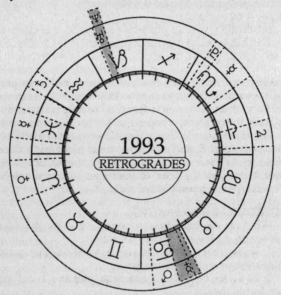

Figure 1

Knowing about the retrograde periods ahead of time enables you to enter them with conscious awareness. The following is a list of the retrograde periods for 1993 and some hints about using the energies constructively.

1993 RETROGRADE PLANETS

Mercury

    Enters Shadow February 13, 1993
    Turns Retrograde February 27, 1993 24 Pisces 13
    Turns Direct March 22, 1993 10 Pisces 17
    Leaves Shadow April 11, 1993

Enters Shadow June 14, 1993
Turns Retrograde July 1, 1993 28 Cancer 15
Turns Direct July 25, 1993 18 Cancer 09
Leaves Shadow August 9, 1993

Enters Shadow October 6, 1993
Turns Retrograde October 25, 1993 22 Scorpio 30
Turns Direct November 15, 1993 6 Scorpio 32
Leaves Shadow December 1, 1993

Mercury's symbolism deals with information gathering, communication, and mental processes such as problem-solving and decision making. When Mercury is moving backwards in the zodiac—retracing its steps, so to speak—then you may take that as a hint to mentally retrace your steps in the endeavors of the past two or three weeks, to see if you have left something undone, or missed some fact important to the future. If possible, you might ask a few more questions before signing important contracts or give some extra thought to the possible effects of important decisions. At this time, it is as if the mental part of you wants a period of time to review or to finish things that you started but haven't finished. This is a great time to carry out research projects, clean out files or closets, repair damaged items, or do the mending that has been piling up.

All three Mercury retrograde periods will be in water signs this year, beginning with the last water sign, Pisces, then in Cancer (first water sign), and finally in Scorpio (second water sign). Mercury, associated with the mind and the breath, and concerned with order and routine, is not at home in water, which symbolizes emotional energy. In this environment, Mercury is flooded with feelings and sentimentality; logic and order are under siege.

If you know ahead of time when Mercury is going to be retrograde, then you can prepare for that period of time by being more careful in your communication. Avoid being embroiled in emotional arguments that you can't win. Plan to have time to finish things and clear the clutter and complexity out of your life. You can be sure that more information will surface as Mercury turns direct and travels through its shadow for the third time.

Venus

> Enters Shadow February 6, 1993
> Turns Retrograde March 11, 1993 20 Aries 01
> Turns Direct April 22, 1993 3 Aries 44
> Leaves Shadow May 26, 1993

The symbolism connected with Venus deals with values, connections, and attractions. Venus is the name of the Goddess of Love; and love always plays a part in these situations. When Venus is retrograde you have the opportunity to see another view of the things and people that you value or love. People may not live up to your expectations; or you may find that something that you thought was valuable turns out to be an imitation. Conversely, what you thought was junk may turn out to be a valuable antique. This is a perfect time to examine your values. When Venus is retrograde something always comes up in your life to give you the opportunity to review your relationships. For instance, new, short-term relationships may appear at this time. This year Venus retrogrades in Aries, where she is not too comfortable. Aries is a fire sign, and is the epitome of excitement and movement and change, but Venus likes to keep things connected and calm and comfortable. And forces will arise to stir things up and challenge your needs for togetherness and stability. The challenge will be to trust your own sense of balance and inner calm to see you through this tense time. Avoid confrontations with others that can make either of you seem wrong. Be aware of the way that you interact with others; be especially conscious of what you expect of others; and don't promise anything that makes you feel uncomfortable.

Use the early shadow time to re-evaluate your relationships with the people in your life whom you value. And most important, examine your relationship with yourself—if you're not living up to your own values, this is a good time to make some plans to remedy this condition. You can take time to evaluate and investigate possibilities, and plan. However, this is not a good time to start a new project—chances are that you will end up with something other than what you really want. Impulsive beginnings won't have staying power at this time. If you can plan ahead of time for Venus retrograde, plan some time to be by yourself. Read some inspirational material, or listen to some dramatic classical music. Write in a journal and ask yourself some burning questions about things that are important to you. Answers are bound to surface after Venus turns direct and moves through the final shadow.

Mars

Enters the shadow September 28, 1992
Turns retrograde November 28, 1992 27 Cancer 37
Turns direct February 15, 1993 8 Cancer 41
Leaves shadow April 22, 1993

Mars symbolism deals with accomplishing your goals and getting what you want; it deals with passion and courage. Mars is a fiery planet, who is not comfortable in the Moon's sign, Cancer; but that is where he will spend this retrograde period. Frustration and temper tantrums will be displayed during this time. If you know about this retrograde period ahead of time, carefully outline what you wish to accomplish during the critical time of Mars' shadow and retrograde, and remind yourself not to overextend yourself or overindulge in emotional traps. The need to defend your nurturing qualities will be great, but really not necessary. Be true to yourself and don't allow others' image of you tempt you to change your own self-image. Don't be too hard on yourself. Be careful not to get caught up in the causes of others, but look to your own needs; and find the courage to stand up for what you believe. You may use the final shadow period to re-examine your goals and to assess what you have already accomplished.

Mars turns retrograde at the same place where Mercury went retrograde in July. You may find that the concepts you were examining at that time will re-emerge and be connected to that which you experience during this Mars retrograde period. Whatever you learned about yourself during Mercury's retrograde period will be of help to you now.

LONG RETROGRADE PERIODS

The Retrograde Periods of the rest of the planets each last more than half of the year. The time periods are longer, but cover a smaller area of the zodiac. We don't experience them in the same way as the other planets; we get used to living with the stress, and take it for granted. The day of the stations and the week or so before and after tend to be more intense, and the recommendation to be more careful with decisions and life changes is valuable at these times. Continue to look for alternate perspectives and collect more information.

Jupiter

> Enters Shadow November 2, 1992
> Turns Retrograde January 28, 1993 14 Libra 42
> Turns Direct June 1, 1993 4 Libra 45
> Leaves Shadow August 29, 1993

Fiery Jupiter retrogrades in the air sign Libra. Jovian energy is expansive and growth oriented, and will feed on Libra's air. Jupiter's symbolism deals with idealism, abstract thought, and the realization of philosophical goals. His retrograde period will bring up questions about honest communication and ideal relationships. The temptation to expand a business without sufficient preparation or analysis of the entire situation can result in reversals after Jupiter leaves his shadow. Be wary of the super deal that must be finalized immediately, without the time to investigate the details. On the other hand, something that was begun before Jupiter entered the shadow may suddenly be completed in a different way than expected.

Jupiter retrograde is a good time to search for information, as people are eager to communicate about abstract ideas, and feel fulfilled by integrating ideas with the facts that support them.

Saturn

> Enters Shadow February 23, 1993
> Turns Retrograde June 10, 1993 0 Pisces 20
> Turns Direct October 28, 1993 23 Aquarius 38
> Leaves Shadow January 31, 1994

Saturn's symbolism deals with authority, time and boundaries. Saturn energy gives you the stimulus to review your organizations—from a large organization to your kitchen cupboards. This will be a good time to examine your opinions and ideas about those in authority in your life. New perspectives and understanding will help you to come to terms with an increased need to question authority.

Saturn turns retrograde just inside the boundary of the watery sign Pisces, where it is not at home; but it spends most of its retrograde period in the last seven degrees of the fixed air sign Aquarius. Saturn works well in Aquarius; communicating proven organizing techniques to help you find order in your life. He will spend the next two and a half years in dreamy Pisces, so take this opportunity to create solid habit patterns now.

URANUS AND NEPTUNE— TOGETHER AT LAST

The last conjunction of Uranus and Neptune was 172 years ago. This year they will conjunct three times—once while they are both retrograde on August 20. So, it is best to look at them together.

Uranus

Enters Shadow January 10, 1993
Turns Retrograde April 26, 1993 22 Capricorn 11
Turns Direct September 27, 1993 18 Capricorn 14
Leaves Shadow January 11, 1994

Neptune

Enters Shadow January 2, 1993
Turns Retrograde April 22, 1993 21 Capricorn 09
Turns Direct September 30, 1993 18 Capricorn 23
Leaves Shadow January 19, 1994

Uranus symbolizes eccentricity and the need for personal freedom. Neptune represents the intuitive side of the mind, and your own personal perspective of reality. Since the Retrograde Period of these two planets fills the entire year, it should be no surprise that these areas of human consciousness are constantly in need of examination.

Both planets spend the year within a degree of each other in earthy Capricorn, which puts the emphasis and a great deal of intensity on practical issues. Introspection must be balanced with a realistic grasp of your place in a shared universe. This is a good time to build peaceful relationships with others. Developing inner strength and self-sufficiency will help you to use these energies constructively.

Pluto

> Enters Shadow November 11, 1992
> Turns Retrograde February 26, 1993 25 Scorpio 31
> Turns Direct August 2, 1993 22 Scorpio 43
> Leaves Shadow November 20, 1993

Pluto, small and distant, retrogrades in its own sign, fixed and watery Scorpio. Pluto symbolizes the energy of power and control. In 1993, Pluto's direct station is in a dynamic aspect to the direct station of Saturn, linking their energies. The process of re-organizing and building new structures must begin with releasing the old. Pluto's retrograde energies are good for acknowledging your power to control, and then using that power to release old, unusable structures in your life. That may mean letting go of relationships that no longer serve you, or throwing out clothes that no longer fit to make room for a new wardrobe.

Retrograde motion is with us to stay, and give us a different perspective of life. Let go of the fear and learn to use this symbolic tool and you can enrich your life.

Notes

1. Lilly, William. *An Introduction to Astrology*. Newcastle Publishing Company, Inc., Hollywood, CA, 1972, p. 344.

2. Bonatus, Guido. *A Guide for Astrologers*, Translated by Henry Coley, The National Astrological Library, Washington, DC, 1964, p. 4.

3. Astronomers have found that the Sun does indeed move in a retrograde motion relative to the center of mass of the entire solar system, but its motion is very small, and there is no change in the Sun's zodiacal position. Astrologers are studying this phenomenon to determine any synchronous events or any correlation to life expression.

Matchmaking with the Sun and Moon

Carolyn Reynolds

In *The Book of Lovers* (Llewellyn Publications, 1992) you will find 288 Sun/Moon personality profiles to help you gain character insights into all your intimate relationships, whether with friends and neighbors, children, co-workers or lovers. In order to get the Moon working for you, you will need to know that there are many planetary configurations in a person's chart. The two most important, however, are the Sun and Moon combinations.

The Sun position on the day of "his" or "her" birth you probably already know: that is the very popular Sun sign astrology. However, the Moon was also positioned in an astrological sign on the day she/he was born. The Sun position explains the character traits of the person (e.g. values, ethics, objectives, approaches to situations), while the Moon explains emotional needs and predisposition or temperament. This *Book of Lovers* is essentially a reference book to all possible combinations of Sun-Moon placements from 1900 to 2000. In addition, it includes a separate table for Rising signs (based on time of birth), which represents the outer personality of the person, or the persona—the self people most often show to the world.

However, in intimate relationships, it is the Sun and Moon which team up to incline people to behave the way they do.

The elements of the Moon are Fire, Earth, Water and Air. People get along best with matching elements. On the following page are charts that show relationships between elements and signs; those combinations that are compatible and those that are not.

The Moon's Elements or the Four Temperaments
Chart 1. Compatible Elements

FIRE	EARTH	AIR	WATER
Aries	Taurus	Gemini	Cancer
Leo	Virgo	Libra	Scorpio
Sagittarius	Capricorn	Aquarius	Pisces

Chart 2. The Oppositions of the Moon

Aries opposite Libra	Cancer opposite Capricorn
Taurus opposite Scorpio	Leo opposite Aquarius
Gemini opposite Sagittarius	Virgo opposite Pisces

These Moons are 180 degrees apart. They are in stressful relationships to one another. They cause the "we live in two different worlds" feeling between people.

Chart 3. Sign Combinations

Harmonious
Aries, Leo, Sagittarius
Taurus, Virgo, Capricorn
Gemini, Libra, Aquarius
Cancer, Scorpio, Pisces

Disharmonious
Aries, Cancer, Libra, Capricorn
Gemini, Virgo, Sagittarius, Libra
Taurus, Leo, Scorpio, Aquarius

Simply put, if you have a Sun in Sagittarius, and your Moon is in Scorpio, look to the mate who has his/her Sun in Scorpio and/or a Moon in Sagittarius. For further possible combinations, look for those who have the same Moon as yours, or Sun or Moon in the same sign, or in a harmonious element as your Sun and Moon (i.e., Fire likes Fire, Air likes Air, and so forth). Whether in love or in friendship, the most compatible relationships are the ones in which the Moon is in the same element. The reason for this is that there is an easy emotional understanding, a harmonious adjustment to each other's habits and feelings. Psychologically, you feel in touch with one another. If your Moon is in the same element as that of the person you are interested in, you will have an easy understanding of him or her.

When your Moon is in the same sign as the Moon of a particular person, whether a friend or lover, co-worker, parent or child, there is very little division between needs. You feel better, emotionally, by their very presence. You are able to communicate emotional patterns and your re-actions to life easily. So easily, in fact, that you often need little discussion about your actions. This may make for a lazy relationship where neither one of you has to reach, grow, or work very hard at developing common ground.

Arnold Schwartzenegger and Maria Shriver are an in-teresting couple who have a fated match with his Leo Sun to her Leo Moon, but I'd like to do some matchmaking from *The Book of Lovers'* personality profile.

One of the things that I stress in *The Book of Lovers* is that you can change your direction, or the form of your rela-tionships, by working with different Sun/Moon combina-tions.

For example, Arnold is one of the most ambitious men of the Zodiac, according to his combination of Leo Sun/ Capricorn Moon, and he is looking for someone who, like himself, is not sniveling but forthright and purposeful. He seeks a woman who is good for his public image. How per-fect for him that Maria not only fills that bill but is sexual, daring, and magnetic. With most men she would be the head of the family, but with Arnold she has found a man who is strong enough to encourage her to stand on her own two feet while being swept off them by his passionate nature.

Someone like Dolly Parton, with her Capricorn Sun and Virgo Moon, could be another match for Arnold if only for a good long-term friendship. With Dolly, Arnold finds a relationship that offers an emotional sharing of their secret insecurities and fears. The hidden parts of their nature are suddenly expressed with one another. If they were to venture into the sexual arena Dolly could find her-self learning about bells ringing and bombs bursting.

Not to leave Maria, a Scorpio Sun and Leo Moon, out, she could find the challenge of a lifetime with Pierce Bros-nan who, according to his Sun in Taurus and Moon in Aquarius, is one of the most genuine, humanitarian men of the zodiac. I predict an eventual move into a humanitarian venture or politics in his distant future. With Pierce, Maria could experience the delightful and unusual life of a pixie; a life where money, possessions, and ambition are secondary, and more ethereal experiences are primary. These two are truly the opposites that attract.

Pierce Brosnan could find Farrah Fawcett a wonderful match with her loving and sensitive nature. According with her Sun in Aquarius and her Moon in Cancer, she is gaining strength in the 90s, and emerging stronger for her prior struggles. Her generosity, sound judgment, and concern for others mirrors Pierce's own.

Clint Eastwood's life could take many twists and turns into his always stellar direction with Kathleen Turner. Clint is a Gemini Sun/Leo Moon, while Kathleen is a Gemini Sun/Aquarius Moon, one of the most fascinating women of the 144 combinations. She is part tomboy, all woman, and very intelligent underneath her often wistful moods. Clint has one of the most appealing combinations and could end up choosing any career path or any number of women for his relationships. One of his most favorable matches could be with Reba McEntyre, an Aries Sun/ Gemini Moon combination who has enough energy to keep up with anyone's schedule. Reba is one woman who tries to have it all and is fully capable in every area of her life. She is hopeful of everyone's best, and is excitingly unpredictable. She could offer Clint something he rarely finds: a challenge.

So, whether you are looking for a challenge, or someone to share your innermost secrets and desires, you can match your Moon to alter the dynamics of your relationships. Happy Matching.

Job Hunting? Let the Stars be Your Guide!

Louise Riotte

Yesterday I called the Minibus, a community transportation service my county provides for the elderly end handicapped for a small fee.

My call was answered by an attractive lady who came to the door to assist me. I am 83 and slightly crippled. As she helped me to the bus she asked, "Do you remember me?" I had to confess that I did not, then she told me that she was one of many people I have helped to find employment. About two years ago she came to me to participate in the free vocational counseling service I offer to the unemployed, which is just a simple matter of typing up a master copy of their work experience which can then be xeroxed for as many copies as needed. We set up a definite time for an interview and I ask them to write out and bring with them a history of their work experience and the names of references. My counseling service covers attitudes, work preferences, dress, and it includes an astrological analysis of my clients' strengths and weaknesses.

I do not draw horoscopes but, having done this for many years, their Sun signs give me a good idea of their abilities and how best I can help them. I also use my current copy of the Llewellyn *Moon Sign Book*, explaining the importance of timing and favorable and unfavorable dates. Then I help them choose dates and times when they are most likely to succeed. There is great theraputic value in this, raising self-esteem and building up confidence for the forthcoming interview.

In counseling I often refer to Linda Goodman's *Sun Signs*, which is very helpful in defining both the employee and employer characteristics of each Sun sign. Another very helpful book, *Cosmic Influences on Human Behavior*, by Michel Gauquelin, often brings to the attention of the client some unexpected talent which may be helpful in changing to another line of work.

As a Libra, I discovered through astrology that I was well suited to a career in both writing and illustration. In the February 1991 issue of *Publisher's Weekly* I was named one of the top twenty garden writers of all-time with one notably successful book, *Carrots Love Tomatoes, Secrets of Companion Planting*, which has now sold over 400,000 copies. This book and all my others have now been translated into a number of foreign languages and they have been turning up even in Australia and New Zealand.

Other books helpful to the job-seeker include *Creative Visualization* (Llewellyn), by Melita Denning and Osborne Phillips; *The Lunar Effect* (Anchor Press, Doubleday), by Arnold L. Lieber, M.D.; *Your Astrological Guide to Health and Diet* (G.P. Putman's Sons), by Carroll Righter; *Body Language* (Wyden Books), by Julius Fast; and an amusing and helpful little book, *Heavens Help The Working Girl* (Franconia Press), by Paige Mckenzie.

Briefly, here are some pointers which may help you to land a job which will not only pay the rent, but also give you personal satisfaction through doing the type of work for which your Sun sign shows you to be best suited.

ARIES (March 21 – April 20)

The Aries native is a natural born innovator and leader, since he/she is not easily defeated or intimidated. Being a go-getter from the moment you wake up in the morning gives you a decided advantage over your competitors; just make sure that your energy does not slow down between the take-off and the finish.

Money, which admittedly is very nice, is never your prime reason for working. You are practical and will insist upon being paid what you are worth, but primarily you are eager to work at an interesting job—if it is in pleasant surroundings and with cooperative people that is just an extra bonus; but you will do well if you like your work—no matter what!

With this in mind you will be selective and waste no time in wondering where to start. Through reading, research and experience you will have a pretty good idea of the type of work for which you are best suited. You are very capable of making decisions, willing to come to work early and often stay late if an exciting project is under way. You are not a clock-watcher and this soon becomes apparent to your employer, who may be watching you more than you realize. However, a tight and repetitive schedule may bore you and could work to your disadvantage.

Make a list of places and jobs that appeal to you when you are seeking work. Get a job application and, if possible, fill it out and get an interview while you are there so you will not waste time retracing your steps. Your self-esteem and self-confidence is usually extraordinarily high compared to other signs, but do not make the mistake of being too aggressive. Watch the body language of the person interviewing you and temper your own accordingly.

The versatile Aries is at home in almost any career or profession, whether it's a greenhouse or a police station, according to Goodman. But whether Aries wears a fire-fighter's hat or a surgeon's mask, he/she must always be in charge. The fields of advertising and public relations are also excellent possibilities.

TAURUS (April 20 – May 20)

Taurus is best characterized by the old adage "slow but sure." Early in life you will come to a full knowledge of your own inner workings, your limitations and your abilities. You may be slow starting out, but in the long run you are virtually assured of achieving your goal. You will build your career step by step. Money is important to you and you may be willing to accept less than ideal working conditions if the pay is good. You are capable of working long hard hours and waiting patiently for your efforts to pay off.

According to Linda Goodman, Taurus is happy working as a florist (remember Ferdinand the bull?), in the live-stock or poultry industry, or in the wholesale food industry. You would also make a good doctor or engineer. You love music and are happy expressing yourself creatively through your senses—but even here you never lose sight of the bottom line when developing and pursuing your artistic talents.

Righter says that many famous artists, actors, and musicians, as well as sculptors, have a Sun sign in Taurus, but if you choose one of these occupations it may take you a little longer than others to master your subject, since you are a very meticulous and methodical worker. In applying for jobs you are also this way, careful to put your best foot forward. Plan for getting the best job available, but you will be willing to start somewhere near it, possibly as an assistant, with the long-term goal of moving up. Carefully research the companies you would like to work for, complete with the names of personnel managers. Take great pains to achieve an attractive resume, which will be very helpful to send with your letter of inquiry and job application. Carefully follow up appointments for job interviews. Once you have found a position to your liking you are quite likely to remain. You are not a "job-jumper," and good work is, in time, quite likely to result in promotion.

GEMINI (May 21 – June 21)

The quick-moving, quick-thinking, Gemini likes variety and this is just as important as money when she/he is job seeking. Geminis have good self-esteem and know that whatever skills are needed can be quickly acquired on the job. Geminis will excel in all fields of communication, and this typically allows for the personal freedom they need.

New situations are adjusted to with ease, but this ability may also be a drawback: a position in a new area which looks interesting may cause this native to throw over a good job for another, resulting in a perpetual loss of benefits and seniority.

Geminis are generally popular with their fellow employees, being of an outgoing temperament and keeping the office entertained with lots of jokes and gay chatter. If this is not overdone their employers appreciate this, as it is good for morale and keeps the workplace pleasant.

Geminis make excellent secretaries, receptionists, and switchboard operators. They are capable of charming people who walk in the door, and being personally pleasant on the phone. Geminis are good salespersons, able to charm people into buying things. But Geminis are careful of their own money and if they do any betting it will be in a situation where they are especially knowledgeable, or else where their wits are challenged, or in which there is the possibility for a quick return on investments.

All of which adds up to the best way for a Gemini to begin job-hunting—by using that charming "telephone voice" of yours to set up interviews and obtain job information. You may wish to begin by contacting friends and acquaintances who are working. Having come across well on the telephone, the job interviews you have set up will get off to a good start. Be careful in selecting the places where you interview—it is likely that you will end up being hired on the spot!

CANCER (June 22 – July 22)

The Cancerian employee is the epitome of loyalty—a characteristic employers often reward with salary increases and promotions. As income rises to equal Cancer's output, output increases due to Cancer's willingness to assume responsibility and concern for others, including the company and his employers.

The Moonchild native, according to Righter, has a sixth sense when it comes to business, especially merchandising. The Cancerian has a better sense of values than most signs, is a cautious buyer and a shrewd trader. They also know where to obtain the best items, and, as they are highly perceptive to the needs of other people, they instinctively know the best way to sell them. Blessed with the gift of psychic faculties, the merchant often travels far and wide while sitting at his desk. As they are highly sensitive people, it may take longer for them to achieve success in a highly competitive business environment. However, they have the tenacity (a crab-like trait) to hold on to both their dreams and their ideals, which will help them achieve success in the long run.

Cancer has a desire for the good things of life, but once having achieved success is not a reckless spender. Always dreading poverty, Cancers accumulate possessions and savings to forestall the possibility of ever being in need.

When the Moonchild goes job hunting his/her best bet is to call on relatives and close friends for help. Take advantage of the fact that you have some favors coming to you for the help you have given in the past. Furthermore, family and friends may be able to give a better accounting of your capabilities than you yourself may be willing to give, because of your modest and reticent nature. Friends too are often helpful in singing your praises and, because they like you, may help you find work where they are themselves employed.

You have a very caring, dependable nature and once you secure a job to your liking you are quite apt to remain there and enjoy your good luck.

LEO (July 21 – August 22)

Leos are not likely ever to be accused of "hiding their light under a bushel." They are beautiful people, magnetic and dynamic, and leadership is a built-in characteristic. Fairly bursting with energy and vitality, Leos plunge into ambitious, long-range projects and carry them through to conclusion with tremendous self-confidence. But Leos are not insensible to the possibility of failure. They would profit greatly from the advice and the reassurances of family members, friends, and associates. All Leos have a wee bit of vanity—they love titles, the bigger and the fancier the better—and sometimes prefer an impressive one to more money. Fortunately for them, a good sense of responsibility, loyalty, and devotion which accompanies Leo's pride are the very qualities likely to be rewarded monetarily. Young Leos, promoted wisely, are often gradually eased into top positions as they mature.

Leos do not work as well in teams, since even the slightest modification of their plans tends to be taken by them as criticism. But once the plan is put into effect, Leos get things done with a flair, and their tremendous physical energy is one of their greatest assets.

Leos do well, according to Righter, as writers and journalists, judges, government officials, brokers, bankers and foremen. Leos usually make good money, but have extravagant tastes and often spend it unwisely, a trait which is usually overcome with maturity. Leos will always aim for the top of any organization and of any profession, or as close to it as their qualifications will permit, and they will always have their ear to the ground hoping to pick up clues from friends who might know of openings; they use informal channels to their fullest advantage, and may make discreet inquiries about job opportunities among professional persons who handle their business affairs. They may even ask their spouses to inventory business associates for possible openings. Once you hear of a desirable vacancy, be ready to call and arrange appointments for interviews, bringing up names of any mutual acquaintances likely to help smooth the way for you. It all helps!

VIRGO (August 23 – September 22)

Virgos like to make haste slowly. The Virgo native seeks perfection and is discriminating in his choice of occupation. They are methodical in their approach to any problems and very conscientious in whatever they do. McKenzie says that they are statisticians par excellence. Payrolls are heaven to statistic-happy Virgo. They love to work under an employer who gives them details to explore, analyze, and experiment with.

From an employer's point of view, they may well be the perfect clerical help, staying with any chore from beginning to end. Virgos learn quickly and don't mind exacting chores or a bit of drudgery, but it must lead to something better. Virgos don't mind starting at the bottom because they realize that their good qualities will soon become apparent, and that they will be upwardly mobile in a short time. A wise employer will see to it that they are well-paid as they advance, for Virgos have a strong sense of equity.

Virgos don't need much help in getting a job. They seem to know instinctively how to appraise the employment field, gathering data from several sources (including government statistical sheets) and analyzing what they have learned. After a thorough evaluation, they will zero in on the best possibility with a direct approach, for example, by advertising for a desired position in the local paper.

While taking the direct approach is generally a good strategy for Virgos, they need to watch themselves a bit more than other signs in personal relations, especially in the workplace. Going straight to the point may sometimes be offensive, whereas practicing social graces will throw a better light on their good qualities. They should be careful not to criticize or make suggestions unless very sure of their ground, since people are apt to misinterpret Virgo's constructive criticisms as "complaining."

LIBRA (September 23 – October 23)

You will be happiest in a position with an attractive environment with cooperative co-workers. But if this is not immediately available you will use your considerable skill in bringing this about. Harmony, says Mckenzie, is as basic as breathing to the Libran nature, peacemaking comes naturally, and you will always seek a neat balance between what is practical and what is beautiful. You are yourself very likely to be attractive in person and charming in manner. This can be a definite asset to your employer as well as yourself, especially if you work as a receptionist. Venus rules the sign of Libra and bestows artistic ability upon those born at this time. Saturn adds constructive skill to the art of Venus; thus Librans often excel in the constructive arts, such as jewelry design, decorating, or architectural drafting. Many entertainers, musicians, and writers have been Libran born.

Perhaps the biggest problem of Libras is their inability to make decisions, which may limit their usefulness in an executive position. Libras strive to see all sides of a question and their efforts to bring about equitable solutions may distort their viewpoint to the point of ineffectiveness.

Sometimes the biggest problem of Libras is deciding where to apply for a job and in what line of work. Try not to spend too much time debating the advantages of an older, larger organization versus a smaller, less formal business. List the pros and cons of both before you ever go near an application. Chances are fringe benefits and salary scales will be greater in the larger companies, but possibly the smaller ones will offer more variety and a greater chance of promotion in a shorter time.

Make up your mind (and don't be too long about it!), which offers the most for you. You are basically perceptive, considerate and have good sense. If you use these qualities you will be able to reach a decision most advantageous to all concerned. Guard against doing anything from a personal or prejudicial point of view; this is contrary to your nature, and if you do, you will regret it.

As a Libra you have good earning power, but you have expensive tastes. Look for a job which will eventually produce good money.

SCORPIO (October 24 – November 22)

The highly developed Scorpio, according to Righter, responds to the qualities of the eagle, and is able to soar above the earthbound and purely physical plane of consciousness with courage, strength and self-control. Scorpio is a fixed water sign and its natives combine these fixed-sign qualities with an analytical, penetrating mind and an aptitude for scientific, philosophic or laboratory research and investigation.

Scorpios are secretive, loving mystery, and will usually reveal their plans only as accomplished projects (which often works greatly to their advantage). They are also go-getters and don't waste time sitting around waiting for opportunities to fall into their laps, although this may appear to be the case since they work behind the scenes pulling the strings to promote themselves. They are also aware of their superior talents and have no false modesty in calling attention to them.

Scorpios are happiest working alone, for they do not like being cooped up in close quarters with others. Scorpios have terrific energy, working tirelessly, and often moonlight a second job. You might expect Scorpio to be aggressive in job seeking. Not so, at least not openly. However a Scorpio goes about it, they will do their hunting quietly. No one will know about the appointments for interviews they make, whether they are successful or not, then one day your Scorpio will simply "be there," quite likely in an excellent position for which there were many applicants. And, once "there," Scorpio's self-assurance will carry them far.

Guard against being too aggressive in a job interview. If you are hired, there will be a better opportunity later to make suggestions to improve the company—by dropping your ideas in the appropriate box.

SAGITTARIUS (November 23 – December 21)

The Sagittarian, says Goodman, is an excellent salesperson, but may have to be trained to curb his/her hasty enthusiasims for s/he is apt to dash out after a challenge and forget to wear his/her caution. Dishonesty is not a Sagittarian weakness, but neither is tact, and they must carefully guard their occasional outbursts of temper.

The active, independent Sagittarian has little regard for money, is not a clock-watcher, but is stifled by the restriction of an eight-to-five regimen. Even so, finances seldom seem to give any real trouble. With many interests she/he often seems to come out on top, no matter what. Perhaps it is because Sagittarians are very optimistic, and set-backs just seem to produce harder effort to succeed.

The Archer works well under pressure, but must guard against an occasional mood of depression if things do not seem to be going well. Soon optimism will take charge again and things will begin to right themselves.

Sagittarius is a travel sign and its natives enjoy movement. Many of this sign, says Righter, participate in sports, either as a profession or for recreation. Highly intelligent Sagittarians become philosophers, pillars of the church, physicians and reputable individuals in any occupation.

The Sagittarian looking for a job goes about it rather casually, generally by spreading the word among their many friends and acquaintances. They may even accept a part-time or volunteer job, if it is interesting.

CAPRICORN (December 22 – Januury 19)

Many Capricorns, says Goodman, make excellent researchers, extremely capable dentists, brilliant engineers and architects. They're clever at merchandising, manufacturing and politics. They are also capable bankers, teachers and bookkeepers.

There is also a strong creative side to Saturn people and you may find your Capricorn friend has a surprising hobby, such as being a Sunday artist, a weekend musician, dabbling in sculpture, selling real estate, gardening, singing in a choir, or belonging to a drama class. Culture is close to the Capricorn heart, and so is Mother Earth.

Capricorns, says McKenzie, are, like Taurus and Virgo, strongly ambitious and willing to work hard to achieve success, following established procedures which have proven successful. This does not mean that they are "in a rut" for they are not averse to new methods—provided they be within the framework of the accepted procedures.

The Goat is self-reliant and self-confident, with a strong sense of responsibility and the strength to follow through on whatever is started, planning carefully, and making his/her plans pay off.

With so much drive and a wide variety of interests it is seldom a problem for a Capricorn to find employment. Your typical Capricorn is a firm believer in the "it's not what you know, it's who you know" school of thought. Having once decided to go to work, whether from need or the desire for an interesting occupation, this native will contact influential friends who are working in good jobs and endeavor to collect information on possible openings. This does not arouse resentment for his/her tactics, which are usually open and above board, as the Capricorn is careful of his/her good name and the respect of others. So don't hesitate to use the names of anyone you know whom you feel can assist you in getting a good position. They won't mind for they are well aware of your good qualities, willingness to work hard and accept responsibility.

AQUARIUS (January 20 – February 18)

Aquarius is a mental sign and the native may prefer a profession or occupation which requires mental application. Being very versatile you are quite adaptable to different circumstances or changing conditions, but you have a surprising penchant for the uncommon or the unusual. If your occupation becomes routine or monotonous, you are apt to inject a note of nonconformity in your attitude toward it or find a different way to do the job, for Aquarius denotes inventiveness and original thinking, being ruled by Uranus, the planet of spontaneity and the new order.

Change is the foundation of your life, for the new and original turns you on. You may be very strongly attracted to the agencies that have sprung up in growing community concern, child abuse, unemployment, homelessness, underprivileged groups and the environment. You do not work to achieve security but to initiate new concepts. Ecology, or any other sort of working toward positive reforms, may be the field that stimulates your fertile imagination. Aquarians have made notable achievements in the fields of aviation, journalism, equal rights, modern astrology, the labor movement, the military, and ever new forms of entertainment. They have achieved fame as violinists, theater stars, singers, authors, and statesmen.

The Aquarian worker will give a full day's work for a day's pay, says Goodman, and he/she is also utterly trustworthy with company secrets, and probably the best customer's person that can be found, because he/she has the ability to make friends with even the most stand-offish clients.

Aquarians, of all the signs, are likely to take the most unorthodox way to find a job, says McKenzie, yet the most direct. They don't go in for the run-of-the-mill job hunting routine but prefer to explore the town or the territory for a likely place to work that will prove to be interesting. Once this is found they will work hard and be patient as they endeavor to find a way to land a job in their chosen place of preference. And you may be reasonably sure that. what they have chosen is both interesting and unusual.

PISCES (February 19 – March 20)

Pisces, a water sign ruled by Neptune is, perhaps, the most contradictory of all the signs, with an ingenious but often irresolute mind. Natives are adaptable, conforming, comprehending, imaginative, intuitive, flexible, sympathetic, and versatile. They are also emotional, changeable, sensitive and impressionable. They are often gifted with psychic powers. With so much sensitivity floating around they may run the gamut—from the depths of escapism and despair, to the heights of spiritual attainment and professional success.

Pisceans have foresight and genius, and alone with a powerful imagination are often endowed with executive ability. Notable Pisceans have been botanists, inventors, physicists, poets, playwrights, painters, sculptors, novelists, judges, philosophers, and atomic scientists.

In the business world the twin-signed Pisces has potential for both personal and financial success, provided that he/she is adept in balancing false optimism with reality, imagination and industry. By some strange process he/she often succeeds in doing just that, often using an original approach to tackle routine chores on a productive basis. The highest problem of the native is often "too much of a good thing"—they are often too generous, too willing, too tolerant or even too compassionate for their own good. But the native will fight for his/her rights with surprising strength.

The Piscean has such a many-sided personality that it may be difficult to decide which side of their personality to display to a prospective employer—and they often run the risk of being either too reticent or too aggressive. When filling out an application, remember that on paper you have the ability to express yourself well and interestingly.

Economic Trends 1993

Jean Innis

Individuals, groups, companies, and government are all important in the determination of economic trends at any given time. People run companies, people are elected to government positions, and people buy and sell. All of these things influence the trends of the economy, for good or for bad.

There are a few simple basics about determining the trends of economic conditions. In order to predict future trends, you must first understand the present. It will also help you to look into the past, because trends (planetary conditions) are always repeated, albeit in a slightly different form. And remember, it's true that as much money can be made in bad times as in good; you just need to know where to invest.

So we look at the planets as they transit the signs (see Figure 2 on page 43) to learn where the strongest forces operate. The slower a planet moves, the more influential the force exerted; therefore, we begin with Pluto.

PLUTO
Driving Force for 1993

On January 1, Pluto is positioned at 24 degrees 38 minutes of Scorpio. Pluto will be a major focus this year, when Saturn makes a square aspect during the months of March and October, and will be approaching the third-and-last-square which will take place in January, 1994.

Keywords for Pluto are transformation and regeneration. Scorpio rules the medical field, sex (including pornography), drugs, violence, organized crime, death, insurance, inheritance, taxes, the IRS, psychiatry and psychotherapy, nuclear and atomic power, martial arts, parapsy-

41

chology and psychic phenomena, detectives and the FBI, garbage and recycling.

Pluto has been transiting Scorpio for over a decade; already we have seen many drastic changes in the matters listed above. To date, we have yet to resolve the abortion issue (sex leading to unwanted pregnancies and ultimate destruction) or to find a cure for AIDS (sex leading to venereal disease). We haven't solved the national drug problem, nor maintained control over organized crime and its association with drugs and pornography. The national debt remains out of control, and the managers of insurance companies and state officials continue to battle fraud. Not until late 1995, when Pluto leaves Scorpio for good and enters Sagittarius, will we be completely aware of all of the changes brought about by Pluto in this intense sign where it acts so powerfully.

During 1993, while Pluto continues to transit through the last 10 degrees of Scorpio, its influence will continue to force fundamental changes in all aspects ruled by Scorpio. We will begin to feel Pluto's influence more strongly in our homes as our sense of personal security and security systems become of increasing importance. As others lose control of their lives through association with drug abuse and crime (organized and otherwise), we will see an even greater need to protect ourselves in our homes.

Scorpio also rules privacy, and Pluto in Scorpio means changes in this area of our lives. Scorpio is a secretive, private sign, and it doesn't like private affairs aired like sheets on a clothesline, flapping in the breeze. Therefore, while Pluto transits the last 10 degrees of Scorpio, changes will be made within the home to protect the private lives of families and individuals. Unlisted phone numbers will become more prevalent, and many of us will begin to guard all forms of privacy more carefully. We are tired of being bothered in our homes when we're trying to relax, and we don't like the idea of being on everyone's mailing list. We are afraid the numbers on our credit cards might be accessed by others and used against our will, so we are beginning to guard these plastic card numbers more carefully. We are finding that we want confidential mail, secret bank accounts, private vaults and safe-deposit boxes—in short, we want more privacy.

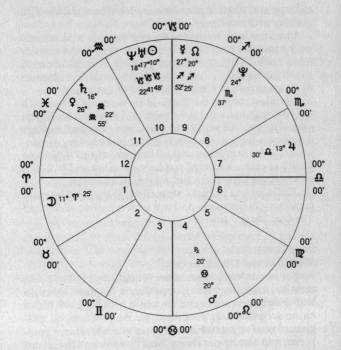

Figure 2
New Year, Jan. 1, 1993
82W36 39N43

The martial arts will become increasingly more popular as a form of exercise and of self protection as Pluto transits through Scorpio, the sign which gives intensity and control. Those who practice the martial arts do so not only to attain physical strength and control, but also mental agility. Those in fields that protect the public—policemen, detectives, firemen, etc.—will be encouraged to learn karate so they will be able to maintain strength and concentration in difficult situations.

We will continue to try to clean up our planet by recycling. Since Pluto has to do with power and recycling, we can expect to see more trash burning power plants and nuclear power plants. Along with the use of these facilities, of course, will be the possibility of more disasters because of carelessness and mishandling of debris. It will become even more important for us to see that each item we're finished with is disposed of appropriately. We will also need to see that products that can be used again (after some sort of transformation) are redistributed as necessary.

Pluto's transiting Scorpio is likely to result in the search for in-depth knowledge of psychological and biological sexual drives. All sexual interests, emotions and feelings are more in the open than ever before in the history of mankind. This information will ultimately help us develop a healthier outlook toward our own sexuality and will help us to release deep fears and repressed attitudes.

The ideal end of Pluto's transiting Scorpio will be more comfort with ourselves and our secrets, our sexuality and our need for privacy.

NEPTUNE
Illusions and Disillusions

Keywords for Neptune are spiritualistic, idealistic, and creative. As the higher octave of Venus, Neptune has to do with love and romance and art, but at a higher level. It also has to do with drugs, chemicals, alcohol, tobacco, oil, pollution, creativity, art and music, styles and fashion, prosperity, and sometimes chaos. Neptune rules all that is not exactly as it appears to be—all that creates an illusion, and all that causes disillusion.

Capricorn on the other hand is materialistic by nature; it rules business and the economy, companies and corporations, politics and government, controls and regulations, occupations and vocations, conservation and ecology, architecture and buildings (the boney, skeletal structures), and cities.

Neptune has been transiting the sign Capricorn since November of 1984. Neptune, as you might have gathered, isn't comfortable in the sign Capricorn—it's like an artist at a board meeting. The artist wonders what he's doing there and he feels extremely uncomfortable in his surroundings; the other board members think the artist is unrealistic at best, and that he'll never understand business matters. Either our Neptune artist must put aside his idealistic, inspirational side and become as cold, practical and conservative as the others, or he must teach them to see beyond cold practicality and into the realm of the spirit.

Some of the confusion of business and the economy over the past several years is because of this confusing influence of Neptune in the sign Capricorn. The fashion industry has been confused: for the first time skirts can be either long or short. The government has been confused: are we going further into a recession or pulling out? Wall Street is confused for the same reasons. We as investors are confused, and it shows in our erratic spending. Our government and elected officials seem to be unsure of what we wish of them—and we wonder if they even care what we want.

Neptune in Capricorn rules patriotism and work, and work ethics. Neptune is showing us the spiritual side of work while Capricorn is showing us the value of conservative economic policies. Workers are more loyal to their companies, and at the same time, managers of big business are trying to make the workplace more aesthetically pleasing.

Neptune in Capricorn helps us to see that there is much value in being frugal and thrifty. We don't have to have as much money as we once thought; we simply have to manage it better. Of course, this has its bad side: we're not spending as we once did, which creates problems for business. If we don't spend, we don't buy as many products; if we don't buy as many products, the company doesn't need as many employees; if the company doesn't need employees, some of us are laid off and have no jobs at all.

Neptune rules drinking and smoking. Capricorn rules sobriety and conscious morality. During the 80s, we have had a resurgence of public response against drunk drivers, e.g. Mothers Against Drunk Driving, as well as more and more strict enforcement against smoking in public areas.

Neptune also brought us preservatives and (inadvertently) pesticides in our foods, some of which have been discovered to be unhealthy. We are becoming more aware of pollution invading our bodies, our homes and our work environment. These concerns will escalate, but by early 1994, when Neptune in Capricorn sextiles Pluto in Scorpio, we should be nearer to some solutions to the problems of waste and pollution.

While Neptune transits Capricorn there will be a continued interest in antiques and collectibles. The more classic, the more traditional will be desired by collectors. At the same time, "antique"—which is nearly synonymous with used—will be in vogue, opening the doors for many new types of business concerns. Anyone with an eye for the intrinsic beauty in the lines of an old chair will be able to make either a fine sale or a worthwhile investment, depending on his situation. Likewise, while artsy Neptune continues to move through frugal Capricorn you will be admired for your fashion sense if you wear used clothing.

The mid-degrees of Capricorn are representative of intense practicality, but with an eye for beauty. If an article is both used and pretty, it becomes more valuable. During 1993 many people will be investing in antiques, wearing used clothing, and they'll also be planting their own gardens, which has become increasingly prevalent during the past few years. By the end of 1993, when Neptune (and Uranus, too) enters the last 10 degrees of Capricorn, health and diet will come more to the fore, and we will see how our intuition (and the planets) has been guiding us toward better health. We will want to grow as much of our own food as possible, and we'll become hesitant to buy anything that contains preservatives. Many of us will grow enough to sell, and will show huge profits from our efforts—as others who can't grow their own foods will want to buy from someone they trust.

The best that will come of Neptune in Capricorn is a blending of the mystical with the realistic, and the realization that the two aren't as far apart as one might assume. You have to have a dream for a dream come true, but Capricorn will teach us that the dream must be realistic too. And Capricorn will learn that with the mystic faith of Neptune, he can fly.

URANUS
Lightning Quick Changes in Business

Uranus represents sudden changes and reversals, disruption, freedom of expression, originality, creativity, unconventionality, technological breakthroughs, inventions, computers and electronics, human rights, revolution, intuition and astrology.

Uranus entered Capricorn in 1988 and will stay until 1994. As discussed under Neptune, Capricorn is materialistic, conservative and economical. Uranus likes to stir things up, while Capricorn likes to work toward preplanned goals. Uranus enjoys new inventions; Capricorn likes the old, tried and true. With Uranus in Capricorn, everything the sign Capricorn represents is changed and jolted by the presence of Uranus. The traditionally conservative Capricorn business concerns are looking toward increasingly innovative ways of doing business. Old, outdated methods are being forced into drastic alterations.

The opportunities Uranus and Neptune bring while they are conjoined in Capricorn are employer/employee involvement and especially an approach which places emphasis on the ideas of employees. Uranus rules groups of people, and these people are going to have to work together to regain the health of their business concerns.

That these ideas are worthwhile for all of us, is indicated by the sextiles of both Uranus and Neptune to Pluto. The sextile aspects point the way out of difficulties indicated by the Saturn square to Pluto. In other words, by sharing our creativity and our ideas we will be able to solve the problems indicated by the square.

SATURN
The Teacher

Whatever sign is being transmitted by Saturn is where we must learn our lessons. Saturn in Aquarius isn't as difficult as most, because Saturn's heavy-handedness is lifted by this humanitarian Air sign. During 1993, Saturn will be in the final 10 degrees of Aquarius; here we learn to care for our partners, co-workers and our employers. The lessons to be learned while Saturn is in Aquarius is to "love one another as we would ourselves." Individuals who have gained prosperity underhandedly in the 1980's will possibly have difficulty dealing with this fact, even if their dishonesty remains undiscovered by the general public.

Saturn in Aquarius can give power and good fortune, especially when connected with friendships, associations, or public affairs. The influence here is more democratic than with other signs, while also maintaining a stability equaled only by Capricorn (ruled by Saturn) or Libra (where Saturn is in its exaltation). When Saturn comes to a square of Pluto, stability antagonizes power. When this aspect is operative, those people, businesses, and governments who have used power unethically or unwisely will find themselves in serious trouble.

Saturn square Pluto is the immovable object meeting the irresistible force. By the end of 1994, we will see humanity taking the reins, trying to control the forces of the banking industry and insurance companies. We will see the results of these takeovers and changes within companies in about two years.

JUPITER
Gentle Giant

Jupiter retrogrades Libra during nearly the first half of 1993. Libra is the sign of partners, marriage, and otherwise. Jupiter in Libra will promote the desire to remain faithful to one's partner and to choose a partner for life. During September, Jupiter will make a square aspect to both Uranus and Neptune, conjoined in the sign Capricorn. This will cause many to over-extend themselves, since Jupiter squares often bring too much of a good thing. Libra rules lawsuits, and anyone who has become involved in fraudulent practices is likely to be tried and convicted during this time. With Capricorn involved, we will learn of embezzlement and fraud in business and government. These suits will be resolved some time in October, when Jupiter moves to a trine of Saturn. This is a very short time indeed, and perhaps indicates that the public will be extraordinarily upset by these crimes.

The shopping season of 1993 should be much more prosperous for merchants, while Jupiter and Saturn are trine in aspect to one another in the compatible Air signs of Libra and Aquarius.

Jupiter enters Scorpio during November, for its approximate year-long transit of that sign. This will help all of the industries influenced by the outer planets, as Jupiter sextiles Uranus and Neptune, and then conjoins Pluto in Scorpio. Look for more optimism and improvements at that time.

AN OVERVIEW

The most important aspects during 1993 are these:

All year: Uranus conjoins Neptune
March and November: Saturn squares Pluto
May: Saturn enters Pisces
June/July: Saturn retrogrades, back into Aquarius in July
September: Jupiter squares Uranus and Neptune

Uranus conjunct Neptune: These planets are moving very close together during the entire year. This conjunction stimulates idealism, inspiration, novel experiences, innovative ideas; astrology and metaphysics continue to be of interest to many people, including those in big business and in the government. To profit from this aspect, you should strive to advance through your ability to combine vision with strength of purpose and through the ability to introduce novelty and innovative ideas into your business and/or personal enterprises.

Saturn square Pluto: This is an aspect of developmental tension; ambitious individuals who have obtained their position by illegal or fraudulent means will be discovered. Those who have gained their position honestly as the result of patient, persistent efforts, have nothing to fear from this aspect other than a temporary setback because of the general conditions of society.

Jupiter square Uranus: Those individuals or businesses that overexpand and overspend will find themselves in difficulty later. Don't be misled by "get rich quick" schemes.

Jupiter square Neptune: This aspect will cause over impulsiveness and delusions in perception of value. Businesses likely to suffer setbacks are connected with publishing, religion, travel; oil and gas concerns. It is of utmost importance to maintain a realistic outlook if involved with these fields.

GENERAL TRENDS FOR 1993:

Real estate: Investments made in January or July should be profitable, although real estate in general will continue to be in a slump until the fall of 1993, when Jupiter makes a trine aspect to Saturn. If you can purchase real estate before that time it would be advantageous, because that is when interest rates will begin to rise; loans will be more easily obtained, however, in September and October.

Business: Capricorn sets the trend in business success and continues to support used items, antiques, etc. Cultural pursuits are supported by Libra in Jupiter; art collections and galleries for investors should remain popular, with the tendency toward purchasers showing more interest in the traditional.

Ecology: We will make some adjustments in our approach to environmental control when Saturn squares Pluto. This is merely a shift in emphasis toward more innovative ideas and applications which should be under control by the end of the year.

Government: While Neptune and Uranus transit the sign of Capricorn, the public will be disillusioned and will want to change the status quo. The trick will be to make changes for the better.

The year 1993 will be a time of continued change. Powerful planetary aspects are in operation, along with the opportunity to learn from recent mistakes and to use the best of what the positions of the planets imply. Saturn in the final degrees of Aquarius should help to solidify the gains we have made so far while under the influence of Pluto in Scorpio and Uranus and Neptune in Capricorn, albeit with some corrections.

Gloria Star

All of the following sign descriptions and forecasts have been written by internationally renowned astrologer Gloria Star. Gloria has been a professional astrologer for twenty years and bases her private counseling practice in the shoreline township of Clinton, Connecticut. In addition to teaching locally, she is a highly sought-after lecturer at regional, national, and international astrological conventions, and has appeared on numerous radio and television programs throughout the United States. She is a member of the Advisory Board of the National Council for Geocosmic Research (NCGR) and has served on the Steering Committee of the Association for Astrological Networking (AFAN) as Secretary.

Ms. Star has authored the *Sun Sign Book* for Llewellyn since 1989 and is the author of the book *Optimum Child: Developing Your Child's Fullest Potential through Astrology*. She is a contributing author to the Llewellyn anthology *Houses: Power Places in the Horoscope*. Her video and audiotape presentations and courses are widely distributed. She is available for personal consultations and lectures for conventions or conferences. You may reach her through Llewellyn Publications.

How to Benefit Most from Sun Sign Astrology

Astrology is a complex system used to clarify your identity and needs. The Sun, Moon, and each of the planets symbolize many levels of need and energy expression. The Sun symbolizes the ego self, the individual drive to be noticed as a significant being. Each sign of the zodiac represents a set of characteristics and traits which modify the energy of the Sun, Moon, and planets, adding color to the personality. Your Sun Sign is only one factor among many which describes who you are, but it is a powerful one!

The following information is based upon the sign the Sun was in at the time of your birth. Although we can examine a number of your needs and life situations from this information, there are many other factors which a professional astrologer would look at to help you guide your life. If you would like more information to accompany the guidelines in this book, you might appreciate the personalized, more detailed help you'll receive from a competent professional (see readings and other services available at the end of this book).

I've described the year's major challenges and opportunities for every Sun Sign in the "Year Ahead" section. The first part of the section applies to all individuals born under the influence of the sign. In addition, I've included information for specific birth dates that will help you understand the inner process of change you'll be experiencing during 1993. The cycles described in this section comprise your fundamental themes for the year ahead. Consider these ideas as underlying principles that will be present throughout the entire year. These cycles comprise your major challenges and opportunities relating to your personal identity. Blend these ideas with the information you find in the monthly forecast section for your Sun and Ascendant Signs.

To best use the information in the monthly forecasts, you'll want to determine your Ascendant or Rising Sign. If you don't know your Ascendant, the Ascendant Tables (following this description) will help you determine your Rising Sign. They are most accurate for those born in the Western Hemisphere between 60-130 degrees longitude (e.g. the Continental United States). Once you've figured out your Ascending Sign, you'll know two significant factors in your astrological chart. Read the monthly forecast sections for both your Sun and Ascendant to gain the most useful information. (To order an accurate natal chart, see Llewellyn's Astrological Services in the back of this book.)

Your "Rewarding and Challenging Days" sections indicate times when you'll feel more centered ("Rewarding") or out of balance ("Challenging"). The Rewarding Days are not the only times you can perform well, but you're likely to feel better integrated! These days support your expression of individual identity. During the Challenging Days, take some extra time to center yourself by meditating or using other techniques which help you feel more objective.

These guidelines, although highly useful, cannot incorporate all the factors influencing your current life situation. However, you can use this information as a form of objective awareness about the way the current cycles are affecting you at an ego level. Realize that the power of astrology is even more useful when you have a complete chart and professional guidance.

1993 marks a year of powerful change on our planet. We are each experiencing the influences of a planetary cycle which occurs once every 170 years, the conjunction of the planets Uranus and Neptune. Not only does this cycle portend major technological, economic and political developments, but a different level of consciousness as well. Concepts such as "virtual reality" are manifesting around us; we make breakthroughs every day. As an individual, you are charged to create a significant reality of your own.

I've attempted to address this cycle for each of the signs in the "Year Ahead" section, so you can find the best ways to use this energy for your personal evolution. Although this cycle *marks a call to awaken*, many will choose to stay in their patterns of self-defeat. You can make the choice, and through your choices, help sound the call for hope.

—Gloria Star

Your Ascendant is the following if your time of birth was:

If your Sun Sign is:	6 to 8 am	8 to 10 am	10 am to Noon	Noon to 2 pm	2 to 4 pm	4 to 6 pm
Aries	Taurus	Gemini	Cancer	Leo	Virgo	Libra
Taurus	Gemini	Cancer	Leo	Virgo	Libra	Scorpio
Gemini	Cancer	Leo	Virgo	Libra	Scorpio	Sagittarius
Cancer	Leo	Virgo	Libra	Scorpio	Sagittarius	Capricorn
Leo	Virgo	Libra	Scorpio	Sagittarius	Capricorn	Aquarius
Virgo	Libra	Scorpio	Sagittarius	Capricorn	Aquarius	Pisces
Libra	Scorpio	Sagittarius	Capricorn	Aquarius	Pisces	Aries
Scorpio	Sagittarius	Capricorn	Aquarius	Pisces	Aries	Taurus
Sagittarius	Capricorn	Aquarius	Pisces	Aries	Taurus	Gemini
Capricorn	Aquarius	Pisces	Aries	Taurus	Gemini	Cancer
Aquarius	Pisces	Aries	Taurus	Gemini	Cancer	Leo
Pisces	Aries	Taurus	Gemini	Cancer	Leo	Virgo

If your Sun Sign is:	6 to 8 pm	8 to 10 pm	10 am to Midnight	Midnight to 2 am	2 to 4 am	4 to 6 am
Aries	Scorpio	Sagittarius	Capricorn	Aquarius	Pisces	Aries
Taurus	Sagittarius	Capricorn	Aquarius	Pisces	Aries	Taurus
Gemini	Capricorn	Aquarius	Pisces	Aries	Taurus	Gemini
Cancer	Aquarius	Pisces	Aries	Taurus	Gemini	Cancer
Leo	Pisces	Aries	Taurus	Gemini	Cancer	Leo
Virgo	Aries	Taurus	Gemini	Cancer	Leo	Virgo
Libra	Taurus	Gemini	Cancer	Leo	Virgo	Libra
Scorpio	Gemini	Cancer	Leo	Virgo	Libra	Scorpio
Sagittarius	Cancer	Leo	Virgo	Libra	Scorpio	Sagittarius
Capricorn	Leo	Virgo	Libra	Scorpio	Sagittarius	Capricorn
Aquarius	Virgo	Libra	Scorpio	Sagittarius	Capricorn	Aquarius
Pisces	Libra	Scorpio	Sagittarius	Capricorn	Aquarius	Pisces

1. Find your Sun Sign (left column);
2. Determine correct approximate time of birth column;
3. Line up your Sun Sign with birth time to find ascendant.

Sign	Glyph	Dates	Ruler	Element	Quality	Nature
Aries	♈	Mar 21-Apr 20	Mars	Fire	Cardinal	Barren
Taurus	♉	Apr 20-May 21	Venus	Earth	Fixed	Semi-Fruitful
Gemini	♊	May 21-June 22	Mercury	Air	Mutable	Barren
Cancer	♋	June 22-July 23	Moon	Water	Cardinal	Fruitful
Leo	♌	July 23-Aug 23	Sun	Fire	Fixed	Barren
Virgo	♍	Aug 23-Sept 23	Mercury	Earth	Mutable	Barren
Libra	♎	Sept 23-Oct 23	Venus	Air	Cardinal	Semi-Fruitful
Scorpio	♏	Oct 23-Nov 22	Pluto	Water	Fixed	Fruitful
Sagittarius	♐	Nov 23-Dec 22	Jupiter	Fire	Mutable	Barren
Capricorn	♑	Dec 22-Jan 21	Saturn	Earth	Cardinal	Semi-Fruitful
Aquarius	♒	Jan 21-Feb 20	Uranus	Air	Fixed	Barren
Pisces	♓	Feb 20-Mar 21	Neptune	Water	Mutable	Fruitful

ARIES
THE RAM

March 21 to April 20

Element: Fire
Quality: Cardinal
Polarity: Masculine/Yang
Planetary Ruler: Mars
Meditation: "I actively pursue the fulfillment of my destiny."
Gemstone: Diamond
Power Stones: Ruby, carnelian, bloodstone
Key Phrase: I am

Glyph: Ram's head
Anatomy: Head and face
Colors: Red and white
Animal: Ram
Myths/Legends: Jason & the Golden Fleece, Artemis
House Association: First
Opposite Sign: Libra
Flower: Geranium
Key Word: Initiative

Positive Expression:
Self-reliant
Energetic
Innovative
Daring
Incisive
Exuberant
Inspiring
Assertive
Exciting
Intrepid
Courageous

Misuse of Energy:
Careless
Rash
Childish
Blunt
Incomplete
Abrasive
Combative
Impatient
Belligerent
Reckless

ARIES

YOUR EGO'S STRENGTHS AND WEAKNESSES:
Your spark and energy ignite the world around you.
Standing in line and waiting for life to happen is not your
style—you're here to pioneer new territory and lead the
way! When new challenges present themselves, you have
the courage to move forward and explore new directions.

When others show hesitation, you're already off and
running. Obstacles frequently dare you to move forward.
Oftentimes you pave the way, but have little time to wonder who's following since you're always looking ahead.

With Mars as your ruling planet, you have the assertiveness and physical drive that create courageous action.
But you also need to be aware that the same energy can feel
sharp or abrasive to others. Sometimes this leads to confrontations from others you failed to anticipate. It's during
these times you can become your own worst enemy by
stirring the hornet's nest. Your fiery temperament can be
inspiring, lighting a path to success and amazing accomplishment. By expanding your awareness of the effect
your actions and words have upon others, you'll find
greater admiration and less confrontation. Taking time out
to enjoy the beauty around you can help widen your perspective, and may even help you avoid running out of
steam!

By using your energy to enjoy life and allowing your
exuberance to keep you ever-young, you have the ability
to create an exceptional reality. Exploring new vistas requires the kind of initiative you possess.

YOUR CAREER DEVELOPMENT: Career development means activity, whether it's physical, mental or emotional. You have the ability to deal with all types of people, but when working closely with others you'll need to find individuals who will not slow your pace. Working independently may appeal to you, and you'll definitely need room to try new ideas. If you lean toward the physical side, athletics, dancing, coaching, fire-fighting, police work or military activity can be positively rewarding. Or you may prefer to use your sharp intellect in pursuits such as politics or medicine. Other good outlets for your energy are auto mechanics or design, metalworking, masonry or welding. Occupations in the travel industry, beauty and hair-design or jewelry-making may suit you nicely. Whatever your pursuits, you have an ability to sell.

YOUR APPROACH TO ROMANCE: For you, much of romance is the conquest. Your impatience may make it difficult to wait for someone to pursue you. Even if another entices you, you like to run the show! Your needs for playful excitement can be attractive to someone who prefers an active love life. If you're allowed the freedom to be yourself, you can maintain a long-term relationship. But you may be very unhappy when you're confined!

You'll probably get along best with the other fire signs—Leo, Sagittarius, or another Aries. Sharing favorite pastimes with Leo can be delightful, but you cannot afford to be disloyal. You're intrigued with Sagittarian intelligence and good humor, and can enjoy a juicy relationship. Another Aries would provide plenty of passion, but may also be too continually challenging.

Taurus' pace may be a bit too slow, but you'll enjoy the sensuality. Virgo's expectations may wear on your patience, even though you enjoy sharing ideas and work well together. Capricorn is definitely intriguing but you may feel inhibited by all those rules. Gemini's wit matches your own, and you'll love the constant diversity. Libra, your provocative opposite sign, can be the perfect partner, but can you meet their demands for perfection? Aquarius' own independence balances your life, and you're likely to feel very comfortable.

The protectiveness of Cancer is great when it comes to meals on the table, but you may run into trouble if you don't show up on time! The intensity of relationship with Scorpio kindles your passion, although in the long-term you may feel you have less power. And with Pisces you can have a failsafe friend, even if you don't always know what to expect.

YOUR USE OF POWER: Since life is more exciting if it's a challenge, you may find you feel most powerful when you're in the process of tackling the job. Once it's done, you're ready for something new! Your greatest power comes when you're taking the lead, whether in independent activities or motivating others. When activity ceases and everyone else has reached a blockade, you're the one with the power to get things moving again. But in many circumstances, maintaining power means heavy responsibility, which is not your cup of tea!

Your approach to handling immovable obstacles or difficult individuals can lead to domineering or selfish behavior on your part. In your desire to get what you want out of life, you may also run rough-shod over someone else, creating trauma through your words or actions. These situations can lead to increased difficulties in relationships with others in both personal and professional arenas unless you can make some changes in your attitudes toward them. Basically, the simple approach is to become aware of the effect your actions have upon the world and those who inhabit it with you!

One of your greatest challenges is to uncover the power that emerges through self-knowledge. This lights your pathway, but also creates a beacon for others who may be unable to see their own way.

FAMOUS ARIANS: Kareem Abdul-Jabbar, Herb Alpert, Johann Sebastian Bach, Pearl Bailey, Marlon Brando, Anita Bryant, Joseph Campbell, Walter P. Chrysler, James Garner, Maxim Gorky, Ann Miller, Dudley Moore, Gregory Peck, Leon Russell, Al Unser, Jr.

ARIES PLACES: Greely, Colorado; Daytona Beach, FL; Peoria, IL; St. Cloud, MN; Dayton, OH; Columbia, SC; Tacoma, WA; Cambodia; Guatemala; Ireland; Spain.

THE YEAR AHEAD FOR ARIES

This is a year for growth, widening your options and moving into uncharted territory — just the kind of year in which you thrive! There are definitely some challenges in 1993, but your courage and initiative will keep you ahead of the game. Relationships may be more demanding than usual, but only if you're taking unnecessary advantage of someone else. You might even benefit from the efforts and resources of others.

Your greatest challenge comes from walking your own path, despite the criticism or misunderstanding of others. This doesn't mean that you have free license to do whatever you want regardless of the impact upon others. But you can no longer compromise your real talents and abilities and hide your true sense of Self. It's time for you to emerge as a positive force which the world around you must acknowledge.

Friends play an important role now, and you may gravitate more toward groups whose interests support your own. It's a great time to get involved in community activities or to support the political ideals to which you adhere. Although staying focused on the present and living in the moment is important, you're looking more toward the long-term goals that can bring you greater satisfaction. This can strongly affect your career path, but can also give you reason to look at the associations you've chosen and decide if they're really good for you.

The Solar and Lunar Eclipse cycles during 1993 emphasize a need for greater cooperative efforts with others, especially in the arenas of resources and finance. When we bring the picture into focus a primary truth emerges: your philosophical approach to the way you're using what you have is crucially important. You may begin to realize how much your use or misuse of what you have effects the quality of your own life. Chiron's travels in 1993 bring your creative expression into use, and stimulate you to find enjoyment in even the most mundane of tasks.

While Jupiter transits in Libra through November 10th, you're experiencing a wonderful chance to see the results of your actions. Relationships with other people, both at work and at home will become more important. If you're involved in a committed relationship, this can be a great year to equalize the relationship and create a healthier emotional environment for both of you. You also need to be careful to avoid taking your partner for granted, since this can lead to major difficulties. If you're seeking a partner, you may have more options than you've ever experienced. You might not like everything you see, since all your old patterns seem to act like a magnet, attracting exactly the kind of person you thought you'd released from your life. But you can break out of that rut by taking a closer look at what you're hoping to gain through connecting with another person. Perhaps you weren't paying as much attention in the past as you are now!

If you were born from March 20th-26th you're likely to find this a year of reaching out to others. This can be accomplished through paying more careful attention to the relations with people you see everyday and solidifying your place within your neighborhood or community. Recognizing better ways to communicate your ideas can also stimulate you to get back into school or pull out the books and get the details you may have skipped over before. It's a wonderful time to fine-tune your skills. Examine the things that are limiting you during January and take actions to expand your horizons throughout the remainder of the year.

Those of you born March 27th to April 5th may find the larger issues are not affecting your sense of self. If you can adhere to the structures you set in place last year, you can experience steady growth without too many disruptions. But initiating too many new projects may scatter your energy to the extent that your hard work seems wasted. By maintaining your concentration and keeping your eyes on the path you've chosen, you can experience positive success in your personal and professional life.

If you were born April 6th to 14th you're ready to diversify and break away from things that are holding you back. The first two months of the year provide you with a good base and may bring some real stability into your profession. Saturn's sextile to your Sun brings the true nature of your responsibilities into focus. Use this base to help you stay focused, since you're entering a period of surprising changes. However, your intuitive guidance can misfire while Uranus squares your Sun if you've not learned ways to recognize your own inner voice. You may wonder whether or not it's safe to follow that voice inside. If you've spent most of your life failing to listen to your intuitive guidance, it may be a very insistent voice this year. However, if you've been developing a strong sensitivity to your inner messages, this can be the time when outside interference is strong. Basically, what you're needing is plenty of room to test your wings, but you want to carry this out within safe territory.

The cumbersome baggage you've created throughout your life seems rather heavy, and if it's unnecessary, it's time to let it go. Your sense of rebellion may be overtaking your good judgement, so be certain you're not throwing something out just because you're fed up with it or with yourself!

To further the uncertainty of the Uranus square Sun cycle, those born from April 6th-14th are also feeling the square of Neptune to the Sun. Your imagination is amplified during this period, and you're ready to bring some of your internal images into real manifestation. It's possible that your creative ideas can truly bear fruit, but your tendency is to go for something before you've thoroughly investigated the possibilities.

This is a superb cycle to get serious about your spiritual life. In fact, taking some extra time to balance your energy and clear your mind is an excellent way to stay focused. But it's not easy to tell who you can trust during this period. All too often you may be tempted to trust the wrong person because you want to believe that what they have to say is the truth. This can bring difficulties into your relationships because you tend to turn your head and look the other way when you know you need to be more attentive. Both these cycles together give you ample reasons to look into your relationship with family and also to examine the ways your early relationships have shaped your current life experience. Your intimate relationships reflect a great deal about the way you feel about who you are.

All Arians are still struggling with the psychological battle between the internal demanding child and the healthy, spontaneous creativity that comes from the same internal space. This is a superb time to examine your inner self through counseling. But those born from the 6th-14th of April have a special dilemma this year. You're likely to vacillate from taking bold, progressive steps to running away from your true Self. To avoid spending this year in a confused haze of rebellion, use your willpower to work more within the creative realm. Recognize that many things are still in formative stages, and it will be difficult to see the whole picture until after this cycle has passed. Remember to take care of your body, since you need it while you're here on the earth plane!

For Arians born from April 11th to 18th life brings a special challenge while Pluto transits in quincunx to your Sun. This cycle provides an excellent stimulus for you to discover your feelings about and use of your power. You're likely to see several areas of abusive power around you through the political realm or even in your work. But you must realize that you don't have to give in to pressures that will compromise your sense of self or what you know to be right. You can be the one who acts as the catalyst for changes in a situation which needs reform. In your personal relationship, this is the perfect time to adjust your attitudes and begin to bring more peace and harmony into your everyday life. Unresolved anger has its way of working to the surface during this cycle. Once you can see these feelings that may have been hidden, you can do something about them! This is the energy of purging. By eliminating your attachment to the elements in your life which are emotionally, spiritually or physically unhealthy you become lighter, more open and can feel more whole. Then your power emerges clear and unemcumbered, giving you the capability of transforming your life.

If you were born from April 13th-20th you're feeling the supportive energy of Saturn transiting in sextile to your Sun throughout the year. During this period you'll find it easier to maintain a stronger sense of Self. This focus gives you direction during times when you're distracted or challenged. Although any Saturn cycle brings work, the more harmonious transits generally bring work you can tolerate! It's a good time to bring your physical health into a higher priority, and you'll be able to strengthen your vitality more easily by maintaining the discipline necessary to stay strong. You may be more willing to make commitments personally and professionally, since you can more readily see the benefit.

Your friends can be highly influential and may be instrumental in helping you realize your goals. It's a great time to give back some of your own good fortune. Use your creativity to find ways that keep you smiling!

TOOLS TO MAKE A DIFFERENCE: With a number of philosophical and political changes occurring in the world, you're also needing to find positive ways to embrace your own beliefs. Contact with others who have similar ideals can be supportive and may also give you a good outlet to explore even more territory. If given the opportunity, take advantage of teaching or inspiring others.

From a psychological viewpoint, you're in a good phase to take a careful look at your Inner Child. It's time to allow your natural spontaneity to emerge. It's also a healthy way to acknowledge some of your early trauma or disappointment and eliminate these wounds from your psyche.

If you're drawn to work with stones or crystals, use your own power stones to help amplify your energy. Wear diamonds, rubies, carnelian or bloodstone to remind your of your inner strength and passion for life. If you're feeling a lack of energy, try wearing red to revitalize you. Plant red and white geraniums in the spring to bring fresh vitality to your garden or windowsill.

If you feel your youthful glow has faded, you're the perfect candidate to use the accupressure points on your face to bring it back. Facial massage is an excellent way to relax. You might also enjoy using cold or warm packs on the face when you're feeling emotionally distraught. Active forms of exercise are always helpful to you, but you also need to spend time in reflection. You'll probably reflect more easily if your body is moving, and might appreciate contemplative forms of exercise such as yoga, Tai Chi or Aikido. Once you've learned how these systems work, you can benefit from teaching them to others.

AFFIRMATION FOR THE YEAR: "I am walking the path of spiritual power."

ACTION TABLES FOR ARIES

These dates reflect the best (but not the *only*) times for success and ease in these activities according to your Sun Sign.

Change Residence	June 2-Aug. 9
Request a Raise	Mar. 23
Begin a Course of Study	May 21, Dec. 13
Visit a Doctor	Feb. 7-Apr. 14; Aug. 26-Sept. 10
Start a Diet	Jan. 11-12; Feb. 8-9; Mar. 7-8; Apr 3-4; May 2-3, 28-29; June 24-25; July 22-23; Aug. 18-19; Sept. 14-15; Oct. 12-13; Nov. 8-9; Dec. 5-6
Begin a Romance	Aug. 17
Join a Club	Jan. 22
Seek Employment	Jan. 2-20; Aug. 26-Sept. 10
Take a Vacation	Jan. 18-19; Feb. 14-15; Mar. 13-14; Apr. 10-11; May 7-8; June 3-4; July 1-2, 28-29; Aug. 24-25; Sept. 20-21; Oct. 18-19; Nov. 14-15; Dec. 12-13
Change Your Wardrobe	Aug. 10-25
End a Relationship	Apr. 6
Seek Professional Advice	Jan. 13-14; Feb. 10-11; Mar. 9-10; Apr. 5-6; May 3-4, 30-31; June 26-27; July 23-25; Aug. 20-21; Sept. 16-17; Oct. 14-15; Nov. 10-11; Dec. 7-9
Have Beauty Treatments	Mar. 23
Obtain a Loan	Jan. 14-15; Feb. 12-13; Mar. 11-12; Apr. 8-9; May 5-6; June 1-2, 28-30; July 26-27; Aug. 22-23; Sept. 18-19; Oct. 16-17; Nov. 12-13; Dec. 10-11

ARIES/JANUARY

PRIMARY FOCUS

Projects that have been pushed aside need attention, especially those around the house! Watch for a surprising change of events that can disrupt your everyday life.

HEALTH AND FITNESS

Concentrate on peaceful moments of relaxation to help you take the edge off stress. Music can be a helpful tool. Watch a tendency to move too quickly from the 13th-21st.

ROMANCE AND RELATIONSHIPS

Family interactions can be volatile, especially near the Full Moon on the 8th. If you change your position on an important issue it could stir up dissent. You're likely to feel rather rebellious early in the month and may take actions just to stimulate reaction—a risky venture! A new romantic attraction from the 5th-22nd can threaten an existing relationship. You may not care whether or not it will lead anywhere since the prospects of enjoyment appear rather delectable. But it's a good idea to move with caution since they may involve someone else! Consult with a friend on the 22nd-23rd if you need another perspective.

FINANCE AND CAREER

Unanticipated changes at work can cause you to wonder where your job is leading. It can be difficult to learn what's expected of you. Move with caution from the 7th-16th, when everything can change overnight. Greater stability comes with the New Moon on the 22nd, although you may still wonder about your level of control over your career path. Reasonable expenditures are necessary now since there can be uncertainty concerning your income.

OPPORTUNITY OF THE MONTH

The 27th-29th are the best times to find out about a productive choice of direction. Keep a close eye on the openings, since you may walk into a peachy circumstance.

Rewarding Days: 1, 5, 6, 9, 18, 23, 24, 27, 28, 29
Challenging Days: 3, 7, 8, 13, 14, 20, 21

AFFIRMATION FOR THE MONTH

"I am in control of my own destiny."

ARIES/FEBRUARY

PRIMARY FOCUS

You have a new perspective on your goals for the future, but need to spend some time nurturing your ideas before you launch into a different direction.

HEALTH AND FITNESS

Looking good becomes a priority and a surface-oriented approach isn't satisfying. Developing a positive attitude toward yourself is crucial now.

ROMANCE AND RELATIONSHIPS

Venus enters a long-term transit in Aries on the 2nd. During this period, you're likely to attract others. The Full Moon on the 6th provides you with a great feeling of bravado, and a bold approach during the week of the 7th can bring exciting results. But you may also have expectations that cannot be met. You're reevaluating the purpose of intimate relationships and may question an existing entanglement. Romance fares nicely from the 18th-20th. However, there's a tendency to overspend or over-indulge. Spend quiet time with your sweetie on the 21st-22nd.

FINANCE AND CAREER

Show your stronger attributes in your career from the 2nd-6th. Taking advantage of changes means thinking quickly, but you have to balance this with planning and good judgement. There's a tendency to spend money from the 8th-21st (try to work within a budget). Strong allies continue to operate on your behalf but may not make an appearance when needed from the 11th-15th. The New Moon on the 21st prompts you to look behind the scenes, where you may discover mismanagement of resources.

OPPORTUNITY OF THE MONTH

Uranus and Neptune conjunct on the 2nd, a time when your clear thinking allows you to use your creative ideas and stimulate action.

Rewarding Days: 1, 2, 6, 14, 15, 19, 20, 24, 25
Challenging Days: 3, 4, 9, 10, 11, 16, 17, 27

AFFIRMATION FOR THE MONTH

"Change is safe."

ARIES/MARCH

PRIMARY FOCUS
Juggling activities can be exhausting this month unless you keep a clear focus on your priorities. Other people have great expectations of you, and those may conflict with your expectations for yourself!

HEALTH AND FITNESS
There's a lot happening, and you may feel you have to move faster just to keep up with your life. Use exercise to give you energy, but watch a tendency to push too much.

ROMANCE AND RELATIONSHIPS
You may feel like you are being drawn and quartered by everyone's demands on you. If you've spread yourself too thin, this is the month you pay the price, since nobody seems to want to take second place! There can be conflict between your parents and your partner, and you may feel there's nothing you can do. By the Vernal Equinox you're taking a stronger stand for your own needs, and can make significant progress on the 23rd, the day of the New Moon. A new romance can be only fascination. Give it time.

FINANCE AND CAREER
Take a careful look at your career growth and consider the best ways to break out of stifling routines. Since Mercury is retrograde until the 22nd you may not feel there's progress being made until the end of the month. It's a great time for background reading, meeting key people behind the scenes and getting caught up on your paperwork. The Full Moon on the 8th arouses undercurrents with your peers or from those you supervise. Initiate your plans for change on the 23rd.

OPPORTUNITY OF THE MONTH
This month's energy is unbeatable for getting rid of excess. That frees you to be ready for new directions on the 23rd and 24th.

Rewarding Days: 1, 5, 6, 13, 14, 18, 23, 24, 28, 29
Challenging Days: 3, 4, 9, 10, 15, 16, 17, 30

AFFIRMATION FOR THE MONTH
"All my actions bring positive change."

ARIES/APRIL

PRIMARY FOCUS

Now you can move forward with those projects and new ideas without feeling that everyone is set to do battle. There are still areas of conflict, but now you're calling the shots!

HEALTH AND FITNESS

Stress mounts, and you need to deal with it directly. Stay active, and increase physical activity after the 16th.

ROMANCE AND RELATIONSHIPS

Questions about love are running busy circles in your heart. It's important that you maintain honesty with yourself about how you really feel toward your partner or lover. The Full Moon on the 6th brings these questions into an expanded focus. Throughout the week of the 4th-10th you may be demanding the impossible from your partner, or vice versa. Talk about your feelings and hopes. Travel after the 15th can bring some new possibilities in the realm of love.

FINANCE AND CAREER

Take special care with your investments or expenditures until after the 22nd. You're likely to be drawn into situations which are entirely overpriced before that time, and may need to do more research before you act. However, it's a good time to sell things you no longer need or to get rid of old clutter! Conflicts with superiors or authorities from the 1st-13th can create difficulties in your career if you're moving along without considering the effect of your actions. After the New Moon on the 21st there's more stability and a greater consistency among those who can influence your career.

OPPORTUNITY OF THE MONTH

The 29th-30th are days of exciting change which arouse your creativity in ways that you find especially gratifying.

Rewarding Days: 2, 10, 14, 19, 20, 24, 25, 29, 30
Challenging Days: 5, 6, 8, 12, 13, 26, 27

AFFIRMATION FOR THE MONTH

"I am moving forward with peaceful intention."

ARIES/MAY

PRIMARY FOCUS

Money, finances and worth seem to play into everything you're doing. Using your resources wisely means applying them in their best possible manner.

HEALTH AND FITNESS

Vitality is strong, and you're ready to play! It's a fantastic time to join a sports team or to become more involved in fitness activities. Recreation helps you feel better.

ROMANCE AND RELATIONSHIPS

Venus and Mars are in the right place to help you improve your love life! An existing relationship benefits from heightened passion. Share your favorite entertainment, the things memories are made of: dancing until dawn, concerts, long romantic evenings. If you're in the market for a relationship, a new love can emerge now. Passion's fireworks can go off near the Solar Eclipse on the 21st. Your head may be turned by an enthralling person from the 25th-31st. Even if the relationship isn't possible, it can be great fun! Just be sure you're not in forbidden territory.

FINANCE AND CAREER

Creativity can carry you to the forefront in your career. Working closely with others on an exciting project can lead to recognition on the 21st. You may also benefit from the good fortune of your partner this month, and need to share the limelight with others. Take a good look at your finances from the 3rd-17th. You're in a good position to reorganize expenditures and make room for greater flexibility. Take special care with spending from the 3rd-6th, when you may be tempted to buy something just because you like it, not because you need it.

OPPORTUNITY OF THE MONTH

From the 21st-23rd you're in a perfect position to make the contacts that can guarantee your success. Stay alert.

Rewarding Days: 7, 8, 12, 13, 17, 18, 21, 22, 23, 26, 27
Challenging Days: 3, 4, 9, 10, 20, 24, 25, 30, 31

AFFIRMATION FOR THE MONTH

"Everything I do brings me joy!"

ARIES/JUNE

PRIMARY FOCUS

In your enthusiasm to make a good impression or to get what you want, you may stir up a negative response. Watch for potholes in the road to your progress.

HEALTH AND FITNESS

An old injury or chronic ailment can be a nuisance this month. New solutions may exist. Deal with problems from the root cause rather then just treating symptoms.

ROMANCE AND RELATIONSHIPS

Some of the sparkle of your love relationship may have dulled due to demands from your partner. You may be accused of a lack of loyalty, when you were really just doing your own thing. At the core of the conflict may be your fear of being controlled. Use the energy of the Lunar Eclipse on the 4th to open the lines of communication between yourself and others. Then, by the time of the New Moon on the 19th you'll feel you've made real progress. There's a potential disagreement with a family member (especially a parent) brewing from the 14th-22nd. Ignoring their overtures will only lead to complications later on.

FINANCE AND CAREER

You may be enjoying financial success now, but need to watch a tendency to misuse your resources from the 8th-14th. If uncertain about the best path to take, consult with experts on the 4th before making a final decision. Watch for power plays by others early in the month. You can take a posture of strength without giving offense and gain the respect of a former enemy on the 22nd-23rd. Disputes over jointly-held property can flare the 26th-30th.

OPPORTUNITY OF THE MONTH

Meetings, conferences and presentations on the 3rd and 4th fare nicely if you're prepared. Your polished approach can make a positive difference.

Rewarding Days: 3, 4, 8, 13, 14, 18, 19, 22, 23
Challenging Days: 2, 6, 7, 16, 20, 21, 26, 27

AFFIRMATION FOR THE MONTH

"I use my resources wisely."

ARIES/JULY

PRIMARY FOCUS

Sorting through misunderstandings in the family can be frustrating during Mercury's retrograde this month. It seems everyone has a language different from your own.

HEALTH AND FITNESS

Take special care to avoid sunburns, insect bites or other irritations of summer. Your body may overreact to such assaults.

ROMANCE AND RELATIONSHIPS

Emotional situations escalate near the time of the Full Moon on the 3rd, and you can feel that you're standing alone. Unfinished family business can take its emotional toll, but you do seem to have an ally in a sibling. The New Moon on the 19th seems to bring a release from the pressure, but it's crucial that you're aware of your responsibility. Romance may have little time to flower this month, although there are some promising developments on the 20th. Consider taking time for leisure, curling up with a good book or taking a long walk on the 28th-29th.

FINANCE AND CAREER

Followthrough on all communications instead of just assuming that everything is running smoothly. When working with superiors, be sure to find out exactly what they expect of you. Avoid making sudden financial or career changes, but do consider new possibilities. It's the perfect time to investigate options. A sudden windfall the week of the 25th may lead to success, but move with care. Changes in personnel after the 23rd can bring vast improvements in your work environment.

OPPORTUNITY OF THE MONTH

If you're frustrated by a lack of progress, try clearing out your closets or your desk this month. Make room for better things. Forward motion arrives on the 28th!

Rewarding Days: 5, 6, 10, 11, 15, 20, 28, 29
Challenging Days: 3, 4, 13, 17, 18, 22, 23, 24, 30, 31

AFFIRMATION FOR THE MONTH

"My thoughts are clear, my mind is open to new ideas."

ARIES/AUGUST

PRIMARY FOCUS

You're looking for a challenge! Find a positive outlet for your competitiveness. When applied to your creativity, this energy stimulates an exciting possibilities.

HEALTH AND FITNESS

Set reasonable goals for your health. If your doctor gives you the go ahead, the energy is right to extend your workouts or join in a challenging sport.

ROMANCE AND RELATIONSHIPS

There's a bit more peace and quiet at home, giving you time to pay attention to more enjoyable activities. This is a good time to make home improvements or decorate. You might enjoy inviting friends to your home the 16th, 20th, 21st or 29th. Romance can be highly enjoyable at the Full Moon on the 2nd. Pleasure travel from the 10th-25th can also enhance your love life. The New Moon on the 17th can bring a new relationship, or bring vitality into an existing relationship. You may feel argumentative after the 12th, try to avoid generating anger from your partner.

FINANCE AND CAREER

Early in the month you're more attentive to details and may prefer to work individually in order to make greater progress. After the 10th your creative ideas can be enhanced through interaction with others. A sudden change of direction from your company after the 17th can open up fresh opportunities, and you'll need extra effort to be sure your special talents are recognized by the right people. Your career growth is supported by understanding what's behind the scenes at the end of the month.

OPPORTUNITY OF THE MONTH

If new directions are presented from the 17th-19th, be sure to look into them. You may change your life significantly.

Rewarding Days: 2, 3, 6, 7, 8, 12, 16, 17, 24, 25, 29
Challenging Days: 10, 14, 15, 20, 21, 23, 26, 27

AFFIRMATION FOR THE MONTH

"My creativity flows from an abundant source."

ARIES/SEPTEMBER

PRIMARY FOCUS

Intimate relationships and partnerships are at the heart of activities this month. It's a time to take definitive action.

HEALTH AND FITNESS

Some extra reading or a class focusing on health concerns would be enlightening from the 1st-10th. Evaluate nutritional support, since you may have increased needs.

ROMANCE AND RELATIONSHIPS

Jumping to conclusions about your partner can lead to trouble. This is a good time to get issues out into the open and seek positive resolution. Existing relationships need TLC, especially near the New Moon on the 15th. Philosophical differences with your partner may raise concerns about making a lasting commitment. Search for common ground instead of continually pointing out your differences. If you've felt that the reins have been too tight, you're likely to bolt midmonth when anything looks better than the confinement you've been experiencing. Spend time with children to rekindle *joie de vivre*.

FINANCE AND CAREER

Communication with co-workers from the 1st-11th improves your job considerably. You may need to form a positive network of support to effectively counteract the changes from management. If you're involved in legal action this month, make a special effort to clarify your position. To avoid legal or financial hassles from the 8th-20th maintain an awareness of the results of your actions. You can benefit from your partner's good fortune this month; be sure to let him/her know you appreciate it!

OPPORTUNITY OF THE MONTH

Clear away the cobwebs and make progress in your dealings with others on the 3rd and then review on the Full Moon on the 30th.

Rewarding Days: 3, 4, 8, 12, 13, 20, 21, 25, 30
Challenging Days: 1, 10, 11, 16, 17, 19, 23, 24

AFFIRMATION FOR THE MONTH

"I am gentle and kind."

ARIES/OCTOBER

PRIMARY FOCUS

This is an excellent time to investigate metaphysics and the ultimate mysteries of life and death. Developing your spiritual path enhances every aspect of your life.

HEALTH AND FITNESS

Chronic ailments can become bothersome, leading you to search for the best way to handle your physical needs. Look into holistic approaches to caring for your health.

ROMANCE AND RELATIONSHIPS

You're not only more willing to be honest about your needs and fears, but also you have a chance to elicit from your partner what s/he needs from you. Your sexual experiences are now driven by a desire to bond with another person, not just to enjoy short-lived passion. It's a good time to explore the best ways to achieve true ecstasy with one another, and to share the magic of intermingling energy. From the New Moon on the 15th until the Full Moon on the 30th you're ready to taste the true sweetness of transformational love.

FINANCE AND CAREER

Your success this month may depend largely upon your ability to work effectively with others. There can be disagreements over the best ways to use the resources of a company or partnership from the 1st-9th. Find ways to eliminate unnecessary programs or expenditures during this time. Talk over ideas with a good friend the week of the 10th. They may help you open exciting new doors! You may feel hard pressed to generate a sense of stability. Take your time finalizing plans after the 25th, when Mercury's retrograde can bring an unexpected outside challenge.

OPPORTUNITY OF THE MONTH

It's fruit basket upset time on the 25th. You may benefit most from careful observation before taking action!

Rewarding Days: 1, 5, 6, 10, 11, 18, 19, 27, 28
Challenging Days: 3, 7, 8, 9, 14, 15, 20, 21, 25

AFFIRMATION FOR THE MONTH

"I am concerned about the needs of others."

ARIES/NOVEMBER

PRIMARY FOCUS

It's crucial to find the best ways to benefit through sharing resources with others. This requires cooperative effort but is well worth the time and energy!

HEALTH AND FITNESS

Schedule a massage the first week of the month to help alleviate accumulated pressure and tension. You might also enjoy health benefits from travel after the 24th.

ROMANCE AND RELATIONSHIPS

Misunderstandings can run rampant this month, so be especially careful to express what you mean. An old love may reenter your life from the 1st-13th, bringing up unresolved issues about money or sex. It's good to allow your feelings to surface and to release your attachment to the past. Past trauma may be the obstacle that's blocked your ability to get close to the ones you love now! By the time of the Lunar Eclipse on the 29th you're feeling the need to change scenery. Consider taking a short trip to clear your mind.

FINANCE AND CAREER

Money matters grow complex now, partly due to oversights and mismanagement. Use Mercury's retrograde through the 14th to review records and balance accounts. A meeting with a financial advisor on the 15th or 16th offers positive insights. Resist increasing your debt load the last half of the month; the price you'll pay later on might not be worth the risk. Presentations or meetings fare nicely after the 23rd. These are also good days to make contacts, write letters and prepare for next month's success.

OPPORTUNITY OF THE MONTH

Plan to travel or spend time in heady discussion with others on the 24th-25th. These are great days for you to inspire others.

Rewarding Days: 1, 6, 7, 14, 15, 19, 24, 25, 29
Challenging Days: 4, 5, 10, 11, 13, 16, 17, 27

AFFIRMATION FOR THE MONTH

"I acknowledge and embrace my inner self."

ARIES/DECEMBER

PRIMARY FOCUS

This is an adventurous month of inspiration and recognition. Teaching or studying provide excellent benefits, especially if you also have a chance to travel.

HEALTH AND FITNESS

Your vitality gets a boost now, and you're raring to get moving. Plan to enjoy your favorite winter sport from the 7th-26th.

ROMANCE AND RELATIONSHIPS

You're ready to find a connection with someone whose ideas about life are similar to your own. Travel can be highly beneficial this month and may provide just the right setting for a romantic interlude. The New Moon on the 13th stimulates you to hold a more open attitude toward others. Throughout that week you seem to have a sparkle that's difficult to ignore. During the week of the 19th seek the company of others who are interested in the same things you are. You may just find the person you've been seeking.

FINANCE AND CAREER

Educational pursuits give your career a boost this month. If you've been needing to take a refresher course or attend a workshop, not only will you improve your skills but also you're likely to enjoy yourself! Your presentations are enthusiastically received by others from the 8th-23rd. Show ways to sustain the programs you're proposing. Legal proceedings run smoothly from the 3rd-26th, but are best the week of the 12th. Watch for jealousy or confrontation on the job during the Full Moon on the 28th.

OPPORTUNITY OF THE MONTH

The 13th is definitely an auspicious day for action leading to prosperity. You're generating much good will from others and need to show independence and generosity.

Rewarding Days: 3, 4, 12, 13, 16, 17, 21, 22, 26, 31
Challenging Days: 1, 2, 6, 7, 8, 14, 15, 28, 29

AFFIRMATION FOR THE MONTH

"I can clearly see the vision of my continued success."

TAURUS
THE BULL

April 20 to May 21

Element: Earth
Quality: Fixed
Polarity: Feminine/Yin
Planetary Ruler: Venus
Meditation: "I am the steward of my environment."
Gemstone: Emerald
Power Stones: Diamond, rose quartz, topaz, blue lace agate
Key Phrase: I have

Glyph: Bull's head
Anatomy: Neck and throat
Color: Green
Animal: Cattle
Myths/Legends: Bull of Minos, Osiris, Ceriddwen
House Association: Second
Opposite Sign: Scorpio
Flower: Violet
Key Word: Conservation

Positive Expression:
 Persistent
 Stable
 Calm
 Steadfast
 Enduring
 Prosperous
 Reliable
 Loving
 Focused
 Substantial

Misuse of Energy:
 Covetous
 Materialistic
 Possessive
 Avaricious
 Lethargic
 Greedy
 Obstinate
 Unyielding

TAURUS

YOUR EGO'S STRENGTHS AND WEAKNESSES:
Your life is a continual building process, with the desire
for stability driving you toward success in your endeavors. When the world feels unsteady, others will flock to
you for strength and reassurance. Your unfaltering devotion toward maintaining security is a haven for those you
love.

Change for its own sake is not appealing to you, since
you don't like to lose precious time or resources. You're
most comfortable when growth is steady and assured,
whether it's in the accumulation of material stability or in
the realm of personal relationships. You look for things
that will endure, and appreciate quality and durability.
Through the energy of Venus, your planetary ruler, you
can express a powerful sense of love and emotion. Beauty
in its natural forms, as well as artistic expression, are important to you. Your own sense of artistry often needs an
outlet for expression.

When you feel threatened, you can become stubbornly
resistant to cooperation with others. Sometimes, you act
against your own best interests in order to simply hold on
to what you possess. Learning to say good-bye to a person
or to any of your possessions can be difficult unless you begin to realize you are more than what you have. This tendency often leads to excessive materialism, especially
when you're feeling emotionally insecure.

You're learning to express steadfastness in a world of
change without falling into a rut, mastering your own

sense of values. As you develop ways to release unnecessary attachments, you make room for even more love to flow into your life.

YOUR CAREER DEVELOPMENT: As a result of your needs for stability, you'll seek a career which allows consistent growth while providing a sound base. With a good head for business, you can recognize a reliable opportunity and have the ability to build a solid financial future. You don't mind working hard if it leads to success. You might enjoy working with your hands, and you have a good sense of structure. These can be applied in the building industry, furniture building or architectural design. Landscape design, gardening, farming, and ranching give you a chance to stay connected to the Earth.

In the arts, you may be an accomplished sculptor, potter or singer. Banking, real estate and investment are appealing areas. You can be an encouraging counselor, whether in business in personal areas. Your love for food might stimulate you to own or work in a restaurant, bakery, or grocery store. The beauty industry (including clothing design, sales or manufacturing), cosmetic industry, or hairdressing can provide satisfying outlets for your creativity.

YOUR APPROACH TO ROMANCE: Your natural sensuality is well-suited to romance. You can be a loyal mate and seek a partner who will enjoy building a home and family. You can be tender yet strong in your physical expression of love.

Commitment in a relationship can bring the positive reward of a love that endures through time. You can also be highly possessive of those you love. To avoid disappointments, watch your tenacity toward trying to keep the status quo instead of allowing the natural changes which occur through the years.

You may be most attracted to Water signs—Scorpio, Pisces and Cancer. Scorpio, your magnetic opposite, appeals to your sensuality and stimulates your passionate side. With Pisces, you enjoy sharing romantic fantasies and can bring dreams into reality. Contentment could be easy with Cancer, who will share your desire for home and family.

The flash and loyalty of Leo are appealing, although

you need to watch a tendency toward competitive ego conflicts. Aries' spontaneity can throw you off balance, while Gemini's versatility challenges you to become more adaptable. With Libra, you share a love for the beautiful things in life, but may feel unstable with his/her indecisiveness. You'll enjoy the generosity of Sagittarius, but may find it difficult to deal with the desire for adventure. Aquarius may live too much in the head for you, as you need more personal attention.

Other Earth signs provide harmony and ease. Another Taurean offers a feeling of steadfast commitment. Virgo understands your need for comfort while Capricorn helps to assure your financial stability.

YOUR USE OF POWER: Your power often comes through building a fortress of strength which no threat can penetrate. This is often accomplished by surrounding yourself with strong material resources, but can also exist within the framework of a loyal company or family. You generate power through maintaining your assets.

Greed or excessive possessiveness can lead to your abuse of power. This usually occurs when you're feeling a threat to your security. You can stand in the way of your own progress when you refuse to change when it's necessary.

Through acknowledging your understanding of the resources of Mother Earth, you can conserve and utilize what you have around you. You also need to learn the value of the people around you, and find ways to share making the most of what you have. By conserving and replenishing Earth's riches, you assure a positive future for your children and future generations. This can be an expression of your endless love which endures beyond time.

FAMOUS TAUREANS: Cher, Fred Astaire, Shirley Temple-Black, Johannes Brahms, George Carlin, Scott Carpenter, Judy Collins, Gary Cooper, Sigmund Freud, Martha Graham, Saddam Hussein, Joe Louis, Nicolo Machiavelli, Jack Nicholson, Benjamin Spock, Mike Wallace

THE YEAR AHEAD FOR TAURUS

Throughout the year you're experiencing an awakening of your faith in yourself. Some of the changes in the world around you may not fit into your old pattern of functioning, but will, instead, call upon your resourcefulness to build strong foundations for future growth. By examining the things which require improvement (including many of your own attitudes) you may find that you're still carrying around some excessive baggage which only serves to slow you down. This is the time to clear away the excess and make way for a less encumbered life.

Balancing hard work with time to enjoy the fruits of your labor can be tricky this year. It may seem that the work load has expanded, but the profit in it has not. This could indicate that you need to take a careful look at your feelings about the ways you've chosen to develop your career. You may very well be using your most creative energy in the least productive tasks. But you have something working in your favor: you can see ways to release the unnecessary and move forward with activities and relationships that bring the sense of stability and security you crave.

1993 is a year of recognizing the pathway to fulfilling your destiny. It's your choice whether or not you want to step onto the path. You're finding different uses for the material things you possess, and may even decide to simplify your life and slow the process of material accumulation in favor of greater peace of mind. This is an especially significant year for Taureans born after May 5th or for those of you who have the Moon, planets or sensitive points in your astrological chart from 15-30 degrees of Taurus.

The Solar and Lunar Eclipse cycles this year emphasize worth and finances, including the resources you share with others. You may feel that other people are not sharing fairly with you. It's also possible that you may be withholding your energy in some ways. Take a careful look at your relationships to determine any areas of unspoken resentment you may be feeling. It's all too easy to hold back when you feel you've been hurt or disappointed in some way. The undercurrent of these events is your own feelings about sharing. Old issues from your early life may be playing a part in your response to the people you care about. Take a look at what you're afraid to lose. This is your time to release that blockage, which only serves to keep you from enjoying the flow of increased possibilities in your own life.

From January through early November, Jupiter transits in the sign of Libra. During this time, you may feel that the rhythm of life is forcing you to move at a pace that's slightly uncomfortable. This discomfort may come from the way you're organizing your priorities. It's too easy during this cycle to become distracted by the bulk of the tasks in front of you. Try to break up these tasks into a manageable size and prioritize them according to their importance. The big picture may simply be too much! Physically, this cycle can also bring along with it a tendency toward self-indulgence. However, you can use this time to improve your health by increasing your focus on activities and a lifestyle which enhances your vitality. Once Jupiter moves into Scorpio in November, you may find it tempting to extend beyond your means, and if you've been gradually inching toward self-indulgence, this cycle can bring a high price to pay. Use this energy to find a heightened sense of self-confidence, but know your boundaries. Feeling the balloon bursting can be a shocking experience!

Taureans born from April 20th-25th are experiencing some relief from much of the inner conflict that has resulted from dealing with the restraints of the world. From April through August you're feeling a positive supportive cycle while Saturn sextiles your Sun. It's up to you to examine your life and make positive improvements now. If you have habits you know to be detrimental to your health, this is a great cycle in which to leave them behind and free yourself of their negative effects! Taking a more responsible attitude toward your career can provide your with the foundation for long-term success With Chiron trine your Sun from September through the end of December, you're feeling more confident about making choices which fulfill your life purpose. Whatever your life path, this is the perfect time to evaluate your long-range goals and put yourself on-track toward achieving them.

If you were born from April 26th-May 4th you've just completed a period of reorganization and change. The endings you experienced during 1992 may have left you feeling somewhat depleted. However, you are now in a positive cycle to move forward and gain some much- deserved recognition. By the end of the year, your resources are more highly diversified and you're feeling like you're finally back on track with your life. Take your time getting started now, since moving too quickly can result in setbacks you hadn't anticipated.

Uranus and Neptune are both trine your Sun this year if you were born from May 5th-13th. This energy stimulates innovative and imaginative possibilities for your life. You can break out of the old image that has kept you feeling trapped and express a more clearly defined projection of your true self. From the psychological standpoint, you're in a period of positive identity crisis, with less resistance from your old inner dialogue. Now you have the opportunity to take a leap of faith and experience a new level of your inner strength. Creative or artistic endeavors take on an exciting dimension now.

This cycle can also bring about changes in your relationships with your parents, particularly your father. Rather than feeling the negative side of the generation gap, you're beginning to experience the positive differences. In your intimate relationships you may feel a need to bring more honesty and spontaneity into your life. Old hurts can easily be resolved now, since you're much more open to forgiving yourself and allowing the pain to dissolve into oblivion. Since you're also feeling a break with the past, you may be confronting some of your fears about taking a stand and living your life on your own terms. Continue to reaffirm the directions you're heading, while gracefully diminishing the need to carry everything with you on this new journey. Saturn's transit is square to your Sun through February, bringing a sense of frustration with the inner desire you feel to break free. From February through December, however, you're ready to surrender to the intuitive voice that can guide you into a reality you never believed possible.

You're experiencing challenges and opportunities,

endings and beginnings all at once if you were born between May 10th-21st. For those born May 10th-13th,
you're still feeling the trine from Uranus and Neptune (see
above). However, you may also find there are obstacles to
achieving the true potential you envision. Most of this results from unresolved feelings of guilt or resentment that
need to finally be erased. It's a wonderful time to do some
positive work on your inner self.

Everyone born from May 10th-21st is experiencing the
transits of Saturn and Pluto to your Sun. This can be a mile-
stone year for you, with the challenge to do with your life
what you feel you must. Now you can't afford compromises that are out of harmony. It's time to eliminate the
things you're holding onto that are outworn or unnecessary to allow yourself the freedom to connect with your
true sense of power. Circumstances can feel beyond your
control, but you do have control of the way you respond to
them. Saturn's square aspect to your Sun can bring a sense
of lowered physical vitality, primarily due to the excessive
responsibilities you may be carrying. Consequently, your
approach to dealing with stress is vitally important.

Pluto opposes your Sun, challenging you to dig deep
and find out who's really hidden at the core of your being.
This cycle brings issues to the surface that may have
haunted you most of your life. It's a great time to clear
away all the debris from your psyche and prepare to fly!
Relationships with people from your past frequently
resurface during this cycle, giving you a chance to reach
closure or to re-connect. You may feel that you're constantly challenged to confront issues from your past without the benefit of dealing directly with the people or circumstances involved. Seeking the support of a counselor
or therapist may be an excellent way to deal with any issues that are overwhelming. At the core, this is a time of
healing. You're transforming and allowing your true essence to emerge pure and free. Because Chiron is also
squaring your Sun until September, you may be feeling a
deep sense of inner unrest and may wonder about the fu-
tility about many of your life choices. Once you clarify
your motivations, this cycle can become quite fruitful, especially in terms of satisfying your deeper needs.

TOOLS TO MAKE A DIFFERENCE: The world around you is in a state of flux and transition, and you can be a participant in the construction of the new order. Your ability to utilize all your resources helps you get through any lean times with more grace than many of your friends. In fact, you can be helpful to others by sharing your knowledge of the practical ways to deal with maintaining stability in a time of unrest.

Since you're likely to feel that your physical system is undergoing a shift, you can use your birthstone and power stones to help you stabilize. Emeralds worn at the neck or near the heart chakra (in the center of the chest) have a positive effect on your sense of vitality. Try working with diamond, rose quartz, topaz or various agates to balance your energy. If you're feeling generally low, use a healing meditation and stones to bring you back into harmony with yourself.

You also respond positively to the color green, and can use the energy of this color when working with visualizations for prosperity and stability. Anytime you're feeling panic or low self-esteem, take a walk through large trees, work in your garden or with your house plants and share some vital life force with the plant kingdom. It's a good idea to keep violets in your home (they usually like kitchen windows). Their evergreen leaves and beautifully colored blossoms are a reminder that you're always continuing to grow.

In your visualizations for 1993, concentrate on the essence of positive growth and development. See yourself walking through an evergreen forest in early springtime after morning rain. Look around you for signs of new life. Become aware of the fragrance of the forest, the moisture in the air. Listen for the songs of birds. Imagine that you are standing in front of an ancient redwood. Nearby, a younger and much smaller tree reaches for the light of the Sun. Feel the symbiosis of the forest, and take with you a sense that time brings growth, and all life is precious.

AFFIRMATION FOR THE YEAR: "I have peace of mind and joy in my heart."

ACTION TABLES FOR TAURUS

These dates reflect the best (but not the *only*) times for success and ease in these activities according to your Sun Sign.

Change Residence	Aug. 10-26
Request a Raise	Apr. 21-22
Begin a Course of Study	Jan. 22, July 19
Visit a Doctor	Apr. 15-May 2; Sept. 11-30
Start a Diet	Jan. 13-14; Feb. 9, 11; Mar. 9-10; Apr. 5, 7; May 3-4, 30-31; June 26-27; July 24-25; Aug. 20-21; Sept. 16-17; Oct. 14-15; Nov. 10-11; Dec. 8-9
Begin a Romance	Sept. 16
Join a Club	Feb. 21
Seek Employment	Jan. 21-Feb. 7; Sept. 11-30
Take a Vacation	Jan. 20-21; Feb. 16-18; Mar. 15-16; Apr. 12-13; May 9-10; June 1-2, 28-29; July 3-4, 30-31; Aug. 26-28; Sept. 23-24; Oct. 20-21; Nov. 16-17; Dec. 14-15
Change Your Wardrobe	Aug. 26-Sept. 10
End a Relationship	May 6
Seek Professional Advice	Jan. 15-16; Feb. 12-13; Mar. 11-12; Apr. 7-8; May 5-6; June 1-2, 28-29; July 26-27; Aug. 22-23; Sept. 18-19; Oct. 16-17; Nov. 12-13; Dec. 10-11
Have a Makeover	Apr. 21
Obtain a Loan	Jan. 18-19; Feb. 26-27; Mar. 13-14; Apr. 9-11; May 7-8; June 3-4; July 1-2, 28-29; Aug. 24-25; Sept. 20-21; Oct. 18-19; Nov. 14-15; Dec. 12-13

TAURUS/JANUARY

PRIMARY FOCUS
Information is your key to success this month. Whether through educational pursuits, networking with others in your field, or making contact with friends and family, this is your time to obtain and share important ideas.

HEALTH AND FITNESS
If you're a winter sports buff, travel to your favorite area to enjoy yourself. Vacationing now is great for your health—perhaps you'd prefer a tropical island. Give yourself a break!

ROMANCE AND RELATIONSHIPS
Contact with siblings looks probable now, with outworn rivalries surfacing near the time of the Full Moon on the 8th. Take a look at your own issues, since that's where the real difficulty resides. Love relationships benefit from time spent away from routine, especially from the 10th-21st. However, there can be squabbles with your partner over finances midmonth. Whether you're already connected or looking for love, travel can provide superbly exciting nuance. Friendship can evolve into deeper ties after the 24th.

FINANCE AND CAREER
Your finances definitely improve, although you do need to budget expenses associated with transportation or education. Limit impulsive expenditures from the 1st-14th. An unexpected reward or gift is likely on the 21st to 22nd. Important presentations fare well the week of the 10th, although an interruption creates confusion on the 14th. Launch a new project after the 22nd.

OPPORTUNITY OF THE MONTH
Stir the imagination of others to elicit their support. Express your ideas on the 12th; manifest them the week of the 17th.

Rewarding Days: 2, 3, 7, 8, 11, 12, 21, 25, 30, 31
Challenging Days: 9, 10, 14, 15, 16, 22, 23

AFFIRMATION FOR THE MONTH
"My mind is open to new possibilities."

TAURUS/FEBRUARY

PRIMARY FOCUS

Your desire to break away from limiting belief systems while avoiding undermining your professional stability creates conflict which reigns supreme this month.

HEALTH AND FITNESS

This is the perfect time to enroll in a fitness or nutrition class. Team sports can be rewarding physically and emotionally.

ROMANCE AND RELATIONSHIPS

What you're expressing may not reflect your real feelings. In fact, you may be harboring secret yearnings about which you can write beautiful verse, yet you may feel blocked when in the presence of your intended beloved. Conflicting emotions can be clarified through some introspective creative activity such as writing. Reasonable caution might be beneficial from the 1st until after the Full Moon on the 6th, when you could find obstacles discouraging. However, the courage to bring your feelings to the surface is much stronger after the New Moon on the 21st.

FINANCE AND CAREER

Finding a way to incorporate new ideas into your current framework may not be easy, but it is possible. Completely overturning the status quo can be self-defeating, while bringing innovation into an existing situation is much more rewarding from the 8th-13th. Business travel is beneficial after the 7th, and fares especially from the 19th-26th. Reconsider your long-range plans when Mercury begins its retrograde cycle on the 27th.

OPPORTUNITY OF THE MONTH

The Uranus-Neptune conjunction on the 2nd stimulates you to reach beyond your current circumstances. Take positive action on the 21st.

Rewarding Days: 4, 5, 8, 16, 17, 21, 22, 26, 27
Challenging Days: 2, 6, 7, 12, 13, 19, 20

AFFIRMATION FOR THE MONTH

"I feel the power of life in everything I say or do."

TAURUS/MARCH

PRIMARY FOCUS

The political scene can have a strong effect on your professional life. Your response to new policies or strategies can strengthen your position, or may open the door to change.

HEALTH AND FITNESS

Get out and experience the healing impact of changing the scenery. Walking would be highly beneficial now.

ROMANCE AND RELATIONSHIPS

Reevaluate your intimate relationships. If you're involved in a committed relationship you may be hungry for a change, but looking outside may not be the answer. You may, instead, find exciting ways to enliven your intimate sharing. A fascination can become a quickly moving entanglement from the 8th-14th, magnified by the Full Moon on the 8th. Watch your friends to learn who really cares about you and who may be using you only to satisfy their selfish needs. Conflicts with family over joint property or other financial issues can arise on the 19th-20th. A stubborn approach on your part will only intensify the situation.

FINANCE AND CAREER

Discontent with your career or the people involved with it can lead you to take strong action. Investigate as many options as possible before making a change, especially while Mercury is retrograde through the 22nd. Things are definitely evolving, and you may even be in the midst of a revolutionary shift. Watch for hidden agenda the week of the 7th. Be aware of undermining from the 19th-24th.

OPPORTUNITY OF THE MONTH

Investigate, inquire and plan. Premature action could be confusing. Allow others to jump off the cliff first.

Rewarding Days: 3, 4, 7, 8, 16, 21, 25, 26, 30
Challenging Days: 5, 6, 11, 12, 14, 18, 19

AFFIRMATION FOR THE MONTH

"I am open to truth and wisdom."

TAURUS/APRIL

PRIMARY FOCUS

Communication, travel and networking can be complex, but rewarding. You're ready to set plans in motion for a change.

HEALTH AND FITNESS

There's a lot of energy seeking an escape route, so some type of physical activity is important. Use extra caution during high-risk activities from the 1st-13th.

ROMANCE AND RELATIONSHIPS

To brighten an existing relationship, plan an amorous vacation between the 1st-15th. You're reviewing and improving love ties. Philosophical connections can make a positive difference, so spend some time sharing your ideas or attending inspiring lectures, concerts or galleries. A new love may be a close as next door, but it's more likely that you'll be attracted to someone whose background is different from your own or who lives far from you. Romance is most exciting from the Full Moon on the 6th until the 10th. However, the New Moon in Taurus on the 21st could also open the door for great improvements in your love life.

FINANCE AND CAREER

Political activities can be extremely important the first half of the month. However, maintain an awareness of the effect rash actions on your part could create from the 1st-11th. A friend can become an important business contact form the 7th-9th. Business travel brings sensational results from the 1st-17th and again on the 21st-22nd.

OPPORTUNITY OF THE MONTH

The Taurus New Moon on the 21st gives you just the boost you need to lay the foundation for strong beginnings. Initiate changes, but expect them to move at a careful pace.

Rewarding Days: 4, 12, 13, 17, 18, 22, 23, 26, 27
Challenging Days: 1, 2, 6, 7, 8, 14, 15, 29, 30

AFFIRMATION FOR THE MONTH

"I am filled with inspiration; my path is clear."

TAURUS/MAY

PRIMARY FOCUS

Activity on the home front multiplies, and can bring turmoil in the family. It's time to break away from the pain of your past.

HEALTH AND FITNESS

Increasing your physical activity level enhances your basic vitality and gives you an outlet to release any anger. To de-stress the 9th-20th try a long walk or good workout.

ROMANCE AND RELATIONSHIPS

The Full Moon on the 5th highlights your partnerships and can intensify any struggles you're having on the romantic front. Any disputes with family can bring tension into your love life, and your only solution is to bring things to the surface. You may find it easier to talk about your feelings from the 4th to 18th. However, your hidden or unspoken response to what you feel can lead to disputes from the 15th-17th. A change of heart after the 25th can lead to new love interests, but you're just playing with fire if you're trying to create jealousy.

FINANCE AND CAREER

Although you know that you're worth more than you're paid, it's difficult to get the point across to the people who matter. Discuss money matters the week of the 9th and then from the 19th-21st. Uncomfortable hidden agendas from the 3rd-10th can lead you to feel you're being compromised. During the Solar Eclipse on the 21st you're ready to seriously consider another way to manage your resources.

OPPORTUNITY OF THE MONTH

Pull together your resources on the 19th and 20th and prepare to take a good look at your financial picture. Necessity may dictate that you curb your spending.

Rewarding Days: 1, 2, 9, 10, 14, 15, 19, 20, 24, 28, 29
Challenging Days: 4, 5, 6, 7, 12, 13, 26, 27, 31

AFFIRMATION FOR THE MONTH

"I carefully utilize my resources."

TAURUS/JUNE

PRIMARY FOCUS

Firm up long range plans. Use progress on the financial front to enhance peace in other areas.

HEALTH AND FITNESS

You're ready to take it easy and might enjoy a vacation. This is a great time to be pampered.

ROMANCE AND RELATIONSHIPS

Venus transits in Taurus this month and your beauty shines through, attracting positive attention and enhancing your loveability. You're also experiencing a long cycle of improved communication. Consider traveling to make the most of your love life but watch out for trouble over power issues from the 10th-18th. A sudden change of scenery turns the tide from the 16th-18th. If you're single, this is a terrific month to make contact with a special person and begin a new love relationship. After the 23rd, love's in the air, the trees, the chocolate strawberries ....

FINANCE AND CAREER

Finances, especially those involving shared resources, can be a source of dispute at the time of the Lunar Eclipse on the 4th which can intensify from the 9th-14th. Consider cutting your losses and breaking free of cumbersome situations. The latter half of the month proves to be more progressive, with an exceptionally good cycle for presentations, sales or communications of importance. Initiate a new program or make fresh contacts after the New Moon on the 19th, but expect a cautious response from the 23rd-26th.

OPPORTUNITY OF THE MONTH

You can make excellent progress on the 15th-16th by taking advantage of a situation that's gone through a radical change.

Rewarding Days: 6, 10, 11, 15, 16, 20, 21, 24 25
Challenging Days: 1, 2, 8, 9, 18, 22, 23, 29, 30

AFFIRMATION FOR THE MONTH

"I clearly communicate my feelings."

TAURUS/JULY

PRIMARY FOCUS

Your tremendous flow of creative energy still may not be enough to help you get beyond your self-doubt. Are you really satisfied?

HEALTH AND FITNESS

Any fitness activities need to be fun, otherwise you won't bother. Dancing, sports, or volleyball games seem much more enticing than sweating it out in a gym.

ROMANCE AND RELATIONSHIPS

You need more passion now, and it may be up to you to provide the stimulus. Consider a trip back to your favorite romantic rendezvous near the Full Moon on the 3rd. A small squabble over money can dampen your romantic plans from the 15th-17th. If you've been wondering when to make the move to connect with the person you've been admiring, you've got the drive and opportunity now. You'll find it easier to draw their attention at the time of the New Moon on the 19th, although you're fairly assertive all month.

FINANCE AND CAREER

While Mercury retrogrades from the 1st-25th you may be experiencing all types of delays or breakdowns in communication. The most frustrating time is from the 15th-25th, when equipment failures can hinder your progress. Be sure to follow through on important matters, since letting things slide now will only lead to dead ends. Get back in touch with individuals or circumstances that were incomplete if you're hoping to see progress. Your creative output is viewed favorably from the 22nd-31st, although progress still feels cautious.

OPPORTUNITY OF THE MONTH

Capitalize on an unexpected change in the system from the 18th-20th.

Rewarding Days: 3, 4, 8, 13, 14, 17, 18, 22, 23, 30
Challenging Days: 1, 5, 6, 11, 20, 21, 26, 27

AFFIRMATION FOR THE MONTH

"I openly express my creativity."

TAURUS/AUGUST

PRIMARY FOCUS
Breaking out of a rut is your key to success. Concentrate on self-improvement, including your relationship with your peers.

HEALTH AND FITNESS
Maintaining optimum health means action now. Spending time outdoors proves to be stimulating from the 2nd-26th.

ROMANCE AND RELATIONSHIPS
Romance is most promising from the 1st-12th. Your eagerness to share your thoughts may be comfortably expressed in phone calls or writing letters to your sweetheart. From the Full Moon on the 2nd until the New Moon on the 17th family responsibilities may get in the way of having a good time, but you can always include your sweetheart. But try not to let these obligations get in the way of your intimate hours. Contact with siblings brings improved relations from the 2nd-10th. Speak from your heart.

FINANCE AND CAREER
The pull between home and career can prove to be highly stressful this month. Take direct action after the 12th to adjust your schedule or realign your priorities, thereby streamlining your productivity in career. Work relationships appear to be strained the latter part of the month, but can be improved by open communication. The second Full Moon of the month on the 31st illuminates possibilities you hadn't previously considered. Contact a friend to discuss different options.

OPPORTUNITY OF THE MONTH
A philosophical change prompts rewarding directions in your career near the time of the Uranus-Neptune conjunction on the 19th.

Rewarding Days: 4, 5, 9, 10, 14, 18, 19, 26, 31
Challenging Days: 2, 3, 7, 16, 17, 22, 23, 29

AFFIRMATION FOR THE MONTH
"I feel stable in the face of change."

TAURUS/SEPTEMBER

PRIMARY FOCUS

Even though the path appears to be rocky, this is an important time to take a leap of faith in your work. Self-improvement is a positive challenge for you this month.

HEALTH AND FITNESS

A tendency to overextend yourself can quickly exhaust your energy. Build stamina while increasing your physical flexibility.

ROMANCE AND RELATIONSHIPS

Although there's romantic activity early in the month, your work may not allow you much time to pursue your desires. Intimacy can blossom through the 11th, but your head may be easily turned midmonth. Are you bored with your partner or with yourself? Increase your show of affection near the New Moon on the 15th to turn the tide. Business travel may tie in to your meeting an intriguing individual. A friendship could become one of your most powerful supports, especially as an ally when things at work may be haywire!

FINANCE AND CAREER

The rate of growth you're experiencing professionally can create a difficult balancing act, so try to avoid taking on more than you can handle. Supportive peer associations are crucial to your success. It may look as though you're pulling everything together on the 7th, only to deal with surprises from government or management by the end of the week. Take heart: things turn around by the 16th (even though you may not like all the changes). Be alert to fireworks in the work place near the Full Moon on the 30th.

OPPORTUNITY OF THE MONTH

You're inspired to take bold steps from the 14th-16th, improving your career options and stabilizing your love life.

Rewarding Days: 1, 5, 6, 10, 11, 14, 15, 23, 28
Challenging Days: 3, 12, 13, 17. 19, 25, 26

AFFIRMATION FOR THE MONTH

"I am confident in all my pursuits."

TAURUS/OCTOBER

PRIMARY FOCUS
Major shifts in the structure of business offer different options. Decide to stabilize by moving forward.

HEALTH AND FITNESS
In order to stay physically healthy, you need to look at the way you're handling stress. Concentrate on releasing tension.

ROMANCE AND RELATIONSHIPS
You're likely to argue more frequently with your partner, or to be the brunt of his/her anger. Under closer scrutiny, you'll probably find that most of the issues have little to do with the person involved, but are connected to outside pressures. If you are ready to break out of a relationship, this is a superb time to say good-bye. New romantic interests flourish the week of the 3rd, or this energy can easily be used to revitalize an existing relationship. From the 25th until the Full Moon on the 30th you're finding excellent ways to express your feelings and open your heart.

FINANCE AND CAREER
Some of the pressures at work may involve social issues, and can bring up some old prejudices you thought were long gone. Use your increased creative flow to get some new programs off the ground (especially from the 15th-30th). Try to keep your foot out of your mouth from the 25th-31st, when your priorities may not synchronize with those of the powers that be. Avoid impulsive spending all month. Finances may be okay, but not too flexible!

OPPORTUNITY OF THE MONTH
While things around you change, you can maintain stability by keeping your priorities clear. Be especially alert on the 26th when a door can swing open, but then close quickly if you fail to act.

Rewarding Days: 2, 3, 7, 8, 12, 13, 20, 21, 25, 26, 30, 31
Challenging Days: 1, 10, 11, 16, 17, 19, 22, 23

AFFIRMATION FOR THE MONTH
"I have ample resources to meet my needs."

TAURUS/NOVEMBER

PRIMARY FOCUS

Interactions with other people seem to take the bulk of your time. Get back in touch and complete unfinished business.

HEALTH AND FITNESS

Unraveling chronic health problems brings success. Examine your dietary habits and consider making a change to lighter fare.

ROMANCE AND RELATIONSHIPS

Misunderstandings can heat up unresolved issues from the 1st-6th. You'll have a chance to smooth things over from the 13th-22nd. Renew or begin a more committed love relationship. The period from the Solar Eclipse on the 13th until the Lunar Eclipse on the 29th is exceptionally good to review "potential" partners. There's plenty of passion to motivate you to express yourself. But when the fires cool, you may find you have a very real connection that's difficult to ignore. This isn't a good time to skim the surface—you're hungry for the whole enchilada!

FINANCE AND CAREER

Disputes over jointly held property or finances can flare. Before you make a final decision, take another look at the whole picture. Mercury's retrograde until the 14th gives you ample time to review the details before making a final judgement. After the 13th you may see things quite differently. A business partnership may bring rewards the latter half of the month, so dissolving all ties may be a rash action. There's certainly plenty of room for improvement, and you have the ammunition you need to renovate.

OPPORTUNITY OF THE MONTH

Look at the other side of a dispute on the 13th. You don't have to give away the farm—just look for mutual benefits!

Rewarding Days: 4, 8, 9, 16, 17, 21, 22, 26, 27
Challenging Days: 1, 6, 7, 12, 13, 19, 20

AFFIRMATION FOR THE MONTH

"My life is filled with joyful new possibilities."

TAURUS/DECEMBER

PRIMARY FOCUS

Get your affairs together for taxes and to review your finances for the year. You'll feel more secure when you know your status.

HEALTH AND FITNESS

Use stress as a positive motivator and find ways to relieve the extra tension. Get to the core of underlying or chronic problems.

ROMANCE AND RELATIONSHIPS

Intimate relationships can often be taken for granted, and it's important to take a careful look at the things you appreciate about your partner. Your yearning for a profound connection can strengthen a relationship or motivate you to look for one! Make contact with your deeper motivations and uncover the areas in your life where you've substituted emotional attachment for real blending. Your approach to fulfilling sexual needs can be rather revealing now. If someone close to you experiences a loss, take time to reflect upon your own mortality. After the 26th you're feeling much lighter, and at the time of the Full Moon on the 28th you're ready to see the world!

FINANCE AND CAREER

You can't afford to ignore financial details. Consult with your accountant or attorney to review your records. In business dealings, the money matters can delay progress if you've failed to account for all the details. The New Moon on the 13th ushers in a good period to seek investors. Business travel may bring lucrative opportunities from the 7th-31st.

OPPORTUNITY OF THE MONTH

The 26th-28th mark an exceptional time to finalize contracts or strengthen important projects. Your persistence pays off!

Rewarding Days: 1, 2, 5, 6, 14, 19, 23, 24, 28, 29
Challenging Days: 3, 4, 8, 10, 11, 16, 17, 30, 31

AFFIRMATION FOR THE MONTH

"I have abundance enough to share."

GEMINI
THE TWIN

May 21 to June 22

Element: Air
Quality: Mutable
Polarity: Masculine/Yang
Planetary Ruler: Mercury
Meditation: "My mind is linked to The Source"
Gemstone: Agate
Power Stones: Herkimer diamond, Alexandrite, Celestite, Aquamarine
Glyph: Pillars of Duality
Key Phrase: I think

Anatomy: Shoulders, arms, hands, lungs, nervous system
Colors: Orange and yellow
Animal: Monkeys, talking birds, flying insects
Myths/Legends: Castor and Pollux, Peter Pan
House Association: Third
Opposite Sign: Sagittarius
Flower: Lily of the Valley
Key Word: Versatility

Positive Expression:
  Skillful
  Articulate
  Perceptive
  Clever
  Flexible
  Rational
  Perspicacious
  Sophisticated
  Inquisitive

Misuse of Energy:
  Unsettled
  Gossipy
  Distant
  Prankish
  Frivolous
  Erratic
  Nervous

GEMINI

YOUR EGO'S STRENGTHS AND WEAKNESSES: A continual sense of curiosity helps you create a life of multiple interests and diversity. Because you're always eager to look into new ideas, you'll project an aura of youth, no matter what your age. It's easy for you to adapt to changes, and you may go out of your way to find them!

Your debonair attitude and strong communicative abilities help you attract people from many backgrounds. A lover of travel, literature, and intelligent ideas, your continued accumulation of information gives you a cosmopolitan air. You're the original networker and a natural negotiator. Your knack for bringing the right people together at the right time can be a strong asset.

It's sometimes difficult for you to do only one thing at a time, since you're usually involved in at least several activities at once. This continual juggling act may keep your life interesting, but is sometimes frustrating to others who aren't sure when you're going to arrive. Your mutability can baffle those who are not accustomed to your multiple-track mind!

The energy of Mercury, your planetary ruler, gives your mental functioning a high priority. Coupled with your strong intuitive abilities, your mind is an exceptional tool through which you develop your special ingenuity. You understand the premise, "What you think, you become," and may need to remind yourself that your mind can be both healer and slayer. Through the link of the mind you connect to the source of all knowledge.

YOUR CAREER DEVELOPMENT: To maintain your interest, your career path needs to be a mental challenge. You're a natural "people-person," and will benefit through developing your communicative skills. Rather than finding just one area of focus, you'll perform better when your life is continually creating new pathways or if your job is highly diversified.

Your fascination with the mind may lead you to a career in counseling or teaching. Public speaking, writing, advertising public relations and broadcasting are all positive expressions of your talents. Highly technological areas can present the right invitation to your need to work with mind and hands together. The performing arts (including juggling, clowning and pantomime) can be a good arena for your natural wit and charm. Also, the automotive or travel industries may have options that pique your interest. Use your manual dexterity in dental, drafting, carving, secretarial or musical pursuits.

YOUR APPROACH TO ROMANCE: Relating is natural for you, and you're thoroughly intrigued by sharing ideas with others. Your sociability gives you plenty of options for partners, but you're only interested in those who appreciate freedom and independence as much as you do! Intellectual repartee can be highly arousing for you. However, it's important to remember that you tend to use ideas and abstractions as a diversion or shield to avoid dealing with or expressing your deeper feelings.

Although you are an Air sign, you may find the Fire signs—Aries, Leo and Sagittarius—to be highly stimulating. However, the attraction and chemistry with your opposite sign, Sagittarius, may lead to a battle if one tries to domineer the other! Aries' independence and assertiveness is invigorating, while Leo's flare for a good time is truly heavenly.

Taurus' sensuality appeals to your need to share touch, but you may find the pace too slow. Another Gemini can bring lots of excitement, but it will be necessary to draw reasonable boundaries about your individual roles in the relationship. The emotional sensitivity of Cancer can be comforting, but s/he may find you too difficult to pin down. Virgo may sometimes be an uncomfortable companion, but is intellectually stimulating.

You'll enjoy Libra's artistry and refinement, and find mutual pleasure in sharing ideas. Scorpio's intense emotionality is engaging, although baffling. Capricorn's controlling nature may be entirely foreign to you. However, Aquarius' unique approach to life is a breath of fresh air. You're often confused by Pisces, but intrigued by their imaginative nature.

YOUR USE OF POWER: The strength of ideas and knowledge provide real power to you. When you're in a situation that calls for a quick solution, you have the power to dazzle them all! In an age when technology and communication are important, you can move into positions of influence. But you need to keep your desire to have diverse experiences in check in order to avoid projecting an air of superficiality. Keeping a focus on your priorities will give others greater confidence in your abilities.

Your aliveness can be contagious, drawing people from all walks of life and cultures. You can identify with the eager spontaneity of the young, and can encourage and inspire young people to manifest their dreams and hopes. Use the power of communication to bridge differences between divergent factions. Celebrate and nurture the continual growth of new ideas. You're here to soar through life, and are keenly attuned to the whisper of Divine Intelligence. Through opening your mind to greater truth you are uplifted, and the spirit of humanity flies with you.

FAMOUS GEMINIS: Alice Bailey, Josephine Baker, Mel Blanc, Bjorn Borg, George Bush, Jacques-Yves Cousteau, Johnny Depp, Ralph Waldo Emerson, Ian Fleming, Marilyn Monroe, Norman Vincent Peale, Phylicia Rashad, Beverly Sills, Donald Trump, Frank Lloyd Wright

THE YEAR AHEAD FOR GEMINI

You have ample opportunities to enjoy the game of life during 1993, and can find abundant outlets for your imaginative ideas. While you may have felt as though you were driving a team of wild horses in 1992, this year provides you with a more definitive sense of direction. Your responses to the other people in your life can generate more favorable support, but you're still faced with the task of upholding your end of the bargain!

Jupiter's transit in Libra, which lasts until November 10th, can be positively supportive to you this year. The key to making this cycle work for you is to find the ways to enjoy whatever you're doing, no matter how mundane the task or circumstance. Bring more light into your life by seeking out experiences which are entertaining and pleasurable to you. Your own Inner Child is likely to be rather demanding during this cycle, and it's an excellent time to openly express your creativity in whatever forms you find comfortable. If you have children, you may find a very special delight in sharing their triumphs and supporting them through their trials. There is a difficult side to this cycle: it's easy to overdo everything. You're feeling the stimulus to push to the limit, but may not recognize those boundaries until you've crossed them!

The Solar and Lunar Eclipses are especially significant for you this year, when the eclipses complete their cycle begun at the end of 1991 in the Gemini-Sagittarius axis. You're continuing to experience an expanded sense of your deeper motivations and needs. Take a careful look at your reasons for commitment (or lack of it!) in relationships. By uncovering the reasons for your choices, you may find that you've actually avoided meeting your needs. This is the year to acknowledge your real feelings about your personal interactions. Your early childhood may also come back into focus. It's a good time to brighten the memory of the joys from your past. You may also uncover some fundamental truths about your past which are less than pleasant. Through the transits signified by the eclipses and the nodes of the Moon, you're in the best possible position to be honest with yourself about your past. Although some realizations may be unpleasant, all of the awareness you're achieving brings release from what was and opens the doorway to what can be.

If you were born from May 21st-24th, you're experiencing a clarified sense of identity. The frustrations of changing directions mid-stream last year are behind you, and now you're in the process of regrouping and getting stabilized. During the months from late May until November of this year you may feel a stronger sense of reverence for yourself stimulated by the energy of the Eclipse near the time of your birthday. Make an extra effort to get in touch with your feelings about your father, especially during the month of June. Pay careful attention to the purpose behind your actions during September and October when Chiron's cycle challenges you to become more purposeful in your choices and actions.

If your birthday falls from May 25th-30th, you may be tempted to jump from one experience into another without giving ample consideration to the consequences of your actions. Uranus' transit is sesquiquad your Sun, and this cycle often brings an unquenchable dissatisfaction with the status quo. The real dilemma is internal, and involves your need to act consciously and creatively. Just following the path set by others is no longer acceptable. You're ready to listen to the inner yearning to express your most soulful desires. This cycle is intensified by the energy of Neptune, which is also sesquiquad your Sun this year. If you've never taken a serious look at your spiritual life, most of the yearning you're feeling will be from the desire to bring the spiritual into your everyday reality. It's not necessary to change everything around you. In fact, jumping from one change to another will only distract you! But it is a superb time to surrender to the voice which urges you to try life on your terms and from your own sense of moral integrity.

For those of you born from May 29th-June 4th, this year provides you with some intriguing revelations about yourself. The lessons you've learned about staying focused are put to the test. Last year, you had some help from the disciplined energy of Saturn, but now you have the choices about how to stay on track. It's easy to allow yourself to be distracted by the complaints of others. Learn to listen to their ideas, but be aware that you don't have to fix their problems! The Lunar Eclipse on June 4th can stimulate you to put someone's needs ahead of your own. This works only if your motivation is pure.

You're feeling the strength and discipline of Saturn's trine to your Sun if you were born from June 5th-21st. This cycle is one of the best to put your priorities in order and eliminate the things that are nonproductive. You may want to get back into school or spend some time fine-tuning your skills this year. It's also a good cycle for extended travel. If you have the opportunity to teach what you know, take it! You'll find that your own knowledge grows exponentially through sharing with others, either formally or informally. Confirm your philosophy of life. Whatever your belief system, it's important to look at the reality behind your ideals. If you've been holding onto an ideology that diminishes your spiritual needs, this is the time to replace your ideals with a system that improves and strengthens your connection to the Source.

For those of you born from June 7th-15th, the Uranus-Neptune conjunction brings a series of unexpected changes into your life. If you've been waiting for everything to be "just right" before you act, you may find yourself feeling forced into action because the fence on which you've been sitting collapses. It's also harder to scatter your energies, since the winds of change are definitely blowing your unfinished projects into a great mess. Now, this is not an impossible time. In fact, it should be rather exciting and can provide you with exceptional creative drive. But you can easily work against yourself if you try to jump from one thing to another without becoming aware of the results of your actions. Your natural ability to cooperate with change works nicely for you during this phase. The difficult part is knowing when to make the adjustments. Fortunately, you do have some help from the Saturn cycle (above) in helping you to keep your priorities straight. Just remember that these priorities are likely to change more than once during the course of the year. Take special care of your health this year, since it's easy to forget about your "human" needs in favor of the more intangible reality that's becoming a large part of your life. Most of the physical changes you're experiencing have a definitive link with the changes in consciousness that you're experiencing. The inventiveness and illumination of this cycle are a great gift. How you use these gifts is up to you! Pluto is transiting in quincunx to your Sun this year if you were born from June 12th-19th. While mysteries of life draw a great deal of your attention, you're also becoming more aware of your own power. Your self-concept can undergo several alterations during this cycle as you become more aware of the need to clarify who you are and where you're going. It's during this phase that you become more aware of your own mortality, while acknowledging the aspect of yourself which is immortal. In the world of work and career, this cycle brings its own special challenges. Others can undermine your progress if you've been ignoring their needs or demands. To use this energy most effectively, concentrate on the improvements which are necessary in your work situation. Ignoring the things which need to be changed can bring unfortunate results. A more intensifed view of your physical health may help you get to the core of any physical complaints and uncover their psychological and spiritual elements.

TOOLS TO MAKE A DIFFERENCE: Several of the cycles for the year present special challenges to your sense of well-being. Instead of making health a negative issue, it's time to become more completely aware of your feeling nature. Some extra time spent in reflection may give you insights that bring vast improvements to your physical health. Spend plenty of time in the fresh air. If you're stuck inside an office or other building, take every opportunity to keep the air moving or to take breaks and change the scenery.

You may respond positively to bright colors and plenty of light in your home and work environments. If possible, keep windows open to allow the circulation of fresh air. Wear your own colors in the orange and yellow spectrum to help revitalize you when you're feeling low. In the springtime, plant various colors of lilies in your garden or have freshly cut lilies nearby. Your flower, Lily of the Valley, is reputed to have special properties. The flowers, soaked in white wine, can be sipped to strengthen memory or can be used as a rub for aching joints. Try rubbing the tincture onto your temples for a headache. The aromatic properties of Lily of the Valley are sometimes used as a mild soporofic. To keep the skin of your hands supple, try a cream with comfrey and marigold. (Always remember to try a patch test before using any herbal creams or remedies just to be sure you're not allergic to them!)

Use your power stones of quartz and alexandrite to help you maintain your energy and concentration. Use deep breathing to help your your mind. This can be achieved through heightened aerobic activity or through concentrated breathing exercises. Yogic pranayamas are especially useful when you're trying to balance your energy.

This is a year of ideas for you, and you need an outlet to bring those ideas into manifestation. Although keeping a journal may seem rather tedious to you, it's still a good idea to have one around for the times when you want to record your reflections. Because you may have more inspiration than you have time to realize it, keep note of those ideas in a special place. Then, if the lean times come later on, you'll have a plethora of ideas to develop! This is also an excellent time to develop your speaking skills. Volunteer to speak for special interest groups, or consider taking courses in public speaking.

You're a natural at creative visualization, and you might also enjoy learning some neurolinguistic programming techniques. Not only can this understanding help you improve your ability to communicate your thoughts and feelings more effectively, but you'll also learn ways to elicit better information from others. One of your best tools to develop this year is the ability to listen more effectively, giving you a better arena for responses that will take you toward fantastic opportunities. In your reflective time, envision yourself in an amphitheater in the presence of a great teacher. You're learning the formula for peace and prosperity. Listen to this inner voice, which is connected to the source of all wisdom. Open your consciousness to accept the information that comes from the All-Knowing Universal Mind.

AFFIRMATION FOR THE YEAR: "I joyfully follow my creative inspiration."

ACTION TABLES FOR GEMINI

These dates reflect the best (but not the *only*) times for success and ease in these activities according to your Sun Sign.

Change Residence	Aug. 26-Sept. 10
Request a Raise	Mar. 23
Begin a Course of Study	Jan. 22, Aug 18
Visit a Doctor	May 4-17; Oct. 1-Dec. 6
Start a Diet	Jan. 15-16; Feb. 12-13;
	Mar. 11-12; Apr 7-8;
	May 5-6; June 1-2, 29-30;
	July 26-27; Aug. 22-23;
	Sept. 18-19; Oct. 16-17;
	Nov. 12-13; Dec. 10-11
Begin a Romance	Oct. 15
Join a Club	Apr. 23
Seek Employment	Feb. 8-Apr. 14; Oct. 2-Dec. 6
Take a Vacation	Jan. 22-23; Feb. 19-20;
	Mar. 18-19; Apr. 14-15;
	May 12-13; June 8-9;
	July 5-6; Aug. 29-30;
	Sept. 18-19; Oct. 22-23;
	Nov. 19-20; Dec. 16-17
Change Your Wardrobe	Sept. 11-30
End a Relationship	June 4
Seek Professional Advice	Jan. 18-19; Feb. 14-15;
	Mar. 13-14; Apr. 10-11;
	May 7-8; June 3-4;
	July 1-2, 28-29; Aug. 24-25;
	Sept. 20-21; Oct. 18-19;
	Nov. 14-15; Dec. 12-13
Have a Makeover	June 4
Obtain a Loan	Jan. 20-21; Feb. 16-17;
	Mar. 15-17; Apr. 12-13;
	May 9-10; June 6-7;
	July 3-4, 30-31; Aug. 26-27;
	Sept. 23-24; Oct. 20-21;
	Nov. 16-17; Dec. 14-15

GEMINI/JANUARY

PRIMARY FOCUS

Money issues can create a wedge in your relationships. Simplify your finances by eliminating unnecessary expenditures.

HEALTH AND FITNESS

Stress plays a major role, and it's critical that you allow time to release tension. Schedule a massage the 8th, 9th or 16th.

ROMANCE AND RELATIONSHIPS

If you've been feeling less connected to your partner, it could be the result of diminshed sexual activity. You may feel you have little time for romantic playfulness. A flirtation from the 1st-9th may create more trouble than it's worth. It's likely to be only a flash in the pan. Romance novels are safer than new entanglements the weekend of the 16th. Reevaluate your feelings after the New Moon on the 22nd, when you're more open to exploring your true affection. Allow time for your inner self on the 31st.

FINANCE AND CAREER

The basis behind your thoughts about money involves the feeling that you're not receiving sufficient reward for your efforts. If your options are too limited in your current job, take a look at other possibilities. The time near the Full Moon on the 8th may be too emotionally charged to make a rational decision about your career. But if you've limited yourself too severely, it's a good time to consider other choices. An educational pursuit can broaden your options after the 21st. Presentations fare best the afternoon of the 22nd or from the 27th to 29th.

OPPORTUNITY OF THE MONTH

You're breaking out of old attitudes about your material needs on the 22nd and 23rd. Use this time for meaningful conversation.

Rewarding Days: 5, 6, 9, 13, 14, 22, 23, 24, 28, 29
Challenging Days: 3, 8, 11, 12, 18, 19, 21, 25, 26

AFFIRMATION FOR THE MONTH

"I honestly acknowledge my feelings."

GEMINI/FEBRUARY

PRIMARY FOCUS

Increased support from others can open new avenues, but you may feel that someone has abandoned you. Still it is a hopeful time.

HEALTH AND FITNESS

If you've been ignoring your health, begin now to gradually increase your activity and evaluate your nutritional needs.

ROMANCE AND RELATIONSHIPS

Your friends play a special part in uplifting your spirits. A romance can result from a connection with a friend, but it may also generate some jealousy. Involvement in group activities can result in an uncomfortable position of leadership. Plan a romantic get-away the weekend of the 6th, which is also a good time to talk about your hopes for the future. Take a different approach to dealing with your parents after the New Moon on the 21st when they may be more open to your ideas.

FINANCE AND CAREER

The Uranus/Neptune conjunction on the 2nd may stir up financial dragons you thought to be fast asleep. Take special care with matters involving taxes this month. Expenditures at work may also be problematic due to mismanagement or oversight, leaving you feeling responsible. You can be highly influential near the time of the Full Moon on the 6th, and if you have political ambitions may want to use this time to take a public stand on an issue. However, plans can backfire if you go into negotiations unprepared from the 11th-20th, so do your homework!

OPPORTUNITY OF THE MONTH

You're in a strong position from the 2nd-6th to turn the tide, bringing others around to your way of thinking. The limelight can be quite beneficial now.

Rewarding Days: 1, 2, 5, 6, 10, 19, 20, 24
Challenging Days: 4, 8, 9, 14, 15, 21, 22

AFFIRMATION FOR THE MONTH

"I speak words of love and hope."

GEMINI/MARCH

PRIMARY FOCUS

Your integrity and sense of moral judgment may be tested by others less scrupulous than yourself. True friends show their support, but you're the one who has to make the final choice.

HEALTH AND FITNESS

Find something you enjoy and commit to stay with it. A fitness class or team sport could be the perfect solution.

ROMANCE AND RELATIONSHIPS

You're ready to experience greater enjoyment in your sex life, although this may create some friction with your current partner. It's easy to get distracted by a more delectable person, who, in the long run, may prove to offer less than you'd thought. A relationship that's reached its completion ends between the 19th-26th. But one that still offers promise can be reborn. Take another look on the 23rd, when you may find the positives outweighing the negatives.

FINANCE AND CAREER

Between equipment failures and breakdowns in communication with your boss, you may be ready to throw it all out the window! Mercury's retrograde until the 22nd is only part of the dilemma. The real issue involves your deeper convictions about your work and the integrity you expect. Carefully explore details before exposing any corruption. New allies surface after the 21st. A tendency toward extravagant expenditures from the 7th-19th can drain your cash reserves. Investigate before you invest. Next month is better.

OPPORTUNITY OF THE MONTH

The New Moon on the 23rd brings a strong ray of hope for meaningful rewards from your career. Listen before you take action.

Rewarding Days: 1, 2, 5, 6, 9, 10, 18, 23, 24, 28, 29
Challenging Days: 4, 7, 8, 13, 14, 16, 20, 21, 26

AFFIRMATION FOR THE MONTH

"My mind is balanced and clear."

GEMINI/APRIL

PRIMARY FOCUS
Just when you thought things couldn't get more complicated, new surprises throw a monkey wrench in the works! Before you rush in to save the day, be sure you're ready for the consequences.

HEALTH AND FITNESS
Nutritional support for your nervous system helps you survive the hectic pace. Allow time to balance activity and relaxation.

ROMANCE AND RELATIONSHIPS
Relationships can be aggravating if you're trying to keep others happy while avoiding fulfilling your own needs. Watch a tendency to leap before you look from the 3rd-14th. Fascination may be fleeting and costly. You're definitely asking questions about the value of maintaining a love relationship. Romantic sparks from a friendship can lead to a passionate encounter near the time of the Full Moon on the 6th. A tendency to say just the wrong things is strong on the 28th-29th.

FINANCE AND CAREER
Money matters are complex, and you may feel you're living too close to the edge. Turn this around by taking time to evaluate where you'd like to be and begin to create the space for that reality in your consciousness. This is the time to turn away from actions that undermine your stability. Although you may be tempted to shop for a new wardrobe or stock your home or office with more fancy gadgets, wait until after the 23rd before you make large purchases. You'll get a better bargain!

OPPORTUNITY OF THE MONTH
Some careful work behind the scenes during the New Moon on the 21st can lead to substantial agreements on the 24th and 25th.

Rewarding Days: 1, 5, 6, 14, 19, 24, 25, 29
Challenging Days: 3, 4, 8, 10, 11, 15, 17, 18, 22

AFFIRMATION FOR THE MONTH
"I honor my intuitive voice."

GEMINI/MAY

PRIMARY FOCUS
Definite decisions are required from you this month. You can't afford a lack of focus or to avoid commitment.

HEALTH AND FITNESS
It's much easier to make time for yourself. To strengthen your vitality, increase your activity level and get outdoors.

ROMANCE AND RELATIONSHIPS
Friendships play an important role, influencing your love life. If you're seeking a relationship, connect with groups who share your special interests. Active pursuit of romance is definitely rewarding this month, but your actions can backfire on the Full Moon on the 5th due to mixed signals. Your roving eye can get you into trouble the week of the 23rd unless you're really free to pursue the object of your desire. Near the time of the Solar Eclipse in Gemini on the 21st you may feel pressured to compromise. Open, honest conversations can lead to a consensus.

FINANCE AND CAREER
Progress in your career path comes through more consistent networking and active communication. Get down to core issues with coworkers or employees on the 5th and 6th. Concentrate on letters, presentations or conferences on the 12th, 13th, and after the 17th. If you run into snags from authorities on the 21st-22nd, regroup and try a more simplified approach. There's some relief on the financial front, but you still need to keep a tendency toward impulsive expenditures in check after the 24th.

OPPORTUNITY OF THE MONTH
During the Solar Eclipse on the 21st you have a special look at the way you can isolate others through too much mental activity.

Rewarding Days: 3, 4, 12, 13, 17, 21, 22, 26, 30, 31
Challenging Days: 1, 2, 6, 7, 8, 14, 15, 28, 29

AFFIRMATION FOR THE MONTH
"I am open to the ideas of others."

GEMINI/JUNE

PRIMARY FOCUS

Even though your days may be full of open conversations with others, the emotions brewing behind the scenes may keep you up at night. Keeping a journal might broaden your perspective.

HEALTH AND FITNESS

Deliberately set aside time for yourself for your own peace of mind. The rush of activities can leave little time for leisure.

ROMANCE AND RELATIONSHIPS

What you desire from your love life may contrast sharply with what you're experiencing! Contemplate your true feelings and needs during the Lunar Eclipse on the 4th. An existing commitment or the consideration of a long-term relationship gives you reason to explore new possibilities. Communication may bog down when it comes to finances. Watch a tendency to project things onto your partner which really belong to your past! By the time of the New Moon in Gemini on the 19th, you're ready to try something different.

FINANCE AND CAREER

Although you're eager to get involved in a more exciting activity in your career, there's red tape holding up your progress. The waiting time gives you a chance to take another look before you move forward. Be sure you're not just following a desire to escape, since your responsibilities will catch up with you sooner or later! Be cautious with expenditures from the 13th-22nd, since there are likely to be hidden circumstances that surface later on. Extravagance proves too costly from the 26th-30th.

OPPORTUNITY OF THE MONTH

The Gemini New Moon on the 19th gives you a chance to start over or step into a new direction. Move carefully.

Rewarding Days: 8, 9, 13, 18, 19, 22, 23, 27
Challenging Days: 2, 3, 4, 10, 11, 16, 24, 25

AFFIRMATION FOR THE MONTH

"I have ample time to do everything I desire."

GEMINI/JULY

PRIMARY FOCUS
There's a lot of activity on the home front, and you may want to move. Take major steps cautiously to avoid financial blunders.

HEALTH AND FITNESS
Your stress level rises, but you feel powerless to do much about it. Use positive affirmations to boost your self-concept.

ROMANCE AND RELATIONSHIPS
Time spent with your sweetheart can be quite enjoyable, but there's the problem of satisfying demands from family. Try to include everyone in your plans, especially from the 15th-17th. A romantic interlude on the 24th or 25th can smooth over some rough edges. Venus transits in Gemini from the 6th-31st, supporting your ability to get in touch with and express your feelings more clearly.

FINANCE AND CAREER
Although you may be attracting greater resources, they may not go as far as you had hoped. Mercury's retrograde cycle through the 25th only serves to complicate matters, since all progress may seem to be dependent on something outside your own influence. Review your finances with an expert, and get caught up with important paperwork. Watch for a surprising development with a partner near the Full Moon on the 3rd. Be alert to an eruption of previously hidden animosity among co-workers or employees mid-month. Take action after the New Moon on the 19th, when you know more of what to expect. Negotiate agreements, and put them into action after the 24th.

OPPORTUNITY OF THE MONTH
Your articulate charm wins support on the 15th, but you may feel most confident about taking risks on the 24th and 25th.

Rewarding Days: 5, 6, 10, 15, 16, 20, 24, 25
Challenging Days: 1, 2, 3, 8, 9, 22, 23, 28, 29

AFFIRMATION FOR THE MONTH
"I deserve to have my needs fulfilled."

GEMINI/AUGUST

PRIMARY FOCUS
With ample reasons to celebrate, you're enjoying a strong period of creative inspiration. The momentum gets going now, and continues for several weeks. Travel looks promising.

HEALTH AND FITNESS
Recreation and heightened activity add sparkle to your life. Get involved in a sport or enjoyable fitness routine after the 8th.

ROMANCE AND RELATIONSHIPS
If you've been out of touch with a brother or sister, take time to connect from the 10th-25th. Each of you can benefit from the support and camaraderie. You uncover common ground at the time of the Full Moon on the 2nd. Significant improvement in your love life from the 13th-17th stimulates positive emotional candor. Conflict can arise on the 19th if you're trying to avoid honest intimacy. If you're ready, this may be the time you discover the depth of your passion.

FINANCE AND CAREER
Incomplete contracts or unfinished business can interrupt your schedule from the 1st-10th. Double-check your figures before you agree to prices. Situations you thought to be stable can suddenly unravel on the 19th, but if you're paying attention to details you can avoid extreme difficulty. Chiseling a more defined niche for your talents becomes a priority at work. If you lose the support of a former ally, better circumstances arise later on. Take initial steps during the New Moon on the 17th to set your plan of action into motion.

OPPORTUNITY OF THE MONTH
Plan an important conference on the 12th to solidify agreements and gain trust. You can be quite impressive.

Rewarding Days: 2, 7, 11, 12, 16, 20, 21, 29
Challenging Days: 4, 5, 14, 18, 19, 24, 25, 31

AFFIRMATION FOR THE MONTH
"My enthusiasm is powered by truth."

GEMINI/SEPTEMBER

PRIMARY FOCUS

Your freshness and ingenuity set you apart from the crowd. Your creative expression is fueled by love, which shines through all you do.

HEALTH AND FITNESS

Your mental attitude is lifting, and health issues improve dramatically. Supportive personal affirmations work wonders now!

ROMANCE AND RELATIONSHIPS

Send loving messages to your sweetheart through expressive, open communication from the 8th-18th. Traveling may draw significant individuals into your field of influence. While Mars and Jupiter both transit through your Solar Fifth House all month you're feeling a tremendous surge of energy propelling you to take leaps in your love life. You may encounter an enthralling love interest midmonth. By the time of the Full Moon on the 30th you've had ample opportunity to find out how you really feel. Children can play a special role, providing the impetus for greater joy.

FINANCE AND CAREER

Concentrate sufficient energy on your career growth. Your presentations or attendance at conferences can make a significant impact on the 3rd, 8th, 9th, 13th and 17th. Regroup at the New Moon on the 15th before taking the stage the next day. Watch financial dealings from the 22nd-29th to be sure you're not just jumping in before you know all the details. Extravagance during this period is likely to result in diminishing your stability.

OPPORTUNITY OF THE MONTH

Take advantage of sudden changes in circumstance on the 16th. These doors may close quickly.

Rewarding Days: 3, 4, 8, 9, 12, 13, 16, 17, 25, 26, 30
Challenging Days: 1, 6, 11, 14, 15, 20, 21, 28

AFFIRMATION FOR THE MONTH

"I am filled with love and joy!"

GEMINI/OCTOBER

PRIMARY FOCUS

Sudden changes can scatter your concentration. By maintaining your priorities you'll still be able to show strong growth in the midst of the confusion that surrounds you.

HEALTH AND FITNESS

Thinking about your health is insufficient. It's time to take definitive action. Break away from the habits undermining your vitality.

ROMANCE AND RELATIONSHIPS

Your favorite romancing may happen at home, where quiet candle-lit dinners and soft moonlight set the stage for more intimate encounter. It's quite possible that your head will be turned by a new arrival the week of the 10th. At the time of the New Moon on the 15th you're in an exceptionally strong phase to try something different in the way of romance. If you're having difficulty in your love relationship, physical intimacy can prove to be more like a battle ground. Anger may open deeper wounds, allowing you to uncover the core of your love (or lack of it!).

FINANCE AND CAREER

Relationships with co-workers can be highly frustrating this month. United efforts seem to work against your best interests. A budgetary crunch may temporarily freeze your financial flexibility. Expect a change in position near the time of the Uranus-Neptune conjunction on the 25th. The Full Moon on the 30th intensifies the situation, although your partner or the efforts of others offers much-needed support.

OPPORTUNITY OF THE MONTH

Your flexibility serves you well. Negotiations on the 15th bring the stability for making changes without overturning the applecart.

Rewarding Days: 1, 5, 6, 14, 15, 22, 23, 27
Challenging Days: 3, 8, 10, 12, 13, 18, 19, 25

AFFIRMATION FOR THE MONTH

"My challenges bring exciting rewards."

GEMINI/NOVEMBER

PRIMARY FOCUS
Requests and demands from others can keep your head spinning. Procrastination can be damaging, so move with great care.

HEALTH AND FITNESS
Get to the core of any physical problems. Knowledge is your best weapon; compassion for yourself, your best healer.

ROMANCE AND RELATIONSHIPS
Every relationship may feel like a "working" relationship. An affair seeks to have greater long-term meaning. A marriage stirs up ancient trauma. And if you're single, you may yearn for a warm caress in the hours of darkness. The real dilemma is within the recesses of your soul. Past situations in which you've managed to side-step intimacy may haunt you. It's a positive lesson, since you come away with the knowledge of the best ways to proceed in the future. By the time of the Lunar Eclipse on the 29th, you're more focused on a healthier way of rediscovering yourself.

FINANCE AND CAREER
Mercury's retrograde until the 15th brings more garbage to the surface. Your real responsibilities become clear. A business partner can be argumentative after the 9th, but at least you know where they stand! Gossip can be demeaning unless you take the time for direct communication. The days near the Solar Eclipse on the 13th are indicative of a need to get serious about your duties. Eliminate nonproductive activities.

OPPORTUNITY OF THE MONTH
Supportive response during conferences or negotiations is likely on the 6th and 7th. If you cannot reach a consensus, finalize these dealings on the 25th.

Rewarding Days: 1, 2, 6, 7, 10, 19, 24, 25, 29
Challenging Days: 4, 8, 9, 13, 14, 15, 21, 22

AFFIRMATION FOR THE MONTH
"I have faith in myself."

GEMINI/DECEMBER

PRIMARY FOCUS
Social activities take a front seat. Your partner's involvement compels you into new situations. At least it's a good forum for conversation!

HEALTH AND FITNESS
With Mars transiting in opposition to your Sun, your engine's revving! Get an early start on your favorite winter sports.

ROMANCE AND RELATIONSHIPS
The need to make a commitment may give you ample reasons to question the value of your on-going relationship. The New Moon on the 13th stimulates the idea of moving into a more exclusive relationship with one another. An existing love can grow into more unified understanding. Frank talk about your sexual needs can be illuminating after the 26th. If you're open, an experience of true ecstasy can await you during the Full Moon on the 28th. But you might also decide to end a relationship if the real bond you require is not possible.

FINANCE AND CAREER
Your interactions with others is productive. Concentrate on activities which bring you into the social scene and increase your recognizability. Business partnerships flourish mid-month, but there may be some dissension over jointly-held properties or finances after the 20th. Inappropriate jealousy in the workplace on the 10th causes problems if unchecked. Seek out investors from the 26th-29th. Legal action fares best the week of the 12th.

OPPORTUNITY OF THE MONTH
Take advantage of contacts with others on the 13th by working cooperatively toward a common goal. Your allies are assets.

Rewarding Days: 3. 4. 8. 13. 16. 17. 21. 26. 27, 31
Challenging Days: 2, 5, 6, 10, 12, 18, 19, 24

AFFIRMATION FOR THE MONTH
"I carefully listen to my intuitive voice."

CANCER
THE CRAB

June 22 to July 23

Element: Water
Quality: Cardinal
Polarity: Feminine/Yin
Planetary Ruler: Moon
Meditation: "Awareness of inner feelings"
Gemstone: Pearl
Power Stones: Moonstone, chrysocolla
Glyph: Breast or crab claws
Key Phrase: I think

Anatomy: Stomach, breasts
Colors: Silver, pearl white
Animal: Crustaceans, cows, chickens
Myths/Legends: Hecate, Asherah, Hercules and the Crab
House Association: Fourth
Opposite Sign: Capricorn
Flower: Larkspur
Key Word: Receptivity

Positive Expression
  Nurturing
  Tenderhearted
  Devoted
  Patriotic
  Protective
  Sensitive
  Tenacious
  Concerned
  Sympathetic
  Intuitive
  Maternal

Misuse of Energy
  Smothering
  Defensive
  Insecure
  Brooding
  Manipulative
  Suspicious
  Anxious
  Moody
  Crabby
  Isolationistic

CANCER

YOUR EGO'S STRENGTHS AND WEAKNESSES:
Growth is the essence of your vitality. Your ability to sustain and nurture is the core of your strength. You may find it easy to provide protection to others and can be positively supportive in times of crisis. Not only does your family count on your devotion, but you may find that others in the work place look to you for comfort and understanding.

Both Cancerian men and women are ruled by the energy of the Moon, and have a natural attunement to the cycles of change. It is also through this energy that a strong domestic sensibility emerges. Your surroundings need to reflect an atmosphere of ease and you may enjoy creating a cozy warmth through crafts, cooking or other related activities. You can generate a feeling of solace in any environment.

Although you may intend to provide sustenance or care, others may interpret your actions as smothering if they're carried too far. Use your psychic sensitivity to help you know when you've reached too deeply into another person's boundaries! Allow your reverence for the past to emerge as part of your inner security, instead of insulating yourself from change or positive growth. And remember that what you instill in those you care for goes with them, even when they've moved out of the nest!

Through your concern for maintaining a high quality of life, you can help to sustain your connection to the essence of the Divine Feminine or Goddess. To keep this energy flowing smoothly, you need only learn the lesson of the cycles—"for everything there is a season."

YOUR CAREER DEVELOPMENT: Through using your awareness of the energy around you, you can assure your success in numerous business or career ventures. Your pride in your nation or community may lead you to pursue a political career. Working in the restaurant business, hotel industry, home furnishings, antiques, or real estate may be lucrative and enjoyable for you.

With your ability to hold onto your assets and possessions, you may become quite wealthy and influential. Any position of prominence suits you, and your aptitude for influencing others can assist your climb up the ladder. Teaching may feel natural for you, and you might also enjoy history and archaeology.

Your attunement to others can also be helpful in counseling. The medical field can be an excellent outlet for your desire to care for others. And you may also find that your enviable green thumb can be useful in the landscaping or floral industry.

YOUR APPROACH TO ROMANCE: You're looking for a love that can mature through devotion and care for one another. It might be difficult to keep positive boundaries in your relationships, since you tend to feel everything that's going on. But you don't have to be responsible for the happiness of the one you love! If you're hurt, you might also withdraw and keep yourself from feeling the very closeness you crave. Give yourself plenty of opportunities to hug. And look for a partner who appreciates your sensuality and desire for sustained lovemaking.

You may find it easier to get along with the other Water signs—Scorpio, Pisces and Cancer. With another Cancerian you may devote much of your energy toward developing a strong home and family life. Scorpio encourages your deeper passions and can facilitate your creativity, while Pisces' mystical imagination stimulates your most profound hopes.

Aries moves so quickly you may often feel hurt, although continually attracted. You're safe with Taurus who gives you the room to develop your dreams. Watch your tendency to mother Gemini, who may have different things in mind! And be wary of losing the spotlight to Leo, who can be fun but may not always give you the appreciation you desire.

Virgo's helpful understanding can provide a good platform for your free self-expression. But Libra can throw you off balance, leaving you wondering what's going on. Sagittarius may feel entirely too unreliable, although you might thoroughly enjoy their presence—while it lasts! An Aquarian friend is a good confidant, but you may feel uncomfortable together in intimate surroundings. You're likely to be most attracted to your opposite sign, Capricorn, whose determination to succeed creates a strong foothold for your own security.

YOUR USE OF POWER: Power comes to you through your emotional nature, which can provide a positive environment for your own growth while encouraging the growth of others. Your energy may provide a haven in the storm, ingratiating others and offering you a wide range of influence. You might find that your most powerful position is within your family. But in a business, you also can engender a feeling of family, forging together a network of devoted individuals who share a common goal.

The traditions from the past can inhibit your own power, unless you can find a way to reshape the traditions to work with current trends. But your true power arises when you feel secure and know that you have shelter from the storm and that those you love are insulated from harm. In order to stay strong, you must maintain an open awareness of your own needs and continue to find ways to remain connected to the Source which fills and sustains you.

FAMOUS CANCERIANS: Arthur Ashe, Bill Blass, Kim Carnes, Edgar Degas, Princess Diana, Harrison Ford, John Glenn, Robert Heinlein, Janet Leigh, Carl Lewis, Art Linkletter, Charles and William Mayo, Marcel Proust, Linda Ronstadt, O. J. Simpson, William Butler Yeats

THE YEAR AHEAD FOR CANCER

This is the year to find out the best ways to utilize all your resources. You're still making changes and moving into new forms of self-expression, but may find that the impact of your actions upon others is more noticeable now. Your security base is expanding, giving you a sense of greater freedom of expression. However, the features of many traditions which once guided you have been altered.

You may feel that the changing priorities of others in your life makes it difficult to keep your own priorities straight. By allowing yourself to move ahead with these changes, it's possible that you'll discover new pathways which would have been closed to you in the past. Relationships are definitely a testing ground this year, but don't have to bring impossible challenges. For the greater part of the year, you're likely to feel that you do have more responsibilities because of the intimate ties in your life. But you're also reaping the benefit of seeing more of yourself reflected through these contacts. This is the time to break out of your old pattern in all relationships. If others have been taking unfair advantage, find ways to avoid falling into the trap of carrying their burdens for them. Working on co-dependency issues may be quite illuminating for you now. The true responsibility that you're taking on supports your personal needs first. This is quite different from always keeping the others in your life happy while you suffer the consequences.

The Uranus/Neptune conjunctions this year are at 18 and 19 degrees of Capricorn. If you have any planets or the Sun or Moon from 13 to 24 degrees of Cancer, you're definitely experiencing a special impact in your life from this powerful conjunction. This opposition aspect can stimulate you to break free of many of the traps you've fallen into throughout your life, giving you a chance to truly free yourself of outworn habits, attitudes or circumstances. But it's also easy to find yourself feeling that your life is out of your control during this cycle. Circumstances may be changing without your consent, but you do have the right to respond to those changes as you wish. By choosing a response which brings you greater self-realization, you'll find this to be a period of exceptional freedom and inspiration.

Jupiter's transit in Libra through November 10th can bring quite a lesson in boundaries. You may feel that you're needing more of everything, but are you really fulfilling a need or just a desire to shelter yourself from your fears? A careful look inside yourself can give you the answer. This is an excellent time to create a shelter of understanding and warmth through your family. Extracting the elements of your upbringing which are still positive in your life allows you to appreciate the true value of improving upon tradition. If you're thinking about moving, be clear about your motivations, since there's a tendency to overextend in this area. Once Jupiter moves into Scorpio in November you may feel much more balanced about your choices, instead of just trying to prove something through indulging in extravagant luxuries you don't even want.

The Eclipses of 1993 are definitely pointing to a need to work on yourself from the inside out. This is an exceptional time to advance your attitudes, especially those which stand in the way of your success and prosperity. Take a careful look at your relations with co-workers or peers, since there's likely to be ample room for enrichment in this area. You may also be drawn to pay special attention to your health. It's basically a question of developing a desire to care for yourself more effectively. Evaluate your current nutritional needs in light of the stresses and strains you're experiencing. You may need to boost your mineral intake, and might also find that you're craving more exercise. The planet Mars transits in Cancer from January through the end of April. This can bring a powerful boost in your energy levels, getting your year off to a great start. But pay attention to your feelings of anger or frustration. Find good outlets to express these feelings rather than repress them. Otherwise, you may be experiencing negative confrontations with others during this period.

If your birth occurred from June 21st-23rd, you're experiencing two different Saturn aspects this year. The year begins with Saturn sesquiquadrate your Sun, challenging you to take conscious action to create a healthier lifestyle. Chronic physical ailments can reach a point of frustration which stimulates you to look into the core of the problem and to work on it through bringing greater power over your own life. From late May until the end of June, Saturn travels in trine aspect to your Sun, giving you a good perspective on the best ways to use your talents. You may also experience improvements in your health, and have a good opportunity to set a firm foundation for your personal evolution.

If you were born from June 24th-28th you'll need to keep your priorities in order to avoid overexerting yourself. The desire to have your dreams of the perfect home life fulfilled can overwhelm the reality of your life circumstances. Certainly making things better is a positive goal, as long as your actions are not out of proportion with your abilities. You're experiencing a long transit of Jupiter square your Sun throughout the spring and early summer, and may find it hard to say "no" to anything. However, for most of the year your self-concept is strong and you may find it much easier to express your personal identity.

For Cancerians born from June 28th-July 6th, this year can prove to be a difficult balancing act. You've been working hard on getting your finances in order, and may have had good success from your creative efforts in the last couple of years. But now you're realizing that a number of changes are required in order to maintain or achieve the level of success you desire. Both Pluto and Saturn are transiting in sesquiquadrate to your Sun. Saturn's cycle brings your relationship with society into a different focus. You may also find your personal relationships, particularly a partnership, to be trying. You need a good outlet for self-expression without compromising your real needs. Communication of your needs is essential. Pluto's cycle challenges you to act in a manner which will bring about a greater fulfillment of your desires. Rather than channeling your desires toward something outside yourself, try to remember that your ultimate desire brings you into greater harmony within yourself. Through this awareness, your creativity can open to a more richly expressive avenue.

If you were born from July 7th-15th you're ready for your own form of personal revolution. The conjunction of

Uranus and Neptune is opposing your Sun in 1993. Fasten your seat belt and get ready for some spectacular changes! If you've been wanting to move into a new direction, this is the perfect time to walk onto a different path. You may simply be ready to allow your real self to emerge after many years of repression. But it's all too easy to fly into a situation for which you feel unprepared, only to discover that not only are you in foreign territory, but you've forgotten your manual. Changes are practically inevitable during this cycle, and your best preparation is to maintain continual awareness of your inner self instead of trying to jump into every new situation which arises. Partners can be unpredictable, and you may feel that you don't want anybody else cluttering your life with their needs. What's really changing is the way you're meeting your own needs. Outworn situations can dissolve. New opportunities can entice. It's time to open your consciousness to a clear vision of what you are and to manifest that vision in harmony with your higher needs.

For those born from July 15th-21st, deeper levels of change are occurring in the heart of your being. Pluto's transit trines your Sun, intensifying your need to extract yourself from the barriers you've erected to protect your vulnerabilities. You might decide to sit back and watch the world change around you—which it will. But you have the power now to stand shoulder to shoulder with those people you've held in high regard. This is the time to use your influence to transform an ailing situation into a thriving one. But you're feeling the frustration from Saturn quincunx your Sun, and may wonder if you have the energy to take the risk. Plant your feet firmly and reach as far as you can to make these changes. You're likely to find that the result is a truly evolutionary experience!

If you were born on July 22nd or 23rd you're in a good cycle to let go of the elements from your past which you perceive to be blocking your progress. Be especially mindful of your obligations this year, since this is a cycle leading to a number of endings and completions. You're preparing for future growth, but must tend to your current obligations before moving ahead. It's time to enjoy a positive sense of Self.

TOOLS TO MAKE A DIFFERENCE: Since there's a great deal of healing happening in your life in 1993, let this be a time in which you facilitate transformation through your own actions and attitudes. Participation in activities with others of like mind can be an excellent support now. It's not a time for isolation, even if you do feel that you want to stand out as a individual.

Try planting a small herb garden, and begin to expand your understanding of the magical healing power of plants. You might especially enjoy brewing herbal teas or using herbal potions in your bath. Legend has it that mint, chamomile or comfrey teas are soothing to upset stomachs. And to invigorate your spirits, bathe in rosemary! Natural fragrances are also harmonious for you, especially the oils of rose, ylang ylang or vanilla. Although larkspur is said to be your flower, you have a special attunement to the entire plant kingdom, and fare better when you have plants around your environment.

You may have always been drawn to pearls, and have a special affinity for these stones. Jewelry, cufflinks or buttons of pearl can have a truly clarifying effect when you're feeling stressed. These miracles from the sea can remind you that you're naturally attuned to the cycles of the Moon, which also controls the tides of Earth's oceans. Moonstones and chrysocolla are also especially effective for you as balancing stones. If you're not wearing them, you might also enjoy artistic renderings using these stones.

Take some extra time this year to listen to your intuitive voice. This is, perhaps, your most valuable tool, and one which you carry with you at all times. If you feel disconnected from this aspect of your Self, spend a few minutes each morning and evening tuning into your feelings. In your meditations, see yourself floating in a tranquil sea. Feel the waves carrying you and surrender to the power of the ebb and flow. When you emerge from the sea, take with you the remembrance of trust and serenity. Know that the changes you're experiencing are a part of this natural flow.

AFFIRMATION FOR THE YEAR: "I feel the strength of my connection with the Source of All Life."

ACTION TABLES FOR CANCER

These dates reflect the best (but not the *only*) times for success and ease in these activities according to your Sun Sign.

Change Residence	Sept. 11-30
Request a Raise	July 19
Begin a Course of Study	Feb. 21; Sept. 16
Visit a Doctor	May 18-June 1; Dec. 7-25
Start a Diet	Jan. 18-19; Feb. 14-15; Mar. 13-14; Apr. 10-11; May 7-8; June 3-4; July 1-2, 28-29; Aug. 24-25; Sept. 20-21; Oct. 18-19; Nov. 14-15; Dec. 12-13
Begin a Romance	Nov. 13-14
Join a Club	Apr. 21
Seek Employment	Apr. 15-May 3; Dec. 7-25
Take a Vacation	Jan. 25-26; Feb. 21-22; Mar. 20-21; Apr. 17-18; May 14-15; June 10-11; July 8-9; Aug. 4-5, 31; Sept. 1-2, 27-28; Oct. 25-26; Nov. 21-22; Dec. 18-20
Change Your Wardrobe	Oct. 1-Dec. 6
End a Relationship	July 3
Seek Professional Advice	Jan. 20-21; Feb. 16-17; Mar. 15-17; Apr. 12-13; May 9-10; June 6-7; July 3-4, 30-31; Aug. 26-28; Sept. 23-24; Oct. 20-21; Nov. 16-17; Dec. 14-15
Have a Makeover	July 19
Obtain a Loan	Jan. 22-24 Feb. 19-20; Mar. 18-19; Apr. 14-15; May 11-13; June 8-9; July 5-6; Aug. 1-3, 29-30; Sept. 25-26; Oct. 22-23; Nov. 19-20; Dec. 16-17

CANCER/JANUARY

PRIMARY FOCUS
Maintaining balance in the face of change can be emotionally distressing if you try too hard to hang onto the past. Keep a clear perspective on the best ways to let go of the unnecessary.

HEALTH AND FITNESS
Watch your digestive system this month, since you may find yourself eating on the run and not really being attentive to your physical needs. Give yourself time to work out and to relax!

ROMANCE AND RELATIONSHIPS
Your love life improves through sharing travel or getting involved in the same inspirational subjects. The Full Moon in Cancer on the 8th is punctuated by a pressing need to have your desires fulfilled immediately. If you've had enough, then you're likely to walk away if you feel nothing more can be done to bring improvements. By the time of the New Moon on the 22nd, you may be willing to take a look at innovative approaches to your love life. But nothing happens without first establishing trust.

FINANCE AND CAREER
A business partnership can bring crazy demands on your time, and you may decide that it's easier to just get back into the system or go it alone. Before you leap into major changes, consider your longer term options. Try a fresh approach to interfacing with the public from the 10th-18th. Take a careful look at your finances after the 22nd, when taxes or insurance may seem to take your "fun" money. Avoid unnecessary expenditures, since they can lead to disappointments.

OPPORTUNITY OF THE MONTH
Keep your ethical standards high when you're doing business on the 7th and 8th. The rewards can be gratifying.

Rewarding Days: 3, 4, 7, 8, 12, 15, 16, 25, 26, 30
Challenging Days: 1, 10, 13, 14, 18, 20, 21, 27, 28

AFFIRMATION FOR THE MONTH
"I move forward with confidence and agility."

CANCER/FEBRUARY

PRIMARY FOCUS

Surprising events can turn the tide. Maintain a broad perspective on what's happening to avoid getting caught in meaningless details.

HEALTH AND FITNESS

You may lose your motivation to stay fit because demands at work or other distractions seem to eat away at your time. Make a fresh effort after the 20th.

ROMANCE AND RELATIONSHIPS

Take some time to talk about your hopes for the future, but be aware that your plans are quite likely to change as new opportunities arise in your professional life. Relations with parents may improve, but watch a tendency to give them the wrong impression regarding your time commitments. A flirtation at work can lead to fireworks after the 21st, but be sure you have a clear field before you set them off! An existing relationship can become more open and intimate on the 21st and 22nd, when you may feel a more spiritual bond that you have experienced in the past.

FINANCE AND CAREER

Disagreements over the best ways to utilize resources can block progress in business dealings from the 1st–10th, although this is most marked during the Full Moon on the 6th. Negotiations which favor your advancement are highly promising after the 19th. Make presentations or attend conferences on the 21st, 22nd or 27th. You may find it hard to hold onto your money this month. Buy what's necessary, but avoid extravagant spending from the 21st–27th.

OPPORTUNITY OF THE MONTH

Finish ongoing projects early this month to be ready to move on a new deal on the 21st or 22nd.

Rewarding Days: 4, 8, 12, 13, 21, 22, 26, 27
Challenging Days: 6, 10, 11, 16, 17, 24, 25

AFFIRMATION FOR THE MONTH

"Change is safe."

CANCER/MARCH

PRIMARY FOCUS
You may feel that you're pulled in several directions with little time remaining for your own needs. Allow your creative ideas and feelings to emerge as a way to make the most of your options.

HEALTH AND FITNESS
Cabin fever breaks! Keep a reasonable pace and watch a tendency to move too quickly. Alertness helps you avoid accidents now.

ROMANCE AND RELATIONSHIPS
Romantic travel enhances an existing relationship. At the least, return to your favorite haunts to rekindle your passion for one another. A new affair has its enticement from the 1st-19th, but it may just be symptomatic of your needs to reach a higher level of intimacy in your current relationship. If you're ready to leave, this is an excellent cycle to let go and move forward, but you must be honest with yourself about your true motivations. If you're free and ready, the Full Moon on the 8th can be just the stimulus you need to signal someone new.

FINANCE AND CAREER
While Mercury retrogrades through the 22nd, you may find that you're spending more time re-hashing what you thought had already been settled. A surprising move from the competition on the 10th-11th can throw you off balance. Patience rewards you, since there are organizational changes that you may not have known about and final deals are much more lucrative and rewarding after the 23rd. Avoid major investments until after the 25th.

OPPORTUNITY OF THE MONTH
Use this retrograde of Mercury to clarify contracts and expand your horizons. Target the 21st and 22nd for final negotiations.

Rewarding Days: 3, 4, 7, 8, 11, 12, 20, 21, 26, 30, 31
Challenging Days: 6, 9, 10, 15, 16, 17, 23, 24

AFFIRMATION FOR THE MONTH
"I honor my intuitive voice."

CANCER/APRIL

PRIMARY FOCUS
It's tempting to burn all your bridges now. Look carefully into your own mirror, since the solution may be within yourself!

HEALTH AND FITNESS
Taking risks which looks exciting, but may prove costly. Investigate and learn before you participate.

ROMANCE AND RELATIONSHIPS
While Venus retrogrades until the 22nd you may be seriously questioning the validity of your relationship. To get what you want, make a special effort to express your needs to your partner. Family pressures on the 6th can exaggerate your discontent, so look carefully at your own agenda before you place blame on someone else. If you've been reluctant to bring change into your partnership, the experimental energy from the 1st-14th can stimulate unusual options. Move with care, since you may run into some of your own hidden vulnerabilities! Talk with a friend or trusted advisor about your concerns on the 21st or 22nd.

FINANCE AND CAREER
You may feel that your current situation is entirely too limiting. If you can work within the system you've chosen, it's a good time to talk with your superiors or realign your responsibilities. Your ideas are likely to be well received, but you may find your presentations are more polished through the 14th. Let your past successes in your career work for you and take steps to create a more favorable path on the 22nd.

OPPORTUNITY OF THE MONTH
Banish routine! Let your uniqueness shine through now. Show your strength and take a position of influence on the 21st-22nd.

Rewarding Days: 3, 4, 8, 17, 18, 22, 23, 26, 27
Challenging Days: 2, 5, 6, 12, 13, 19, 20

AFFIRMATION FOR THE MONTH
"I freely express my individuality."

CANCER/MAY

PRIMARY FOCUS
It's time to gain favor with your superiors and to take your responsibilities seriously. You can make a positive impression by concentrating your efforts where you know they'll do the most good.

HEALTH AND FITNESS
Increasing your stamina and endurance pays off this month. Join a class or team sport from the 4th-17th.

ROMANCE AND RELATIONSHIPS
You're likely to attract the attention of someone special through your career or a public appearance. This can lead to a strong friendship or may even develop into a romance if you're available. Spend some extra time with your friends early in the month, and give yourself ample room to share your talents with others near the time of the Full Moon on the 5th. Applaud the accomplishments of children this month. By the time of the Solar Eclipse on the 21st you may desire to spend a little time alone. It's a good time to reflect, and can be a satisfying period of spiritual strength.

FINANCE AND CAREER
Career progress is promising, but you may feel you're competing for the brass ring. Clarify the expectations of your superiors early in the month, since there's a tendency to miss the boat due to misjudgment from the 1st-7th. Look for the unusual solution to dilemmas the week of the 9th. You're likely to desire some changes in your home environment by the end of the month, so allow some cash in your budget for your special decorative touch.

OPPORTUNITY OF THE MONTH
Business meetings on the 24th and 25th can bring satisfying results. Your uniqueness magnifies your worth.

Rewarding Days: 1, 2, 5, 6, 14, 15, 19, 24, 25, 28
Challenging Days: 3, 4, 8, 9, 10, 17, 18, 30, 31

AFFIRMATION FOR THE MONTH
"I love my work and my work loves me."

CANCER/JUNE

PRIMARY FOCUS

It's easier to express yourself this month, and you may find that your words and actions have a stronger influence on others.

HEALTH AND FITNESS

An attitude of enjoyment toward exercise helps you stay fit. Seek answers to your health questions and take appropriate actions to stay well.

ROMANCE AND RELATIONSHIPS

Getting your message across is important now. Send cards or make phone calls that will help others to clarify your feelings. Romance can develop quickly after the 13th. A revised approach to partnerships and commitment brings greater satisfaction after the 20th. You may feel that your lover is competing with your friends for your attention on the 28th-30th. Special times with friends are part of the action now, but be careful you're not using this to shield you from deeper intimacy with your sweetheart!

FINANCE AND CAREER

The Lunar Eclipse on the 4th may bring some issues with coworkers to the surface. Games of manipulation tend to backfire. Work carefully with others behind the scenes to launch plans for improvement after the 19th. Finances can improve, since you're more aware of the best ways to use your resources now. Future growth seems promising. But watch a tendency toward impulsive spending from the 10th-19th.

OPPORTUNITY OF THE MONTH

The best times to work on plans that will lead to future success is from the 3rd-14th. You'll have ample time to improve your ideas or products before their final release in August.

Rewarding Days: 1, 2, 10, 11, 12, 15, 16, 20, 21, 24, 25, 29
Challenging Days: 5, 6, 7, 13, 14, 23, 26, 27

AFFIRMATION FOR THE MONTH

"My words and actions are guided by Divine Wisdom."

CANCER/JULY

PRIMARY FOCUS
Travel seems inevitable this month, although you may have to deal with frustrating delays or breakdowns. Be prepared.

HEALTH AND FITNESS
Your nervous system may be working overtime. Try increasing B-vitamin rich foods. A vacation now can take the edge off; keep your plans simple and flexible.

ROMANCE AND RELATIONSHIPS
The Full Moon on the 3rd highlights partnerships, and may be an excellent time to consider making a new commitment or to renew old vows. Talk about the issues you face together before taking the plunge. You may decide that you're not ready to go further, and may want to wait until Mercury turns direct on the 25th before you make a final decision. You'll feel more confident about major life issues after the New Moon in Cancer on the 19th. A flirtation from the 17th-27th can lead to trouble. Watch your signals!

FINANCE AND CAREER
Networking is the key to your success this month, but you may find it difficult to connect with the right people. Equipment breakdowns or inaccurate communications can bring delays in important negotiations after the 14th, but you can use these to your advantage after the 19th. Contracts signed now may have to be renegotiated later on. Watch for hidden power plays midmonth which can dismantle the status quo. As long as you keep your priorities, these changes can work to your benefit.

OPPORTUNITY OF THE MONTH
Taking bold steps on the 19th can bring a turn-around in a stalemate circumstance. You may have to take the initiative.

Rewarding Days: 8, 9, 13, 14, 17, 18, 19, 22, 26, 27
Challenging Days: 3, 4, 10, 11, 24, 25, 28, 30, 31

AFFIRMATION FOR THE MONTH
"I deserve to have my needs fulfilled."

CANCER/AUGUST

PRIMARY FOCUS
Finances are a special concern, whether you're looking for the best ways to spend or to get more for what you're offering.

HEALTH AND FITNESS
Projects around the house may be taking the time you usually spend on fitness. During your "off" time, you're more likely to indulge in the sweet things of life. Try to avoid excess.

ROMANCE AND RELATIONSHIPS
Venus transits in Cancer, enhancing your sensibilities and increasing your desire to have more love in your life. The key to this cycle is allowing greater self-acceptance. You may also be feeling quite frisky from the 14th–23rd, when you're eager to experience a more thrilling love life. Whether you're creating more time for intimacy with your partner or seeking a new love, this cycle can bring a wonderful playfulness. Flirtation can cause trouble; watch for potential misunderstanding on the 20th–21st.

FINANCE AND CAREER
Your judgment in money matters is swayed by your emotions near the Full Moon on the 2nd. There's a temptation to spend more than necessary on an impulse from the 9th–13th. These are good days to reconsider your image or listen carefully to the competition, but you need to establish a firm foothold before you reach into foreign territory. Mid-month, you can take advantage of the climate for change and establish a new position. You're strongly suited to take the lead in negotiations the 24th–27th.

OPPORTUNITY OF THE MONTH
Maintain contact with individuals whose aims support your own on the 19th. Together your actions may have far-reaching impact.

Rewarding Days: 4, 5, 9, 14, 15, 18, 19, 22, 23, 31
Challenging Days: 3, 7, 8, 20, 21, 26, 27, 28

AFFIRMATION FOR THE MONTH
"I am filled with love and joy!"

CANCER/SEPTEMBER

PRIMARY FOCUS

Changes in your home environment can turn things upside-down. Even carefully planned moves can be full of surprises!

HEALTH AND FITNESS

It's easy to push beyond your physical limitations, only to find that you're paying a very dear price. Pace yourself, since it's all too easy to overexert your body and emotions.

ROMANCE AND RELATIONSHIPS

Family squabbles on the 1st-8th can lead to disagreements with your partner from the 9th-13th. Most of the issues center around who's in charge. Throughout this period, honor your own needs, and try to avoid allowing someone else to dictate them for you! If you compromise on important issues, the resulting resentment can create distance between yourself and those you love. Take time to talk about alternatives near the time of the New Moon on the 15th, but circumstances may still dictate changes you had not anticipated. True colors from your friends shine through on the 28th-29th.

FINANCE AND CAREER

Discontent in the workplace can be the result of longstanding difficulties which are finally percolating to the surface. Intense power struggles can emerge from the 3rd-5th, and may lead to a reorganization by the 16th. If you want to be included in the new structure it's critical that you clarify your position. Conferences fare nicely from the 5th-9th, and may resume on the 23rd. Be wary of the quick fix on the 30th. It can lead to disappointment.

OPPORTUNITY OF THE MONTH

Plan important meetings on the 14th-15th in order to determine the expectations and positions of everyone involved.

Rewarding Days: 1, 5, 6, 10, 11, 15, 19, 28, 29
Challenging Days: 3, 4, 16, 17, 21, 23, 24, 30

AFFIRMATION FOR THE MONTH

"I respect my own value and value my own needs."

CANCER/OCTOBER

PRIMARY FOCUS

Throughout this period of shifting priorities, your creative inspiration remains strong. Let joy stimulate your creativity.

HEALTH AND FITNESS

Your vitality appears to be stronger now. Find the most enjoyable outlets for your fitness activities. And don't forget the importance of entertainment in your physical and emotional health!

ROMANCE AND RELATIONSHIPS

The cycles this month help you to open your expressivity. Open lines of communication, and take the initiative with your sweetheart now. Explore deeper intimate experiences. Travel to places that allow you to be more free. Children may feature more prominently than usual. Begin a new family tradition with the New Moon on the 15th. And strive to achieve a better understanding of one another near the time of the Full Moon on the 30th. A party with friends on the 30th-31st can be a ticklish delight!

FINANCE AND CAREER

To make progress in your career instigate some changes mid-month. A change of the guard can leave some options wide open, but you have to create the wedge to move yourself into them! Manifesting stronger financial stability through your creative efforts is highly promising this month. But watch for power struggles after the 24th, when misunderstandings may run rampant. Mercury's retrograde after the 25th gives you a chance to try again.

OPPORTUNITY OF THE MONTH

If you need to wield influence, schedule an important meeting or conference on the 8th. Your words can be a catalyst for change.

Rewarding Days: 3, 7, 8, 12, 13, 16, 17, 25, 30
Challenging Days: 1, 2, 11, 14, 15, 20, 21, 27, 28

AFFIRMATION FOR THE MONTH

"I find joy in every moment!"

CANCER/NOVEMBER

PRIMARY FOCUS

Enterprises begun last month expand. Your love life takes a front seat and can be the stimulus for much of your creativity.

HEALTH AND FITNESS

Adjustments in your schedule may affect your health. Arrange time to take care of yourself, so you'll have ample energy to do it all.

ROMANCE AND RELATIONSHIPS

A love affair may change shape, and can end early this month if you feel that it's not meeting your needs. If you've been repressing your feelings or indirect about your desires, this can be part of the problem. A more gentle approach near the time of the Solar Eclipse on the 13th can help you trust your feelings more. If you're available, a new love may enter the picture mid-month. Circumstances may prevent you from being together, but these can be resolved with patience and planning.

FINANCE AND CAREER

Projects keep your nose to the grindstone this month, and you may fail to notice some of the things going on around you. Step back and get a clear perspective on your job now. You're in a good position to consider making a change, but first you have to complete the things that you're agreed to do. While Mercury retrogrades until the 15th, finish those old projects. Be aware of your relations with peers or coworkers near the time of the Lunar Eclipse on the 29th, when unspoken expectations can stir up trouble.

OPPORTUNITY OF THE MONTH

By clearing out old debris from your life (physically and psychologically), you're making room for greater reward. Make this a priority from the 1st-6th.

Rewarding Days: 4, 5, 6, 9, 12, 13, 21, 22, 26
Challenging Days: 7, 10, 11, 16, 17, 18, 24, 25

AFFIRMATION FOR THE MONTH

"I am an instrument for the Divine Creator."

CANCER/DECEMBER

PRIMARY FOCUS

Find ways to improve your health. Some extra reading, a class, or workshop can be enlightening.

HEALTH AND FITNESS

Your body requires maintenance, and this is the time to do something nice for the temple of your soul. Watch a tendency to push too far beyond your limits the week of the 12th.

ROMANCE AND RELATIONSHIPS

Travel can be exciting through the 7th. This might also be a good way to meet someone new. If you can't plan a long trip, try a weekend away or a special evening of entertainment from the 10th-12th, when you're ready for a break from all the hustle and bustle. The later part of the month focuses on partnerships, and you can avert disagreement by spending some extra time with your spouse throughout the month. By the time of the Full Moon on the 28th a repressed situation can become explosive. But this is a good time to air your differences and begin again with fresh resolve.

FINANCE AND CAREER

Working with others can be highly productive now. Listen to their concerns and pay attention to power struggles to keep operations running smoothly from the 12th-25th. Most business negotiations will fare better after the 27th, but you are in a good position to discuss proposals on the 2nd, 3rd, 6th and 20th. Your best investment now is in yourself. Evaluate and update your insurance coverage to bring yourself greater peace of mind.

OPPORTUNITY OF THE MONTH

You're most influential on the 1st, 2nd and 28th. Use these days to reach agreements or make a stand on important issues.

Rewarding Days: 1, 2, 5, 6, 10, 18, 19, 24, 25, 28, 29
Challenging Days: 4, 8, 9, 14, 15, 17, 21, 22

AFFIRMATION FOR THE MONTH

"I and healthy and vibrant."

LEO
THE LION

July 23 to August 23

Element: Fire
Quality: Fixed
Polarity: Masculine/Yang
Planetary Ruler: The Sun
Meditation: "Self glows with Light from The Source"
Gemstone: Ruby
Power Stones: Topaz, Sardonyx
Key Phrase: I will

Glyph: Lion's tail
Anatomy: Heart, upper back, sides
Color: Gold
Animal: Lions, large cats
Myths/Legends: Apollo, Helius, Isis
House Association: Fifth
Opposite Sign: Aquarius
Flower: Marigold
Key Word: Magnetism

Positive Expression:
Loyal
Creative
Regal
Dramatic
Bold
Honorable
Benevolent
Self-confident
Dynamic
Gracious

Misuse of Energy:
Egocentric
Arrogant
Domineering
Pompous
Insolent
Ostentatious
Chauvinistic
Selfish

LEO

YOUR EGO'S STRENGTHS AND WEAKNESSESS:
166Although you may have many talents, it's your
warmth and radiance that people remember. Your dynamic and dramatic self-expression can act as a guide to
those who need leadership, or you can stand alone in the
spotlight when your opportunity comes along. It seems
natural for you to be the center of attention.

You can be regal or flamboyant, polished or garish, and
may have plenty of opportunities for a wide range of self-
expression. You definitely need room for your ofttimes
legendary creativity and playfulness. Your loving and
generous nature draws others to your life, and you enjoy
being the object of their affection. But when you feel unap-
preciated, you can lash out and demand attention in negative ways. Your luster is brightest when you see evidence
of loyalty from those you love. It can be difficult to share
the limelight; you can act outrageously dejected.

You're big-hearted, and seek ways to express your generosity. Those individuals and circumstances to which
you're committed can count on your devotion. Honor
ranks high in your priorities. You can be a powerful champion, and have plenty of courage to stand firm when the
going gets tough. But when this need is misplaced you can
become excessively prideful and stubborn. Positively using your magnetic power to create your life on your own
terms imbues you with confidence. Your life lesson centers
around placing your ego at the disposal of your higher nature in order to create a true monument to Divine Power.

YOUR CAREER DEVELOPMENT: You're a natural in a position of leadership and authority. It can be highly important to receive recognition for your achievements. As Chairman of the Board, CEO or Union President, you can excel when you reach the top. You can also be an inspiring teacher, and can give others a real sense of their own importance. You might function very well as a foreman or supervisor, and you're a natural promoter.

If you're drawn to the performing arts, you may excel as a musician, actor, or model. You can also be an effective producer or director. Since you like to be in places where other people are enjoying themselves, you might successfully develop businesses such as restaurants, clubs, amusements or theaters. Politics may also be a choice, but you might prefer to promote and direct a candidate rather than become one!

YOUR APPROACH TO ROMANCE: You love being in love! Whether you're in elegant or humble surroundings, romance with you can be royal. You can be lavish with your affection, and love the attention intimate surroundings brings your way. Once you've extended your love to another, you can be eternally loyal, and you may find it difficult to end relationships. But when you do find the right partner, you can keep your love alive by rekindling warm romance on a regular basis.

As a Fire sign, you enjoy relationships with others who like to be active. Your attraction to your opposite, Aquarius, can tug at your heart strings. You'll learn about equality and autonomy in this relationship! You may find fiery Aries spontaneously attractive, but can wonder about their loyalty. Taurus attracts but you may not enjoy feeling like their possession.

The wit and intelligence of Gemini stimulates your imagination and you can be excellent traveling companions. While the nurturance of Cancer feels comforting, you may not be turned on. Love with another Leo can be hot, but you each need your own spotlight. Virgo's attention to perfection inspires you; Libra's refined beauty and charm entices. With Scorpio you enjoy sensual delights but may feel overwhelmed by the intensity. Sagittarius' sense of adventure harmonizes with your desire to play. Although Capricorn may be good for business, you may feel too restrained romantically. And Pisces woos you into an alternate reality which can be distracting if you lose your bearings!

YOUR USE OF POWER: Your ruler, the Sun, is the energy which stimulates and sustains life force, the essence of the Power of Life. You're eager to tap into this energy and shine as brightly as possible, and may be fueled by the recognition and acknowledgment you gain from others. You're most comfortable when you're radiating that power to others through leadership, inspiration or authority.

Whether at home or at work, you can be a benevolent ruler. Your natural magnetism feels safe and comforting to those around you, and can inspire them to follow their own special talents. But if you're too far out of control, you can become a dictator, stealing power from others to maintain your own. Watch the effect you have upon others as a good guideline to your ability to wield power. And remember that you can become self-absorbed to the extent that the efforts and needs of others may not be as noticeable to you as they once were.

Your path is not always an easy one, since you may feel that your only ally is often the will of the Creator. Through maintaining a communion with this power, your own light can shine as a beacon of hope and love.

FAMOUS LEOS: Melvin Belli, Vida Blue, William Gillette, Amelia Earhart, Jerry Garcia, Dorothy Hammill, Woody Harrelson, Mick Jagger, Alan Leo, Sydney Omarr, Sally Struthers

THE YEAR AHEAD FOR LEO

While the world changes its political climate, you're feeling a need to take a different approach to your own way of getting what you want out of life. Others will definitely have their agendas, but you're finding positive ways to operate within your own parameters without getting pulled into someone's expectations. It's time to work toward achieving a more purposeful existence. You're uncovering the layers that have shrouded the intrinsic meaning of your life. The answers you find are likely to be quite simple, giving you plenty of room to clear away the debris and create a concept that expresses your true identity much more clearly.

A different level of personal honesty can emerge throughout the year, while you take a careful look at the effect your attitude has on shaping your reality. There are always lessons to learn, but you may just now be realizing how effective you've been in writing many of your own tests! During these testing cycles, we often feel that time slows down, but you're probably feeling more like your clock has a short circuit. Staying in the present moment is more important than ever, because so much is happening during the magical moment of now. Your nature is one of expressivity, and you can feel the frustration of suppression of your creativity reaching an all-time high. Look for outlets. Avoid compromise. Open up and play the most important role in your personal drama—the Real You!

All the circumstances for clear sailing may not be present now. In fact, there is likely to be a blockade from the old line challenging you to take care of your responsibilities and do the right thing. Appropriate and ethical behavior may not always be easy, since you may run into some dishonesty in others that you cannot approve. But you have the right energy to make adjustments and use the current situation to your benefit. The challenge of Uranus and Neptune for you in 1993 may be as simple as finding a healthy outlet for self-improvement. But you may also have to face the dragon and decide if you can teach her to dance!

Jupiter's transit in Libra through mid-November can stimulate an excellent support for your need to make contact with others. This is a superb time to get your ideas out to other people. Travel. Make contact with individuals or groups you've found fascinating but have felt reluctant to approach. Polish your communicative skills. Let this be the year to expand your base of operations. If you've wanted to study a subject but haven't had the time, this is a good year for a crash course! By the time Jupiter moves into Scorpio on November 10th you may have had enough of gadding about and shift your focus to broadening your security base. But watch a tendency toward arrogant self-indulgence which can isolate you rather than support your desire to build a stronger level of emotional security.

The Eclipses in 1993 emphasize your need to identify long-term goals. How are your current actions and circumstances helping you move toward these goals? Time with others who share your ideals can be encouraging and supportive, and you may find that you have an opportunity for leadership in a group. You may be moving away from old comrades and into a new area of interest. Your home also begins to take on an expanded focus in the fall, when your family takes a higher priority. While your role in the family transforms you, you may also be responsible for the formulation of some new traditions.

If your birth occurred from July 23rd-25th you're experiencing a year of clearer self-concept. You may need to make some minor adjustments in your routine during the middle part of the year to keep your life running smoothly. Stress can creep up on you, so watch your physical and emotional responses to situations. Throughout most of the year the slower moving planets are not forming any strong aspects to your Sun, giving you some breathing room in terms of personal identity. You're putting the knowledge you've acquired during the last two years to the test now, and need only fine-tune from April through September while Saturn is quincunx your Sun.

Leos born from July 26th-30th are in for a special treat from April through July of 1993. Jupiter cycles in supportive trine to your Sun, giving you an added boost in confidence and optimism. If you've been waiting for a good time to shine, this is it! Contact with influential individuals can be especially favorable, or you may find that others seek your support and influence. The increased recognition you're receiving can give you a boost in your career, and is also helpful if you're involved in community or political activities. If you want to take a bold step forward, you're likely to discover that you can move further more quickly than in the past. The obstacles this cycle presents are often those which can occur through over-indulgence or excessive spending. Keep your priorities in line and you'll find this to be an exceptional period of well-being.

For those born July 31st-August 7th, a period of rebuilding and stabilization finally arrives. After the onslaught of challenges last year, you may have wondered if things would ever straighten out. There may still be tests and obstacles, but you're not worrying so much about how you fit or if you're being ignored. It's time to uncover some of your hidden talents and incorporate them into your current life situation. You may also find that you're more appreciated at home, which gives you the satisfaction of feeling that many of your efforts to hold your life together have been worth it after all.

If you were born from August 8th-15th you have a series of challenges during the year. The year begins with Saturn in opposition to your Sun, testing your resolve and encouraging you to leave behind those things you no longer need. This is a period of endings, and you may find that guilt is a frequent companion. Seek out the core of these feelings, since you may not really feel guilty at all, but your old psychological programming has you believing that you don't deserve to make these changes and feel good about them! Listen carefully to your inner voice when doubts and fears arise. Speak loving words of encouragement to yourself.

You're also feeling the frustration of Uranus and Neptune both traveling in quincunx to your Sun. Trust becomes an issue, since you can bump into so many surprises during this period. As with all astrological cycles, the changes are really occurring inside you, even though you may feel that everything is happening all around you. You're ready to release many of the barriers that are blocking your progress, but may not know exactly how to proceed. Try concentrating on your feeling about what's happening with your life. You may discover that you've been ignoring some of your true feelings about situations, and that now you can release many of the obligations that no longer belong to you. Not only is your level of awareness enhanced during this phase, but you'll find that you're changing your priorities. Allow plenty of time to release the past, since you're ready to forgive and move forward. Your focus about your work is changing, since you're seeking ways to bring more of your individuality and imagination into your job. Peer associations can be important, but you're just as likely to break away from some groups and move toward individual accomplishments! Pay attention to your physical responses to gather important information about your deeper feelings. Your vitality is undergoing several levels of adjustment, and you may be sensitive to substances that weren't a previously a problem. This can be a healing phase, and you may find key answers to many of your questions about staying well.

If your birth occurred from August 14th-21st you're meeting many challenges which you may describe as "ultimate." While Pluto transits in square aspect to your Sun you may be facing up to many of the issues that have been buried since your childhood. Your relationship with your father can be a critical factor now, even if you feel you had a positive relationship while you were growing up. You're seeing many of your early wounds, and may uncover some resentment or disappointment that has lain beneath the surface for decades. Whether or not you choose to openly confront your dad is not important. You need to look at the things you projected onto your father that now you must own for yourself. It's only through acknowledging and owning both the positive and negative aspects of your being that you can accomplish meaningful success. The issue of power is primary now—whether it's your own power or dealing with someone else who seems to have overwhelmed your abilities. Anything that's outgrown its usefulness can be eliminated from your life during this phase. In a primary way, this involves your own attitude toward yourself. This may be one of the best times to get rid of habits that undermine your vitality and turn your life around. The only problem is that you may resist giving up some old pain in favor of renewed joy.

If you were born from August 13th-23rd, you're experiencing a transit of Chiron in Leo, helping you to clarify and define many of your motivations. Wounds of a psychological or physical nature sometimes accompany this cycle as part of your awakening. It's time to be brutally honest with yourself about the things that you've used as excuses for not being true to yourself. Investigate what it means to be whole, since this is the time to know that feeling and carry it forward with you into your future.

TOOLS TO MAKE A DIFFERENCE: Since this is a year of change, your first approach can be one of opening to the possibility that your life can stand a bit of improvement. Allow your relationships with others to be an instrument for personal growth, since some of your best information may come to you through those who relate to you on a daily basis. Find better ways to communicate your thoughts and feelings to be sure you've really understood. You might enjoy learning about neurolinguistic programming as a technique for better communication. Not only can you learn to express yourself more directly and honestly, but you can get better information from others!

To strengthen your vitality, eat a heart-healthy diet. Increasing your physical activity can also be helpful now, but you need to be sure to work within your own limitations. If you're feeling low, try wearing rubies to remind you of your self-confidence. Gold may also carry a special charge for you. You may find that your jewelry helps you change your mood. Plant marigolds and sunflowers around your house. You might even enjoy using powdered marigolds as a soothing skin powder, or, added to water, as a hair-brightening rinse. Get plenty of energy directly from the Sun, but remember to safeguard your skin! Pay special attention to exercises that will strengthen your back and heart, since these areas are often your Achilles heel. In your meditations, spend time focusing on your deepest center. To help your concentration, imagine that you're looking directly into the light of the Sun. Focus on the center of that light, absorb as much energy as you can from the Source and know that it really resides deep within your own Being.

AFFIRMATION FOR THE YEAR: "I am whole, radiant and powerful."

ACTION TABLES FOR LEO

These dates reflect the best (but not the *only*) times for success and ease in these activities according to your Sun Sign.

Change Residence	Oct. 1-Dec. 6
Request a Raise	Aug. 17
Begin a Course of Study	Mar. 23; Oct. 15
Visit a Doctor	Jan. 2-20; June 2-Aug. 9
Start a Diet	Jan. 20-21; Feb. 16-17; Mar. 16-17; Apr. 12-13; May 9-10; June 6-7; July 3-4, 30-31; Aug. 26-27; Sept. 23-24; Oct. 20-21; Nov. 16-17; Dec. 14-15
Begin a Romance	Dec. 13
Join a Club	May 21, June 20
Seek Employment	Jan. 2-20; May 4-17
Take a Vacation	Jan. 27-28; Feb. 24-25; Mar. 23-24; Apr. 19-20; May 16-18; June 13-14; July 10-11; Aug. 6-7; Sept. 3-4, 30; Oct. 1, 27-28; Nov. 21-22; Dec. 21-22
Change Your Wardrobe	Dec. 7-25
End a Relationship	Aug. 2
Seek Professional Advice	Jan. 22-23; Feb. 19-20; Mar. 18-19; Apr. 14-15; May 12-13; June 8-9; July 5-6; Aug. 1-3, 29-30; Sept. 25-26; Oct. 22-23; Nov. 19-20; Dec. 16-17
Have a Makeover	Aug. 17
Obtain a Loan	Jan. 25-26; Feb. 21-22; Mar. 20-21; Apr. 17-18; May 14-15; June 10-11; July 8-9; Aug. 4-5, 31; Sept. 1, 27-29; Oct. 25-26; Nov. 21-22; Dec. 18-19

LEO/JANUARY

PRIMARY FOCUS

There's a lot brewing beneath the surface and behind the scenes. Clarify before you take final action. Safeguard your blind side!

HEALTH AND FITNESS

Stress can mount this month, and you're needing extra time for rest and relaxation. A new approach to stress reduction proves helpful. Schedule a massage mid-month.

ROMANCE AND RELATIONSHIPS

You can harbor a secret desire for someone who appears to be unattainable. In actuality, you're likely to be seeking an escape from the ordinary, and can incorporate some unusual fantasies into your romantic life. Proceed with caution if you're investigating or beginning a new relationship. But if you're already involved, allow some extra time to explore your deeper feelings for one another. This is a time to enjoy the ecstasies of love. Talk about your needs with your partner after the New Moon on the 22nd.

FINANCE AND CAREER

Jointly held resources may appreciate this month, although there is a tendency to suspect others of not giving you your fair share. In all contracts and negotiations, make sure that the details are clearly defined; but be especially careful from the 4th-11th. The Full Moon on the 8th can pinpoint an evasive action, and may expose the culprits you suspect. Be sure you can support your end of the bargain. Business dealings are likely to be more talk than action, but do hold promise. Schedule meetings on the 19th and 28th.

OPPORTUNITY OF THE MONTH

Help someone in whose work you trust and respect on the 18th or 19th. This favor can bring unanticipated gratification.

Rewarding Days: 1, 5, 9, 10, 13, 14, 18, 19, 28, 29
Challenging Days: 3, 4, 15, 16, 21, 22, 23, 30, 31

AFFIRMATION FOR THE MONTH

"I am grateful for the love that fills my life."

LEO/FEBRUARY

PRIMARY FOCUS

Pressures from other people seem to take all your time, leaving very little room for your personal priorities. Be clear about the expectations of others before you make agreements.

HEALTH AND FITNESS

Outdoor sports can be refreshing, but there's a tendency to push beyond your limits. Concentrate on staying flexible, and be aware of what's in front of you.

ROMANCE AND RELATIONSHIPS

Travel can have romantic overtones, and may be the key to a new love by the end of the month. An existing relationship is enhanced through sharing your philosophical ideals or joining in cultural activities together. Traveling together from the 1st-7th or from the 18th-25th can bring you closer. The Full Moon in Leo on the 6th emphasizes your deeper needs, and is an excellent time to talk about your hopes and fears. Single Leos may fall in love with love at the end of the month. Only time will tell if it's real.

FINANCE AND CAREER

Promoting an idea or product can be highly successful from the 3rd-11th. But you may run into resistance from someone who's been swayed by your competitor on the 12th-14th. These set-backs seem to strengthen your resolve, and can provide you with the perfect edge after the New Moon on the 21st. Finances are more flexible this month, leading you to believe you have ample room to indulge in extravagances. But be cautious with spending after the 20th.

OPPORTUNITY OF THE MONTH

Take advantage of the extra attention you're receiving on the 5th and 6th. Be sure to express your gratitude when it's appropriate.

Rewarding Days: 1, 2, 5, 6, 10, 14, 15, 24, 25
Challenging Days: 4, 12, 13, 17, 18, 19, 20, 26, 27

AFFIRMATION FOR THE MONTH

"I am inspired by Truth."

LEO/MARCH

PRIMARY FOCUS

Reconsideration of your beliefs and ideals may result from the actions of others. Be true to yourself, since the other party is out to save their own skin!

HEALTH AND FITNESS

Any chronic physical ailments can be worrisome. However, this cycle can bring solutions that resolve long-term problems.

ROMANCE AND RELATIONSHIPS

A problematic relationship undergoes careful scrutiny. The tendency to be distracted by a new love interest from the 8th-14th can stir up trouble in an otherwise stable relationship. You may simply need to talk about your unfulfilled needs, especially in the sexual arena. You're ready for more intensified intimacy, and it can be that you have some fears stemming from old trauma that are preventing you from experiencing what you desire. By the New Moon on the 23rd you may feel more safe about exploring different possibilities. A new romance begun now is likely to be short lived.

FINANCE AND CAREER

Circumstances at work can be filled with discord, especially if there are power struggles brewing between the hierarchy and the workers. Little resolution occurs, despite new promises made the week of the 7th. The Full Moon on the 8th brings financial matters into play, and may signal a dispute over joint resources, taxes or insurance. Postpone contracts until after the 20th, once Mercury has moved into direct motion. You may reverse your decision!

OPPORTUNITY OF THE MONTH

Some clarity on the 23rd and 24th gives you a break. If you're uncertain, postpone final actions until you can be sure.

Rewarding Days: 1, 2, 5, 9, 13, 14, 23, 24, 28
Challenging Days: 6, 11, 12, 16, 18, 19, 25, 26

AFFIRMATION FOR THE MONTH

"My actions are guided by Truth and Love."

LEO/APRIL

PRIMARY FOCUS
The temptation to act quickly to make changes can get you into hot water if you're moving forward unprepared. Proceed with care.

HEALTH AND FITNESS
A positive attitude is your best insurance toward improving your health. Pay attention to your dreams as indicators of your emotional and spiritual health.

ROMANCE AND RELATIONSHIPS
A breakthrough in communication improves all your relationships after the 15th. However, contact with a sibling or neighbor appears to be important near the time of the Full Moon on the 6th. Even though your philosophies may be different, it may be necessary to reach an agreement. A love relationship needs a broader focus on the 19th-20th, when sharing travel or an inspiring conversation can bring a better understanding. A different look at your parents can add to your tolerance of their viewpoints on the 21st.

FINANCE AND CAREER
Legal entanglements can prove to be frustrating this month. You may not reach a final agreement until after the 23rd. To avoid legal battles in the future, be sure that your current arrangements provide for a broad range of contingencies. Power struggles behind the scenes can be responsible for changes at work the week of the 4th. If you're not directly involved, try to remain an observer. Travel or conferences open new avenues for growth after the 16th.

OPPORTUNITY OF THE MONTH
You're ready to forge into new territory on the 29th, but need to allow time for careful planning. Use the new discoveries midmonth to aid your preparation for these changes.

Rewarding Days: 1, 2, 5, 6, 10, 19, 20, 24, 29, 20
Challenging Days: 3, 7, 8, 14, 15, 22, 23, 27

AFFIRMATION FOR THE MONTH
"I live in harmony with Divine Law."

LEO/MAY

PRIMARY FOCUS

You may feel like you've been supercharged, and begin to see some room for progress. Stay clear about your goals and you'll prosper.

HEALTH AND FITNESS

With Mars now transiting in Leo all month, you have more fuel for your vitality. Increasing your activity level gives you a positive edge. Sports can be highly gratifying.

ROMANCE AND RELATIONSHIPS

If you've been waiting for the right time to let someone know you're ready for love, this is it! There is a tendency to proceed in too strongly an assertive manner, so stay alert to the responses you're receiving to be sure you're not generating animosity instead! Traveling can open the door to a new love from the 1st-8th and then again after the 23rd. The Full Moon on the 5th can rekindle old conflicts at home. But by the time of the Solar Eclipse on the 21st you're ready for some new input!

FINANCE AND CAREER

Although you're ready to move forward, there is a tendency to alienate others by stepping on the wrong toes from the 4th-17th. However, you may have to ruffle a few feathers to get the job done now. Your patience with the status quo has grown thin, and you may feel that it's time for a change of the guard. A friend can be the key to finding a new career direction after the 22nd. In fact, a favor done can result in the kind of loyalty that binds eternally.

OPPORTUNITY OF THE MONTH

During the time of the Solar Eclipse on the 21st you're in an exceptional position to step into a new direction. Your radiance outshines the competition.

Rewarding Days: 3, 4, 7, 8, 17, 18, 21, 22, 26, 27, 30
Challenging Days: 1, 5, 6, 10, 11, 12, 13, 19, 20

AFFIRMATION FOR THE MONTH

"I move forward with confidence and joy."

LEO/JUNE

PRIMARY FOCUS

You're still feeling strong, but may run into obstacles from your past. Honesty is the best policy now, since cover-ups can get excessively sticky.

HEALTH AND FITNESS

Stress to perform at your peak levels can drain your physical vitality. Your best method to recharge may be exercise, but a few relaxing breaks throughout the day can also charge your batteries.

ROMANCE AND RELATIONSHIPS

Your playfulness near the time of the Lunar Eclipse on the 4th can be endearing to a friend, but you may find that your lover is jealous or put off by what appears to be a lack of consideration. This is a great time to enjoy your favorite forms of entertainment. If you're involved with children, include them as much as possible in your activities. A new love relationship is tested by your devotion to your career, but a partner might appreciate the results of your efforts. Talk about your plans and dreams on the 19th.

FINANCE AND CAREER

You can gain the favor of a mentor or superior, but need to be aware that your efforts appear to be threatening to those who feel insecure in their positions. Squabbles over property from the 6th-17th can jeopardize your financial security. Carefully examine the investments you've chosen, since you may find that releasing a property can prove lucrative.

OPPORTUNITY OF THE MONTH

Cooperative efforts on the 3rd and 4th can bring progressive rewards. By taking a position of leadership you may not only benefit yourself, but can open the door for others.

Rewarding Days: 3, 4, 13, 14, 18, 22, 23, 26, 27
Challenging Days: 1, 2, 6, 8, 9, 15, 16, 29, 30

AFFIRMATION FOR THE MONTH

"I willingly release the pain of the past."

LEO/JULY

PRIMARY FOCUS

You may feel scattered in several directions. By making the completion of old projects a higher priority, you'll have more room for your new creative opportunities when they arise later on.

HEALTH AND FITNESS

This is a great time to get involved in a team sport or fitness class. Concentrate on building up your stamina while increasing your flexibility.

ROMANCE AND RELATIONSHIPS

An introspective few days around the Full Moon on the 3rd can help you alleviate a gnawing sense of apprehension. However, social activities with your friends can be quite enjoyable. This might be a good way to meet someone new during the week of the 11th. You may feel like withdrawing during Mercury's retrograde through the 25th, but you might also simply enjoy sharing more quiet evenings or long walks in the park or on the beach. Once the Sun moves into Leo on the 22nd you're likely to feel much livelier.

FINANCE AND CAREER

With Mars transiting your Solar 2nd House there's a strong urge to spend impulsively. The best way to use this energy is through making the most of your resources, not to simply deplete them! In business matters, watch out for a surprising about-face from the 17th-31st. By preparing for change, you'll be ahead of the game instead of standing idly by while fortune blows past you.

OPPORTUNITY OF THE MONTH

You're in a great position to take advantage of changing circumstances on the 28th and 29th. Let your creative ideas guide the way to your success.

Rewarding Days: 1, 2, 10, 11, 15, 16, 19, 20, 24, 28, 29
Challenging Days: 4, 5, 6, 13, 14, 18, 26, 27, 31

AFFIRMATION FOR THE MONTH

"I use all my resources wisely."

LEO/AUGUST

PRIMARY FOCUS

Let others know where you stand by clearly communicating your ideas. But be cautious before you take others into your confidence.

HEALTH AND FITNESS

You may be running in high gear, and can quickly deplete your store of vital nutrients. Evaluate health needs the 14th-18th.

ROMANCE AND RELATIONSHIPS

The Full Moon on the 2nd brings partnership issues to the surface. Your ideas about marriage are changing, and you're looking for better ways to build the trust and compassion you seek. Take extra time to talk with your partner about your feelings and needs from the 10th-25th, when it's easier for you to express yourself more clearly. Share new experiences on the 17th and begin to build more positive connections. Travel on the 20th-21st grants you a different perspective on your relationship. Take time to share your fantasies during the Full Moon on the 31st.

FINANCE AND CAREER

While circumstances at work may be in an uproar, you can lead the way to more peaceful settlements after the 12th. Beware of the things you don't see directly ahead of you from the 15th-20th, when you can be blind-sided by your own ambition. You can make progress now, but may find that the rewards for your efforts are not apparent until the end of the month. Contracts made mid-month may be altered before they go into effect.

OPPORTUNITY OF THE MONTH

You're in a good position to take the lead in an important meeting or conference on the 16th-17th, but need to offer fresh ideas if you're going to keep the loyalty of your supporters.

Rewarding Days: 6, 7, 11, 122, 16, 17, 20, 21, 24, 25
Challenging Days: 1, 2, 5, 9, 10, 22, 23, 27, 28, 29, 30

AFFIRMATION FOR THE MONTH

"I am determined, honest and successful."

LEO/SEPTEMBER

PRIMARY FOCUS

While you're seeking ways to amplify your self-worth you can also win the support of others who can be vital to your success. It's a time to reach out, make contact and express yourself.

HEALTH AND FITNESS

In general, your vitality should be more consistently strong. It's a good time to get out in the open air. Walking, skating or bicycling might be perfectly delightful.

ROMANCE AND RELATIONSHIPS

Your self esteem gets a boost while Venus is in Leo through the 21st. You're experiencing an exceptionally positive cycle for romance, whether you're interested in improving an existing relationship or beginning a new one. In general, the social scene may be more gratifying than usual. Traveling about can broaden your options. If you're wondering where to search for love, open your eyes. The perfect person may be right next door! A surprising communication on the 16th can turn the tide and give you insights about the perfect way to proceed. Watch for conflict at home.

FINANCE AND CAREER

This is the time to attend meetings, conferences and workshops to put you in touch with those who are key in your field. If you're needing to brush up on skills, this is also a great time to take refresher courses. Financial planning makes sense now, and you may be looking for ways to put your money to work for you. Avoid jumping in too quickly from the 8th-21st.

OPPORTUNITY OF THE MONTH

Although you may be eager to make your move on the 13th, wait for the changes on the 16th before you decide which way to proceed.

Rewarding Days: 3, 4, 8, 12, 13, 16, 17, 20, 21, 28
Challenging Days: 1, 5, 6, 11, 18, 19, 23, 25, 26

AFFIRMATION FOR THE MONTH

"My words are inspired by love."

LEO/OCTOBER

PRIMARY FOCUS

Turmoil on the home front can be the result of unresolved issues from your childhood. Take an honest look at your responses. Pridefully refusing to change can lead to disappointment.

HEALTH AND FITNESS

It's easy to hold on to tension, resulting in physical and emotional stress. Concentrate on flexibility and resilience.

ROMANCE AND RELATIONSHIPS

Misunderstandings can lead to volatile arguments this month. You're probing into your most vulnerable aspect of yourself—your need for security may feel threatened. Remind yourself that you have everything you need, and be careful of the temptation to blame someone else if you're disillusioned with your life. Family, especially parents, can be the source of tension. A sibling may offer inspiration on the 15th. Use the Full Moon on the 30th to heal old wounds instead of creating new trauma.

FINANCE AND CAREER

It's easy to bring your personal problems into your business, which can make it difficult to concentrate. However, this is a good time to do some research or look into problem areas, which could give you a chance to be alone with your thoughts. Mercury's retrograde begins on the 25th and may signal a period of uncovering deception. If you're liquidating property, be aware of the tendency to under-evaluate its true worth.

OPPORTUNITY OF THE MONTH

It's time to let go of the things from your past that you've outgrown. Use this cycle to free yourself of attitudes that block your success.

Rewarding Days: 1, 5, 6, 10, 14, 15, 18, 19, 27
Challenging Days: 2, 3, 8, 11, 16, 17, 22, 23, 30, 31

AFFIRMATION FOR THE MONTH

"I am safe and secure."

LEO/NOVEMBER

PRIMARY FOCUS

Your humor is your saving grace this month, and gives you a much better frame of reference for the changes in your life. Continue to clear out debris to make room for new bounty.

HEALTH AND FITNESS

Avoid the temptation to stuff your feelings early in the month. Exercise and recreation is appealing and fun after the 9th.

ROMANCE AND RELATIONSHIPS

Through the time of the Solar Eclipse on the 13th there's likely to be continued emotional strife at home. Much of what's happening may be a simple power struggle. Review your priorities. Perhaps it would be more productive to tear down the barriers and get to the core of the issue. Your need to play can improve a love relationship, or may also be the source of more quality time with your children after the 10th. The Lunar Eclipse on the 29th offers creative inspiration and better support of your ideas.

FINANCE AND CAREER

The power base at work is likely to be shifting now. Watch for competitive tactics, which can be downright nasty early in the month. By concentrating on completing the tasks before you you'll make room for a more creative endeavor next month. Avoid making investments this month, since your attention needs to be focused on eliminating rather than accumulating potential liabilities. Review any budgets for home improvement and look for hidden costs.

OPPORTUNITY OF THE MONTH

The light at the end of the tunnel on the 29th comes through yielding to your need to be creative. Take in a game or concert.

Rewarding Days: 1, 2, 6, 10, 11, 14, 15, 24, 29
Challenging Days: 4, 7, 12, 13, 17, 18, 19, 20, 26, 27

AFFIRMATION FOR THE MONTH

"I honor my own feelings and support my real needs."

LEO/DECEMBER

PRIMARY FOCUS

You're searching for ways to enjoy yourself more, and may find that others are also seeking out your creative expertise to brighten their holidays.

HEALTH AND FITNESS

Participating in or watching your favorite sports indulges your need to play now. Boost your vitality through pure enjoyment. Watch stress levels after the 27th.

ROMANCE AND RELATIONSHIPS

It's about time that something wonderful happened in your love life! This is an exceptional period for romance and pleasure. Entertaining at home or attending parties with friends may be memorable. You may decide that you want to share this special time with the ones your hold close to your heart. It's a time when giving is easier. By the time of the New Moon on the 13th you're ready for travel or recreation. Consider a vacation. The quality of life improves by your own expression of love and joy.

FINANCE AND CAREER

Speculative ventures fare better from the 3rd-25th. you may be the one with the inside information the week of the 12th. Cooperative efforts at work are also running more smoothly, and communication has definitely improved. If you're considering making a change, look for a situation which allows more time for creative expression. Work gets busier after the 27th. Arguments can arise during the Full Moon the 28th. Avoid becoming the antagonist!

OPPORTUNITY OF THE MONTH

Take steps to get a new project off the ground on the 13th. If you have lain the foundation, the launch should go smoothly.

Rewarding Days: 3, 4, 8, 12, 13, 21, 22, 26, 30, 31
Challenging Days: 2, 10, 11, 16, 17, 23, 24

AFFIRMATION FOR THE MONTH

"I am filled with creative inspiration!"

VIRGO
THE VIRGIN

August 23 to September 23

Element: Earth
Quality: Mutable
Polarity: Feminine/Yin
Planetary Ruler: Mercury
Meditation: "Experience love through service"
Gemstone: Sapphire
Power Stones: Peridot, rhodochrosite, amazonite
Glyph: Greek symbol for "virgin"
Key Phrase: I analyze

Anatomy: Abdomen, intestines, gall bladder, duodenum, pancreas
Colors: Taupe, bluegray
Animal: Domesticated animals
Myths/Legends: Demeter, Astraea, Hygeia
House Association: Sixth
Opposite Sign: Pisces
Flower: Pansy
Key Word: Perfection

Positive Expression:
Precise
Methodical
Discriminating
Practical
Helpful
Conscientious
Humble
Efficient
Meticulous

Misuse of Energy:
Skeptical
Nervous
Superficial
Tedious
Intolerant
Hypochondriacal
Self-deprecating
Hypercritical

VIRGO

YOUR EGO'S STRENGTHS AND WEAKNESSES:
While your desire to be the best you can be drives you toward your goals, you keep an eye on the most practical ways to achieve them. You're the efficiency expert with an eye for detail and quality. Your observational skills keep you ahead of the game while others are distracted by the obvious. Your desire to learn takes a high priority, and may be your lifelong quest. You may be a quick study, and find ways to apply what you've learned to your everyday life experiences.

Although Virgos have a reputation for tidiness, if it takes too much time, you can easily stuff it in a closet or drawer in favor of concentrating on what you perceive to be more important. But that doesn't stop your critical eye from noticing when someone else is a slob! For the most part, you can be an easy companion as long as others allow you to do things your way. You love to share what you know, and have a knack for teaching and guiding others.

To avoid the reputation of nitpicking, try to find the things you appreciate or value about another person or situation. Then you can use your discriminating nature to determine more harmonious actions and words. Your admiration for quality and expertise may lead you into intellectual pursuits which can isolate you from the "outside" world. But your real lesson draws you to find ways to develop your own expertise within the world while allowing others to make their own way.

YOUR CAREER DEVELOPMENT: The pleasure of a job well done ranks high in your priorities. Rather than simply getting a job, you may seek a calling which challenges your mind and allows you to improve the quality of your life. Use your natural planning abilities in office management, secretarial service, administration, accounting, systems analysis or research. Let your desire to share your knowledge come forth through writing, speaking or teaching.

Since you're particular about the way you like things done, consider the possibility of running your own business. If you're drawn into service-oriented fields, you might enjoy social work, nursing, dental hygeine, or medicine (don't forget "non-traditional" options!). You may find a fascinating career in herbology, and can be a thorough dietician. A crafts-oriented occupation could also be quite satisfying, since you're probably rather adept at using your hands. You may develop several career options throughout your life, and can probably juggle more than one occupation at a time. Whatever your choices, you can be counted on to do your best.

YOUR APPROACH TO ROMANCE: Before you get to the romantic stage, you have a list of priorities to satisfy. But once you've opened the door, you can be a highly sensual lover. Loving, tender touching can be a magical experience. And your curiosity about the human body can lead to playful scenarios in the bedroom.

You seek a love relationship that has plenty of room for growth, and can be quite adaptable if you're dedicated to making it work. Like all earth signs, you're willing to take your time if the relationship seems worthwhile. Your opposite sign, ethereal Pisces, can be quite mesmerizing, but you may feel that they're too unrealistic. But you're strongly drawn toward the water signs—Cancer, Scorpio and Pisces. With Cancer, you may feel both a strong friendship and powerful physical bond. Scorpio helps you reach a depth of passion that can be thoroughly satisfying.

Aries' playfulness is exciting, but may distract you from your work. You're comfortable with Taurus, whose earthy sensuality feels stabilizing. Although you're drawn to Gemini's intellectual curiosity and wit, their changeability can be confounding. Leo's drama and warmth are comforting, but you may prefer being friends.

With another Virgo you can be yourself—just leave plenty of time to grumble to yourselves and avoid getting occasionally discontented with life. You can be objective and open with Libra, but may wonder where you stand with one another. Talking over tea with Sagittarius is exciting, and there can be a strong bond even if you don't see much of one another. You admire Capricorn's determination to succeed and can build a sensually satisfying and lasting relationship. With Aquarius, there can be fireworks and spiritual strength, but you may sometimes feel left out on the cold when you're ready to settle into a sweet caress.

YOUR USE OF POWER: Even though you may not seek power for its own sake, you're drawn to the idea of influencing others and changing the course of events. You see the power of the mind as primary, and value information and wisdom. Others may not recognize the breadth of power you possess, since you tend to make things appear to be effortless. But you can enjoy the fact that you've finely-tuned your skills and abilities and need to learn to give yourself praise for a job well done.

If you're drawn to minister to the needs of others, be careful of your motivations. Performed in healthy ways through outlets that allow you to both give and receive, you can help others help themselves. You may also feel compelled to call attention to mankind's inhumanity to other life forms, and may discover that you have the power to speak for those who cannot speak or act for themselves. In these ways, you use the power of service to help improve the quality of life.

FAMOUS VIRGOS: Ingrid Bergman, Leonard Bernstein, Edgar Rice Burroughs, Brian DePalma, Rebecca DeMornay, Antonini Dvorak, Scott Hamilton, Mark Harmon, Michael Keaton, Rue McClanahan, Van Morrison, Peter Sellers, Twiggy, Hank Williams

THE YEAR AHEAD FOR VIRGO

While last year provided the impetus to expand your options, this is the year to take the steps that will help to solidify your life path. The changes in the world around you can stimulate exciting opportunities, and it's important to keep in mind that you have a choice about your responses to these alterations. You're seeing the true evolution of yourself into a whole person, and can create a focus that will give you ample room to express your talents.

The awakening stimulated by the Uranus-Neptune conjunction in Capricorn may not bring about easy circumstances for anyone. It's time to take bold steps and be true to yourself. But there are several indicators that this cycle will bring a creative burst of energy into your life that allows you to appreciate yourself more fully. Your job is to stay open to this creative flow and allow it to penetrate every aspect of your life. You can recognize the value of even the simplest tasks now, and your attitude changes are likely to bring a richness to your life that gives deeper meaning to your existence. By making your spirituality an everyday practice instead of an isolated event, you'll find that the opening of consciousness stimulated by this cycle can bring clarity and direction.

Jupiter's transit in Libra lasts until November 10th, broadening your sense of self. You may feel that everything is okay, even if consistent stability doesn't seem to be present. The optimism accompanying this cycle is an optimism about yourself. You're learning that you do have all you need to make your life work. You can build your worth during this cycle. Take care to utilize your resources wisely, since it's all too easy to take them for granted. Wasting your energy can also be part of this phase, especially if you've been scattered or irresponsible. Allow plenty of time to express your gratitude to the Universe. Remind yourself how precious your life experiences have become. Build a storehouse of joy. Once Jupiter moves into Scorpio in November you may find that you're eager to know more, and that learning becomes a higher priority. If you've planned effectively in the first three quarters of the year, you may actually have accumulated sufficient resources to travel, get back into school or buy that new car.

The Solar Eclipses during 1993 bring a shift in your awareness of the need to accept the vast array of culture and heritage available to you. The variety of people gracing the face of the planet can intrigue you, and you may have an opportunity to merge with ideas or experiences that were previously unavailable. Philosophical interests can become a powerful feature, stimulating you to look carefully into the belief system you've adopted. This is an excellent time to study or attend school, but it's just as positive for re-weaving your own ethical and moral attitudes. At the core of this cycle is a desire to understand yourself more fully. You're also feeling a need to communicate more effectively. Not only do you need to reach out to others, but you're eager to feel more connected to Divine Intelligence.

If you were born from August 23rd-25th, you're experiencing a cycle of clarification. For most of the year, you may find a mixture of endings and new beginnings. But you're feeling a pressing need to complete the things that you know are holding you back. From April through August you're feeling the opposition of Saturn transiting your Sun. By becoming more accountable for your own actions and using your energy wisely, this time can be one of tremendous stabilization. But you may also feel that you're being tested. In truth, you are testing yourself. All your old doubts about your abilities can surface now, and the only way to answer these is with honesty and love for yourself. Additionally, Chiron moves into a conjunction with your Sun this fall, amplifying the need to become more aware of your motivations and choices. It's time to leave behind the excuses and circumstances which are holding you back and plant your feet on a path to self-realization.

If you were born from August 25th-31st you're challenged to move forward without unraveling the work you've so carefully completed thus far. During this year you're feeling some frustration while Uranus and Neptune transit in sesquiquad aspect to your Sun. This can be a period when your dreams seem to be just beyond your reach, but you know you have to keep stretching. It's tempting to jump into new circumstances entirely unprepared, or to be attracted to people or situations which can lead to trouble. You can definitely get a boost into more creative circumstances, but you may not know the price you're paying until you get there. The best way to work with this cycle is to allow more time to listen to Divine guidance. And with Chiron conjunct your Sun from October through December, you're pruning yourself to open for more abundant growth. It's no longer necessary to sacrifice yourself so that others can't have their needs fulfilled. You're learning the ways to cut away from your life the things that are debilitating and self-defeating. Eliminating the things that have undermined your vitality you can reach the core of your physical problems and experience a new level of wholeness.

If your birth occurred from September 1st-5th, you're digging deep into yourself to find the keys to your power. Pluto transits semisquare to your Sun this year and can be a powerful motivating energy for your personal and professional growth. Your self-concept is transforming, and you're seriously probing into the more profound meaning of life. By reaching into the abyss of your consciousness, you may discover hidden talents. You're also likely to uncover some dreams that have lain dormant since childhood which can be your springboard to positive life changes.

For Virgos born from September 6th-9th, concentrate on making the adjustments necessary to keep your life flowing smoothly. This is a time of fine-tuning, especially during the early part of the year while Saturn completes its quincunx transit to your Sun. You may find that some of your greatest opportunities arrive in August and September, when you have strong support to extend your influence and enjoy the fruits of life. Clarity about your identity helps you maintain your focus this year.

If you were born from September 10th-15th, you're experiencing the energy of Uranus and Neptune transiting in trine to your Sun. This cycle has historically been linked to powerful awakening, and can bring a profound difference in your sense of self. If you've been dreaming of making changes in your life, this is the year to break away from the ordinary and try something completely new. Your ability to manifest your dreams is exceptional. Others who had previously overlooked your talents can see you now (that includes your improved appreciation for yourself!). Express your inner child by allowing greater spontaneity of expression. Your love life improves dramatically simply from the standpoint that you've decided it's better to enjoy yourself than it is to take everything so seriously. You're also feeling the need to clarify health issues and take responsibility for your physical needs while Saturn transits in quincunx to your Sun. Adjustments in your schedule or in your health habits can honestly make a difference. You can't afford to ignore signals from your body that tell you something's amiss, because you're too excited about having the time and opportunity to realize your dreams. With the heaviness lifting, you may finally be able to use those wings you've been hiding beneath your overcoat.

If you were born from September 15th-21st, you're feeling the energy of Pluto helping you shed your fears and guilt while it travels in transiting sextile to your Sun. This is a time of positive healing, and you'll find that you're probably driven to clean out everything in your life. This clearing energy operates internally through stimulating a need to get to the core of your attitudes about life, and to meet your fears with courage and conviction. You'll probably discover that previous intimidations have been reduced to a size you can easily handle. And if you need assistance, this is an energy that opens the doors so you can request aid from those who can help you make a difference. This is a period of powerful creative vision and insight. Other people will begin to seek your expertise and assistance, and may even show their appreciation! Saturn is also transiting in quincunx to your Sun, keeping you mindful of the need to pay attention to your health and take your responsibilities seriously. It's a time to clean out closets, internally and externally, and make room for a new level of abundance and prosperity.

If your birth occurred from September 22nd-23rd, you're feeling the irritation of Saturn quincunx your Sun through the year. This can be an excellent time to get rid of all the junk in the attic or garage, and marks a period of positive self-improvement. It's necessary to pay special attention to your health, since you may feel that you don't have the physical vitality to do everything on your exhausting list of duties. By reviewing the responsibilities you've undertaken you'll probably discover that you're carrying burdens for others. It may be time to relinquish those in favor of a your own needs. The fine-tuning during this time can also include making the final touches on a creative project that's been waiting for completion. You're making way for the things that are truly nourishing and fulfilling.

TOOLS TO MAKE A DIFFERENCE: This is the year to use what you know! For example, your knowledge about the healing effect of food can bring all kinds of positive improvements into your life. You may even enjoy sharing this with your friends and family or through teaching a class.

Work with your power stones—sapphire, sardonyx and peridot—to help balance your digestive processes and strengthen your vitality. These can be worn as jewelry or can be placed directly on your body while you visualize drawing energy and light into yourself. You might also enjoy surrounding yourself with art or sculptures which display or utilize these stones in exciting ways.

Just as many people do not recognize your power, the positive attributes of your birth flower, the pansy, are often overlooked. In addition to its bright colors, which add a delicate touch to a gourmet meal or salad, the petals and leaves are often used for their medicinal effect for the skin. Its astringent properties can be used in the bath, rinses for the hair in lotions, creams and ointments to soothe the skin. The fresh leaves can be applied directly to blemishes or irritations.

In your visualizations, see yourself in a position of strength and wholeness. Envision yourself standing proudly atop a mountain awash in a brilliant ray of light from the Sun. Feel the warmth penetrating your body. Look down on the roads you've traveled and remember the love and joy you've brought with you to this place in your life. Know that throughout your journey you'll have the vision and clarity to create your life on your own terms.

AFFIRMATION FOR THE YEAR: "My mind is filled with Truth. Divine Guidance shows me the best path to follow."

ACTION TABLES FOR VIRGO

These dates reflect the best (but not the *only*) times for success and ease in these activities according to your Sun Sign.

Change Residence	Jan. 1; Dec. 7-25
Request a Raise	Sept. 16
Begin a Course of Study	Apr. 22, Nov. 13
Visit a Doctor	Jan. 21-Feb. 6; Aug 10-25
Start a Diet	Jan. 22-23; Feb. 18-20; Mar. 18-19; Apr. 14-15; May 11-12; June 8-9; July 5-6; Aug. 1-3, 29-30; Sept. 25-26; Oct. 22-24; Nov. 19-20; Dec. 16-17
Begin a Romance	Dec. 27
Join a Club	July 19
Seek Employment	Jan. 21-Feb. 7; May 18-June 2
Take a Vacation	Jan. 3,-4; 30-31; Feb. 26-27; Mar. 25-27; Apr. 22-23; May 19-20; June 15-17; July 12-14; Aug. 9-10; Sept. 5-7; Oct. 2-4, 30-31; Nov. 26-27; Dec. 23-24
Change Your Wardrobe	Jan. 2-20; Dec. 27-31
End a Relationship	Aug. 31
Seek Professional Advice	Jan. 25-26; Feb. 21-22; Mar. 20-22; Apr. 17-18; May 14-15; June 10-12; July 7-9; Aug. 4-5, 31; Sept. 1-2, 27-29; Oct. 25-26; Nov. 21-22; Dec. 18-20
Have a Makeover	Sept. 15-16
Obtain a Loan	Jan. 27-29; Feb. 24-25; Mar. 23-24; Apr. 19-21; May 17-18; June 13-14; July 10-11; Aug. 6-8; Sept. 3-4, 30; Oct. 1, 27-29; Nov. 23-24; Dec. 21-22

VIRGO/JANUARY

PRIMARY FOCUS

The energy you're putting into your friendships opens new pathways for your personal growth. However, you're changing your priorities, and some friendships will end while others solidify.

HEALTH AND FITNESS

Support your nervous system by adding foods which are rich in B-vitamins and minerals to your diet. A new exercise program or dietary plan can add vitality at the New Moon on the 22nd.

ROMANCE AND RELATIONSHIPS

There can be competition for your time among your friends, but your first priority needs to be to your creative, intimate relationships. Children may provide surprises from the Full Moon on the 8th through the 13th. Be wary of flirtations or infatuation from the 3rd-22nd, when you may only see the exciting part of the picture while missing the true nature of the other person. An existing love relationship needs more playfulness midmonth to avoid getting stuck in the rut of everyday humdrum.

FINANCE AND CAREER

Changes in your work environment can be disconcerting, and you may feel distracted from your primary obligations by the week of the 17th. But it's critical that you remain flexible when unplanned activities demand your time. Watch your finances, and review your insurance options this month. The temptation to speculate on future growth can be costly, so investigate before you invest.

OPPORTUNITY OF THE MONTH

Your influence on the 11th and 12th can lead to others changing their position by the end of the week. Be prepared to follow through with a definitive plan of action.

Rewarding Days: 3, 4, 7, 8, 11, 12, 15, 16, 20, 21, 30, 31
Challenging Days: 1, 5, 6, 10, 14, 17, 18, 19, 25, 26

AFFIRMATION FOR THE MONTH

"My life is filled with abundant joy!"

VIRGO/FEBRUARY

PRIMARY FOCUS

The actions of others seem to dictate your own course all too often this month, and can bring frustrating complications. Watch your own responses, and be sure to say, "No," when you mean it!

HEALTH AND FITNESS

Emotional stress drains your vitality, and can signal a need for more rest and relaxation. Take plenty of breaks to soften the hectic pace, especially near the Full Moon on the 6th.

ROMANCE AND RELATIONSHIPS

If volunteer activities take a toll on your time, review your commitment. Spend time talking with your partner after the 8th to alleviate your anxieties about how you're feeling about one another. Your sensual and sexual needs rank high on your list, and you may be eager to try a more fun-loving approach to your sex life. A new relationship begun now is likely to be more of a friendship than "in-love," but it can be a healthy and fulfilling interaction. Partnership is emphasized after the New Moon on the 21st, when you may decide to take commitment more seriously.

FINANCE AND CAREER

Stubborn attitudes from co-workers can be frustrating early in the month. But the energy is right for negotiation and consensus the week of the 14th. Differences in opinion about the best way to spend shared resources escalate after the 18th, when you may end up spending more than you intended. If you're considering an investment or major purchase, be sure of the long-term obligation.

OPPORTUNITY OF THE MONTH

Listen carefully to others now, since their requests or demands can play an important part in your success.

Rewarding Days: 4, 7, 8, 12, 13, 16, 17, 26, 27
Challenging Days: 1, 2, 6, 14, 15, 21, 22, 28

AFFIRMATION FOR THE MONTH

"I value my own ideas and respect those of others."

VIRGO/MARCH

PRIMARY FOCUS

Watch a tendency to allow others to influence your choice of direction. The pressure to meet another's expectations can be crippling.

HEALTH AND FITNESS

Getting involved in a fitness class or team sport can provide hours of enjoyment and increased vitality. Let your motivation be guided by your need to feel more alive.

ROMANCE AND RELATIONSHIPS

The intricate nature of maintaining close relationships is complicated by the reevaluation of your deeper needs. Improve intimacy through communicating your real feelings. But watch a tendency to sidestep uncomfortable issues, even though these are the very circumstances you're eager to change. The Full Moon in Virgo on the 8th highlights the balance of power in your intimate relationships. If you're considering (or reconsidering) marriage, it's crucial to be honest about your needs.

FINANCE AND CAREER

Work relationships can be compromised by political changes and power struggles. Although you may not be personally involved, you may feel dragged into the conflict by the 19th. Keep a firm foothold, realizing that it's time to clear away unfinished business and get ready for a new agenda. Poor judgment undermines financial decisions. Spend time in research and reevaluation until the 22nd, when Mercury turns direct.

OPPORTUNITY OF THE MONTH

It's time to take a closer look at your priorities. Prosperity comes most easily by making room for change throughout the month.

Rewarding Days: 3, 4, 7, 8, 11, 16, 17, 25, 26, 30
Challenging Days: 1, 2, 6, 13, 14, 19, 20, 21, 28, 29

AFFIRMATION FOR THE MONTH

"I accept and honor my feelings."

VIRGO/APRIL

PRIMARY FOCUS
You may feel that there's not enough time to do all the things required of you. It takes a lot of time and energy to sort through surprising changes in your personal life.

HEALTH AND FITNESS
Your emotions can upset your body this month, and you may feel that you've been short-circuited. Take plenty of time to balance through yoga or other similar centering activities.

ROMANCE AND RELATIONSHIPS
A direct confrontation with a friend early in the month can lead to a break in your relationship. But watch a tendency to jump to conclusions before reaching a final decision. The Full Moon on the 6th can bring up areas of jealousy with your sweetheart, and you may not feel that you've reached a resolution until after the 21st. Take a careful look at your expectations of yourself and others. You may be lashing out because you're feeling unhappy with yourself! The changes you're hoping to achieve are basically up to you and can actually improve the nature of your intimate ties.

FINANCE AND CAREER
An eagerness to jump into a speculative venture can contribute to neglecting important details. If you need to act fast from the 1st-11th, just be sure you've done your research! Those phantom details can surface the week of the 25th, and may leave you with a lot to explain. This is a great time to clear out old inventory or have a garage sale. Avoid purchasing things you don't really need.

OPPORTUNITY OF THE MONTH
Balance your checkbook and look at finances on the 22nd. You may discover funds you had previously overlooked.

Rewarding Days: 3, 4, 7, 8, 12, 22, 23, 26, 27
Challenging Days: 2, 9, 10, 11, 17, 18, 24, 25

AFFIRMATION FOR THE MONTH
"I eagerly release what I no longer need."

VIRGO/MAY

PRIMARY FOCUS

Broaden your contacts with others through study, workshops or travel. As your responsibilities may be increasing, you need better options for delegating responsibility.

HEALTH AND FITNESS

Inner turmoil can deplete your physical vitality unless you break away from routine and concentrate on "inner" fitness.

ROMANCE AND RELATIONSHIPS

Approach your sexual needs as a healthy way to develop a stronger bond with your partner, but also allow yourself to experience the positive nature of your own pleasure. Philosophical discussions from the 3rd-17th can lead to a deeper understanding of your relationship, and may even be the key to allowing more passion in a new love or friendship. Consider taking a short trip near the time of the Full Moon on the 5th, although simply getting away for lunch could be enticing! By the time of the Solar Eclipse on the 21st you may be drawn to reconsider unfinished business with your family, especially parents. Resolution is promising on the 29th.

FINANCE AND CAREER

Working with others toward a common goal shows promise early in the month. However, you may be tempted to go outside the influence of the group after the 24th, when their ideas may seem confining to your creativity. Clarify or rectify your financial liabilities by the 21st, since you may want to head into a fresh enterprise.

OPPORTUNITY OF THE MONTH

Breaking away from routine on the 28th can bring encouraging results, but only if you've cleared a new path for yourself.

Rewarding Days: 1, 2, 5, 6, 9, 10, 19, 20, 28, 29
Challenging Days: 4, 7, 8, 14, 15, 21, 22, 23

AFFIRMATION FOR THE MONTH

"Expressing my gratitude to others is easy."

VIRGO/JUNE

PRIMARY FOCUS

Getting more involved in your community gives you opportunities to take a position of leadership. Your actions as a representative for others or for a specific ideal are met with success.

HEALTH AND FITNESS

Negative mental attitudes can have an undermining effect on your health. Face your fears and focus on the positive to create change.

ROMANCE AND RELATIONSHIPS

Family and friends play an important role now, and may even provide the substance through which you establish a more healthy form of stability. If you're looking for romance, travel can provide interesting options, whether you're amplifying an existing love or seeking someone new. The Lunar Eclipse on the 4th brings a time of encouraging improvement in family relations. A direct line of communication brings clarity on the 19th. A sudden change of heart after the 17th can lead to greener pastures, but only if you're really finished with your old issues!

FINANCE AND CAREER

The financial front improves dramatically, although you may be spending on improved technological support. Educational pursuits, workshops or conferences provide a solid basis for career growth. Watch for competitive dialogue from the 7th-11th, when your rivals are out in full force. Your creative ideas give you the advantage the week of the 13th, although you may not see results until the 24th. Investments fare smoothly after the 23rd.

OPPORTUNITY OF THE MONTH

Your ingenuity works to your advantage on the 24th-25th. Manifesting your desires works, so be sure you know what you want!

Rewarding Days: 1, 2, 6, 7, 15, 16, 20, 21, 24, 25, 29
Challenging Days: 3, 4, 9, 10, 11, 12, 18, 19

AFFIRMATION FOR THE MONTH

"Joy fills my heart and opens my mind."

VIRGO/JULY

PRIMARY FOCUS

You may be backtracking most of the month, since many of your old connections are the key to your current success. Spend time in review and research before moving into entirely new directions.

HEALTH AND FITNESS

While Mars transits in Virgo all month you may be feeling a stronger boost in your physical vitality. Plan enjoyable recreation this month, particularly after the 21st.

ROMANCE AND RELATIONSHIPS

Second thoughts about a new relationship can lead you to mistrust your feelings. Share time with your sweetheart enjoying your favorite forms of entertainment near the time of the Full Moon on the 3rd. Allow plenty of time for your children, or at least indulge your own inner child. Then, after the New Moon on the 19th you may begin to see some substantial emotional growth. Romantic evenings may be the norm the week of the 25th, when your faith in yourself is finally restored.

FINANCE AND CAREER

With Mercury retrograde through the 25th you're probably running into a few snags in your progress. Even if you think you've got everything under control, surprising changes after the 16th can lead you on a wild goose chase. Stay organized and use this time to clear out the debris in your closet, on your desk and behind the door. Promising developments on the 19th may actually open the way for significant advancement.

OPPORTUNITY OF THE MONTH

A shift on the 19th may seem like the end of the rainbow, but give yourself until the 26th to decide if you'll pursue the option.

Rewarding Days: 3, 4, 13, 14, 18, 19, 21, 22, 26, 27, 30
Challenging Days: 1, 2, 8, 9, 15, 16, 20, 28, 29

AFFIRMATION FOR THE MONTH

"I am connected to the Source through my intuitive mind."

VIRGO/AUGUST

PRIMARY FOCUS

Fasten your seat belt—it's time to take off into an exceptional period of self-realization! Create the path you've dreamt about and manifest your innate talents.

HEALTH AND FITNESS

Examine your diet and concentrate on preparing and eating foods that are healing and invigorating. Build stamina and endurance.

ROMANCE AND RELATIONSHIPS

Special time with your friends adds a sense of warmth and support which cements your connection with one another. Your love life improves through more open expression of your feelings, and you can expand your experiences together to include memorable travel or unique pleasures. From the time of the New Moon on the 17th through the Full Moon on the 31st you're in a spontaneous and playful cycle. Surprising changes can help you release the blocks to experiencing life at its fullest. Let your inner child sing and dance!

FINANCE AND CAREER

Shifts in your fortune can be quite promising, bringing golden opportunities. But watch a tendency to spend before the money has arrived! Planning major investments or expenditures is crucial to avoid diluting your financial stability. The Full Moon on the 2nd brings some tense situations at work into the light. Realign your responsibilities, and avoid taking the rap for someone else. Attention to details on the 22nd-23rd pays off on the 27th.

OPPORTUNITY OF THE MONTH

Taking a creative risk brings recognition for your expertise on the 18th and 19th. You're realizing remarkable progress in multiple areas, and can increase your influence on the 31st.

Rewarding Days: 9, 10, 14, 15, 18, 19, 22, 23, 26, 27
Challenging Days: 2, 4, 5, 6, 11, 12, 13, 24, 25, 31

AFFIRMATION FOR THE MONTH

"I am filled with joy!"

VIRGO/SEPTEMBER

PRIMARY FOCUS
Keep an eye on your finances. You can increase your material holdings, but be sure you're spending in harmony with your needs.

HEALTH AND FITNESS
You may be feeling a bit lazy and make excuses for inactivity. Balancing relaxation with sufficient exercise gives you energy.

ROMANCE AND RELATIONSHIPS
While Mercury transits in Virgo through the 11th you may find it easier to talk about yourself and your needs. This is a good period to travel or attend meetings or conferences, and you can connect with others of like mind more readily. But you may feel reticent to initiate a relationship and prefer to spend some quiet time alone from the 11th-21st. The New Moon in Virgo on the 15th is suited toward indulging in your favorite distractions. Your discontent with the status quo on the 14th may create a wedge between yourself and others. Sharing your feelings is easier after the 22nd.

FINANCE AND CAREER
You can easily deplete many of your resources if you've not researched your expenditures. Avoid strictly impulsive expenses, since you may be operating only from your emotions. Managing your time at work can also be difficult, since it's easy to become distracted by a more interesting project. Make a careful analysis of the tasks at hand early in the month, and allow some time for something different in your schedule!

OPPORTUNITY OF THE MONTH
You're needing to branch out into more creative directions, but may be unsure of the best path. Evaluate on the 15th, and prepare for changes next month.

Rewarding Days: 5, 6, 10, 11, 14, 15, 18, 19, 23, 24
Challenging Days: 1, 2, 8, 9, 13, 20, 21, 27, 28, 29

AFFIRMATION FOR THE MONTH
"I use my resources wisely."

VIRGO/OCTOBER

PRIMARY FOCUS

Changes around you provide significant opportunities for growth. Network to broaden your support.

HEALTH AND FITNESS

In order to keep up with your schedule, you need to stay in good health. Change the scenery. Walk, bike or exercise outdoors.

ROMANCE AND RELATIONSHIPS

You may find it easier to draw experiences that make you feel more complete and worthwhile. Your ability to express yourself is enhanced, while your charisma and charm are more noticeable. A previous distancing or misunderstanding with a sibling comes to the surface early in the month and can be resolved if you'll talk about it Traveling, sharing your ideas or working on a project together can bring you closer. Time spent with children also brings more joy, especially near the Full Moon on the 30th. You don't have to look too far for love this month!

FINANCE AND CAREER

Power struggles at work grow intense by the 9th, when reorganization creates confusion. You may have a good solution to calm the chaos, and need to trust your creative imagination. Put forth your proposal on the 13th, and enact it with the New Moon on the 15th. Restoring positive lines of communication is promising, but can be troublesome after Mercury turns retrograde on the 26th. Plan your business travel or meetings early in the month. Finances are more settled this month with investments showing promise.

OPPORTUNITY OF THE MONTH

An inspiration on the 4th can lead to fulfillment on the 21st. Make the contacts you know will have an impact on your success.

Rewarding Days: 3, 4, 7, 8, 12, 13, 16, 17, 20, 21, 30, 31
Challenging Days: 1, 4, 5, 11, 18, 19, 23, 25, 26

AFFIRMATION FOR THE MONTH

"My words are inspired by Divine Intelligence."

VIRGO/NOVEMBER

PRIMARY FOCUS

Expanding your field of influence may include improving your skills. It's an excellent time to teach or learn.

HEALTH AND FITNESS

Much of your activity centers around home and family. Alleviate tension by stretching your body and relaxing your mind.

ROMANCE AND RELATIONSHIPS

Through the time of the Solar Eclipse on the 13th you're likely to feel that you're not really being heard by those you're reaching toward. Perhaps it would help if you spent some time in reflection and inner awareness of your priorities. The love you're putting into your home and family does have its own reward mid-month, and can provide a positive base for lasting stability. But you may feel a confrontation with your past looming during the Lunar Eclipse on the 29th, when unresolved emotional pain can block the joy. Find a healthy outlet for your anger, and seek out support from a friend.

FINANCE AND CAREER

Finish the paperwork that's been piling up while Mercury's retrograding through the 14th. This time is best spent clearing out incomplete projects and getting back in touch with those you've been putting off. You may discover a gold mine which wasn't ready for development until now. Your tribute for sharing your ideas can lead to good fortune, especially after the 17th. If you're tempted to sign contracts be sure to read the fine print, since you may be obligated for a long period of time!

OPPORTUNITY OF THE MONTH

The period from the 13th-29th provides exceptional understanding and can be the basis for real wisdom. Investigate.

Rewarding Days: 4, 5, 8, 9, 12, 13, 16, 17, 26, 27
Challenging Days: 1, 2, 7, 14, 15, 20, 21, 22, 29, 30

AFFIRMATION FOR THE MONTH

I speak words of love and encouragement."

VIRGO/DECEMBER

PRIMARY FOCUS

Your attention turns to the home front, when stabilizing ties with family and friends can be highly rewarding. Conflict can arise if power becomes an issue instead of realizing your commonality.

HEALTH AND FITNESS

Stress can build up if you fail to seek ways to alleviate the tension. Increased activity may be your best option, but a massage can be highly effective the weekend of the 18th.

ROMANCE AND RELATIONSHIPS

Family conflict can result from property disputes, but you don't have to get in the middle of it all! Unforeseen circumstances come to light at the time of the New Moon on the 13th when you may find it more effective to observe instead of trying to take control. You're probably dealing with too many cooks in the kitchen. Romance is most promising near the time of the Full Moon on the 28th, but you're ready to make your move by the 21st!

FINANCE AND CAREER

Contracts signed from the 1st-6th show promise. These are also good days to schedule meetings or make presentations. Socializing can have a positive effect on your business on the 10th-11th, although you may not feel comfortable unless you're hosting the event. Direct confrontation with your superiors is not a good idea this month, although you feel that someone is threatened by your presence. Take them to lunch on the 28th!

OPPORTUNITY OF THE MONTH

Since you're pulled in several directions, you may need a good time to rejuvenate. Take some time on the 5th to get away and be alone with your thoughts. The clarity will come in handy!

Rewarding Days: 1, 2, 5, 6, 10, 14, 15, 23, 24, 28, 29
Challenging Days: 4, 12, 13, 16, 17, 18, 19, 26, 27

AFFIRMATION FOR THE MONTH

"My home is a loving and comfortable place."

LIBRA
THE SCALES

September 23 to October 23

Element: Air
Quality: Cardinal
Polarity: Masculine/Yang
Planetary Ruler: Venus
Meditation: "Creating beauty and harmony"
Gemstone: Opal
Power Stones: Tourmaline, kunzite, blue lace agate
Glyph: Scales, Setting Sun
Key Phrase: I balance

Anatomy: Kidneys, lower back, adrenals, appendix
Color: Blue
Animal: Brightly plumed birds
Myths/Legends: Hera, Venus, Cinderella
House Association: Seventh
Opposite Sign: Aries
Flower: Rose
Key Word: Harmony

Positive Expression:
Sociable
Gracious
Refined
Impartial
Agreeable
Logical
Considerate
Artistic
Diplomatic

Misuse of Energy:
Distant
Unreliable
Placating
Argumentative
Indecisive
Critical
Inconsiderate
Conceited

LIBRA

YOUR EGO'S STRENGTHS AND WEAKNESSESS:
Your agreeable manner draws many people to you, and you can bring a sense of charm and elegance into any circumstance. You radiate grace under pressure, and have a knack for brightening your surroundings and creating beauty. When it comes to diplomacy, you have a natural talent for seeing both sides of an issue, and can possess a tremendous objectivity. As a mediator, you can be an impartial judge and positive representative for a person or an idea.

Seeking logical alternatives often brings you into enviable circumstances. Your concern for the impact of your presentation of yourself and your life is apparent to those who enjoy the beauty of your home and are the recipients of your good taste. Always seeking symmetry and harmony, you may be viewed as a highly artistic individual.

Everything is relative for you, and you need to keep a perspective on the whole picture to avoid getting thrown out of balance. Preserving your equilibrium in relationships is sometimes difficult, since you're always looking for perfection in yourself and others. When that ideal is not met, you may feel off-center. Your life lesson is to learn how to relate to others and to the world around you without losing your sense of self. This can be more easily accomplished if you spend more time harmonizing with your inner partner, maintaining more constant contact with your Higher Self.

YOUR CAREER DEVELOPMENT: Your appreciation for the finer things in life may lead you into a career in the arts. This can be accomplished through your own artistry or through representing and maintaining the arts and literature through museums, galleries or conservatories. As a natural in public relations, you might also enjoy personnel management or counseling others. Relationship counseling would be a logical choice, although you could also be an effective attorney or judge.

A career in the fashion or beauty industry might also be enjoyable. Your ability to see and enhance the strengths of others can help you in areas such as image consulting and counseling, but can also be expressed in more dramatic arenas such as costume or set design. Whatever your career choice, you'll accomplish it with a special touch of class.

YOUR APPROACH TO ROMANCE: You're known for your relationships, and may have plenty of stories to tell about your conquests and losses. But one thing is clear—you love to be with others and have a strong ideal when it comes to romance. Love and marriage may be intertwined for you, but the ideal doesn't always work out! You can be the quintessential partner, but can vacillate between absolute involvement and holding back. You may fear you'll lose part of yourself if you lose the relationship.

In sexual encounters, you're most comfortable when you're in a beautiful, safe place. Once you open to your innermost desires, you can thoroughly enjoy the dance of love. The attraction you feel to Aries can bring a high level of excitement, but you may sense that you don't have an egalitarian relationship! Sharing the beautiful things in life with Taurus can feel stable and secure, but you may not like the underlying agenda of control issues. Gemini, whose airy nature like your own enjoys sharing ideas, can be a fabulous companion.

You may feel uncomfortable with the tenacity and sentimentality of Cancer. But Leo's passion for life inflames your own passionate desires. While Virgo is grounding, you may not feel consistently romantic together. Another Libran can be a comfortable companion, but you may not feel consistently secure. The intensity from Scorpio can often overwhelm, although you can become unbelievably intertwined. With Sagittarius, you're drawn to see the world and share the adventure of life. Capricorn's attraction is often powerful, but you can really push each other's buttons if you're not open with one another. Aquarius, another Air sign, offers freedom and can be highly supportive and romantic in ways you appreciate. The high emotionality of Pisces maybe uncomfortable when you're wanting space, but you might adore sharing a romantic interlude.

YOUR USE OF POWER: You need some time to get used to the idea of power before you can acknowledge that you even want any. Once you're clear about it, you may begin to realize that your power comes from using an impartial and logical approach to any circumstance, rather than allowing your emotions to take over and get you into trouble. Unfortunately, this approach often makes you appear distant, and you can deliberately project a cold shoulder when you're hurt.

The perfection you seek in yourself you also look for in the outside world. But your tendency to compare yourself and your life situation with others can undermine your power. Know what you want for yourself, and allow yourself to feel good about these needs. You cannot become anything other than *you!* Once you've established your own boundaries, you can begin to use your power to create life on your own terms, sharing yourself as a whole person with the world around you.

Your attunement to the world and her people can inspire improvement and change where it's needed. Your ability to see the other side gives you hope that change is possible. When you're centered in the energy that flows through you from the Source, your outer life reflects a more stable, balanced reality. You can then blend the perfect colors and textures which become a beautiful portrait of your life.

FAMOUS LIBRANS: Julie Andrews, Hafez Assad, Annie Besant, Lindsey Buckingham, James Clavell, Jimmy Carter, Chevy Chase, William Faulkner, Lee Iacocca, Jerry Lee Lewis, Groucho Marx, Christopher Reeve, Pierre Trudeau, Barbara Walters, Moon Unit Zappa

THE YEAR AHEAD FOR LIBRA

You're eager to expand your field of influence and may feel that the sky's the limit this year. But you realize that there's a price to pay for your hopes and may be more willing now to balance what you're getting with the real cost. As a result, there's a tremendous opportunity for personal success which can extend into every area of your life. You've grown tired of all the talk, and are feeling the necessity of taking appropriate action.

Concentrate on radiating a sense of hope and optimism, a theme which is supported by several cycles occurring in 1993. The Solar and Lunar Eclipses emphasize a shift in your priorities. You're completing a cycle of careful scrutiny about your self-worth and can begin to network with others who share your viewpoint and your ethical standards. You may feel the desire to travel growing stronger this year, but just as importantly, you're ready to look at the different cultures surrounding you and find ways to embrace them as part of your reality. Your own beliefs may be tested as a result of exposure to different concepts, but the core of your identity can withstand the test!

The expansive, fortuitous energy of Jupiter is working to your benefit this year while this planet transits in Libra through November 9th. Your confidence gets a major boost, and you may find more things to appreciate about yourself. Take a look back to 1981, the last time this cycle occurred. You may have a chance to renew some of the dreams that were not completed during that time. But it's also possible that you're finally reaping the rewards for the efforts begun at that time. This is an exceptional period for studying, traveling or teaching, and can provide the excellent advantage of your being in the right place at the right time. If you've been waiting for the right time to expand a business, advertise your services or seek advancement, your efforts can be met with great success. But it's also tempting to fall into a cycle of self-indulgence and costly extravagance. Everything may seem to be going your way, and it's easy to drop the oars and just float downstream. Staying balanced has never been more important, since the opportunities, the contacts and the joy can carry you into long-term success through prudent use of your good fortune.

The Uranus-Neptune conjunction of 1993 can bring a disruptive influence, much like a major quake in the foundation of your life. Not only are you exposing much of your past, but you're finding that the security base you've always relied upon is no longer serving your needs. It's time to forgive yourself for the real or imaginary transgressions of your past and move forward onto a base that can support your creativity and happiness.

If you were born from September 23rd-29th you may be feeling that your life is a little out of step with your internal rhythms. Saturn's aspects by transit to your Sun are indicative of a period of inner unrest. It may seem that your judgment is impaired. It's almost like the partial blindness you experience when going from the light of day into a dark room. You can see, but it takes a period of adjustment. Because of the adjustments you may be feeling internally, it's generally a better idea to be extremely careful when making major life changes. Relationships can be quite a juggling act during this phase, and you need to be blatantly honest with yourself about your true feelings about others in your life. You may find that you've been projecting things onto someone else that are totally inappropriate. And you may have been playing a role that doesn't fit your real needs. Seeing things as they really are does require a period of adjustment, since the truth can be temporarily blinding!

If you were born from September 28th-October 2nd you're experiencing a longer period of Jupiter transiting in conjunction to your Sun. The impact of this cycle lasts from April through July, giving you plenty of time to reach out and expand your boundaries. You may feel that your values are shifting, and need to take a careful look at your motivations. It's easy to get yourself into trouble by spending your resources before they arrive. Operating on promises is dangerous during this time, so try the reasonable approach whenever possible. However, the general feeling of this cycle is one of enhanced confidence, which, when appropriately used, can be the key to opening to a limitless horizon.

For Librans born from September 30th-October 7th, the pressure to pull your life together is growing intense while Pluto transits semisquare your Sun this year. This is an excellent time to clear away the debris from your past that's been accumulating while you've been moving forward. Treading through the left-overs can slow you down, and you're ready to make progress. From an internal level, this period brings you in contact with any old guilt or resentment that have blocked the fulfillment of your needs—especially in the arena of relationships. It's time to peel away the tight layers that have inhibited your self-esteem and locate the center of your being. From this standpoint you can begin to relate on your own terms, since you're uncovering the essence of your deepest needs.

You're feeling a period of some relief from the pressure to experiment, let go and be yourself if you were born from October 8th-10th. The dust has settled and you may even feel more familiar with the uncharted territory you've been exploring. Although there may be changes occurring in other areas of your life, your sense of self should now be stronger, allowing you to feel more confident about your choices and definitely more free in your actions. Jupiter conjuncts your Sun for all of January, February, late August and early September, bringing an excellent time to reach further with your changes and reap the rewards of a job well done. Watch your level of impatience, however, since Mars does square your Sun from January through March, and you may feel that you're driving a team of wild horses! Pace yourself.

You're in the midst of a major change if you were born from October 11th-16th. Several long-lasting cycles are influencing your life this year, and may stimulate some complex transitions. Uranus and Neptune are both transiting in square aspect to your Sun, and can bring intensive special effects. You're feeling the urge to break free and take chances with your life. Playing it safe may seem like death warmed over. You do have some good support while you're making these changes. But it's easy to get lost in the haze, where you feel like you're making significant progress until the fog lifts and you discover you've been going in circles. The first line of transition comes from the things you've counted on as your security. You may finally be willing to let go of circumstances from your past that no longer have relevance. This gives you room to incorporate new elements and experiment with your own lifestyle. This cycle can be a stormy one if you've been imprisoned in a situation that has stifled your growth. But if you've been staying in touch with your needs, you may find that this period gives you a boost into a more highly individualized expression of yourself.

It's all too easy to ignore your physical needs since life has more interesting things to offer than watching your health. But attention to nutrition and a healthy lifestyle can help assure the freedom you need to experience life at its fullest. Mentally, you can appear to be making changes that others find difficult to grasp. You've been experiencing these shifts at an inner level for quite some time, but now you're ready to express them externally. Communication can resolve many of the concerns that others have for you. Spiritually, this is a period of awakening which stimulates changes on all levels. Your job is to stay in the center of your own power while modifying your life.

Saturn transits in harmonious trine to your Sun if you were born from October 10th-23rd. This energy supports focus and self-discipline, and can be especially helpful if you're also feeling the effects of the Uranus-Neptune square (above). Welcoming your responsibilities makes sense during this phase, and it's imperative that you learn to be accountable for yourself, your thoughts and your actions now. This is an excellent period to be in school or involved in some type of disciplined study. But it's also a great time to complete an important project or solidify a business. Taking care of yourself now may mean that you're finally willing to let go of habits you know to be self-defeating. You're ready to make the commitment to yourself to live life in the real world, but on terms that support your needs.

For those of you born from October 16th-21st, you're also feeling a need to restore a positive sense of personal power while Pluto transits in semisextile aspects to your Sun. It's easy to look into the deeper part of yourself now, and you may find that you're willing to deal with issues that have been buried for a long time. Bringing old trauma to the surface can be especially healing during this cycle.

But you can also allow more room in your life for creative activities that you do to satisfy only yourself. It's time to take off the mask and let your beauty shine through.

TOOLS TO MAKE A DIFFERENCE: Since this is a year to grow, you'll be more comfortable seeking out a variety of situations that may have previously seemed unreachable. Give yourself plenty of opportunities to travel, read or connect with others whose ideals support your personal evolution.

Pay extra attention to your kidneys, lower back and adrenals. Strengthening these sensitive areas now can help you while you're making changes in your life. Remind yourself that you have the emotional stability you need to move forward. Your flower, the rose, has many uses in addition to its vibrant beauty. The fragrance is emotionally balancing. A rose tonic is beneficial for the beautification of the skin, since the astringent action is positively stimulating. Rose oil could be an excellent choice of perfume, since the aromatic properties not only balance the emotions but can also have a calming effect. Rosehip tea has long been a favorite of herbalists. Not only is the fruity ambrosia delightful, but it is a rich source of vitamin C.

Librans are among the few individuals who seem to have a positive relationship with the energy of the beautiful opal. These stones, along with tourmaline and kunzite, are not only lovely as jewelry, but have remarkable clearing and harmonizing effects on the emotional and physical body. Wear tourmaline near the throat to help keep this area of the body open and clear.

Use creative visualization to help you connect with inner beauty and strength. Imagine that you are a rosebud, feeling the warmth of the springtime Sun. Little by little, feel yourself opening up until you have become a fully blossoming rose. Know that you emanate the essence of love, radiating an energy which pleases you and which others enjoy. Realize that you continue to repeat this process of blossoming over and over again, and that all things in your life cycle through change.

AFFIRMATION FOR THE YEAR: "I am considerate of my own needs and the needs of others."

ACTION TABLES FOR LIBRA

These dates reflect the best (but not the *only*) times for success and ease in these activities according to your Sun Sign.

Change Residence	Jan. 2-20; Dec. 26-31
Request a Raise	Oct. 15
Begin a Course of Study	May 21; June 20; Dec. 13
Visit a Doctor	Feb. 7-Apr. 15; Aug. 26-Sept. 10
Start a Diet	Jan. 25-26; Feb. 21-22; Mar. 20-21; Apr. 17-18; May 14-15; June 10-11; July 8-9; Aug. 4, 5, 31; Sept. 1-2, 28-29; Oct. 25-26; Nov. 21-22; Dec. 18-20
Begin a Romance	Jan. 22-23
Join a Club	Aug. 17-18
Seek Employment	Feb. 7-Apr. 14; June 2-Aug. 9
Take a Vacation	Jan. 5-6; Feb. 1-2, 28; Mar. 1-2, 28-29; Apr. 24-25; May 21-23; June 18-19; July 15-16; Aug. 11-12; Sept. 8-9; Oct. 5-6; Nov. 1-2, 28-30; Dec. 26-27
Change Your Wardrobe	Jan. 21-Feb. 7
End a Relationship	Sept. 30-31
Seek Professional Advice	Jan. 27-29; Feb. 24,-25; Mar. 23-24; Apr. 19-21; May 16-18; June 13-14; July 10-11; Aug. 6-7; Sept. 3-4, 30; Oct. 1, 27-29; Nov. 23-25; Dec. 21-22
Have a Makeover	Oct. 15
Obtain a Loan	Jan. 3-4, 30-31; Feb. 26-27; Mar. 25-27; Apr. 22-23; May 19-20; June 15-17, July 13-14; Aug. 9-10; Sept. 5-7; Oct. 2-4, 30-31; Nov. 26-27; Dec. 23-25

LIBRA/JANUARY

PRIMARY FOCUS

Changes on the home front disrupt your plans, but there are also power issues in your career that can enhance the instability you're feeling at home. Give yourself time to make final decisions.

HEALTH AND FITNESS

Work off stress through increased activity, but watch a tendency to push yourself too far. Pace yourself.

ROMANCE AND RELATIONSHIPS

Most of your emotional tension seems to be coming from family and parents. You're eager to leave the past and continue to move toward the future, but your family may resist the change, especially near the time of the Full Moon on the 8th. It will be easier to express your ideas and feelings after the 20th, when resistance diminishes. Romance comes back to life after the New Moon on the 22nd, when a new love or an existing relationship takes on a more imaginative dimension. Spend time in intimate surroundings on the 30th, when you may be hungry for delectable love-making!

FINANCE AND CAREER

Although you may feel that you know where you've heading, others around you may have different ideas. Power struggles can emerge from the 5th-11th, especially if you've been perceived as a threat. By maintaining an awareness of your responses, you can use this time to advance in your career, or may choose to change directions. Be honest about your motivations. Concentrate on improving your situation, and you'll find ample rewards.

OPPORTUNITY OF THE MONTH

An inspiring creative project or romantic interlude on the 22nd-23rd can bring a pivotal change in your life direction.

Rewarding Days: 5, 6, 9, 13, 14, 18, 19, 22, 23, 24
Challenging Days: 1, 7, 8, 16, 20, 21, 26, 27, 28

AFFIRMATION FOR THE MONTH

"I seek harmony in the face of conflict."

LIBRA/FEBRUARY

PRIMARY FOCUS

Demands from others continue to provide complications, but may also offer significant opportunities. Stay clear about the reasons behind your changes.

HEALTH AND FITNESS

Looking into your health is a good idea. Establish a baseline for assessing your nutritional and physical needs.

ROMANCE AND RELATIONSHIPS

You may change your mind about a significant relationship, and need to examine whether or not your involvement is meeting your needs. Improve your partnership through sharing your appreciation of one another instead of simply finding fault. Disagreements escalate near the time of the Full Moon on the 6th, and you may break your ties by the 12th if working toward a solution seems futile. Look before you leap into something new late in the month. Your expectations can overwhelm the reality of the connection.

FINANCE AND CAREER

The conflicts from others at work can draw you into situations that impair your ability to get much accomplished. Listening to the concerns of those working under your supervision can provide you with the insights you need to hasten improvements by the time of the New Moon on the 21st. Curtail impulsive expenditures midmonth to avoid undermining your stability. You may be tempted by purely emotional motivations, which interfere with your ability to make a rational choice from the 12th-21st.

OPPORTUNITY OF THE MONTH

Working with groups or in concert with a good friend toward a common goal provides recognition from the 5th-7th.

Rewarding Days: 1, 2, 6, 7, 10, 11, 14, 15, 19
Challenging Days: 3, 4, 13, 16, 17, 21, 24, 25, 27

AFFIRMATION FOR THE MONTH

"I deserve to have my needs fulfilled."

LIBRA/MARCH

PRIMARY FOCUS

Accommodating other people may become tedious if you're not allowing room or time for your own preferences. Set a limit.

HEALTH AND FITNESS

Your energy level may be a bit low, and still you can have difficulty resting. Allow time each day to stretch and relax. Avoid excessive sweets.

ROMANCE AND RELATIONSHIPS

Your planetary ruler, Venus, moves into retrograde motion on the 11th, drawing your attention to the need to reevaluate your intimate relationships. You're working on self-improvement and may feel dissatisfied if your partner is stuck in the same old ruts. This can lead you to take a severe turn toward an entirely new love from the Full Moon on the 8th until the 15th. You may wake up to find you've jumped from the frying pan into the fire! Rekindling the flame can work, but you have to keep your expectations at a reasonable level. Try to reach a consensus on the 23rd.

FINANCE AND CAREER

Your judgment in financial matters can be faulty. Be on the alert for excessive spending or impulsive decision-making. Staying within your budget can be tough, and you need to allow room for unexpected necessary expenditures. At work, misunderstandings create difficulty, and paperwork can be frustrating. Mercury turns direct on the 22nd, when the chaos begins to subside—slowly.

OPPORTUNITY OF THE MONTH

Careful evaluation of your life uncovers resources you'd forgotten, but you have to make the most of them now! Finish those dangling projects and clear out room for something new.

Rewarding Days: 1, 5, 6, 9, 10, 13, 18, 28, 29
Challenging Days: 3, 4, 12, 15, 16, 17, 23, 24, 30

AFFIRMATION FOR THE MONTH

"My heart is filled with joy."

LIBRA/APRIL

PRIMARY FOCUS
The dissatisfaction you're feeling with your life may be due to the fact that you've sought to find yourself and fulfill your needs through all the externals. It's time to turn your life around!

HEALTH AND FITNESS
Your health improves now as you adopt a more self-supportive role and take greater responsibility for your own sense of well-being.

ROMANCE AND RELATIONSHIPS
An existing relationship or new love can be wounded by impulsive actions or words. Be especially mindful of your needs while considering the feelings of another during the Full Moon on the 6th. The best option is to satisfy both of you, but your old agendas can bring up complications that make direct honesty difficult. An attraction on the 6th-10th can feel magical, but you'll need to allow some time before you make a commitment. You're definitely looking for change, but it has to fit your needs.

FINANCE AND CAREER
Business partnerships are rocky. Be sure you've been carrying your own weight, and if you find that you've shouldered too much of the responsibility, renegotiate. You're ready to break away from career circumstances that inhibit your growth and autonomy, and you may meet some resistance to those changes early in the month. Before you step into a new situation, be sure your foundation is stable. Thoroughly investigate your options on the 21st, when you may have a chance to move forward.

OPPORTUNITY OF THE MONTH
Your most significant time of forward motion is from the 21st-29th. Agreement on your terms is most likely on the 29th.

Rewarding Days: 1, 5, 6, 10, 14, 15, 24, 25, 29, 30
Challenging Days: 4, 8, 12, 13, 17, 19, 20, 26, 27

AFFIRMATION FOR THE MONTH
"I am flexible and considerate."

LIBRA/MAY

PRIMARY FOCUS
A position of leadership within your community or among your friends can arise, affording you the chance to create further opportunities for advancement.

HEALTH AND FITNESS
Insight into a chronic physical ailment may offer the key to improvement in your health early in the month. Consider an extended vacation for rejuvenation after the 20th.

ROMANCE AND RELATIONSHIPS
Frank talk about your sexual needs from the 3rd-17th can unlock some of the barriers to the achievement of intimacy with your partner. A secluded, romantic getaway can be the perfect setting to open the doors to ecstasy near the Full Moon on the 5th, or you may simply want to transform your own surroundings to achieve the same effect. Whether you seek a new relationship or desire to improve an existing connection, travel from the time of the Solar Eclipse on the 21st through the 31st can be inspiring and advantageous.

FINANCE AND CAREER
You're finally realizing some progress in your career, but still need to watch out for the competition. You're tempted to carry your ideas too far the week of the 23rd, and can alienate the more conservative faction at work. But if your aim is to break out and move into different territory, you have just the ammunition you need following the Solar Eclipse on the 21st. Keep your ethical standards high and safeguard your finances after the 26th.

OPPORTUNITY OF THE MONTH
You're in an excellent position to influence others or move into profitable circumstances on the 21st and 22nd.

Rewarding Days: 3, 4, 7, 8, 12, 13, 21, 22, 23, 26, 30, 31
Challenging Days: 1, 6, 9, 10, 14, 16, 17, 24, 25

AFFIRMATION FOR THE MONTH
"My actions and words are guided by love and wisdom."

LIBRA/JUNE

PRIMARY FOCUS
Spending extra time learning more about your craft or trade this month leads to future advancement. Travel broadens your options.

HEALTH AND FITNESS
Team sports or group fitness activities can provide both health benefits and solidify friendships. Mental stress may accelerate now, and you may need to enhance your nutritional support.

ROMANCE AND RELATIONSHIPS
While you may be more demonstrative of your affections, you might run into old fears that prevent you from trusting your feelings. Consideration of your partner's needs can bring you closer, but your own desires are also pressing. Talk about your ideals and beliefs during the Lunar Eclipse on the 4th, when you may find the missing link in your bond with one another. Jealousy from a friend from the 6th-19th can lead to crisis, or may expose deception. Clarify your motives and make a fresh start on the 19th, when you discover a more meaningful quality in your relationship.

FINANCE AND CAREER
Getting your ideas across to your superiors can be frustrated by surprising twists from the 15th-18th. Financial disputes can be the result of circumstances beyond your control midmonth, but you still have to come up with a plan of recourse. Uncovering the real value of a product or service may be determined by what the other party is willing to pay. Bargains are scarce now, since the other guy is holding firm and you may not be willing to budge, either!

OPPORTUNITY OF THE MONTH
The New Moon on the 19th marks the most significant time to reach agreements or launch creative projects.

Rewarding Days: 3, 4, 8, 9, 18, 19, 22, 23, 26, 27
Challenging Days: 2, 5, 6, 13, 14, 20, 21, 29

AFFIRMATION FOR THE MONTH
"I listen carefully to others."

LIBRA/JULY

PRIMARY FOCUS

Your reputation may vacillate while others make choices about your value to their cause. Promote your best attributes!

HEALTH AND FITNESS

Energy expended toward inner fitness provides you with a quiet confidence in the face of stress.

ROMANCE AND RELATIONSHIPS

Family conflicts can lead you to withdraw from contact since you're seeking support and may not feel that it's forthcoming. But it's time to take a serious look at your deeper feelings about your roots. Honestly evaluate your past and the ways you're currently choosing to fill your needs during the Full Moon on the 3rd. Differing value systems may be at the heart of your disputes in any relationship midmonth, but if you can clearly express your ideals, you'll make great strides in eliminating an unhealthy agenda that's kept you from getting what you need.

FINANCE AND CAREER

After the 6th you may feel more confident about expanding your options. Schedule important conferences on the 15th, 19th, 20th or 24th, when you'll find a more receptive audience for your ideas. Travel during the week of the 11th or the 25th can put you in contact with expeditious circumstances. However, since Mercury is retrograde until the 25th, you might prefer to postpone final decisions until the last week of the month. Examine contracts with care, and investigate emerging investment opportunities.

OPPORTUNITY OF THE MONTH

Clear out the cobwebs and finish your paperwork, since you're needing plenty of room to expand next month.

Rewarding Days: 1, 5, 6, 15, 16, 20, 23, 24, 28, 29
Challenging Days: 3, 4, 8, 10, 11, 13, 17, 18, 30, 31

AFFIRMATION FOR THE MONTH

"I respect my intuitive guidance."

LIBRA/AUGUST

PRIMARY FOCUS

Everything remains in a state of flux, but your willingness to experiment places you in touch with those who can help you fulfill your dreams for success.

HEALTH AND FITNESS

You'll need the energy boost coming your way after the 12th, and need time to be active. Emotions powerfully effect your health.

ROMANCE AND RELATIONSHIPS

Your friends can be your best allies mid-month, when you may seek their counsel during a time of emotional crisis. The Full Moon on the 2nd brings your love life into focus and marks an important cycle for revitalizing and enjoying your love encounters. But there are distractions brewing from the 15th-20th which can be symbolic of your discontent with the status quo. It's not the best time to run away from the issues, since they'll follow you even if you change partners. But you feel the breath of new life once you open to the spontaneous urges that propel you toward change and growth.

FINANCE AND CAREER

A turn-about on the 1st-2nd can create a need to look toward a different direction in your career. If you're wanting to expand, make connections from the 10th-25th with those who value your work and may be able to give you a boost. Greater rewards for your work are manifesting now, although you need to be careful to avoid putting all your eggs in one basket. Diversify.

OPPORTUNITY OF THE MONTH

The New Moon on the 17th opens your eyes to the fact that your dreams can become reality. Balance risks with good judgment.

Rewarding Days: 2, 3, 11, 12, 16, 17, 20, 21, 24, 29
Challenging Days: 4, 6, 7, 14, 15, 23, 26, 27, 28, 31

AFFIRMATION FOR THE MONTH

"I am an honorable friend."

LIBRA/SEPTEMBER

PRIMARY FOCUS

Community activities provide positive avenues toward building your reputation and broadening your influence.

HEALTH AND FITNESS

While Mars continues its transit in Libra until the 27th you may feel a recharge in your power supply. Pacing yourself is crucial, since moving too quickly can result in unexpected set-backs.

ROMANCE AND RELATIONSHIPS

An existing relationship grows through sharing common interests, and may also be enhanced through travel. If you're seeking a new love, turn your attention to situations which hold your fascination where you may find the person of your dreams. Talking about your feelings and needs works its own magic after the New Moon on the 15th, and may lead to a deeper level of commitment by the Full Moon on the 30th. However, you can jump into a volatile situation on the 10th-11th. Seek support and counsel from friends if you feel you're in over your head.

FINANCE AND CAREER

Make the most of changing circumstances by initiating an exciting idea or project in your career. You're in perfect circumstances to take the lead from the 8th-18th, but need to watch for a shift in financial support. You're simply changing tracks, not falling off the mountain! Your fresh approach stirs the imagination and support of others on the 21st-22nd. This can lead to more stable finances.

OPPORTUNITY OF THE MONTH

After interruptions and delays, some things are beginning to turn around. Be prepared before stepping into the spotlight on the 16th.

Rewarding Days: 8, 9, 12, 13, 16, 17, 20, 21, 25, 26
Challenging Days: 1, 3, 4, 10, 11, 23, 24, 30

AFFIRMATION FOR THE MONTH

"My consciousness is connected to The Source of All Wisdom."

LIBRA/OCTOBER

PRIMARY FOCUS
Building your financial worth can help provide a sense of enhanced stability this month. Pay attention to all the details.

HEALTH AND FITNESS
This is the perfect time to concentrate on increasing your physical flexibility while enhancing your endurance and stamina.

ROMANCE AND RELATIONSHIPS
Your creative projects, love life or children may prove to be rather costly this month. The simple approach to romance can be the most comfortable, since quiet evenings unfold to intimate encounter by midmonth. A romantic get-away on the 15th can result in surprises. Your ability to get in touch with a greater sense of self-worth allows you to appreciate others more fully from the 17th-31st. Family pressures can lead to a temporary change of heart after the 25th, and you may feel a disturbing emotional distance from family. It's time to release the past and move forward.

FINANCE AND CAREER
Through careful planning you can use this time to liquidate or eliminate debt, but it's also tempting to overspend. The most prudent course of action will be the most gratifying. Counting on a situation before the final contracts are drawn or paid can bring disastrous results, since there can be a major shift by the 25th that nobody anticipated. Get new projects moving on the 15th and 16th to offset the possibility of change between the 25th-30th. Take comfort in team efforts, which fare nicely after the 17th.

OPPORTUNITY OF THE MONTH
The Libra New Moon on the 15th is the perfect time to get down to negotiations, personal or professional.

Rewarding Days: 5, 6, 10, 14, 15, 18, 19, 22, 23
Challenging Days: 1, 3, 7, 8, 17, 20, 21, 25, 27, 28

AFFIRMATION FOR THE MONTH
"I am loving, gentle and kind."

LIBRA/NOVEMBER

PRIMARY FOCUS

Financial confusion is likely until after Mercury goes direct on the 15th. Conserve your resources.

HEALTH AND FITNESS

Weekend getaways can be your salvation this month. Take time to enjoy a change of pace and bring some variety into your life.

ROMANCE AND RELATIONSHIPS

Appreciate the smoothly operating circumstances to avoid getting caught in the doldrums. From the 1st-9th you have a remarkable period of positive self-worth emerging which can support you in taking the steps to express feelings you've long ignored. Welcome contact with a sibling on the 10th or 11th by taking the first step in reaching out to one another. Although you may feel a bit withdrawn during the Solar Eclipse on the 13th, you're more willing to open up the next day. Reaffirm your connection with your Higher Self during the Lunar Eclipse on the 29th, and realize the ways in which you're bonded to others through this energy.

FINANCE AND CAREER

Double-check all your financial figures early in the month, since it's all too easy to miss important details. You can vastly improve your financial worth now by repairing, reusing or recycling some of your goods or resources instead or buying new. Career improves through putting energy into sharpening your skills, attending workshops or conferring with others in your field after the 10th. Make important calls on the 29th or 30th.

OPPORTUNITY OF THE MONTH

It's time to probe into your motivations behind your spending patterns. You may find that you don't need as much "stuff" now!

Rewarding Days: 1, 2, 6, 7, 10, 11, 14, 15, 19, 20, 29, 30
Challenging Days: 4, 5, 9, 13, 16, 17, 18, 23, 24

AFFIRMATION FOR THE MONTH

"I have everything I need."

LIBRA/DECEMBER

PRIMARY FOCUS

It's time to communicate, travel and make contact with the world. Teaching, writing or studying can be extremely rewarding.

HEALTH AND FITNESS

Staying active is important now. This is a great time to take a vacation, especially if you make it a healthy one!

ROMANCE AND RELATIONSHIPS

All your relationships undergo vast improvement through the 25th. Use the energy of the New Moon on the 13th to get your message of love across in an unforgettable manner. Travel from the 12th-26th can bring a new love interest, but it can also be the key to invigorating an existing relationship. Show your feelings to your friends, and reconnect with those you love who may be separated by distance on the 7th, 8th, 12th, 13th 16th or 27th. Be honest with yourself about your feelings toward family during the Full Moon on the 28th, when you may need to mend fences through forgiving yourself for your differences.

FINANCE AND CAREER

You may be filled with "brotherly love," and need to watch a tendency to give away the farm. You can demonstrate some shrewd financial maneuvers from the 1st-6th, but you may be swimming with sharks, so move with caution! Business deals fare well on the 12th and 13th, when you may be at your peak in diplomacy. You're in good company on the 16th and 17th, when you may find the support of others in a creative project can lead to unexpected success.

OPPORTUNITY OF THE MONTH

Your willingness to reach out and make contact can turn the tide on the 13th. This can be a time of serendipity.

Rewarding Days: 3, 4, 8, 9, 12, 13, 16, 17, 26, 27, 31
Challenging Days: 1, 2, 6, 14, 15, 19, 21, 22, 28, 29

AFFIRMATION FOR THE MONTH

"I speak words of love and wisdom."

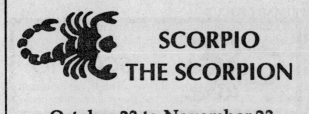

SCORPIO
THE SCORPION

October 23 to November 23

Element: Water
Quality: Fixed
Polarity: Feminine/Yin
Planetary Ruler: Pluto
Meditation: Mastery through transformation
Gemstone: Topaz
Power Stones: Obsidian, citrine, garnet
Anatomy: Reproductive organs, genitals, rectum
Key Phrase: I desire

Glyph: Scorpion's tail
Color: Burgundy, black
Animal: Reptiles, scorpions, birds of prey
Myths/Legends: Hades and Persephone, Shiva, Ereshkigal
House Association: Eighth
Opposite Sign: Taurus
Flower: Chrysanthemum
Key Word: Intensity

Positive Expression:
  Regenerating
  Erotic
  Sensual
  Incisive
  Healing
  Transforming
  Penetrating
  Passionate
  Investigative

Misuse of Energy:
  Violent
  Jealous
  Extreme
  Vengeful
  Destructive
  Obsessive
  Overbearing
  Lascivious

SCORPIO

YOUR EGO'S STRENGTHS AND WEAKNESSES:
Your interest in what's happening beneath the surface
comes from your enhanced perceptivity. Life's mysteries
continually stimulate your creativity, inviting you to find
what lies at the vital center of all existence. Your natural
charisma both fascinates and mystifies others. You can be
intriguing, and you like it that way.

Because your sensibilities alert you to hidden agendas,
some people may be uncomfortable around you. Your insight into human nature is keen, since you know firsthand
about inner conflict. Although you may appear to be detached, you prefer to keep the volcano of emotion brewing
beneath the surface under control. This can lead others to
feel wary or mistrustful of you, since they know there's
something going on, but can never tell exactly what it is!

When devoted to a principal or ideal, you can rise to he-
roic action. However, that same zeal can lead toward destructive vengeance if you've been deeply wounded in
some way. Your planetary ruler, Pluto, is an energy of
powerful transformation. Through this energy, you are
carried along the path of the healer through the heights of
joy and the depths of despair. One of your primary life lessons here on earth is to learn forgiveness of yourself and
others through releasing resentment, guilt and shame.

YOUR CAREER DEVELOPMENT: Your work and career need to provide a sense of bringing about change.
You're well-suited to a career which involves renovation,

research or scientific probing. Through expressions of artistry in painting, writing or music your work may have a rejuvenating or transformational effect upon others. Healing arts such as counseling or medicine can be fulfilling.

In the entertainment field, you can become an exceptional producer or performer, but may prefer the role which gives you the greatest influence. You also have a knack for making the most of the resources of others, and might enjoy career management, financial counseling or insurance sales. History and archaeology are natural choices for you, whether as a career or as a hobby. However you direct your career, you are especially talented in taking what appears to be useless and transforming it into something of beauty and value. You might even make a tidy profit!

YOUR APPROACH TO ROMANCE: When you're ready for love, you can weave an enticing and mesmerizing romantic web. You may long for the person who will share the depths of your soul, and then be unwilling to unlock the doors once you've sent out the invitation! Until trust has been established, you're likely to keep your feelings hidden away. Once hurt, you can close the door to love forever, which protects your vulnerability, but also leaves you longing for tenderness.

Your search for the partner who accepts and shares your desires can be frustrating, but may also lead to rich rewards. With you, the art of lovemaking can be a continually intriguing experience, which unlocks to doors to true ecstasy. Your zodiac opposite, Taurus, demonstrates a sensuality and a steadfast nature which may be highly attractive to you. Just try to avoid battles, since you're both exceedingly stubborn!

You're most at home with the emotionally sensitive Water signs—Cancer, Scorpio and Pisces. With Cancer, the connection is meaningful, but you're the one with the power. Pisces draws you into fanciful creative romance. Another Scorpio encourages extremes, from passion to volatility.

You may feel like Aries is just asking for trouble, since you don't appreciate being teased. And Gemini's entertaining wit can become distracting when you seek continuity and support. Leo's magnetism shivers your timbers, but you may find them to be too self-centered. The friendship and support you feel from Virgo can grow toward lasting passion.

Libra seems to know what intrigues you, but drives you nuts trying to make decisions. The lusty adventurous Sagittarian is inviting, but you may have difficulty in the long-term unless you can relinquish some controls. Capricorn's earthy practicality encourages your growth and supports your success. And although Aquarius may intrigue you, there's likely to be too much distance to achieve the far-reaches of passion together.

YOUR USE OF POWER: If anyone understands power, it's you. Even in your youth you may have been drawn to powerful people, and probably felt a strong fascination with super heroes. You seek power over your emotions, but may fail to recognize that this power is not achieved until you give in to your deeper needs! You have an innate understanding of the natural transformational rhythms of life, the processes of life and death, and know that these changes are merely a part of existing. Through accepting and integrating this understanding, you can use your power to help others deal with these changes in their own lives. You possess the power to act as a catalyst for healing.

Instead of searching deep within your own soul for your true needs, you may have built a massive shield against the rich experiences of life. Once you've reached into that inner realm, you'll find that at the core of your being there resides a powerful warrior spirit which is constantly guarding you from harm. This power does not have to emerge as threatening or vengeful toward others, once you find the honesty to know that you deserve to have your own needs fulfilled. Through compassion for yourself, you can reach out toward others and toward the world and bring about the changes which impart growth and hope.

FAMOUS SCORPIOS: Charles Bronson; Danny DeVito; Sally Field; Art Garfunkel; Terry Gilliam; Billy Graham; Goldie Hawn; Grace Kelly; Vivian Leigh; Rene Magritte; Annie Potts; Will Rogers; Theodore Roosevelt; Jonas Salk; Grace Slick; Henry Winkler; Alfred Woodard

THE YEAR AHEAD FOR SCORPIO

You may be wrestling with fundamental questions about the meaning of your life during 1993 while you're discovering a deeper level of faith in yourself. This is a time of opening your mind to different viewpoints, allowing the penetration of new ideas which can enhance and revitalize your creativity. It's not necessary to erase your sense of identity, instead, you're getting to the core of your essence and experiencing rebirth.

The phenomena of Uranus and Neptune conjoining in the heavens can have a positive impact this year. If you've been making alterations in your life, this cycle can illuminate a path toward heightened opportunity through broader connections with others. Your uniqueness can be an asset to your success. And you cannot afford to remain stuck in the past when you're feeling pulled toward change. Although your friends and loved ones can be supportive, you're likely to find that many of the decisions and changes are entirely up to you. Work toward clear communication of your needs and ideas in order to manifest a reality that suits your changing consciousness.

The Solar and Lunar Eclipses during 1993 heighten your awareness of your deeper values, but also draw your attention to the need to become more balanced in your relationships with others. Your feelings about your own self-worth are critical to getting what you want from life, especially now. Take a careful look at the ways you've held yourself back, and be more aware of the issues you've projected onto others in your life. Regain control of your responses to your feelings about your life circumstances. During the Solar Eclipse in Scorpio on November 13th you may feel more acutely vulnerable, but you're also ready to eliminate the structures which inhibit your ability to fulfill your real needs. During this period of self-reflection, take off your mask and get a clear view of your strength and convictions.

Jupiter's cycle in Libra lasts until November 10th, and can bring a profound sense of inner peace during outer turmoil. This phase provides a strong connection with the

realm of the intangible. You are more attuned to your part
in the human drama, as a member of the collective humanity. You may also need to withdraw from the chaos of everyday life during this cycle, spending more time in contemplation and reflection. Pay special attention to your
dreams, and take the time to listen to your inner voice. This
is a time of surrender to Divine Intelligence and harmonize with the continuum of life. You are preparing to
emerge with increased confidence and optimism when Jupiter moves into Scorpio on November 10th, beginning a
year-long cycle of self-expansion.

For Scorpios born from October 23-25th, many of the
challenges you've worked hard to overcome now seem to
be less threatening. You're building toward the future, carrying your responsibilities with greater ease. From May
through July you're experiencing a supportive trine from
Saturn to your Sun, marking a time of more positive real-
ism. This is an excellent time to improve your health and
institute programs which support your fullest levels of vitality. You're also experiencing an assimilation of your
past, finding an appreciation for the value of your accomplishments and the structures that can support you in your
future growth. You're setting the foundation for the realization of your long-term goals.

If your birth occurred from October 26th-28th, you may
be feeling fewer challenges to your sense of self during
1993. During the early part of the year, Saturn's cycle
brings a positive sense of recognizing certain elements of
your destiny, but you do have choices about the way you
respond to this phase. Through accepting the manifestation of what you've created through your life choices and
attitudes, you can learn more about how to have a more
complete sense of fulfillment. This is the time to embrace
the essence of your being with love and acceptance.

You're experiencing a year of utilizing your unique talents and abilities if you were born from October 29th-No-
vember 2nd. Uranus and Neptune are both transiting in
quintile aspect to your Sun, providing you with the opportunities to exercise your own special gifts. This is a good
time to seek out guidance to help you fine-tune your talents. But if you've been mastering the technicalities, it's
quite possible that you'll realize a very positive shift in

your abilities now. It's the difference between knowing the notes of a composition and giving a masterful performance.

If you were born from November 3rd-9th, you're working with the energy of Saturn in a minor aspect to your Sun. Although there may not be a lot of externals giving you cause to ponder the meaning of your life, you may feel that you're being pulled into some circumstances in a fateful way. You have a wide range of choices, but you may have to work within the limitations and with the materials that the Universe has provided. This is one of those periods when you take the bitter with the sweet and find that you can make a pretty exceptional concoction!

You're experiencing the impact of changing ideals and opening consciousness if you were born from November 10th-16th. The transits of Saturn, Uranus and Neptune are all having a powerful impact in your life. Saturn's transit in square to your Sun lasts through February, marking a period of struggle with the status quo. You can learn a great deal about your fears during this time, and may feel that you're unfairly limited by the actions of others or by circumstances beyond your own control. Since this is a completion of a cycle which began last year, it's important to finish projects you started. Getting rid of the things you no longer need is also part of this period, since you're simplifying and clarifying the best way to handle the necessities. The energy of Uranus transiting in sextile to your Sun will help to speed this release along quite nicely!

Most of all, you're feeling a new level of excitement brewing. This is your time to shine, and once you've paved the way, you may find that nothing in your life is ever the same again. The energies of Uranus and Neptune both sextile your Sun can be used to launch you into a time of exciting change and great awakening. Although you may be affiliated with others who are also making changes, it's really time for you to allow your own spark to ignite enthusiastic new options for your creativity and imagination. You may feel more comfortable operating independently, unless you're in relationships which allow you a lot of room for change. It's easy to take this time for granted, since you seem to have a knack for being in the right place at the right time. This can be a period of tremendous for-

ward motion. You can revitalize relationships or begin
anew, changing the patterns you've felt to be unhealthy
and unrewarding and expressing your needs more clearly.
Your choices about actualizing yourself may have never
been this exciting.

If your birth occurred from November 14th-20th,
you're feeling Pluto's conjunction to your Sun. This cycle
can occur only once in your life, and marks a period of
clearing away the debris and helping you locate the core of
your being. Whether you experience a period of powerful
success or intense destructiveness depends upon the way
you've accepted yourself in the past and the manner in
which you go about allowing your personal transformation to take place. One thing is certain: it's a time of intense
self-awareness. Your sensibilities are intensified. You may
experience enhanced psychic perception. More importantly, you're feeling a need for increased honesty with
yourself. Your feelings have always been a powerful an-
tenna, but now they're tuned into both external and the
deeper internal levels. You have a chance to release any
old guilt, resentment or pain that has kept you from having what you really want from life. This transformation to
a purified expression of yourself gives you the option of
walking away from the pain of your past into a bright and
promising future of self-actualization. You're more capable of accepting your own power, which may have been
hidden away in some dark corner of your psyche waiting
for the right time to emerge. This is the time.

You're also feeling the square of Saturn to your Sun,
amplifying the needs to clarify your life issues. If you were
born from November 9th-22nd, you're feeling the pressure from the Saturn square. Although you may feel restriction or inhibition during this cycle, it can be a time of
marked accomplishment. Watch your health, since your
vitality may not be up to par. Eliminate the things that are
undermining your well-being, or get to the core of chronic
problems. You cannot run away from your responsibility
toward yourself and your true needs. But neither can you
carry the burden for others during this cycle. You must
find the courage to break away from behaviors and attitudes which have pulled you into negative beliefs, fears or
ideals. Sometimes this cycle stirs up old power struggles

with parents, particularly bringing up unfinished emotional issues. Although it's not necessary to physically confront your parents, you need to recognize that you're terminating a certain level of connection. You're being set free, emerging with the gifts which belong to you.

TOOLS TO MAKE A DIFFERENCE: Your way of viewing the world is changing, and you need to find supports that will allow you to grow into these changes and still recognize yourself! Take a look around and clear away debris that's just taking up space. Cleaning closets, attics and desks may not only provide a welcome sense of relief, but can also make room for something new and alive.

For physical purification, work toward eliminating substances that drain your energy. This is a good year to study and utilize fasting methods, under the direction of a professional. At the least, be sure your intake of liquids (particularly water) is adequate to aid your physical purification process. Use herbal baths and potions to stimulate or soothe as necessary, and consider working with aromatherapy to ease stress. Your flower, the chrysanthemum, makes a wonderful hair tonic or rinse (be sure you're not allergic!), and is sometimes added to herbal conditioners and shampoos. Enjoy the vital color of these flowers in and around your home.

The legendary power of the black obsidian, which is reputed to help individuals face the darkness within, may be a welcome facilitator in changing your consciousness during 1993. Wear your power stones of garnet and citrine in jewelry, to help you focus on drawing positive energy and emanating strength and courage. Build a shield, using your power stones and other objects to remind you of your connection to all the elements of the earth. In your visualizations during 1993, take time to feel the presence of a protective energy around you. Express gratitude to your spiritual protectors and guides. Clear the energy around your home and belongings and create protective shields. A ritual such as smudging done in Native American ceremonies can help you stay clear and draw only pure and positive energy toward you.

AFFIRMATION FOR THE YEAR: "I am a channel for the healing energy of love."

ACTION TABLES FOR SCORPIO

These dates reflect the best (but not the *only*) times for success and ease in these activities according to your Sun Sign.

Change Residence	Jan. 21-Feb. 7
Request a Raise	Nov. 13-14
Begin a Course of Study	July 19
Visit a Doctor	Apr. 16-May 3; Sept. 11-30
Start a Diet	Jan. 27-29; Feb. 24-25; Mar. 23-24; Apr. 19-20; May 17-18; June 13-14; July 10-11; Aug. 6-8; Sept. 3-4, 30; Oct. 27-29; Nov. 24-25; Dec. 21-22
Begin a Romance	Feb. 21-22
Join a Club	Sept. 16
Seek Employment	Apr. 16-May 3; Aug. 10-25
Take a Vacation	Jan. 7-8; Feb. 4-5; Mar. 3-4, 30-31; Apr. 26-27; May 24-25; June 20-21; July 1-18; Aug. 14-15; Sept. 10-11; Oct. 7-8; Nov. 4-5; Dec. 1-2, 28-29
Change Your Wardrobe	Feb. 8-Apr. 14
End a Relationship	Apr. 21-22
Seek Professional Advice	Jan 3-4, 30-31; Feb. 26-27; Mar. 25-26; Apr. 22-23; May 19-20; June 15-17; July 13-14; Aug. 9-10; Sept. 5-7; Oct. 2-3, 30-31; Nov. 26-27; Dec. 23-25
Have a Makeover	Nov. 14-15
Obtain a Loan	Jan. 5-6; Feb. 1-2, 28; Mar. 1-2, 28-29; Apr. 24-25; May. 21-23; June 18-19; July 15-16; Aug. 11-13; Sept. 8-9; Oct. 5-6; Nov. 1-2, 29-30; Dec. 26-27

SCORPIO/JANUARY

PRIMARY FOCUS

The year begins with concrete concepts for future growth. You're making progress staying in touch with the right people. Traveling can be lucrative and illuminating.

HEALTH AND FITNESS

Staying active gives you the vitality you need to accomplish your tasks. Watch a tendency to scatter your energy mid-month.

ROMANCE AND RELATIONSHIPS

The climate for romance is clear, with plenty of energy for cuddling beneath the comforter with your favorite sweetie. Your tendency to seek out greener pastures can lead to trouble from the 1st-17th, unless you really are free to roam. If so, take your time. Send love letters, deliver flowers or make romantic calls from the 3rd-20th. Plan something exquisitely romantic during the Full Moon on the 8th. Time spent with children is inspiring and gratifying the week of the 17th. Family obligations take extra time after the 22nd, but can bring ample rewards.

FINANCE AND CAREER

While launching your plan of action, remember to plan for the expenditures which fall into the "miscellaneous" category. Investments fare nicely, but there's a tendency to pay too high a price from the 12th-19th, so be sure you're getting the best deal before you reach final agreements. An innovative approach or utilization of new technology adds a boost to your progress from the 19th-23rd. Excessive optimism can be damaging on the 29th.

OPPORTUNITY OF THE MONTH

You're in an excellent position to make a positive impact on the right person on the 7th, 8th or 16th. Trust your instincts.

Rewarding Days: 7, 8, 11, 12, 15, 16, 20, 21, 25, 26
Challenging Days: 2, 3, 5, 9, 10, 19, 22, 23, 30, 31

AFFIRMATION FOR THE MONTH

"My mind is focused on creating solutions."

SCORPIO/FEBRUARY

PRIMARY FOCUS
Your desire to spend some time alone may not fit with the expectations of others. Take care to avoid alienating the wrong person. Get things straightened out at home.

HEALTH AND FITNESS
Allowing some extra time to relax may be difficult. Schedule a massage before the 6th to help ease the stress you feel from work.

ROMANCE AND RELATIONSHIPS
Unfinished family business can drag you down, especially near the time of the Full Moon on the 6th. By taking an objective, independent viewpoint, you may be able to speed progress. Disputes with parents or disagreements over tradition can create a wedge between yourself and your partner. It's easier to work out your differences after the 19th, when you're in a more playful mood. Romantic intrigue may arrive in full flourish after the New Moon on the 21st. An existing relationship grows stronger. But if you're looking for someone new, there's great promise from the 21st-25th.

FINANCE AND CAREER
Opposition from the conservative faction in your career can slow your progress. You can make an impact by bringing a different viewpoint which works within traditional boundaries. By becoming aware of your competition, you can create a more viable option or a better product. Use the energy on the 21st to make a break through. Creative or artistic ventures fare well now, but you're also in a good position to work harmoniously with others.

OPPORTUNITY OF THE MONTH
Use your influence and connections to get things moving on the 21st and 22nd. Success can follow, but may require a few revisions.

Rewarding Days: 3, 4, 8, 12, 13, 16, 17, 21, 22
Challenging Days: 1, 2, 6, 19, 20, 26, 27

AFFIRMATION FOR THE MONTH
"I am willing to honor my responsibilities."

SCORPIO/MARCH

PRIMARY FOCUS

Your creative ingenuity and imagination are working overtime this month. Many of your ideas are in their infantile stage and need further development. Others just require a few frills.

HEALTH AND FITNESS

It's easy to overlook your health in favor of having a good time. There's a tendency to vacillate between overindulgence and excessive activity.

ROMANCE AND RELATIONSHIPS

Your fantasies may be competing with the reality of your love life. It's easy to lead yourself (and someone else!) into a fanciful circumstance which can never be fully consummated. A serious relationship may need more imagination and honesty, even though your head may be turned by an enticing possibility the week of the 7th. Talk over your dilemma with a friend before you take a chance. You may have a complete change of heart by the 26th!

FINANCE AND CAREER

Since Mercury retrogrades until the 22nd, you may run into delays or breakdowns which interfere with your progress. Get your paperwork out of the way, and concentrate on smoothing over the rough edges with co-workers, although your greatest struggle may be with management or government on the 19th. There's hope for improvement following the New Moon on the 23rd. Avoid impulsive purchases or investments after the 11th, when you may attract circumstances which are not worth the price you're asked to pay.

OPPORTUNITY OF THE MONTH

Make improvements in a product or idea early in the month. Your sensibilities on the 8th give you the right direction.

Rewarding Days: 3, 4, 7, 8, 11, 12, 16, 20, 21, 30, 31
Challenging Days: 5, 6, 9, 18, 19, 25, 26, 27

AFFIRMATION FOR THE MONTH

"My creativity is inspired by love."

SCORPIO/APRIL

PRIMARY FOCUS
Work-related travel can be productive, but may also create additional mental and physical stress. Maintain a balanced schedule to avoid burn-out.

HEALTH AND FITNESS
Take care of your health near the Full Moon on the 6th, when you may need some extra time to yourself. Simple TLC goes a long way!

ROMANCE AND RELATIONSHIPS
Articulating your feelings breaks the ice early in the month. The expectations in your intimate relationship can get in the way of honest communication. Whether you're single or involved, it's an excellent time to improve your own attitudes about fulfilling your deeper needs. Travel can lead to romance through the 10th. But this is also an excellent period to nurture your spiritual yearnings. The feeling of marriage and commitment may be changing for you, so keep your awareness levels open. Consider what you really want from a partner on the 22nd-23rd, and know what you're willing to give.

FINANCE AND CAREER
The demands on your time from clients or co-workers can force you to reevaluate your commitments. Your ethical standards may not mesh with those of others around you, and it's imperative to uphold your own values and ideals. This is a good time to expand your horizons and diversify your career options, but avoid circumstances that can jeopardize your reputation the week of the 4th. Equalize responsibilities in partnerships the week of the 22nd.

OPPORTUNITY OF THE MONTH
A radical shift in your viewpoint from the 4th-8th can give you cause to look toward a new direction in your career.

Rewarding Days: 3, 4, 7, 8, 12, 13, 17, 18, 26
Challenging Days: 1, 2, 6, 14, 15, 22, 23, 29, 30

AFFIRMATION FOR THE MONTH
"I have faith in my ideals."

SCORPIO/MAY

PRIMARY FOCUS

Satisfying the demands from others can be frustrating, especially if you have little room for negotiation. Search out the factions agreeable to your efforts.

HEALTH AND FITNESS

Insight into dealing with a chronic ailment can help you reach the core of the problem. Look for answers the week of the 23rd.

ROMANCE AND RELATIONSHIPS

You may feel you're fighting against an antiquated tradition within your family, and it can directly affect your partnership. It's time to look at your motivation, and clarify who you're trying to satisfy through your actions. Bring the issues out in the open on the Full Moon in Scorpio on the 5th, and ask for the intervention of Divine Wisdom in the process. By the time of the Solar Eclipse on the 21st the alchemy you've created through your intimate relationship may manifest as a positive rebirth of love.

FINANCE AND CAREER

Open contact with those who work under your supervision leads to a better working relationship by the end of the month. However, you may find some opposition to your programs from someone who feels threatened by your position. Be alert to undermining which can lead to direct confrontation from the 12th-17th. You may have to give in to pressure because of financial limitations the week of the 23rd, but at lest you're making some progress. Investments are best postponed until you feel more flexible.

OPPORTUNITY OF THE MONTH

Listening with care can provide you with excellent insight this month. Be attentive to the unspoken expectations on the 19th-20th.

Rewarding Days: 1, 5, 6, 9, 14, 15, 24, 25, 29
Challenging Days: 3, 4, 11, 12, 13, 19, 20, 26, 27

AFFIRMATION FOR THE MONTH

"I am honest about my intentions."

SCORPIO/JUNE

PRIMARY FOCUS
An objective analysis of your finances can reveal areas in which you need to expand your opportunities. This is a good time to set forth a plan to increase your income.

HEALTH AND FITNESS
Stress in your career takes a bite out of your vitality. Since you're putting forth greater effort, find time to step back and rejuvenate as frequently as possible.

ROMANCE AND RELATIONSHIPS
Harmony between yourself and your partner improves, although you do need to make an extra effort to express your gratitude to one another. The discovery of some fundamental differences in your politics or belief systems near the time of the New Moon on the 19th stimulates a search for deeper meaning in the relationship. But the truth you seek is within yourself and the connection you feel with the center of your being. Setting forth on this path leads to a realization that brings clarity of vision.

FINANCE AND CAREER
The theme of the Lunar Eclipse on the 4th revolves around your finances. Evaluation of your spending habits may reveal patterns that can help you get your finances back under your own control. Schedule significant conferences or meetings from the 13th-29th, when you're in a good position to influence others on your behalf. Travel fares nicely midmonth, but you may not finalize agreements until the 28th-29th. Compromise can be costly on the 29th.

OPPORTUNITY OF THE MONTH
Unfulfilled promises on the 1st-2nd may lead to significant professional growth on the 29th. Look for the unique angle.

Rewarding Days: 1, 2, 6, 10, 11, 20, 21, 25,
Challenging Days: 8, 9, 13, 15, 16, 22, 23

AFFIRMATION FOR THE MONTH
"I easily acknowledge the worth of others."

SCORPIO/JULY

PRIMARY FOCUS

Time spent with friends and others who share your beliefs can be encouraging. A position of leadership paves the way for success.

HEALTH AND FITNESS

Get involved in fitness classes or team sports now to generate greater confidence. Increased activity pays off with stronger vitality and endurance.

ROMANCE AND RELATIONSHIPS

The Full Moon on the 3rd signals a period of travel and interaction with others outside your normal frame of reference. An old love may reenter the picture for a brief period, although it's probably just a test to see how you really feel now that time has changed your perspective. If you have questions about your past, this is a good month to get back to your roots and see how you feel about them now. Your viewpoints are changing, and can bring improvements in all your relationships near the New Moon on the 19th. It's easier to speak from your heart after the 22nd.

FINANCE AND CAREER

To improve your financial outlook, review the contacts from your past that have been on hold. You may have some success getting the rust out during Mercury's retrograde cycle through the 25th. Review of programs or projects is revealing, and may lead you to abandon an idea in favor of a simpler concept. Generating enthusiasm from others works well this month, and it's a good time to seek out investors or other support. Finalize contracts on the 26th-27th. Consider postponing your own investments until after the 25th.

OPPORTUNITY OF THE MONTH

The New Moon on the 19th reveals an exciting path. Investigate and then take action on the 26th-27th.

Rewarding Days: 3, 4, 8, 9, 17, 18, 22, 26, 27, 30, 31
Challenging Days: 5, 6, 13, 14, 19, 20, 21

AFFIRMATION FOR THE MONTH

"I follow the path of wisdom and truth."

SCORPIO/AUGUST

PRIMARY FOCUS
Reaching beyond your limitations can be accomplished more easily. It's a time to broaden your horizons while testing your loyalties.

HEALTH AND FITNESS
Although you may increase your activity level early in the month, your sense of well-being is stabilized through positive "inner" fitness. Pay extra attention to your psychological health.

ROMANCE AND RELATIONSHIPS
Travel is a plus for romance from the 2nd-26th, and may lead to a change in your love life. Explore the spiritual essence of a relationship to heal many of the doubts and fears that limit intimacy. Your need for greater spontaneity can be exciting from the 15th-23rd, but you can alienate your lover if you carry this too far. Mounting family pressure from the Full Moon on the 2nd through the New Moon on the 17th, can be the result of unrealistic expectations. Establish your own landmarks!

FINANCE AND CAREER
Business expansion through contacts with others outside your normal field of reference is emphasized from the 1st-11th. You're continuing to build a strong network throughout most of the month, but need to be aware of surprising changes in procedure or policy from the 16th-20th. Ignoring the change can lead to disputes over control on the 23rd and 24th. New connections formed after the 26th provide an entirely different perspective. Legal matters fare better from the 1st-10th or after the 24th.

OPPORTUNITY OF THE MONTH
You're moving into exciting new territory during the Full Moon on the 31st. Coordinate your efforts with others who understand you.

Rewarding Days: 4, 5, 14, 15, 18, 19, 22, 23, 26, 27, 31
Challenging Days: 1, 2, 7, 9, 10, 16, 17, 25, 29, 30

AFFIRMATION FOR THE MONTH
"I am safe and secure."

SCORPIO/SEPTEMBER

PRIMARY FOCUS
You may be known by the company you keep. Many of the things you're doing behind the scenes may not be noticed, but they're an important part of your preparation for future success.

HEALTH AND FITNESS
Restless energy can drain your vitality. Take breaks often, and be sure to find time to work out.

ROMANCE AND RELATIONSHIPS
Friends provide a great source of inspiration and support. Take time to celebrate their unique accomplishments early in the month. You may withdraw from the limelight, but are in the perfect mood for a clandestine liaison the week of the 12th. Covering your tracks can be difficult, since jealousy from another can be troublesome from the 14th-17th. Know your reasons for pulling away, since your inattentiveness can suggest that you don't care.

FINANCE AND CAREER
If you're feeling married to your job it's probably because so much seems to be riding on it now. Work relations can be filled with double-entendre, making it difficult to know which direction to concentrate your efforts. Political action or group activities can generate opportunities for advancement near the New Moon on the 15th. If you choose to take the responsibility, be sure you have the time and energy to fulfill the obligation. Target your allies early, since you may need their help and support to complete the task at hand. Assign jobs before the Full Moon on the 30th.

OPPORTUNITY OF THE MONTH
A change of the guard may leave an opening on the 15th. Creating a power machine may suit you better than wearing the crown.

Rewarding Days: 1, 10, 11, 14, 15, 18, 19, 23, 28, 29
Challenging Days: 3, 5, 6, 12, 13, 25, 26, 30

AFFIRMATION FOR THE MONTH
"I am a vital link in the chain of life."

SCORPIO/OCTOBER

PRIMARY FOCUS

You can move into a position of power during this time of change and upheaval. Even if you're only maintaining a steadfast position, you may still be the one called upon to lead the charge.

HEALTH AND FITNESS

Mars transits in Scorpio all month, promoting your strengthened vitality and enhanced endurance. Get a good fitness program going.

ROMANCE AND RELATIONSHIPS

You'll probably feel more at home with friends, and can fortify a romantic relationship by developing greater unconditionality. You need to feel that there is mutual support of your goals in a partnership. By allowing yourself time to withdraw during the New Moon on the 15th, you may gain the objectivity you need to take an important step in building a more intimate level of trust. Partnership is stressed during the Full Moon on the 30th.

FINANCE AND CAREER

Changing your attitude toward your work allows greater success. Although you may finally be receiving ample reward for your efforts, the circumstances of the job may be in a state of flux. Watch the power plays, since you may be the one chosen to run the offensive maneuvers! Your ideas can make the difference in turning around a previously unworkable situation from the 25th-31st. Use Mercury's retrograde after the 25th to consider improvements.

OPPORTUNITY OF THE MONTH

Making the right connections on the 8th can place you in virgin territory—just the right spot for an ambitious Scorpio!

Rewarding Days: 7, 8, 12, 13, 16, 17, 20, 21, 25, 26
Challenging Days: 1, 2, 3, 10, 11, 22, 23, 27, 30, 31

AFFIRMATION FOR THE MONTH

"My words are sincere."

SCORPIO/NOVEMBER

PRIMARY FOCUS
This is a period of completion opening the way to new direction and growth. You're beginning a cycle of fortuitous circumstance which can set the stage for long-term abundance.

HEALTH AND FITNESS
Concentrate on increasing your stamina, since you'll want to have plenty of energy to take advantage of your opportunities.

ROMANCE AND RELATIONSHIPS
You're likely to feel a bit apprehensive approaching the time of the Solar Eclipse in Scorpio occurring the 13th. However, the energy during this period presents a remarkable support for leaving behind the useless portions of your life and proceeding with great success and prosperity. You can attract the love and support you need because you're finally recognizing your own worth. Although some relationships may end during this phase, you're really just making room for more auspicious and rewarding connections.

FINANCE AND CAREER
Until Mercury completes its retrograde cycle on the 14th you may be uncertain of the progress you're making. The key action now is completion! You can demand greater reward for your efforts, although you mush be careful to avoid undervaluation of the products of others near the Lunar Eclipse on the 29th. Interesting investment possibilities are likely to emerge midmonth. Contracts are most auspicious on the 17th and 22nd.

OPPORTUNITY OF THE MONTH
Your influence can be the catalyst for vast changes in relationships at work and at home on the 12th and 13th.

Rewarding Days: 4, 5, 8, 9, 12, 13, 16, 17, 21, 22
Challenging Days: 1, 6, 7, 19, 2-, 26, 27

AFFIRMATION FOR THE MONTH
"Every action I take is in harmony with my highest needs."

SCORPIO/DECEMBER

PRIMARY FOCUS

Your enthusiasm can lead you to waste some of your resources now, since you may feel that everything is safe. Proceed with care and deliberation in order to assure maintaining your success.

HEALTH AND FITNESS

Pace yourself. You can easily vacillate between pushing too hard and stifling inactivity. Time outside can be invigorating now.

ROMANCE AND RELATIONSHIPS

The dust is settling and you're in a good position to clarify your feelings and hopes from the 1st-6th. Some of your motivations may be purely selfish mid-month, but you're in a more cooperative frame of reference after the 21st. There's a tendency to fall in love with love, not fully discovering the other person until later. Romance fares best from the 20th-31st, with an emphasis on travel or short jaunts away from the everyday. Reaching out to a friend on the 28th can bring a pleasant surprise.

FINANCE AND CAREER

Money and the best ways to spend it are foremost in your mind from the 2nd-26th. Finding the best ways to use all your resources, including your time, become a critical issue the week of the 12th, when you're likely to find you've overstretched your range! Use the New Moon on the 13th to make financial plans for the future. Target the period after the 20th to make connections with key individuals.

OPPORTUNITY OF THE MONTH

The three days around the Full Moon on the 28th are highly significant for clarifying your aims and getting in touch with the people who can support your efforts. Reciprocal actions pay off.

Rewarding Days: 1, 2, 6, 10, 11, 14, 15, 18, 19, 28, 29
Challenging Days: 3, 4, 5, 12, 16, 17, 21, 23, 24, 25, 31

AFFIRMATION FOR THE MONTH

"I use my resources wisely."

SAGITTARIUS
THE ARCHER

November 23 to December 22

Element: Fire
Quality: Mutable
Polarity: Masculine/Yang
Planetary Ruler: Jupiter
Meditation: "All things in harmony with Higher Law are possible"
Gemstone: Turquoise
Power Stones: Lapis lazuli, sodalite, azurite
Glyph: Archer's arrow
Key Phrase: I understand

Anatomy: Hips, thighs, sciatic nerve
Colors: Royal blue and purple
Animal: Fleet-footed animals
Myths/Legends: Athena, Chiron
House Association: Ninth
Opposite Sign: Gemini
Flower: Narcissus
Key Word: Expansion

Positive Expression:
Understanding
Adventurous
Philosophical
Tolerant
Generous
Optimistic
Wise
Jovial
Philanthropic
Athletic

Misuse of Energy:
Blunt
Extravagant
Self-righteous
Over-zealous
Condescending
Gluttonous
Opinionated
Foolish
Bigoted

SAGITTARIUS

YOUR EGO'S STRENGTHS AND WEAKNESSES:
The grand adventure of life is continually fascinating for
you. Your enthusiastic optimism often provides a buoyant
inspiration to those around you. In any circumstance, you
can be honest, direct and steadfast in your belief that the
truth will set you free. You strive to reach understanding,
and strongly admire those who possess wisdom.

Your delight in exploring the world and her people
stems from a desire to experience as much of life as you
possibly can. You're the philosopher of the zodiac, and
may constantly question and expand your base of knowledge in your quest for understanding. Your fascination
with other cultures may lead to a desire to master at least
one foreign language, and can be your stimulus to travel.

In your search for broader frontiers, you may leave behind those who yearn to be with you. You're always looking forward, and can grow impatient when the pace of life
fails to keep up with your ideals. Through your generosity, you can create an atmosphere of trust and understanding. But you need to watch a tendency to expect more from
others than they can deliver. You can also undermine your
own growth through feeling that you should be more than
you are.

Your zeal can blaze a path to wisdom, but it can just as
easily lead you toward self-righteousness and judgmental
fanaticism. The greater truth may be that you don't really
know everything, and, more importantly, that you don't
have to! During your life on Earth, you carry the flame of

hope and desire to achieve unity with higher spiritual law. Through your expressive talents with words and rhetoric, you can illustrate this wisdom to the world.

YOUR CAREER DEVELOPMENT: As the opportunist of the zodiac, you're happiest in a career which offers unlimited potential and room for independent action. Your ability to relate to people from varied circumstances may pique an interest in foreign affairs. You're a natural promoter, and may enjoy work in sales, advertising or as an agent for others.

Your needs to express ideas and share information may lead you to a career in writing, journalism or publishing. And with your ability to sway others through your speech, you may also be drawn to law or the ministry. Speculative investments may also be lucrative for you, whether in sports or racing or in other markets such as stocks. Your constant desire to learn and teach may stimulate you to seek a profession in teaching or in higher education, where you can stimulate incentive in your students to reach high levels of personal mastery. No matter what your career choice, you think big!

YOUR APPROACH TO ROMANCE: Stalking the right lover may become a delightful game, as long as you call the shots and don't get caught in the lair (until you're ready!). Love is an adventure, and may be most alluring if the other person has a background distinctive from your own. The ultimate relationship for you offers honesty, shared philosophies and independence.

Although you can be highly sensual, you might prefer to know the other person's way of thinking before you get physical. Once you're ready to commit to a relationship, you can be steadfast. But until then, you may leave your former lovers behind in a cloud of dust. The attraction you feel to your opposite sign, Gemini, may stem from sharing highly creative ideas. However, you can each act rather childish in the face of disagreement! You're generally easy going, especially around other Fire signs, Aries, Leo and Sagittarius. Spontaneous passion with Aries can be invigorating, and Leo charms and warms your heart. Another Sagittarian may be an exceptional companion who shares your love of reading and travel.

The slow pace of Taurus can feel entirely too cumbersome, while Cancer's need to take care of you can become claustrophobic. Although you may appreciate Virgo's ideas, your wider vision can lead to disagreements. You're fascinated with Libra's refined manner, and may enjoy a long relationship. And you may have to stay on your toes to avoid falling victim to the allure of Scorpio. While Capricorn offers steadfast security, you may not feel completely open. The independence of Aquarius can be highly compatible and supportive. Pisces' imagination can be interesting, but you may not feel you can trust the relationship.

YOUR USE OF POWER: You feel most powerful when you're free to exercise your own ideas and actualize your potential. Although you may seek wisdom, it takes time to develop. Sometimes getting through all the foolish double-talk and working from the core of an idea seems impossible, but you're willing to put forth the effort if you can achieve the understanding you seek. Although you want the best from life, you're unwilling to sacrifice your freedom.

You realize that the truth does, indeed, set you free. And although you may seek the truth, you have to be careful to avoid shutting your mind and looking for truth only as you see it. To have the abundant life, you may first be required to harmonize your actions with your Higher Needs. Otherwise, you can fall into a trap of hedonistic desire or fanatical beliefs that become, in themselves, your own prison.

The power of wisdom may come in many forms for you. Through travel, study, writing, teaching or inspiring others, you may recognize the your real power is connected to shaping the future through improving the understanding among humankind. Use your gifts and energy to unlock the minds of humanity to higher truth.

FAMOUS SAGITTARIANS: Louisa May Alcott; Kim Bassinger; Ludwig von Beethoven; David Carradine; Terry Cole-Whittaker; John Davidson; Susan Dey; Chris Evert; J. Paul Getty; Katarina Witt

THE YEAR AHEAD FOR SAGITTARIUS

Throughout 1993 you're experiencing a strong emphasis on getting in touch with your feelings about yourself, your life choices and your ideals. Your associations with others may lead to opportunities for leadership or recognition that were previously blocked. New chapters are opening for you now, and you're in an excellent position to stabilize while moving forward.

By all accounts, the larger cycles indicate that this is a year of profound change and healing among the people on our planet. One of those cycles, the conjunction of Uranus and Neptune, is helping you unravel your values while you're taking a look at the way you really feel about your own worth as a person. The more intangible elements may seem to take priority over the material. But most importantly, you're experiencing an awakening in your attitude toward the use of all your assets. Through imaginative use and sharing of your resources, you may find that you are experiencing a more positive form of abundance. However, it's also easy to make choices which deplete your financial or emotional stability if you act without investigative forethought. Balancing your actions with clear analysis is not easy, since it does slow you down, but it may save you some major hassles later on!

You're feeling the uplifting and optimistic energy of Jupiter's cycle this year in the realm of realizing some of your goals and manifesting greater reward from your career endeavors. Many of the responsibilities you added last year are now paying off through recognition and positive financial success. Choosing to become more involved in community activities or with special interest groups can be highly profitable. Your friends may provide exceptional support and encouragement now, although it's easy to take these associations for granted. Through extending your appreciation for their support, you not only give back, but will find that you solidify the bond you share with one another. Be careful to avoid scattering your energy, since you may be requested to do more than you have time to accomplish.

The Solar and Lunar Eclipse cycles this year emphasize the Sagittarian dilemma. Reaching out in ways that will provide healthy outlets for future growth involves long-range vision of the impact of the changes. As you may have discovered, it's easy to drop everything and move into a new direction only to discover the value of what you've left behind when you can no longer retrieve it. For you, this is a cycle of enhanced self-awareness, which can give you a clearer perspective of your current life circumstances. But you're also feeling a need to observe the effect your actions and choices have upon your relationships. Communication with others about your needs and desires can help to make the difference in the quality of feedback you're experiencing from them. Before you decide to venture into new circumstances, take a careful look at your current involvements. Be sure you're not cutting the cord to something or someone you truly need.

Chiron's influence during 1993 may have a strong impact upon your real connection with your Higher Self. By deliberately working toward creating your life in harmony with higher law, you can reach a more profound sense of your life purpose through this cycle. It's like forming a partnership with Divine Intelligence. You become the conduit for the information, and in the process, you have a chance to assimilate the energy that's been flowing through you.

If you were born from November 23rd-25th, you're experiencing a year of defining your options and taking on new responsibilities. Throughout the Spring and Summer months, you're feeling the pressure of Saturn transiting in square to your Sun. You're seeing the results of many of the choices you made in 1985-86. If you're happy with your life circumstances, this is the time to stabilize, make any necessary adjustments and continue with your plan of action. But if you're dissatisfied, then it's time to find out what lies at the core of your dissatisfaction. Simply changing your outer world may not be sufficient. It's a period of self-testing, when you define your identity and life direction. Keep your priorities clear to facilitate your choices. Pay careful attention to your physical needs, since this can be a time when you're feeling a high level of stress and need to give your body what it requires to stay healthy and strong.

If you were born from November 26th-30th you're feeling the impact of Uranus and Neptune transiting in semi-square to your Sun. This period may require that you take a leap of faith, which can be especially troubling if you're uncertain or confused. If you've been clear about maintaining a strong sense of self-awareness and personal honesty, then this can be a time of moving into an exciting direction which fulfills many of your dreams. Your own uniqueness may be the key to opening the right doors, so trusting yourself is a key issue. But you may also be drawn into situations which prove to be merely a disruption and lead only into chaos or distraction. The different pathways are rarely easy to distinguish, since your enthusiasm runs high now and can block your recognition of important details. But you're experiencing a strong protective energy from Jupiter's transit from April through July which can help you locate positive support systems during this time of change. However, your best choice is to look deep within yourself before you take the leap!

For those born from November 30th through December 7th, the support and optimism of Jupiter's cycle is especially powerful. You're also experiencing the deep changes in your ability to stay in touch with your feelings, a cycle emphasized by the Lunar Eclipses in May and November. Your awareness of the impact of your personal relationships increases, which can lead you to balance your commitments within the parameters of both of your emotional needs. This cycle can strengthen a relationship which supports growth, but may lead to the unraveling of a counter-productive relationship. You're also getting in touch with unresolved issues with your parents.

If you were born from December 8th-22nd, you're experiencing a supportive transit from Saturn to your Sun. This cycle is stabilizing, but it does carry some limitations. You may be discovering that your wings have been clipped, although you can still fly! Saturn's sextile to your Sun brings real growth defined within the boundaries of your personal limitations. This is an excellent time to complete major undertakings, such as school or entry-level positions at work. Once you've met your obligations, the accomplishments from this period can provide the foundation for substantial growth and prosperity. Now's the time to define your life direction and take careful steps to be sure you're gaining what you want from your efforts. The ultimate responsibility for your success is primarily yours now. You're ready to take on the commitments, but only those which are honestly yours. One factor in your growth now may involve getting a few monkeys off your back and returning them to their rightful owners!

If you were born from December 9th-16th, you're also feeling the impatience and idealization generated while Uranus and Neptune aspect your Sun this year. The semi-sextile transit of these planets to your Sun brings a different perspective on your priorities. You may need to branch out into areas that complement, but which are uniquely different from what you've done in the past. This is the time to add your imagination and creative vision to your career, relationships and self-expression. You don't have to take giant leaps, but can, instead, step into the realization of exciting possibilities while still maintaining your balance. If you've had a desire to move into a direction which allows you to use your special talents, this can be the time to take some important steps. Take advantage of situations which allow you to meet influential individuals or those who can help your fine-tune your own skills.

You're feeling some deep pressures to release the things in your life that you no longer need if you were born from December 15th-20th. Pluto is transiting in semi-sextile aspect to your Sun, stimulating a look at your internal motivations and hidden desires. This can be a time of rediscovery of your power and the healthiest ways to use it. You may be drawn to a more contemplative lifestyle, although you can just as easily bring your enhanced perceptibility into your everyday life. Personal honesty is crucial now, and you may be disappointed in others who fail to maintain their own integrity. You're exposing life at its core elements, and can emerge with greater freedom to actualize and manifest your real self.

TOOLS TO MAKE A DIFFERENCE: Taking advantage of this period of balanced growth requires increased awareness on your part. Develop a stronger sense of your feelings through contemplative or meditative activity. You might prefer an active form of meditation such as t'ai chi, and may even find that your best times to commune with your inner self occur when you're in the great outdoors. No matter where you find the right circumstances or most effective techniques, the important factor is to take the time to tune in!

Because your basic sense of life involves the feeling that there's always a potential for improvement, you need to find ways to continually reinforce this understanding. You might enjoy becoming involved in the natural cycles of plants and trees, either simply as an observer or an active gardener. Especially during the fall, take some time to become aware of the meaning of the season which marks your birth cycle. Celebrate the bounty of the harvest, reminding yourself of the natural ebb and flow of abundance. Plant narcissus, jonquils, daffodils or other bulbous plants in the fall, knowing that they hold the promise of the first colors of spring. Your natural affinity for turquoise and lapis lazuli is not accidental. These stones, when either worn in jewelry or placed in your home can become channels through which you draw positive energy toward yourself. The colors connect you with the plane of pure thought and divine protection.

One of your most powerful options this year involves your connection with others. This is the time to get involved. If you have a political interest, write letters, join committees or campaign for reform. Simply stating your point of view may not seem like enough. You need to feel like you're taking action to bring about change. You may also discover that unless you're supporting your own special interests that your access to them may diminish! This is the year to make an investment in yourself.

During your periods of visualization, envision yourself standing on a mountaintop. Feel yourself surrounded by a clear blue sky and the bright warmth of the sun. Look out over the horizon and feel the vastness. Take that feeling into yourself, for you are limited only by your vision of your horizon. Know that you are not alone. Rather, you're standing together with others who share the hope and joy for life that helps to perpetuate growth. Feel a communion with these individuals, who, when joined together, form a powerful coalition for releasing the past and moving forward into a brighter future.

AFFIRMATION FOR THE YEAR: "I have faith in myself and my vision for a bright tomorrow."

ACTION TABLES FOR SAGITTARIUS

These dates reflect the best (but not the *only*) times for success and ease in these activities according to your Sun Sign.

Change Residence	Feb. 8-Apr. 14
Request a Raise	Dec. 13-14
Begin a Course of Study	Jan. 22; Aug. 17
Visit a Doctor	May 4-17; Oct. 1-Dec. 6
Start a Diet	Jan. 3-4, 30-31; Feb. 26-27; Mar. 25-27; Apr. 22-23; May 19-20; June 15-16; July 13-14; Aug. 9-10; Sept. 5-7; Oct. 3-4, 30-31; Nov. 26-27; Dec. 23-25
Begin a Romance	Mar. 23-24
Join a Club	Oct. 15
Seek Employment	May 4-17; Aug. 26-Sept. 10
Take a Vacation	Jan. 9-10; Feb. 6-7; Mar. 5-6; Apr. 1-2, 29-30; May 26-27; June 22-23; July 19-20; Aug. 16-17; Sept. 12-13; Oct. 10-11; Nov. 6-7; Dec. 3-4, 30-31
Change Your Wardrobe	Apr. 16-May 2
End a Relationship	Nov. 29
Seek Professional Advice	Jan. 5-6; Feb. 1-2, 28; Mar. 28-29; Apr. 24-25; May 21-22; June 18-19; July 15-16; Aug. 11-13; Sept. 8-9; Oct. 5-6; Nov. 1-2, 29-30; Dec. 26-27
Have a Makeover	Dec. 13
Obtain a Loan	Jan. 7-8; Feb. 3-4; Mar. 3-4, 30-31; Apr. 26-27; May 24-25; June 20-21; July 17-18; Aug. 14-15; Sept. 10-11; Oct. 7-9; Nov. 4-5; Dec. 1-2, 28-29

SAGITTARIUS/JANUARY

PRIMARY FOCUS

Surprises on the financial front can bring confusion if you've been disorganized or uncertain about your assets and liabilities.

HEALTH AND FITNESS

Emotional stress plays a larger part in your physical well-being early in the month. Give yourself some time to get away and relax.

ROMANCE AND RELATIONSHIPS

Concentrate on bringing greater harmony into your home and family life. Enjoy sharing time with friends or siblings on your own turf. A party on the 14th, 18th, 23rd or 24th could warm up any relationships that have lost their luster. Contacts which began with promise on the 1st or 2nd can be renewed after the New Moon on the 22nd, when you'll be better able to see where they might lead. Taking the time to catch up on letters or phone calls on the 23rd, 28th or 29th can satisfy your need to know how you both feel.

FINANCE AND CAREER

Pressure from others can throw your financial stability out of balance from the 1st–9th. If you've been projecting an idea or proposal, you may run into objections from others about the costs involved near the time of the Full Moon on the 8th. This gives you a chance to iron out the contingencies and submit a revision, which might be well received on the 22nd or 23rd. A meeting with an ally can open the door to new possibilities on the 29th, but get the facts before you move into virgin territory.

OPPORTUNITY OF THE MONTH

Although raring to go on the 18th, you may not be fully prepared to move forward. Organize, then get things moving on the 23rd.

Rewarding Days: 1, 9, 10, 13, 18, 19, 22, 23, 24, 28, 29
Challenging Days: 3, 5, 6, 8, 11, 12, 25, 26, 30

AFFIRMATION FOR THE MONTH

"I use all my resources wisely."

SAGITTARIUS/FEBRUARY

PRIMARY FOCUS

The desire to bring greater enjoyment into your life can lead to pursuing a creative interest. Increasing your involvement in community or special interests can benefit your career.

HEALTH AND FITNESS

Worrisome circumstances at home drain your vitality. Work to the core of the problems. It's a good time for psychological house-cleaning.

ROMANCE AND RELATIONSHIPS

While Venus transits your Solar 5th House this month you may want to put romantic experiences into a higher priority. Keeping your personal and professional life in balance can be a drag, since friends and lovers are ever more interesting and invigorating than work, especially near the Full Moon on the 6th. Sexual politics can be frustrating midmonth, when your desires can be misunderstood. Clarify your feelings and expectations on the 15th and 19th. Listen to your partner. You may be the one who needs to loosen up a bit!

FINANCE AND CAREER

Network from the 1st-19th to build your reputation and generate the support you need to accomplish your aims. Contacts or proposals accomplished before the 13th are likely to move along more smoothly. Use the second half of the month to gather facts and handle details, since you may have some explaining to do next month! Unexpected expenditures early in the month may deplete your cash reserves. It's best to keep spending to a minimum.

OPPORTUNITY OF THE MONTH

A friend or business contact may introduce you to an unforeseen chance to improve your career options on the 6th.

Rewarding Days: 5, 6, 10, 11, 14, 15, 19, 20, 24
Challenging Days: 1, 2, 8, 12, 17, 21, 22, 27, 28

AFFIRMATION FOR THE MONTH

"I am clear about my immediate goals."

SAGITTARIUS/MARCH

PRIMARY FOCUS
It's time to take a second look at your personal relationships. Unresolved emotional situations need your special attention now.

HEALTH AND FITNESS
Your physical health is closely related to your emotional and spiritual well-being this month. It's time to accomplish a release from the pain of your past and heal those ancient wounds.

ROMANCE AND RELATIONSHIPS
A careful examination of your early life may give you some clues to the blocks in your current love relationship. Use the energy of the Full Moon on the 8th to help you release family patterns that have inhibited the fulfillment of your needs. A flirtation from the 1st-15th may be a flash in the pan, although exciting! If you're committed, your partner's expectations can seem inhibiting. Explore different ways to relate on intimate levels during the New Moon on the 23rd when it's time to rejuvenate your love life.

FINANCE AND CAREER
The confusion during this retrograde of Mercury until the 22nd can be especially frustrating. Continual changes make it difficult to know which way to jump, so stay flexible in your position at work! Investment opportunities may not bring anything substantial, but investigating them can lead you to look into something you hadn't previously considered. Next month is a better time for financial risks, since you can easily undermine your stability by risking more than you can afford now.

OPPORTUNITY OF THE MONTH
Wait until the New Moon on the 23rd to take the risk of trying something entirely different.

Rewarding Days: 5, 6, 9, 10, 13, 14, 18, 23, 24
Challenging Days: 1, 2, 4, 7, 8, 12, 16, 20, 21, 28, 29

AFFIRMATION FOR THE MONTH
"I deserve to have the love I need."

SAGITTARIUS/APRIL

PRIMARY FOCUS

You're in the mood to enjoy life, and may spend more time pursuing your favorite pleasurable activities.

HEALTH AND FITNESS

Avoid pushing yourself too intensely now, even though it's tempting to "go where no one has gone before." Balance risk with reasonable caution and preparedness.

ROMANCE AND RELATIONSHIPS

While Venus continues its retrograde cycle in your solar 5th House through the 22nd, you're taking a very careful second look at your love relationship. Take time to talk over your feelings with a good friend near the Full Moon on the 6th, when you may be more aware of your needs. It's tempting to push your partner too far from the 1st-11th, resulting in alienation or hurt. You may feel that your own needs have been short-changed. A mending can take place from the 15th-21st, when frank talk leads to understanding.

FINANCE AND CAREER

A shift in priorities from an investor or partner can create a change in your plans from the 1st-13th. Attempt to clarify the long-range goals involved. You may discover that your viewpoint differs widely from that of your superiors. But by the time of the New Moon on the 23rd, you're in a good position to make the necessary adjustments and get moving along a more reasonable path. Plan important meetings or presentations for the 29th-30th, when you'll be greeted by greater optimism and support.

OPPORTUNITY OF THE MONTH

Take inventory of your situation on the 2nd, and plan to make an important move on the 29th. The gates are opening!

Rewarding Days: 1, 2, 5, 10, 11, 14, 15, 19, 20, 29, 30
Challenging Days: 3, 4, 6, 8, 13, 17, 18, 24, 25

AFFIRMATION FOR THE MONTH

"I am honest about my feelings."

SAGITTARIUS/MAY

PRIMARY FOCUS

Travel can bring the affirmation of your hopes. You're ready for a fresh approach to your life, and may feel more open to change.

HEALTH AND FITNESS

Make an assessment of your health status. Consider adjusting diet or exercise habits to accommodate your schedule changes.

ROMANCE AND RELATIONSHIPS

Improve an existing relationship through sharing inspirational activities. Travel or philosophical discussions can initiate a better understanding. The Solar Eclipse on the 21st emphasizes your link with others, and may bring hidden disputes to the surface. This can also be a time when you're rethinking your needs in a partnership. A new love may enter the picture after the 24th but you may also find positive changes in an existing union. Time spent with friends can also be highly beneficial, and may be the catalyst for positive change in your love life. Increasing social activities after the 22nd brings personal and professional satisfaction.

FINANCE AND CAREER

Discuss grievances with co-workers or employees from the 1st-14th, but be aware of the tendency toward heightened emotionality interfering with clear communication during the Full Moon on the 5th. A revision in schedules can create havoc midmonth, and may generate an undermining power play. Greater openness after the 19th changes the focus. However, you may feel restricted by the demands of others near the 21st.

OPPORTUNITY OF THE MONTH

By taking the initiative on the 8th you may be able to thwart the competition or halt opposition to your plans.

Rewarding Days: 3, 4, 7, 8, 12, 17, 18, 26, 27, 30
Challenging Days: 1, 2, 6, 14, 15, 20, 21, 22, 23, 28, 29

AFFIRMATION FOR THE MONTH

"My ideals are in harmony with my highest needs."

SAGITTARIUS/JUNE

PRIMARY FOCUS
Reflecting upon your past relationships may reveal a surprising pattern. Examine your motivations.

HEALTH AND FITNESS
To maintain optimum health, use the extra energy you're feeling now in heightened activity. Sports can be quite enjoyable now.

ROMANCE AND RELATIONSHIPS
Your feelings about the meaning of marriage are emphasized during the Lunar Eclipse on the 4th. Personal honesty is your best assurance of getting to the core of these feelings so you can begin to fulfill your partnership needs more effectively. Heightened emotionality about sexual issues may interfere with clear communication. Your hopes or fantasies may contrast sharply with the reality you're experiencing. By the time of the New Moon on the 19th you may feel more comfortable about bridging this gap. Acknowledge any anger within your family or toward parents which emerges on the 24th to avoid creating an unwelcome barrier.

FINANCE AND CAREER
Financial matters can be worrisome, since the inconsistency makes it difficult to plan ahead. This is an excellent time to confer with a financial expert and sort through paperwork. Double-check tax and insurance records. If you need to gain the support of investors, plan to make presentations on the 4th, 8th, 9th or 14th. You may have to do some juggling to come up with the right numbers, but progress is promising on the 22nd.

OPPORTUNITY OF THE MONTH
The Moon's Eclipse on the 4th offers an excellent time for reflection and self-awareness. Take a good look in the mirror.

Rewarding Days: 3, 4, 8, 9, 13, 14, 22, 27, 28
Challenging Days: 2, 6, 10, 11, 16, 17, 18, 19, 24, 25

AFFIRMATION FOR THE MONTH
"I let go of the attachments which inhibit my growth."

SAGITTARIUS/JULY

PRIMARY FOCUS

Your desire to expand your career options may stem from a need for greater acknowledgment of your worth. Be careful to avoid stepping on the wrong toes in your climb up the ladder!

HEALTH AND FITNESS

Stress at work can deplete your vitality. Seek physical and emotional support to alleviate the tension.

ROMANCE AND RELATIONSHIPS

Misunderstandings with your partner can be heightened through the 25th. Signals can easily be misinterpreted; emotions can interfere with clear communication. If arguments over finances occur near the Full Moon on the 3rd, be sure it's really about money. You may be dealing with a partner who feels unsupported, or you may feel that you've been too inhibited by their demands. Watch for foot in the mouth syndrome from the 15th-31st. Keep your sense of humor! Talk with a friend on the 11th if you need a different perspective.

FINANCE AND CAREER

Money matters can be crazy during this retrograde of Mercury from the 1st-25th. You may be in the midst of circumstances beyond your control which make forethought difficult. Get to the core of the problems that emerge now, so you can avoid them in the future. An investor or supporter may drop out of the picture by midmonth, but you may be able to recover by targeting a new venture after the New Moon on the 19th. Investigation is necessary before moving forward.

OPPORTUNITY OF THE MONTH

Staying on top of the details can make the difference between success and disappointment. Move forward on the 28th-29th.

Rewarding Days: 1, 2, 5, 10, 11, 19, 20, 24, 28, 29
Challenging Days: 4, 7, 8, 9, 14, 15, 16, 18, 21, 22

AFFIRMATION FOR THE MONTH

"I happily release the burden of my past."

SAGITTARIUS/AUGUST

PRIMARY FOCUS
Your career provides greater rewards and may even offer the opportunity for travel. Political or special interest activities motivate you to expand your goals.

HEALTH AND FITNESS
Take the edge off of stress by getting involved in a fitness class, working out with a friend or joining in a team sport.

ROMANCE AND RELATIONSHIPS
At the time of the Full Moon on the 2nd you may be inspired to travel with your sweetheart to distant horizons. Enjoyment and ease in traveling are best supported from the 10th-25th. Revitalizing an existing relationship or experiencing the first blush of new love is promising on the 17th. Share your ideals with one another, since philosophical discussions, cultural exchanges or intellectual pursuits can cement your bond. Unrealistic infatuation on the 18th can be dangerous if it interferes with an honest relationship.

FINANCE AND CAREER
Contacts made on the 2nd open doors. You're getting things back in balance financially after the 10th, when new prospects emerge. You may be singled out for recognition after the 15th, which can lead to advancement. You're less likely to meet with competitive resistance after the 12th, and may find that outside threats have diminished. If you're ready to move into a new position, take advantage of your contacts through friends and colleagues. But be aware of criticism during the Full Moon on the 31st.

OPPORTUNITY OF THE MONTH
Use the powerful open energy of the New Moon on the 17th to expand your influence and broaden your territory.

Rewarding Days: 2, 3, 6, 7, 8, 16, 17, 20, 21, 24, 25, 29
Challenging Days: 4, 5, 10, 11, 12, 13, 23, 31

AFFIRMATION FOR THE MONTH
"I have faith in my future."

SAGITTARIUS/SEPTEMBER

PRIMARY FOCUS

Forward progress is highly promising. This is an exceptional time to travel, promote ideas, write or teach. Even from a "learning" position, you may still be involved in guiding others.

HEALTH AND FITNESS

Increasing your physical activity may give you the edge you need to accomplish everything on your long list of goals. Stay centered.

ROMANCE AND RELATIONSHIPS

Friends provide motivation and encouragement, but may also challenge your goals. Sudden changes can prompt an end to a relationship late in the month, but your intuition may be giving you signals long before. Your search for love may be rewarded now, although you may feel some doubt about the longevity of the relationship. A fickle attitude frustrates your contentment the week of the 19th. However, honest talk can give you a promising direction near the time of the Full Moon on the 30th.

FINANCE AND CAREER

Although you're making remarkable career progress, you still have the obstacle of different viewpoints to conquer early in the month. Connections with others outside your normal field of reference through travel, correspondence or conferences can give you the missing pieces from the 1st-21st. However, outside indecision and distraction from the 9th-12th is frustrating. Meet with superiors after the New Moon on the 15th, and finalize contracts before the 30th.

OPPORTUNITY OF THE MONTH

By maintaining high levels of integrity you're attracting the types of circumstances that elevate your status. Be ready to move forward on the 21st.

Rewarding Days: 3, 4, 12, 13, 17, 20, 21, 25, 30
Challenging Days: 1, 2, 8, 9, 14, 15, 19, 24, 27, 28

AFFIRMATION FOR THE MONTH

"My aim is clear."

SAGITTARIUS/OCTOBER

PRIMARY FOCUS

Inner level changes result from actively pursuing a release of the past. You're reaching a strong level of emotional self-support.

HEALTH AND FITNESS

Take a mental health break this month, and create an internal environment of healing and self-acceptance.

ROMANCE AND RELATIONSHIPS

If you're involved in a love relationship, share your innermost thoughts and feelings with your partner. You may also need some time to withdraw without feeling that this action compromises your relationship. Your friends may be the source of your inspiration near the time of the New Moon on the 15th. If you're single, you might prefer to keep it that way for a while, since you're feeling more self-oriented and independent. But be sure you're not shutting out others who are really close, especially near the time of the Full Moon on the 30th, when you may need some extra hugs.

FINANCE AND CAREER

You're generating good feelings from those who see you operating in the outside world, and can make strong career progress now. Far-reaching changes may be in the works, which can require that you get a lot done behind the scenes or in your off-work hours. Safeguard important documents or material which needs to be kept secret, since there may be unseen forces at work waiting to take advantage of a weak link. But remain positive, since paranoia works against your success. Keep spending to a minimum.

OPPORTUNITY OF THE MONTH

An exciting promise on the 15th can lead to positive changes in your career. Take time to uncover the consequences of a change.

Rewarding Days: 1, 10, 11, 14, 15, 18, 19, 22, 27, 28
Challenging Days: 4, 5, 6, 8, 9, 12, 13, 17, 25, 26, 30

AFFIRMATION FOR THE MONTH

"I have a powerful storehouse of joy!"

SAGITTARIUS/NOVEMBER

PRIMARY FOCUS

Advancement in your career may provide a larger arena for your growth. You may prefer to keep a strong line drawn between your public and personal life to avoid feeling over-exposed.

HEALTH AND FITNESS

Your vitality improves. Gradually increase your activity. Slow down to avoid stumbling over your own two feet.

ROMANCE AND RELATIONSHIPS

The appeal of a clandestine relationship may be strong, and could be the best way to avoid outside pressure. But be sure you're aware of the other person's needs and motivations, since you could get into hot water by the end of the month! Feelings about your own commitment may be filled with intricate complexity near the time of the Solar Eclipse on the 13th. If you fail to direct these needs, you may run into open conflict by the time of the Lunar Eclipse on the 29th, when you're reaping what you've sown.

FINANCE AND CAREER

Recognition or advancement in career from the 1st-8th is the result of your persistent optimism. However, there may be factions working against you, especially if you allow misunderstandings to go unanswered. Follow-through on important communications and double-check appointments during Mercury's retrograde through the 14th. There may be some delay in getting projects off the ground all month. Use this time to plan, investigate and get everything in order.

OPPORTUNITY OF THE MONTH

A breakthrough in your personal feelings about the way you share love can renew an intimate relationship on the 24th.

Rewarding Days: 6, 7, 10, 11, 14, 15, 19, 23, 24
Challenging Days: 1, 2, 8, 9, 13, 17, 21, 22, 29, 30

AFFIRMATION FOR THE MONTH

"I listen to my intuitive voice."

SAGITTARIUS/DECEMBER

PRIMARY FOCUS
Many of the obstacles which were previously blocking your progress are gone, allowing you to move forward and accomplish your goals. It's a great time to travel and enjoy the beauty of nature.

HEALTH AND FITNESS
You may feel more integrated and aware. Assess your health, and take measures to strengthen your vitality and build stamina.

ROMANCE AND RELATIONSHIPS
You may feel as though you're emerging from darkness into the light, giving you much more confidence about expressing your needs to your partner. Your love life undergoes a vast improvement, and you're radiating more of the warmth and good humor you're known to possess. Stay socially active. Plan a party for the 12th, 16th, 21st, 22nd or 31st. The New Moon in Sagittarius on the 13th marks an important time to turn over a new leaf and decide you can have what you want after all!

FINANCE AND CAREER
Old-line resistance remains, but may be cracking. Get involved in expanding your territory or making new contacts through the 23rd. But watch for conservative attitudes, especially by the Full Moon on the 28th, when your far-reaching plans may seem impossible to those who can only think in terms of what has been instead of what can be. It's up to you to take the lead, without getting distracted in the process and losing valuable time or support. Stay focused on your goals.

OPPORTUNITY OF THE MONTH
By far, your best time to get things moving is in the early hours of the 13th, when you may feel that the world's your oyster.

Rewarding Days: 3, 4, 8, 9, 12, 13, 16, 21, 22, 30, 31
Challenging Days: 2, 5, 6, 11, 18, 19, 26, 27

AFFIRMATION FOR THE MONTH
"I create my own reality."

CAPRICORN
THE GOAT

December 22 to January 21

Element: Earth
Quality: Cardinal
Polarity: Feminine/Yin
Planetary Ruler: Saturn
Meditation: "Mastering the challenge of the physical plane"
Gemstone: Garnet
Power Stones: Diamond, quartz, onyx, black obsidian
Key Phrase: I use

Glyph: Head of goat, knees
Anatomy: Knees, skin, skeleton
Color: Black
Animal: Goats, thick-shelled animals
Myths/Legends: Pan, Vesta
House Association: Tenth
Opposite Sign: Cancer
Flower: Carnation
Key Word: Structure

Positive Expression:
Conscientious
Sensible
Patient
Disciplined
Ambitious
Responsible
Frugal
Prudent
Cautious

Misuse of Energy:
Repressed
Fearful
Rigid
Controlling
Machiavellian
Repressed
Miserly
Melancholy

CAPRICORN

YOUR EGO'S STRENGTHS AND WEAKNESSES:
You operate most effectively when you're the one in charge. A focused and persistent individual, you have a good sense of structure. Success comes to you through reliable and responsible action, making the most of all the materials at hand. Other people may remember your dry wit, but your desire to achieve mastery may be the trait which sets you apart from the crowd.

Your ambition to achieve the ultimate can keep you moving forward when everything around you has come to a standstill. You like challenges and deadlines, and perform best when there's a bit of pressure to beat the clock. Through the energy of Saturn, your planetary ruler, you learn that manifesting your dreams requires building a strong foundation. But you can allow inhibition and fearfulness to block your path. By getting back to the basics, you can always step into the right position to put you on track.

Your desire to be in control can lead you to take unnecessary advantage of others. You're more than happy to provide rules, and to change them as it suits your needs. Although you can be highly realistic, you may also grow melancholy when reality overwhelms your hopes. By balancing your realistic thinking while maintaining a vision of your goals, you can persist in moving ahead. You're working toward mastery over the physical plane without losing your connection with your Higher Self. In this way, you can create a pattern for success which serves you well and which others may choose to follow.

YOUR CAREER DEVELOPMENT: You're likely to have the edge in business or educational situations, where your astute judgment and sense of responsibility are strong assets. Positions of management and authority are your preference, since you're at your best when you're in control, and you're adept in delegating responsibilities to others. Although your administrative and executive abilities can shine when working for others (or for the government), you might prefer to own your business.

Your ambition may lead you into positions as diverse as politics or the ministry. Or you may be drawn into the practice or teaching of physics, geology, life sciences or medicine. Chiropractic medicine, naturopathy and herbology are excellent choices, and you're a natural metaphysician. Your teaching abilities can pull you toward the field of education or administration.

In the construction industry, you may be drawn into contracting, design or development. Managing a farm or ranch may answer your needs to get back to nature. But whatever your choices, you're determined to make them successful!

YOUR APPROACH TO ROMANCE: Since your self-worth may be tied up with your success in the outside world, you may feel inhibited in romance until you've established a foundation in your career. But once you open up and allow yourself to receive love, you may find that the sensual pleasures can be your forte. Beneath the mask of control, you can be a highly sensitive lover.

Stability is an important factor in relationships, and you'll be most comfortable in a love which gradually takes shape and grows over time. The Water signs—Cancer, Scorpio, and Pisces—may be the most alluring. Your opposite sign, Cancer, helps you maintain a stable existence and can be a patient partner. Scorpio's enticing sensuality appeals to your understanding of the alchemy of love. And Pisces' mystical imagination provides the perfect escape from the everyday.

You're challenged by Aries, whose playfulness is compelling but can sometimes get in the way when you have to get to work. Taurus, whose earthiness gets your motor running, can be the perfect long-time lover and partner. Gemini's fickleness may be too frustrating. Before you decide if it can last with Leo, try to define who's in charge and get your territories established before it's too late.

Virgo can help you design your plans for the future and can be an easy companion. Libra's refinement and good taste are attractive, but you may feel baffled by their detached attitude. Sagittarius' search for the best things in life is inspiring, but you have to give them freedom. Another Capricorn may be a dedicated partner, good for business, but you may both feel that the relationship gets too stuffy if you fail to allow time for play. With Aquarius, you have a lifelong friend and learn to let go of expectations.

YOUR USE OF POWER: Your quest for power may be involved in gaining greater control, although you may have to learn that control does not equal inflexibility. Struggling to keep the structure you've established in tact can lead to conflict if someone else wants to create change. But by incorporating periodic review and evaluation, you may find that you can assess and initiate revisions on your own. You can easily undermine your own power by ignoring the need to change and by holding rigidly to patterns or traditions which have outlived their usefulness.

Other people may look up to you, and you can easily influence the lives of children or those who see you as their mentor. Once you've established the position of respect you desire, others are quite likely to seek your counsel and guidance. But you may also find those control issues lurking behind the mask of guiding others. Remind yourself that you really cannot be in charge of anyone's life but your own. However, by selflessly offering support and direction to another, you have the power to help them positively shape their destiny.

FAMOUS CAPRICORNS: Robert Bly; Victor Borge; David Bowie; Carlos Castaneda; Paul Cezanne; Conrad Hilton; Cary Grant; Sandy Koufax; Rush Limbaugh; Susan Lucci; Dolly Parton; J. R. R. Tolkein

THE YEAR AHEAD FOR CAPRICORN

While the world continues to reshape and reorganize politically and economically, you may find that there's a special place for your abilities. With your sense of structure and economy, a circumstance which needs rebuilding or improvement can benefit from your judgment as to its soundness. More importantly, on a personal level, you're experiencing a strong movement toward a brighter and less encumbered life situation. Your own life structure may now include more room for free expression, allowing you to receive greater abundance on every level. And you're learning better ways to utilize your resources, which imparts a stronger sense of stability and financial security.

Even though the revolution in consciousness indicated by the Uranus/Neptune conjunction in Capricorn is affecting the core of human society, for Capricorns this is an especially notable cycle. You may feel the urge to break away and leave behind the aspects of your life that have become too inhibiting. But there's an old guilt that may be creeping into the back of your mind that says you should be doing something else! This is a time to forgive yourself and release attitudes that get in the way of manifesting the reality you desire. But watch a tendency to avoid your responsibilities, since you may easily undermine a relationship or situation that needs to be strengthened instead of abandoned. You need to be blatantly honest with yourself now, since it's all too easy to feel that you're the only one who really matters.

The Solar Eclipse cycles during 1993 emphasize your need to take a look at your hopes and dreams and the self-expression necessary to fulfill them. Much of your work can be done on an inner level, since you're experiencing a stronger feeling about your place in the larger scheme of things. Your growing connection to your spiritual needs can be a source of great inspiration. Yet if you look around you, you'll find that you gain support and inspiration from your friends, and that your spirit soars when you look into the eyes of a child filled with joy. Take some time to gaze into your own eyes and find the part of you that needs to play and dance in the joy of your own accomplishments.

Jupiter's transit brings broader horizons in your career and an expanded influence to your reputation. If you've established a strong foundation, this is the time to reach further through teaching, learning, travel or advertising. You may find more doors opening for you, but you can also be vulnerable to traps. These traps are most dangerous if your ego gets in the way of recognizing your own limitations. However, by maintaining a balanced perspective on your long-range plans you may more easily decide which opportunities can bring growth and which will only weight you down. After Jupiter moves into Scorpio on November 10th, you're likely to move toward more palatable circumstances.

If you were born on December 22nd-24th you may see marked results for your efforts. This is especially notable from May through July, when Saturn moves into the sextile to your Sun. You're also needing to take a careful look at the way you're maintaining your health, since the Solar Eclipse in May draws your attention to the way you feel. You're also in the midst of establishing a better sense of your destiny, and may be feeling more inclined to make decisions based on your spiritual needs once Chiron moves into Virgo in September.

For Capricorns born December 25th-January 5th, the tendency to push yourself (and others) beyond your limits is tempting. The transits of Venus, Mars and Jupiter are all bringing broader opportunities your direction through August of 1993. You're also feeling the impact of a powerful cycle while Saturn and Pluto both transit in semi-square aspect to your Sun. This cycle can create a feeling that everything you're doing has a special effect on the fulfillment of your destiny. The impact of this transit is generally not fully realized until the cycle is over, when you can survey the width and breadth of the leap you've taken. But it does mark a period of a release from the levels of consciousness which have held you hostage for most of your life. You can repair wounded relationships by honestly listening to the needs of others. And you can facilitate healing within yourself through accepting your feelings and needs without judgment. Avoid getting caught in the trap of rules and regulations that could stultify your growth. Cooperating with the law of the land is important, but more importantly, you're finding the necessity of cooperation with the Laws of the Universe. Circumstances in which you've taken unnecessarily harsh or egotistical attitudes are likely to come back to haunt you now. During this time, you need to maintain as much flexibility as possible to avoid getting stuck with someone else's problems! The real temptation of 1993 comes from a long-lasting square from Jupiter to your Sun (until August). Although you may meet all the right people and reach out in many directions, many of these will not bear fruit. But the stimulation to get out of a rut and incorporate new ideas, better services, or enhanced products is generally worth the risk. The most difficult aspect of this cycle involves the tendency to allow your ego to get out of control. You may discover the limits of your own power simply by abusing it. Lessons learned in this manner are rarely forgotten. You can experience far-reaching influence and general good fortune. Just keep in step with the rhythm of your heart and you'll do fine.

If you were born from January 6th-20th, you're feeling a strong urge to express your creative energies in the outside world. Some of you will also feel the need to make radical changes in your sense of self (see Jan. 7th-14th below). You're stimulated by Saturn's transit in semi-sextile to your Sun which can be frustrating, but generally results in a period of marked accomplishment. You can make positive strides in establishing your expertise while setting up a sound base for financial success. However, if you've been wasteful in utilizing your resources, this can also be a period of financial struggle, or at the least, frustration. Your issue is attached to making the most of what you've got—that includes all your resources (time, money, relationships, health, even ideas!). With persistent effort, this can be a year of strengthening of self and appreciable accomplishment.

If you were born from January 7th-14th, you're experiencing the force of Uranus and Neptune exactly in conjunction to your Sun. It's time to make a definitive statement about your identity, and to break away from the circumstances of your past which are preventing the self-realization you may crave. If you've fallen victim to negative patterns in relationships, this can be a time of release and forgiveness, allowing you to gradually establish more healthy choices. This is a time of recovery and awareness. But it's also a period of imagination, hope and futuristic thinking. The limitations you were once willing to accept may seem completely unpalatable now. Your first choice of action may be to step into the abyss of the unknown completely unprepared (highly un-Capricornian!). By realizing that you can take many of your accomplishments from the past into your new reality, you may be less willing to jump off that cliff without your hang-gliding equipment. Take a careful look within yourself. Your most powerful challenges come from beliefs about your worth and identity that you may be discovering to be untrue. This type of awakening brings phenomenal change, and it can also bring great confusion. You may wonder who you are, where you're heading and why the world seems to be such a different place. It's more than the changes you hear about in the news. You're feeling the fundamental change that comes from accepting your destiny and taking it on under your terms while working in harmony with Higher Law. Be prepared for your own personal revolution. It might help if you offer a few hints to the other people involved in your life, since their support can be crucial to the quality of your life changes.

If you were born from January 13th-18th, you're feeling the deeper level evolution which accompanies Pluto's transit in sextile to your Sun. Through conscious choice, you can make this a period of marked growth on all levels. You're eliminating the unnecessary, making the load much lighter. This can be a period of profound healing, physically and emotionally. Self-acceptance is enhanced by the support and caring you feel from your friends. You may also be attracted to political efforts or community activities. These can not only enhance your reputation, but may give you the opportunity to make your mark in history.

TOOLS TO MAKE A DIFFERENCE: To take advantage of this period of personal awakening, find ample outlets for your creative inspiration. Allowing extra time in your schedule to enjoy a hobby or your favorite recreational activities can give you a greater sense of vitality and even increase your energy levels. Get back to nature this year. Take walks in the woods or create a small garden. Touching your element, earth, is a centering experience for you.

If you have a chance, take in museums or exhibits which give you a sense of the slow evolution of life which occurs throughout time. While you're on your nature walks, look for your gemstone, garnet. They're more abundant than you think! These stones work on a level which uplifts the spirit and help to maintain the natural flow of energy in the body. Deep level massage is also a good idea for you. In fact, giving a massage may be just as helpful to you as receiving one!

Your flower, the carnation, also has many useful properties. The oil from carnations is helpful in relieving skin problems, which often are a burden when you're under stress. Carnation wine is reputed to be an aphrodisiac. This long-lasting flower is a bright addition to the home or office.

This year provides many invitations to master your task of meeting the challenge of the physical plane. Your best tool is the development of a positive attitude and the realization that you can break out of a system that may have stifled your individuality or imagination. When you feel stuck take some time to reflect on the best ways to get beyond your limitations. Keep in mind the prancing persistence of the goat, always looking for a better viewpoint. Goats operate much better if they have some free range. And, not surprisingly, so do you!

In your visualizations for 1993, concentrate on obtaining a clear view of the path ahead. Once you're relaxed, allow your mind's eye to take you on a journey toward your inner teacher. You may find this teacher in any life form, or perhaps in the form of a crystal being. Spend time in the presence of your teacher, just feeling the energy exchange between the two of you. You may become aware of a purely fragrant aroma emanating from this being. Remind yourself that the wisdom of this teacher is always accessible to you, since this being is part of your consciousness.

AFFIRMATION FOR THE YEAR: "I can create everything I need to make my life complete."

ACTION TABLES FOR CAPRICORN

These dates reflect the best (but not the *only*) times for success and ease in these activities according to your Sun Sign.

Change Residence	Apr. 15-May 3
Request a Raise	Dec. 27
Begin a Course of Study	Feb. 21; Sept. 16
Visit a Doctor	Jan. 1-2; May 18-June 1; Dec. 7-25
Start a Diet	Jan. 5-6; Feb. 1-2, 28; Mar. 1-2, 28-29; Apr. 24-25; May 21-22; June 18-19; July 15-16; Aug. 11-12; Sept. 8-9; Oct. 5-6; Nov. 1-3, 28-30; Dec. 26-27
Begin a Romance	Apr. 21-22
Join a Club	Nov. 13-14
Seek Employment	May 18-June 1; Sept. 11-30
Take a Vacation	Jan. 11-12; Feb. 8-9; Mar. 7-8; Apr. 3-4; May 1-2, 28-29; June 24-25; July 22-23; Aug. 18-19; Sept. 14-15; Oct. 12-13; Nov. 8-9; Dec. 5-6
Change Your Wardrobe	May 4-17
End a Relationship	Jan. 8; Dec. 28-29
Seek Professional Advice	Jan. 7-8; Feb. 3-4; Mar. 3-4, 30-31; Apr. 26-28; May 24-25; June 20-21; July 17-18; Aug. 14-15; Sept. 10-11; Oct. 7-8; Nov. 4-5; Dec. 1-2, 28-29
Have a Makeover	Dec. 26-27
Obtain a Loan	Jan. 9-10; Feb. 5-6; Mar. 5-6; Apr. 1-2, 29-30; May 26-27; June 22-23; July 19-20; Aug. 16-17; Sept. 12-13; Oct. 10-11; Nov. 6-7; Dec. 3-4, 30-31

CAPRICORN/JANUARY

PRIMARY FOCUS
With so much energy propelling you toward change it will be difficult to stand firm. Flowing with the changes is one thing, but watch a tendency to cut off your nose to spite your face!

HEALTH AND FITNESS
You may be experiencing a great deal of nervous energy which interferes with your sleep or rest periods. Take the time to exercise, which will alleviate some of the stress and help you balance your energy.

ROMANCE AND RELATIONSHIPS
Marriage and partnership interaction tends toward volatility, especially near the time of the Full Moon on the 8th. Hidden anger surfaces, which gives you a chance to clear the air and get to the core of your dissatisfaction. You may be the target for your partner's inner discontent, but you can just as easily project your unhappiness onto them. This cycle also points toward room for progress and repair, which is the best step before you decide to bolt and run! Honest conversation about your needs fares well from the 11th-22nd. Find time for tenderness on the 30th-31st.

FINANCE AND CAREER
New ideas or general improvements can give you hope that your economic situation is taking a turn for the better. But move cautiously and with adequate preparation from the 1st-8th and again on the 14th and 15th, since it's easy to jump into a situation before you're ready. Networking pays off from the 3rd-20th. Seek more effective uses of your resources after the New Moon on the 22nd.

OPPORTUNITY OF THE MONTH
The burst of energy on the 7th and 8th can give you just the push you need to manifest your dreams.

Rewarding Days: 3, 11, 12, 15, 16, 20, 21, 25, 26, 30
Challenging Days: 1, 5, 7, 8, 13, 14, 24, 27, 28

AFFIRMATION FOR THE MONTH
"I am flexible in the face of change."

CAPRICORN/FEBRUARY

PRIMARY FOCUS
Disagreeable attitudes from others can block your progress. By responding to complaints with positive action, you can use the dissension to your benefit.

HEALTH AND FITNESS
Stress looms large, and you may have little time to think about taking care of your body. Give yourself a break. Take time out for a massage on the 13th or 18th.

ROMANCE AND RELATIONSHIPS
Your attempts to bring more peace onto the home front may be thwarted by circumstances beyond your control. Sexual issues can be the source of your disputes, but they may surface as arguments over money during the Full Moon on the 6th. Talking about your feelings is easier on the 16th and 17th, and may lead to more promising dialogue after the New Moon on the 21st. Be aware of the ways you're trying to meet unrealistic expectations. Align your priorities with your current needs and maintain your hopes.

FINANCE AND CAREER
Getting to the root of misuse or abuse of your business resources from the 1st-5th may expose corruption in the system. Restore sound finances by building on your reputation and making an effort to reach out into new territory. You may have better success from the 21st-26th. However, you can use Mercury's retrograde which begins on the 27th to your benefit by following through on projects already underway.

OPPORTUNITY OF THE MONTH
By capitalizing on the climate for radical change this month, you can pave the way toward successful diversification.

Rewarding Days: 7, 8, 12, 16, 17, 21, 22, 26, 27
Challenging Days: 2, 3, 4, 6, 9, 10, 24, 25

AFFIRMATION FOR THE MONTH
"My mind is open to new ideas."

CAPRICORN/MARCH

PRIMARY FOCUS

Avoid getting caught in the crunch of political change by keeping a lower profile. Keep in touch with the people who can make a difference, but avoid unexplored territory unless you have a guide.

HEALTH AND FITNESS

Scattering your energy can lead to exhaustion. Take time to center before you face the world each day.

ROMANCE AND RELATIONSHIPS

Changing circumstances in the outside world can affect the roles you carry in your intimate relationship. Arguments about who's in control may be irrelevant if you fail to accomplish meeting your basic needs! You may need a new spark, and can seek it outside a current commitment this month. Before you stray, be sure the risk is worth the price you'll pay if it doesn't work out. Restoring an existing relationship now can be just as exciting and may prove to be more rewarding. Renew vows after the New Moon on the 23rd.

FINANCE AND CAREER

Even though Mercury continues its retrograde cycle through the 22nd, you still have ample room to expand your professional aims. But the structures are undergoing deep level changes, and you may decide to leave one system in favor or one with stronger integrity. Talk over your hopes with a colleague on the Full Moon, the 8th. There may be a way to salvage your business before you move on. New investments are best postponed for a while, since you need most of your resources to make ends meet.

OPPORTUNITY OF THE MONTH

Getting back in touch with a former colleague or business associate on the 7th-8th can expedite a sound financial picture.

Rewarding Days: 7, 8, 11, 12, 15, 16, 20, 25, 26
Challenging Days: 3, 4, 6, 9, 10, 19, 23, 24, 30, 31

AFFIRMATION FOR THE MONTH

"I openly evaluate all possibilities."

CAPRICORN/APRIL

PRIMARY FOCUS

Although the confusion may be lifting and mechanical operations improving, there are still conflicts over who's in charge. Unresolved past issues are finally reaching the surface.

HEALTH AND FITNESS

Nervous tension multiplies early in the month. Concentrate on improving your flexibility.

ROMANCE AND RELATIONSHIPS

Unspoken expectations create problems through the 9th. Watch for those which originate from your parents on the Full Moon on the 6th. But be aware that an intimate relationship can be filled with anticipation as well. Your defensive tendency can overwhelm the situation through the 10th. Try to address problems directly without barking orders. You're feeling more centered after the New Moon on the 21st, when you may just need to spend some quiet time enjoying your favorite pastime. Romance can work nicely on the 22nd and 23rd, when you're feeling more open to enjoying yourself.

FINANCE AND CAREER

A business partnership may rip apart early in the month. Your ideas may simply require more independent action. If you work within a larger system, this may be a period of unrest and changes in the hierarchy. Although you may be interested in social climbing, take a careful look at your motivations to avoid getting caught in the crunch of larger egos. Take care to avoid wasting your financial resources from the 3rd-9th.

OPPORTUNITY OF THE MONTH

Better ideas for long-term financial success emerge on the 20th, but meet a more responsive audience on the 21st and 22nd.

Rewarding Days: 3, 4, 7, 8, 12, 13, 17, 18, 22, 23
Challenging Days: 2, 5, 6, 15, 19, 20, 26, 27

AFFIRMATION FOR THE MONTH

"I respect the boundaries of others."

CAPRICORN/MAY

PRIMARY FOCUS
Inspiring the interest of others can lead to sharing their resources. Know the obligations before making changes.

HEALTH AND FITNESS
Getting to the core of chronic physical complaints can become a driving force now. Cut out habits which undermine your vitality and block your energy.

ROMANCE AND RELATIONSHIPS
Although relationships may be improving, you may still feel uneasy. Part of this may stem from the fact that you've reached a level of intimacy which is more rewarding, but leaves you feeling more vulnerable. The real intimacy is with your own deeper needs, and can be a source of spiritual strength during the time of the Full Moon on the 5th. This is also a powerful period to solidify a love relationship. If you're seeking a new love, keep your eyes open the week of the 23rd, when you may meet an absolutely intriguing person. Cherish the possibility of change.

FINANCE AND CAREER
Capitalize on your imaginative and more expressive ideas or services from the 4th-17th, when you may find that your unique approach stirs strong interest from others. Conferences or meetings on the 14th and 15th can provide the right connections to get things moving after the Solar Eclipse on the 21st. Seek out better ways to support the needs and interests of those who work for you, since without their efforts your success could be quickly curtailed.

OPPORTUNITY OF THE MONTH
By shifting to a more positive outlook on the 5th you can turn the tide and generate greater reward from your work.

Rewarding Days: 1, 2, 5, 9, 10, 14, 15, 19, 20, 28, 29
Challenging Days: 3, 4, 8, 16, 17, 24, 25, 30, 31

AFFIRMATION FOR THE MONTH
"I am grateful for all I have."

CAPRICORN/JUNE

PRIMARY FOCUS

Although this is a month of hard work, cooperative interaction with others opens the way for an ease in the stress you've been feeling. Duty calls before pleasure.

HEALTH AND FITNESS

A close look at your health now pays off in the long term. Both emotional and physical needs may require closer investigation.

ROMANCE AND RELATIONSHIPS

Your social life may demand more of your time, and some of these situations can disrupt your carefully planned schedule. New information may bring surprises about your partnership to light mid-month. Although this can be a good month to share your favorite forms of entertainment, be sure not to overlook the deeper needs of an intimate relationship. Your sexual encounters can strengthen your bond to one another, but they can also be the source of dispute from the 9th-14th. Miscommunication runs rampant from the 15th-19th, so try to think before you speak.

FINANCE AND CAREER

Work relations can be filled with excessive competition near the time of the Lunar Eclipse on the 4th. But you're in a good position to calm the water on the 6th and 7th. Since you may not reach final resolution to problems until after the New Moon on the 19th, take the time to investigate the details. Your positive effectiveness in generating new business after the 7th can open the way for more consistent financial success. Plan carefully.

OPPORTUNITY OF THE MONTH

Make presentations or attend critical meetings on the 24th and 25th, when contracts and agreements pay tribute to your efforts.

Rewarding Days: 2, 5, 6, 7, 10, 11, 15, 16, 24, 25, 29
Challenging Days: 1, 13, 14, 18, 20, 21, 26, 27

AFFIRMATION FOR THE MONTH

"I enjoy my work!"

CAPRICORN/JULY

PRIMARY FOCUS
Listen carefully, since Mercury's retrograde until the 25th and may complicate communications or interfere with agreements. It's a great time to renegotiate and investigate.

HEALTH AND FITNESS
Your energy level is more balanced now. Incorporate both exercise relaxation into your schedule. A vacation is in order this month.

ROMANCE AND RELATIONSHIPS
The spotlight's on your needs during the Full Moon on the 3rd, when you're drawn to achieving a more balanced relationship. One-way issues only add fuel to the fire, and may push you toward seeking satisfaction elsewhere. New relationships begun now are likely to be filled with confusion or unreasonable expectations, and may end just as suddenly as they begin. To repair an existing relationship, consider taking time away from your routine. And if you're traveling, keep the plans simple and be prepared for delays or changes in your schedule.

FINANCE AND CAREER
Bringing legal issues to a close can be tough. You'll be less frustrated if you use this time to search out details and investigate all your options, rather than rushing in to make a final decision. A turn-about by the opposition can leave you wide open to take advantage of better circumstance on the 19th. But be aware of your own vulnerabilities, since it could be a ploy to throw you off guard! Save your big ammunition for the 25th-31st.

OPPORTUNITY OF THE MONTH
This can be a time when fundamental ethical issues work to your benefit. Keep your standards high, and make your move on the 26th.

Rewarding Days: 3, 4, 8, 13, 14, 22, 23, 26, 27, 30, 31
Challenging Days: 1, 6, 10, 11, 17, 18, 20, 24, 25

AFFIRMATION FOR THE MONTH
"I respect the Laws of the Universe."

CAPRICORN/AUGUST

PRIMARY FOCUS

You're benefiting from the resources of others, and can put yourself in a good position for career advancement. Look into the most personally fulfilling circumstances.

HEALTH AND FITNESS

Learning about your body's needs can stimulate you to make some changes in your habits now. Seek the advice of an expert.

ROMANCE AND RELATIONSHIPS

Consider traveling from the 1st-11th to help revitalize an existing relationship or to open to a new love. During the days near the Full Moon on the 2nd you may feel drawn to an exotic hide-away where you can share an intimate encounter. Clarify where you stand with your sweetheart early in the month, since your romantic urges from the 9th-12th can lead you to project unrealistic options. Arguments over finances from the 17th-22nd can create a wedge in your relationship. Talk it over with a friend on the 23rd.

FINANCE AND CAREER

Conferences or meetings held early in the month provide the backdrop for positive changes after the New Moon on the 17th. Incorporate the needs of your sponsor or client into your plans this month, since you may be creating a long-term ally. But be aware of your tendency to limit your focus to only one interest. Restricting your viewpoint is likely to curtail the broader options opening up for you on the 26th and 27th. Move forward with new ideas on the 19th.

OPPORTUNITY OF THE MONTH

You're in the strongest position for success from the 26th-31st. Take advantage of being in the right place at the right time.

Rewarding Days: 4, 5, 9, 10, 18, 19, 22, 23, 26, 27, 28, 31
Challenging Days: 2, 6, 7, 8, 14, 15, 20, 21

AFFIRMATION FOR THE MONTH

"I honor my intuitive guidance."

CAPRICORN/SEPTEMBER

PRIMARY FOCUS
A strong push in your career can bring you the recognition and reward you deserve. Avoid antagonizing those who can help you in your climb up the ladder. Watch for surprises at work.

HEALTH AND FITNESS
Although you usually move at a reasonable pace, it's easy to get ahead of yourself this month. Remind yourself to slow down.

ROMANCE AND RELATIONSHIPS
Sharing inspirational experiences deepens a love relationship, and may be a positive source of revitalization. The experience of traveling can help you open to your needs, and a new love or a better approach to an existing relationship can take root at the time of the New Moon on the 15th. Emotional tension is high from the 14th-16th, when you may resist the intrusion of intimacy. By clarifying what's behind your resistance, you may discover a link which allows you to make great strides in fulfilling your desires.

FINANCE AND CAREER
You may be in a highly fertile situation with your work, and need to take advantage of the best options. But watch for confrontation from superiors or others who may feel threatened by your ambition, since their actions can thwart your progress. You can seize the lead through careful negotiation and convincing rhetoric. A sudden shift of opinion can turn the tide on the 10th, but forces beneath the surface can bring greater change mid-month. Keep your standards high on the Full Moon of the 30th.

OPPORTUNITY OF THE MONTH
The power you're feeling on the 15th may be the impetus you need to make a significant change in your career.

Rewarding Days: 1, 5, 6, 14, 15, 18, 19, 24, 28
Challenging Days: 3, 4, 9, 10, 11, 16, 17, 22, 30

AFFIRMATION FOR THE MONTH
"I am confident and optimistic."

CAPRICORN/OCTOBER

PRIMARY FOCUS
Political action, whether confined to a special interest or broader influence, may consume a large portion of your time. You are strongly identified with your aims and hopes for the future.

HEALTH AND FITNESS
To increase your energy levels, devote a regular interval of time to physical activity. Team sports can be highly positive now.

ROMANCE AND RELATIONSHIPS
You may need to forge a different response to your contact with your parents. Whether this is externally, in the way you relate to them directly, or internally through your inner programming, it's time for you to act in accordance with your individual needs. Friends play an important role this month, too, and your interactions with them can help you fine-tune the manifestation of your dreams. The value of unconditional love becomes increasingly important by the Full Moon on the 30th. This can be a highly romantic period, and can become a time of increasing trust.

FINANCE AND CAREER
Making strides in your career may involve taking a leadership position on political matters. Wide-ranging changes can create the feeling of being caught in the middle of something that's beyond your control. However, these changes may bring about the opening you've needed to move into a position of influence. Although meetings and conferences are promising all month, there can be confusing communication once Mercury changes direction on the 25th.

OPPORTUNITY OF THE MONTH
This month revolves around long-range plans and targeting future growth. Take definitive action on the 16th.

Rewarding Days: 3, 4, 12, 13, 16, 17, 20, 21, 25, 30, 31
Challenging Days: 1, 2, 7, 8, 9, 11, 14, 15, 23, 27, 28

AFFIRMATION FOR THE MONTH
"I am confident about my goals."

CAPRICORN/NOVEMBER

PRIMARY FOCUS

Your friends may become the cornerstone of your ability to gain greater influence and respect. But you're also planting seeds for your long-term stability, and need to dust off your dreams.

HEALTH AND FITNESS

By the 9th you may feel more inclined to withdraw from higher activity levels and work on inner fitness. Focus on balance.

ROMANCE AND RELATIONSHIPS

Improve your love life by expressing needs more directly. If you're seeking a relationship, begin with friends. You may experience a few false starts until Mercury turns direct on the 15th, but there's no need to paralyze yourself! The Solar Eclipse on the 13th provides a powerful stimulus for you to listen more carefully to your inner voice. In matters of the heart, this is the only voice that may speak the truth! If you're reluctant to act on your feelings, test the waters by socializing in comfortable surroundings.

FINANCE AND CAREER

Power struggles early in the month may result from breakdowns in communication. Failing to attend to the root cause can undermine your progress and create difficulty later on. If you're making changes in your career, connect with colleagues and friends from the 12th-18th. A previously planned expenditure or investment may have hidden costs which surface from the 9th-16th. Stay within your budget to avoid a crunch after the 27th.

OPPORTUNITY OF THE MONTH

It's time to be honest with yourself about your life choices. Playing a role because it's safe is not nearly as rewarding as fulfilling your needs. Take an inner inventory on the 13th.

Rewarding Days: 8, 9, 12, 13, 16, 17, 21, 22, 26
Challenging Days: 2, 4, 5, 7, 10, 11, 23, 24, 25

AFFIRMATION FOR THE MONTH:

"I believe in myself."

CAPRICORN/DECEMBER

PRIMARY FOCUS
Behind-the-scenes preparation early in the month puts you in the perfect position by the Solstice. Make room for success.

HEALTH AND FITNESS
Continue to allow time for relaxation through the 19th. But once Mars enters Capricorn on the 20th, you're eager to get busy.

ROMANCE AND RELATIONSHIPS
Your secret desires may lead you to fantasize about all sorts of possibilities in your love life. Use your imagination to bring about improvements in your own ability to achieve satisfaction within yourself. Then, you may experience a significant change from the 20th-26th, when you're not only ready, but willing, to take the risk of deeper levels of intimacy. The Full Moon on the 28th marks a significant period of self-realization, and can extend your ability to balance your needs with those of someone else.

FINANCE AND CAREER
Secret communications from the 1st-4th may have powerful possibilities, but need to be carefully investigated before you take action. You're getting everything in order, and can be ready to launch a completely new program on the 26th. Use your influence in the community to benefit charitable concerns from the 2nd-25th. Consider the possibility of setting up a long-range structure to help meet these community needs in the future. Investments fare best on the 24th and 27th. You may see a return from previous investments on the 28th.

OPPORTUNITY OF THE MONTH
It's time for review and reconciliation. Once you're satisfied, make your move forward on the 23rd or 24th.

Rewarding Days: 5, 6, 10, 14, 15, 18, 23, 24
Challenging Days: 1, 2, 4, 7, 8, 21, 22, 28, 29

AFFIRMATION FOR THE MONTH
"I set myself free through forgiveness."

AQUARIUS
THE
WATER-BEARER

January 21 to February 20

Element: Air
Quality: Fixed
Polarity: Masculine/Yang
Planetary Ruler: Uranus
Meditation: "Creating new paths by focusing the mind"
Gemstone: Amethyst
Power Stones: Aquamarine, chrysocolla, black pearl
Color: Violet
Key Phrase: I know

Glyph: Waves of water or electricity
Anatomy: Ankles, circulatory system
Animal: Birds
Myths/Legends: Deucalion, Ninkhursag, John the Baptist
House Association: Eleven
Opposite Sign: Leo
Flower: Orchid
Key Word: Unconventional

Positive Expression:
Liberal
Ingenious
Futuristic
Progressive
Humane
Unselfish
Altruistic
Autonomous
Friendly
Unconditional

Misuse of Energy:
Thoughtless
Deviant
Detached
Fanatical
Rebellious
Anarchistic
Aloof
Undirected
Intransigent

AQUARIUS

YOUR EGO'S STRENGTHS AND WEAKNESSES:
Your unique self-expression sets you apart from the
crowd. You may use your inventive mind in many ways,
and may become a pioneer for the unusual. With a natural
grasp of the extraordinary, you possess the ability to see
things from a universal perspective. Your friends are the
jewels of your life, and it is through your associations with
them that you may gain the greatest recognition for your
special talents.

Anyone who knows you well can attest to the fact that
you can be full of surprises! You value freedom and may
champion the cause of human liberty and individual
rights. In music and the arts you appreciate the unusual
and more abstract forms of expression. Even though your
own creative efforts may seem unusual now, you may set a
precedent for what later becomes classical style.

You're willing to step outside the boundaries of the
mainstream and risk being different. However, you can be
rebellious or negligent when focused only on your own
selfish interests. Through connecting with the untamable
energy of your planetary ruler, Uranus, you may feel ali-
enated from many of the traditions which have been used
by others as an excuse for lack of progress. Trust your intuitive guidance to help you determine whether you are
part of a gradual evolution or if you are called to carry the
torch of revolutionary change.

Maintaining a balance between eccentricity and the Bo-
hemian can be a challenge for you. Your aloof posture can

alienate others, even though your intention may be to maintain objectivity. You're learning ways to remain aware of your personal connection with Universal Love. This unconditional attitude can illuminate the path toward a brighter future for all of humanity.

YOUR CAREER DEVELOPMENT: Keeping your mind busy is a top priority in your career path. You need plenty of room to exercise your originality and express your ideas. The scientific fields may fascinate and reward you well; areas such as computer science, electronics, theoretical mathematics, astrology, meteorology, aviation or the space industry may be appealing. Writing may be a special talent, whether technical or fanciful. Your talents may also reside in working with people through advertising, public relations, broadcasting or the news media.

Politics, especially in the areas of civil rights, may hold your interest. You might enjoy owning a unique business marketing your own or uncommon creations. In fine arts, your talents may range to visionary art to original music using the ultimate in technology. Whatever your career choice, your special touch is unlikely to be overlooked.

YOUR APPROACH TO ROMANCE: Your need for closeness may not be apparent to those who, at first glance, see only your independence. You seek a companion who can be both a friend and lover, and insist on equality. Once your own electrical energy is charged by contact with the right person, it's difficult to resist experimenting and moving toward romance. Your intuition tells you if it's love. But beware: your mind may try to talk you out of getting involved!

You're at ease with the other Air signs—Gemini, Libra and other Aquarians. The allure of Gemini's wit and intelligence is hard to resist. You're encouraged to share and open your heart to Libra's charm and refinement. Another Aquarian may be difficult to reach at an intimate level, but if you do connect, you may be able to create a remarkable life together.

On your toes with Aries, you may love the excitement and passion. Taurus' need to hold on to everything may feel too heavy. Your independent nature is not quite compatible with Cancer's need for contact. Your opposite sign,

Leo, is highly engaging and playful, although challenging at time. And although Virgo may inspire you to search your soul, it may be difficult to truly appreciate one another. With Scorpio you may reach an uncomfortable feeling that you're never quite at the same level. Sagittarius brings hope and complements your need for freedom. Friendship with Capricorn may be easier then romance, since control issues can get in the way. Similar ideals may connect you with Pisces, although you can easily get lost in the vapors of a different reality with one another.

YOUR USE OF POWER: You're quick to spot a misuse of power, and may resist moving into positions of great power and influence until you feel you're ready. Rather than seeking power for the sake of personal recognition, you might be more comfortable in a situation which allows you to represent a common cause or universal ideal. You understand the power of the human mind and spirit, and may be drawn to merging in consciousness with a higher source.

Once you've been recognized for your outstanding abilities, others may boost you into a position of influence. Through winning the trust of others, you can generate clear new directions for a group, company, or government. Your altruistic spirit may stimulate you to champion causes for those who are in need. However, you may also find yourself in positions of notoriety which can damage your efforts if your personal actions have offended the sensibilities of society.

Because you possess the power of vision, you may feel very lonely stepping into directions that are foreign or uncomfortable for others. The future is quite real for you, and you can create ways to make that future brighter for the generations that follow.

FAMOUS AQUARIANS: Hank Aaron; Alfred Adler; Alan Alda; Helen Gurley Brown; Alice Cooper; Charles Darwin; James Dean; Charles Dickens; Hugh Downs; Betty Friedan; Rick James; Jack Lemmon; Charles Lindbergh; Paul Newman; Ronald Reagan; Burt Reynolds

THE YEAR AHEAD FOR AQUARIUS

Through consistent focus on your goals and support of your own ideals, you may find this year to be one of landmark significance in your personal and professional growth. You're clearing away the barrier of others' expectations in favor of finding your own path toward accomplishment. Responsibilities cannot always be chosen, but you may find it easier to accept those which are required of you. Many of the changes in the world around you can create options you had not previously considered. But you can also instigate your own changes which result in exceptional rewards for your efforts.

Many of the processes which spur you to bring changes are a result of a shift in consciousness. Your inner experiences can become a rich source of inspiration and hope, and it is through an awakening to a different view of your inner self that you find the courage to make the external changes you desire. The conjunction of Uranus and Neptune stimulates wide-ranging changes politically and economically during 1993. But your experience of letting go of the outworn or repressive attitudes from your past signifies the personal impact you feel from this energy. Many of the structures that once supported your lifestyle may no longer be functioning, or you may find that you no longer need them. It's tempting to use past support systems as a crutch, but the challenge now is to walk with freedom and confidence under your own support.

The Solar Eclipses of the year provide an interesting backdrop, since you're moving into a greater awareness of the importance of building a firm foundation through your creative efforts. Become aware of those whom you hold as mentors, since you may find that your own path may be obscured by holding on to their image as the only way to accomplish your aims. Or, you may feel that you cannot fully express your individuality without dishonoring their teaching. You can still keep these individuals in a place of honor and respect, but not to the exclusion of your own personal truth. You're also beginning to see your family and roots in a different light, and may be formulating your own structure for security from the fragments of your past. There is a powerful dynamic operating which may bring strong images into your dreams, but can also generate exceptional messages from your everyday existence. Watch for the signals that confirm the directions you're choosing.

Jupiter's cycle in Libra stimulates tremendous hope for you this year. Your horizons are opening to broader views, and you may feel that you need to reach out and ask more from life. Travel, study, writing and sharing ideas can bring satisfaction and may also give you the impetus you need to expand your career. Your confidence can be helpful in stabilizing your long-range goals. But in asking more from the Universe, remain grateful for your gifts. You can build on this strong foundation, but need to avoid taking unnecessary advantage of your good fortune through waste or disregard of others.

Chiron's transit in 1993 challenges you to become more aware of the way you relate to others. You may discover that you've left yourself open to psychological injury through your old pattern of relating. If you've had problems with co-dependency issues, these become apparent to you, giving you a chance to recover from this form of self-abuse. There's a tendency to become either repelled by others who are "wounded" or hypnotically drawn to them during this cycle. It may be time to reach out and help. But you cannot be of service if you're compromising your own needs in favor of the desires of another. True altruism is rare, since motivations are often more self-serving than restorative. But if you do hear the call to help, be honest about the reasons behind your actions.

If you were born from January 20th-24th, you're in a good position to build on your previously established circumstances. The responsibilities you've taken on during the last two years may be operating more smoothly. Use this year to extend your special talents and develop the skills and contacts necessary to take advantage of your best attributes. Take careful steps forward during the summer months, when you may need to reorganize or shift your focus. Your greatest challenge to your commitment may arrive this fall, when Jupiter's square to your Sun tempts you to overextend.

If you were born from January 25th-29th you're in a positive cycle of expansion and growth from April through August. These are excellent months to teach, write or travel. Jupiter's trine to your Sun can bring the blessing of contentment, but you may also feel a lack of motivation to move forward. By taking advantage of this time and reaching beyond your previous limitations, you can make significant headway in realizing your goals and achieving success.

For those born from January 27th-February 4th, this year marks a period of consistent self-focus. Although you have made important choices in the past, you may not feel that you have to take any definitive steps to make changes in your sense of self. The lack of outside interference may be a welcome relief after several years of questioning and conflict. But if you utilized the energy of Saturn's transit last year to stabilize, then you can enjoy calmer waters during 1993.

If you were born from February 5th-11th, you're feeling some internal friction, and may feel like it's time to do some inner housecleaning. This can be a time of definitive stability in your work and sense of self while Saturn completes its conjunction to your Sun. But you're experiencing the jolt of energy from Uranus and Neptune cycling in semi-sextile to your Sun. Many of your unconscious mechanisms may be more apparent to you now, making this an excellent time for psychological analysis or other forms of inner work. But you cannot remain comfortable simply staying on an interior level. You need to find an outlet which expresses your newly found sense of freedom. It's time to try your wings, but not from heights that would inhibit your first steps. Working from surroundings which feel familiar or comfortable will give you the confidence to take a different approach. Begin at an inner level, visualizing the effect of the changes you're considering before you actualize them. Once you've entered your new environment, your old support systems may simply inhibit your efforts. By releasing the things from the past you no longer need, this can be a time to inner joy and strong accomplishment.

For those born from February 10th-20th, this year marks a period of powerful completion and exceptional

transformational change. You're experiencing the stabilization and challenge of Saturn conjuncting your Sun, but
you're also feeling the tension from Pluto's square to your
Sun if you were born from February 11th-17th. At no other
time in your life have you felt such a need to break free and
become your true self. And you're facing fears and feelings
which have been such long-time companions that you
may not have recognized their negative effects. Relationships, especially with parents and authorities, can be exceedingly frustrating. You can no longer satisfy another's
demands if they mean compromising your integrity or inhibiting your true creative self-expression. The most difficult aspect of this cycle is the sense of vulnerability you
may feel. You're looking at the reflection of your life and
facing yourself squarely. You may not like what you see.
But you may also find that you prefer the image of your
true self to the image you've maintained for too long.

This cycle challenges you to become completely honest
with yourself. You're learning to examine your motivations and answer only to the desires which take you into
positive evolutionary change. Your health may become an
issue if you've ignored your physical needs. But if you've
been caring for yourself, then this can be the time when solutions to chronic problems emerge, allowing you greater
freedom and stronger vitality. Not only are you taking on
greater responsibilities during this period, but you're also
eliminating the liabilities which have kept you from reaching your goals. Old patterns in relationships that have
compromised your needs may no longer work, since
you're becoming more honest about what you will or will
not do to maintain. Circumstances which are no longer
useful to your growth are dying, and you're reaching an
end to those situations. From an emotional standpoint,
this can be a period of grieving for the losses. Even though
you may be able to see the positive reasons for endings, a
process of grief is likely to accompany the change. By acknowledging this process and making space to let go, this
can be a period of exceptional healing, restoration and rebirth.

TOOLS TO MAKE A DIFFERENCE: To facilitate the
changes you're experiencing, take time for yourself. The
cycles this year can be highly opportunistic, but you're let-

ting go as much as you're moving forward. During such remarkable changes, it's easy to feel your old resistance emerging. To cooperate with yourself, focus on developing greater physical and psychological flexibility. Spend plenty of time stretching in balance to the time you spend building strength. Learn techniques that will bring a sense of inner calm, such as t'ai chi, breema, yoga or chi gong.

Use substances with which you have a special affinity to bring a greater sense of calm. Take time to soak in the negative ions from the ocean, or at least manufacture them in your environment through an ion generator or humidifier if you can't get close to the ocean. Your tendency to be in touch with technology more than nature can be detrimental this year, and time spent in natural surroundings can revitalize and inspire you. Stand barefoot in the grass, and walk in the woods. Listening to songbirds helps your spirits soar.

Wear your colors in the purple to violet spectrum to help you contain your creative energy when you feel scattered. At least a touch of these colors in your personal environment can be helpful. You may also enjoy cultivating your birth flower, the orchid. Paintings of orchids can also be inspiring, but there is very little to compare with the velvet luster of the real thing! You're also strongly attuned to the fragrance of vanilla, and may enjoy inhaling this aroma in potpourri (or in the kitchen!). The energy of amethyst can also be healing for you, and may be used in body therapies or worn as jewelry to help you maintain a sense of inner calm when everything around you is changing. During your periods of contemplation, envision traveling in a small space craft toward Earth. Upon landing, you carefully open the hatch and peer out at the environment. Carefully observe what you see. Step out onto the surface, becoming aware of what you feel around you. Know that you bring with you a special gift of objective awareness. When you return to your normal waking consciousness, remember the keen awareness you felt during your visualization. Keep your senses and consciousness open to new and inspiring information from the world around you.

AFFIRMATION FOR THE YEAR: "My heart is open to joy!"

ACTION TABLES FOR AQUARIUS

These dates reflect the best (but not the *only*) times for success and ease in these activities according to your Sun Sign.

Change Residence	Apr. 26-May 9
Request a Raise	Feb. 10
Begin a Course of Study	Apr. 10, Oct. 4-5
Visit a Doctor	Jan. 2-20; June 2-Aug. 9
Start a Diet	Jan. 7-8; Feb. 3-4; Mar. 3-4, 30-31; Apr. 26-27; May 24-25; June 20-21; July 17-18; Aug. 14-15; Sept. 10-11; Oct. 7-8; Nov. 4-5; Dec. 1-2, 28-29
Begin a Romance	May 21, June 19
Join a Club	Dec. 13
Seek Employment	June 2-Aug. 9; Oct. 1-Dec. 6
Take a Vacation	Jan. 13-14; Feb. 9-10; Mar. 9-10; Apr. 5-6; May 3-4, 30-31; June 26-27; July 24-25; Aug. 20-21; Sept. 16-17; Oct. 14-15; Nov. 10-11; Dec. 7-9
Change Your Wardrobe	May 18-June 1
End a Relationship	Feb. 6-7
Seek Professional Advice	Jan. 9-10; Feb. 5-6; Mar. 5-6; Apr. 1-2, 29-30; May 26-27; June 22-23; July 19-20; Aug. 16-17; Sept. 12-13; Oct. 10-11; Nov. 6-7; Dec. 3-4, 30-31
Have a Makeover	Jan. 22
Obtain a Loan	Jan. 11-12; Feb. 8; Mar. 7-8; Apr. 3-4; May 1-2, 28-29; June 24-25; July 21-22; Aug. 18-19; Sept. 14-15; Oct. 12-13; Nov. 8-9; Dec. 5-6

AQUARIUS/JANUARY

PRIMARY FOCUS

Keeping your job confined to the work day may be difficult, although the extra time should pay off later on.

HEALTH AND FITNESS

Watch your health near the Full Moon on the 8th, when you're tempted to burn the candle at both ends. Balance your activity with adequate relaxation and recreation.

ROMANCE AND RELATIONSHIPS

The road to romance is rocky unless you're open about your inner feelings. Ghosts from the past can appear in the form of guilt over enjoying your present circumstances. You're feeling more confident about accepting your own worth, and can use this improved self-concept to enhance a love relationship or attract a new love. Demands from work can interfere with romance from the 5th-12th. It may be easier to make connections with others after the New Moon in Aquarius on the 22nd. A short trip on the 27th-28th can enliven a romance.

FINANCE AND CAREER

Unreliability from co-workers or those under your supervision can delay the accomplishment of your aims. Avoid complications by looking into complaints before they lead to negative confrontation. Your willingness to look for novel solutions can lead to a surprising reward midmonth. Plan meetings, conferences or special presentations after the 22nd, when you're in a good position to provide succinct, effective ideas for improvement or change.

OPPORTUNITY OF THE MONTH

Amplify your assets on the 22nd and 23rd, concentrating on getting things moving. Attend to details later on.

Rewarding Days: 1, 5, 6, 13, 18, 22, 23, 24, 28
Challenging Days: 2, 3, 4, 9, 10, 11, 15, 16, 30, 31

AFFIRMATION FOR THE MONTH

"I enjoy my work."

AQUARIUS/FEBRUARY

PRIMARY FOCUS

Take in the larger picture this month. Your perspective can give you the insights you need to instigate major new programs or innovations.

HEALTH AND FITNESS

Learning more about your health may include taking in a class or some form of instruction about your special needs. Stay centered.

ROMANCE AND RELATIONSHIPS

Stubborn attitudes inhibit open communication early in the month. A difference of opinion is not sufficient reason to limit a relationship, but if you're looking for an excuse, it may give you a way out. The Full Moon on the 6th marks a time of inflexibility, although the value of listening as a form of communication becomes apparent! Explore your spiritual viewpoints on the 10th and 11th to expose a common bond. Talking with a friend midmonth helps you gain objectivity, but allow space for a romantic rendezvous on the 24th-25th. Take the time to make room for the future.

FINANCE AND CAREER

Monetary issues become increasingly important this month, when the details of your finances can get lost in the everyday shuffle. Although you may find better ways to use your resources, avoid taking risks before you've investigated. Business travel, meetings or conferences fare nicely this month, although you are becoming more keenly aware of the competition. Use your contacts to form a positive network of support. Together you can open more doors.

OPPORTUNITY OF THE MONTH

Your optimistic attitude can be influential on the 24th, when new solutions to old problems are the only answer.

Rewarding Days: 1, 2, 10, 11, 14, 15, 19, 20, 24, 25
Challenging Days: 4, 5, 6, 7, 12, 13, 17, 26, 27

AFFIRMATION FOR THE MONTH

"I clearly communicate my ideas."

AQUARIUS/MARCH

PRIMARY FOCUS

Establishing stronger links with your support network in your career helps to assure more consistent success this month. Pay attention to the details in money matters.

HEALTH AND FITNESS

Job stress can undermine your vitality if you fail to allow time to rejuvenate. Schedule changes are likely to upset your routine.

ROMANCE AND RELATIONSHIPS

Self-expression flows with greater ease, helping you to smooth over the rough spots in a relationship. But you may have questions about the validity of your commitment, and are likely to view your partner from a different perspective. Instead of escaping the pressure, take a look at the real needs that propel you toward particular patterns in your love life. Whether single or attached, you may meet someone who seems to exemplify your ideals. Sexual honesty allows deeper bonding during the Full Moon on the 8th. You're ready to try a fresh approach to intimacy after the 23rd.

FINANCE AND CAREER

With Mercury retrograde until the 22nd, you need to keep a closer watch on your finances. It's easy to overlook the fine print, which can leave you feeling low when you have to pay the price later on. Travel can carry hidden costs from the 1st-20th, and may also bring complications into business deals. Be wary of the quick fix deal the week of the 7th, since crucial data is likely to be "lost" until it's too late to take action. Stay flexible on the 19th-20th.

OPPORTUNITY OF THE MONTH

Postpone major agreements until after the New Moon on the 23rd, when you have a much better perspective on your options.

Rewarding Days: 1, 2, 9, 13, 18, 23, 24, 28, 29
Challenging Days: 3, 4, 5, 6, 11, 12, 17, 19, 20, 25, 26

AFFIRMATION FOR THE MONTH

"I am honest with myself."

AQUARIUS/APRIL

PRIMARY FOCUS

Hopeful signs of progress emerge, but are only workable if you expend the effort to take advantage of the opportunities. Communication and travel are key elements in your success now.

HEALTH AND FITNESS

Emotional stress resulting from the demands of others grows stronger this month. Maintain your focus, and pay special attention to your need for time alone.

ROMANCE AND RELATIONSHIPS

Changing attitudes about your needs in a relationship can result in direct confrontation with your partner. It's easier to talk about your feelings near the Full Moon on the 6th, when a sense of fairness overrides pure selfishness. Be aware of the effect old emotional injury plays in your responses. Your tendency may be to get away from the pressure of repairing an emotional wound the week of the 4th. Inner insight after the 24th stimulates a different approach, resulting in an increased openness to receiving love.

FINANCE AND CAREER

Working behind the scenes to renovate or repair problems at work gives you the leading edge early in the month. Jealousy from co-workers can emerge from the 1st-13th, and can create problems unless you go through proper channels. You're in a good position to negotiate changes on the 15th, but still have some pressing issues from the past. Network, attend meetings and correspond with those who can help you make a difference.

OPPORTUNITY OF THE MONTH

Schedule important meetings or presentations for the 19th, when you're in a good position to wield a positive influence.

Rewarding Days: 6, 10, 14, 15, 19, 20, 24, 25
Challenging Days: 1, 2, 7, 8, 22, 23, 29, 30

AFFIRMATION FOR THE MONTH

"I am an insightful communicator."

AQUARIUS/MAY

PRIMARY FOCUS

Relationships with others take on greater significance. Ego conflicts and competitive urges ruffle feathers at work and at home. You're ready for broader horizons.

HEALTH AND FITNESS

Channel increased physical energy into heightened activity levels, since you'll feel frustrated and uneasy if you try to contain it.

ROMANCE AND RELATIONSHIPS

Open conflict with a partner can clear the air, but watch a tendency to drag in debris from the past from the Full Moon on the 5th until the 18th. If home and family issues arise, deal with them directly instead of projecting them onto an unsuspecting partner or lover! Your insights are more clear during the Solar Eclipse on the 21st, when you may see your needs in a different light. Your creative urges are strong, and need an outlet for expression. New love blossoms, or an existing love gains momentum after the 23rd.

FINANCE AND CAREER

Although the pressure to stay in the game continues to mount, your persistence does finally pay off after the 21st. Until then, watch out for power plays from your competitors and be alert to communication problems with those who work under your supervision. It's time to use the reorganization of your business to your advantage, and get rid of those things which are not producing. Bring in new energy on the 22nd to balance these changes.

OPPORTUNITY OF THE MONTH

A time of introspection during the Sun's Eclipse on the 21st can give you the insight you need to create something truly unique.

Rewarding Days: 3, 4, 7, 8, 12, 17, 21, 22, 23, 30, 31
Challenging Days: 5, 6, 10, 19, 20, 26, 27

AFFIRMATION FOR THE MONTH

"My words and actions are guided by Divine Wisdom."

AQUARIUS/JUNE

PRIMARY FOCUS

Inner conflict arises, since you're wanting to immerse in creative activity, but other people seem to have "plans" for you.

HEALTH AND FITNESS

Learn better ways to take care of your self. Enroll in a fitness class, subscribe to informative publications, and make a commitment to yourself to stay healthy.

ROMANCE AND RELATIONSHIPS

Open turmoil with a partner can lead to a break in the relationship unless you're consistently honest about your needs and feelings. Concentrate on the things you enjoy about one another during the Lunar Eclipse on the 4th, and watch a tendency to compare your needs with another's situation. A parent may be pressuring you to make changes or take actions you feel to be inappropriate from the 6th-14th. Your perspective is much clearer during the New Moon on the 19th. Stay open to the miracle of love.

FINANCE AND CAREER

Although this is a time when your individual effort is important, you may be called upon to get involved in so-cial situations which take time away from your special projects. An assertive approach to the things you know to be important can make a difference the week of the 6th, but be sure your actions will not backfire. Surprising change the week of the 13th can disrupt your work schedule, but may actually provide the basis for better effort. Pay atten-tion to details to avoid being saddled with extra work.

OPPORTUNITY OF THE MONTH

Changes on the 18th may provide an unexpected chance for you to step into the limelight on the 19th. Be pre-pared.

Rewarding Days: 3, 4, 8, 9, 13, 18, 19, 26, 27
Challenging Days: 1, 2, 6, 14, 15, 16, 22, 23, 29, 30

AFFIRMATION FOR THE MONTH

"I trust my Higher Self."

AQUARIUS/JULY

PRIMARY FOCUS

Take a careful look at your finances, especially in the area of insurance and taxes. You may find that you're paying too much!

HEALTH AND FITNESS

A direct approach to any chronic or sensitive physical problems can uncover the underlying cause. Be comprehensive.

ROMANCE AND RELATIONSHIPS

If you've been dissatisfied with your sex life, this may be the month you come to terms with what you're really wanting. Fearful attitudes which are based on old trauma can be dealt with directly. And those feelings which stem from unfounded fears can be explored for their roots. Take a look inside through meditation or time alone during the Full Moon on the 3rd. Talk about your needs and feeling with your partner after the 6th, and plan a romantic interlude for the 15th-16th. Give yourself time to adjust.

FINANCE AND CAREER

Misunderstandings with co-workers or those under your supervision can escalate this month. Although Mercury completes a retrograde cycle on the 25th, communication difficulties are likely to continue all month. Mechanical breakdowns can be problematical after the 18th, but trouble-shooting exposes the riddle. Make an effort to stay on top of your paperwork and complete projects that have been dragging. Jointly-held finances or property can be an issue, and you may need to put some extra money into a creative project. Set forth a plan that satisfies your partner.

OPPORTUNITY OF THE MONTH

This is the time to get to the core of old issues. Take an honest look at yourself and find ways to improve your life.

Rewarding Days: 1, 2, 5, 6, 10, 15, 24, 28, 29
Challenging Days: 4, 12, 13, 14, 19, 20, 26, 27

AFFIRMATION FOR THE MONTH

"I am healthy, strong and powerful."

AQUARIUS/AUGUST

PRIMARY FOCUS
Cooperative efforts can be demanding, but you can also benefit from the resources of others now. Look for ways to expand your career horizons.

HEALTH AND FITNESS
General vitality levels improve after the 12th. Take mini-vacations midmonth. Spend time outdoors as much as possible.

ROMANCE AND RELATIONSHIPS
Complicated circumstances may make it difficult to have the quality time you want with your sweetie until after the 13th. But try to spend some time together during the Full Moon on the 2nd. If you're single, this is a good time to be around other people who share your viewpoints. You're in the process of some powerful internal changes which can affect your desires in relationship. By focusing on your spiritual aims, you may reach a consensus. Stubborn attitudes create delays the week of the 15th, and you're more clear about your needs after the New Moon on the 17th.

FINANCE AND CAREER
Clear up tax problems before the 10th. If you're involved in legal disputes, you may uncover the background information you've needed early in the month. Direct confrontation may force you to take a stand, but you can withstand the pressure and may even turn the tables the week of the 15th. Avoid alienating those who can support your position, since their energy can make the difference between success and defeat.

OPPORTUNITY OF THE MONTH
Sudden changes on the 19th can lead to unusual opportunities on the 20th-21st. Be aware of the long-term obligations involved.

Rewarding Days: 2, 6, 7, 11, 12, 20, 21, 24, 25, 29
Challenging Days: 3, 9, 10, 16, 17, 22, 23, 30

AFFIRMATION FOR THE MONTH
"I am honest with myself about my needs."

AQUARIUS/SEPTEMBER

PRIMARY FOCUS

Travel and education are strongly emphasized. It's a great time to turn around a slow-moving project or make contact with an influential individual by getting beyond your own backyard.

HEALTH AND FITNESS

If you can't take a vacation, then take on an attitude of joy in your work. Celebrate life. Know that you deserve to be happy.

ROMANCE AND RELATIONSHIPS

Any relationship can be transformed through focusing on the higher aspects of your connection with one another. But a partnership is especially open to improvement now. If you're involved in a love relationship and have not made a commitment, then consider the reasons why you're avoiding it. It's time to take action to either move forward or break away by the New Moon on the 15th. A new love or surprising developments in an existing love relationship brings sparkle into your life now. Enjoy it!

FINANCE AND CAREER

Your vision is more clear and you're ready to explore a broader horizon in your career. It's a great time to advertise, make presentations, attend conferences or network within your community. Your influence and originality carry you into arenas that can sustain for a long time to come, but you must be willing to do the work involved. A partner proves to be highly beneficial this month, but watch a tendency to take them for granted from the 12th-18th. Such an attitude can be highly detrimental to your success.

OPPORTUNITY OF THE MONTH

The Full Moon on the 30th marks a time of strong success, and is an excellent time for travel, teaching or writing.

Rewarding Days: 3, 8, 9, 16, 17, 20, 21, 25, 26, 30
Challenging Days: 1, 5, 6, 12, 13, 18, 19

AFFIRMATION FOR THE MONTH

"I am attuned to my Higher Self."

AQUARIUS/OCTOBER

PRIMARY FOCUS
Adopting an assertive attitude in your career is almost inevitable, but be careful to avoid stepping on the wrong toes.

HEALTH AND FITNESS
It's easy to push yourself beyond your normal limitations, which can result in over-tiredness. Balance activity and relaxation.

ROMANCE AND RELATIONSHIPS
Family and parental pressures may allow little time in your life for romance, but you may feel that you should be the one calling the shots. There are some fundamental issues emerging now, and you are in no mood to allow someone else to dictate the circumstance for your personal happiness. Psychologically, this is a period of deep inner insight. It may be time to release those old messages and move into greater control of your own destiny. The situation improves near the New Moon on the 15th, when your higher ideals offer a better way to cope with dissent.

FINANCE AND CAREER
Your drive to succeed can put you shoulder to shoulder with the top brass. You can deal with them effectively once you realize that you're all part of the human race. But there can also be open confrontation from others who see you as a threat to their own power. Your attitude will make the difference in the outcome. A reorganization in your business early in the month can result in a shake-up in the power base by the 25th. Be sure you really want to stick around. You might be ready to make a break.

OPPORTUNITY OF THE MONTH
You're in the best position for negotiating or taking a stand on the 15th. But you'll probably not find complete agreement.

Rewarding Days: 1, 5, 6, 14, 15, 18, 19, 22, 27, 28
Challenging Days: 2, 3, 9, 10, 11, 16, 17, 25, 30, 31

AFFIRMATION FOR THE MONTH
"I am filled with the power of Divine Love."

AQUARIUS/NOVEMBER

PRIMARY FOCUS
Your ambitious drive to get your career moving in the direction you desire gains momentum. Stay centered during the power plays.

HEALTH AND FITNESS
Increased muscular tension early in the month is likely to be the result of job stress. Plan to get involved in a fitness class or team sport after the 10th. The elevated activity will feel great.

ROMANCE AND RELATIONSHIPS
Review the reasons for your drive to the top, since an imbalance between work and your love life can create major problems. An honest look at your feelings about your parents is stimulated by the Solar Eclipse on the 13th. Not only are you experiencing deeper feelings about them, but you're getting a clear picture of the way your early conditioning is still playing a part in your life. Personal satisfaction and support from friends is emphasized by the Lunar Eclipse on the 29th. Be aware that you don't have to choose one over the other!

FINANCE AND CAREER
While Mercury continues its retrograde through the 14th you may find it difficult to finalize career plans. The difficulty in making connections with the top brass can be a blessing in disguise, since the power plays at work may involve a complete reorganization. Wait for the dust to settle before you make your final move. Target the 23rd-30th for special conferences and presentations.

OPPORTUNITY OF THE MONTH
A conservative approach to changing the system works to your benefit on the 29th-30th. You can create a revolution later.

Rewarding Days: 1, 2, 10, 11, 14, 15, 19, 20, 24, 29, 30
Challenging Days: 4, 5, 6, 7, 12, 13, 26, 27

AFFIRMATION FOR THE MONTH
"I am driven by the desire to serve my Highest Needs."

AQUARIUS/DECEMBER

PRIMARY FOCUS

Reward for your career efforts can result in recognition and advancement. It's time to make new long-range plans.

HEALTH AND FITNESS

Physical vitality improves. Consistent activity keeps you strong early in the month. But after the 19th you'll need to pull in the oars and coast during the holidays.

ROMANCE AND RELATIONSHIPS

Friends and those who share your ideals and interests play a powerful role now. Plan a get-together on the 8th, 9th, 12th, 16th 17th, or 26th. The New Moon on the 13th emphasizes a different direction in a friendship, and can mark a good time to evaluate the ways you're expressing unconditional love to those around you. A love relationship benefits from better communication, and can be enhanced by getting outside your normal frame of reference. You may decide to spend time alone during the Full Moon on the 28th, since contemplation and reflection bring greater inner harmony.

FINANCE AND CAREER

Listening and gathering information may serve you better from the 1st-5th than trying to change the opinions of those who are resistant. Openness to new ideas is more promising from the 7th-23rd. Your optimistic attitude can lead to unnecessary spending this month, when a budget would be a good idea. Travel expenses may fit into your business budget if you plan ahead. Look into your financial records after the 27th to expose waste and excess.

OPPORTUNITY OF THE MONTH

Initiate an important project on the 13th, when you're ready to get moving on a unique plan for success.

Rewarding Days: 8, 9, 12, 13, 16, 17, 21, 22, 26, 27
Challenging Days: 3, 4, 6, 10, 11, 15, 23, 24, 30, 31

AFFIRMATION FOR THE MONTH

"I am confident in my ability to create the life I desire."

PISCES
THE FISHES

February 20 to March 21

Element: Water
Quality: Mutable
Polarity: Feminine/Yin
Planetary Ruler: Neptune
Meditation: "Surrendering to the heart of Divine Compassion"
Gemstone: Aquamarine
Power Stones: Bloodstone, tourmaline, amethyst, sugilite
Anatomy: Feet, lymphatic system
Key Phrase: I believe

Glyph: Two fish tied together, swimming in opposite directions
Colors: Violet, sea green
Animal: Dolphin, whale, fish
Myths/Legends: Aphrodite, Buddha, Jesus of Nazareth
House Association: Twelfth
Opposite Sign: Virgo
Flower: Water lily
Key Word: Transcendence

Positive Expression:
Idealistic
Visionary
Compassionate
Poetic
Empathetic
Idealistic
Impressionable
Tenderhearted
Imaginative

Misuse of Energy:
Susceptible
Confused
Addictive
Escapist
Victimized
Self-deceptive
Co-dependent
Unconscious

PISCES

YOUR EGO'S STRENGTHS AND WEAKNESSES:
Your sensitivity and imagination add a touch of the mystical to your personality. Through your visionary awareness, you sense the possibilities, and have tremendous faith in your perceptions. You're the chameleon of the zodiac, constantly adapting to the energy around you. The subtle plane of vibration is real for you, and extends to your enjoyment of music and the arts. The magic of sunrise, the light in the eyes of a child and the tender touch of love inspire your faith in the continual process of life.

Where there is despair, you can bring compassion and calm. The cries of suffering pull at your heart, and may draw you to reach out to those less fortunate. But you can become victimized by illusion or deception, and must safeguard against unscrupulous individuals who would misuse your tenderheartedness. You can be unassuming, and may prefer a quiet life or may even withdraw into seclusion. To stay healthy, you must carefully scrutinize the substances your put into your body. You may feel drawn to escape from the heaviness of the physical plane, but can harm yourself in the process if you lose touch with reality. You can fall prey to addiction, whether in the form of substances or relationships.

Despite occasional feelings of vulnerability, you can always imagine different possibilities. Your faith in your beliefs is strong, and often carries you through when others are trapped in their own despondency. Through learning when to surrender to a Higher Source, you can become a vehicle for divine compassion and transcendent inspiration. Forever seeking to return to your spiritual home, you can easily connect with that place inside yourself through developing compassion for yourself and for others.

YOUR CAREER DEVELOPMENT: For you, the ambition which drives so many to succeed in the world may not be a strong incentive. You're seeking to express your vision of life through your career and need an open arena for your talents and imagination. Your gift of attuning to the universal or collective aspects of life can aid your success in the businesses of advertising, media or movie-making. But you may also be a highly talented artist, musician, actor, photographer or dancer. Fashion design, make-up artistry or hairdressing can be excellent outlets.

Bringing beauty into environments may draw you to work in landscape design, the floral industry or interior design. Or you may have a taste for the restaurant business. Counseling, social work, medicine or the ministry can be outlets for your desire to uplift the human spirit. An attunement to animals may inspire you to seek a career focusing on their needs. Whatever your choices, you're happiest when you're staying in the flow.

YOUR APPROACH TO ROMANCE: You're right at home in the arms of someone you love, experiencing the full fragrance and delight of romance. You may seek a soul mate through your relationships, and can be easily deceived in affairs of the heart. Your openness and trust may not always be met by another who understands your depth. But you continue to seek the enchantment of love, and can create a truly magical space into which you and your truelove retreat from the hardships of the outside world.

Although you may be strongly attracted to your opposite sign, Virgo, you may lose your fascination amidst all the necessary details! You're most emotionally at ease with the Water signs—Cancer, Scorpio and Pisces. Another Piscean understands your special dreams and desires and will share your appreciation for the quiet beauty of life. You're comfortable opening to your creativity with Cancer, and enjoy the feeling of care you receive. Scorpio's intense sensuality inspires your romantic fantasies.

Relating to Aries will stimulate, but you may feel frustrated by their abrasive nature. Taurus' inherent steadfastness and sensual earthiness are highly appealing. Gemini's wit may escape you, although you may enjoy their flexibility. Leo may want all the attention, even though you share a love of entertainment.

Libra's elegance and charm are interesting, but you may not be able to meet their requirements for perfection. Sagittarius' spiritual yearning inspires you, even though you may not see much of one another. Capricorn's stability feels good, but you can fall victim to being used. And a friendship with Aquarius may be a better choice than romance, since they can be difficult to reach, even when you use your imagination!

YOUR USE OF POWER: You can feel the power from the Source flowing through you, surrendering to the powerful natural rhythms of the cycles of life. That energy which sustains and inspires magnetically draws you into the power of Unity with all life. You are becoming an instrument of divine love, which conceives and nourishes life itself.

Staying in the flow of the ocean of creativity keeps you charged with vitality, helping you become a radiant vision of faith and hope. To strengthen your link with Divine Love, you may practice a spiritual path which requires great devotion. Sometimes, it's easy to lose yourself and your direction in this release. You're realizing that the true spiritual teacher is within you. Focusing your energy will aid you in finding true illumination.

Touching the Source, you can be empowered to return to the physical plane to share this transcendent experience with others. You can become a vehicle for Divine Compassion, acting through the power of All that Is to help heal the pain of the world.

FAMOUS PISCEANS: Mario Andretti; Jon Bon Jovi; Johnny Cash; Cyd Charisse; Elizabeth Barrett Browning; Mikhail Gorbachev; Rex Harrison; Jack Kerouac; Michaelangelo; Chuck Norris; Rudolph Nureyev; Ben (Bugsy) Segal; Dinah Shore; John Steinbeck

THE YEAR AHEAD FOR PISCES

While you're completing many of your previous commitments, you're also finding hope for a brighter future during 1993. You're getting in touch with your foundations, evaluating the motivations that have driven you to fulfill your desires. You're learning better ways to care for yourself, and can strengthen your vitality by dedicating more time to the fulfillment of your creative abilities. But you're also challenged to release the things you don't need anymore, since hanging onto old baggage will only slow your progress.

The Uranus-Neptune conjunction and Saturn-Pluto square, which stimulate major changes in the outside world during 1993 can have a beneficial effect upon your life. Although your primary obligation is to yourself, you may also find more effective ways to make a difference in your community. Through associations with others who share your ideals, you can go a long way toward accomplishing what may seem impossible to those who are less inspired. You're seeing the need to make room for a greater variety of people and life experiences, and, as a result, may meet some inspiring new friends this year. You're also allowing more flexibility in your plans for future growth, and can see the importance of looking at different pathways in your life journey. In many ways, the changes you're experiencing are helping you crystallize your dreams.

Jupiter's cycle in Libra, which lasts until November 10th, can generate a series of temptations. Even though you may know deep within your heart that you need to let go of some old habits or unnecessary attachments, you can find it difficult to walk away completely. However, you're experiencing a powerful period of support from the efforts and energy of others, and can use this cycle to give you a strong boost. Evaluate to be sure you're working to your own best advantage within the system, especially in financial matters. But within the context of this cycle lies a trap: it's the boundary between the miraculous and the addictive. You may not be able to hold onto all the people or resources that manifest, because their purpose is likely to be one of setting the stage for greater awareness. You're realizing values that have been there all along. Once Jupiter moves into Scorpio in November you may find it easier to utilize what you've learned. But until then, keep an honest, open heart and shine the light of truth before you.

The Solar Eclipses bring an emphasis to your need to understand more about your consciousness, particularly your higher mind. This link with the Source of all Wisdom is always there, but sometimes you can forget how to use it! Concentrate some special energy on finding better ways to commune with your Higher Self. You may also feel drawn toward the classroom, either as a student or teacher. If you have the opportunity, travel can enhance your life this year, but it may take on the essence of a pilgrimage rather than simply a joy ride. The transiting Lunar Nodes draw your attention to your feelings about home and family, but may also stimulate a different feeling about your teachers or mentors. Chiron's cycle during 1993 also marks a period of shifting focus, and beckons you to look at your responses to the demands of others. The purposes served by your relationships need to be evaluated, since you may be asking from others what you are not capable of giving yourself.

If you were born from February 19th–21st, you're feeling the energy of Saturn transiting in conjunction to your Sun this year. This cycle is particularly strong from May through July, but you'll feel it throughout the year. You're gaining a strong sense of what's necessary, and may find that you have to let the more frivolous elements of your life take a lower priority. Taking responsibility for yourself and your actions is one of the best ways to work with this energy effectively. In your work, you may experience advancement, but also have to deal with the accompanying increased duties. If you resent or resist this urge to "grow up," then the time seems to drag and your burdens feel much heavier. But by accepting and choosing those obligations which are in harmony with your higher needs, you'll find many of your life circumstances actually improving. Relationships with family may change, and you may be sharing decisions which previously excluded you. Just as importantly, you're finding ways to let go of carrying burdens that don't actually belong to you. If you've been struggling with co-dependency issues, this can be the year you find the key to your recovery and reclaim your power.

If your birth occurred from February 21st to 27th you're feeling the stimulus to spring into a more highly individualized and imaginative life circumstance. Uranus and Neptune are transiting in semi-square to your Sun, helping your break away from the resistance that has blocked your achievements and personal growth. This can be an exciting time, helping you to launch into a more fulfilling life circumstance. But there are some difficulties which rest in your attachment to the past. You cannot afford to remain stuck in a rut. Your hopes for the future are hanging in the balance, you're the only one who can extract the illusion from the more substantial vision of hope. This is a cycle in which to take action, and is not a time that affords you the luxury of waiting around for something better. You're the creator. Make it better.

If you were born from February 28th-March 6th, you're in the midst of a cycle which does not challenge your sense of identity. The slower-moving planets are not providing the inner dynamic to make across the board changes, since you've already been turning your life upside down! Now's the time to add substance to those changes and extend their influence by using what you've learned. Your time to test the validity of these changes is coming next year, so get your fine-tuning out of the way and be prepared to turn them on with style and confidence.

For those born from March 7th-13th, this can be a year of invigorating and inspiring change. The planets Uranus and Neptune are transiting in sextile to your Sun, bringing an inner sense of confidence and heightened awareness about your unique talents and abilities. You can improve your skills by using them more effectively. If you've been hiding your light, let it shine! Give yourself a positive arena in which to express yourself, which can mean making some changes in your career or even in your relationships. Career shifts which focus on greater room for creative expression are likely to manifest, but you have to choose to change. Getting involved in your community, spending more time with your friends, helps you interface with the people and circumstances that inspire you to realize your dreams. And on the level of intimate relationship, you can experience a new level of freedom and openness. Growth-inhibiting relationships and life circumstances are likely to fade away, leaving a clearer path to self-realization. It's like using wings: not only can you fly with this energy—you can soar above the previous limitations you had accepted for yourself. This is a time of awakening and inspiration. If you use it well, you will learn how to maintain your gifts throughout time.

If you were born from March 13th-19th, you're feeling the power of Pluto's transit in trine to your Sun. Although this is a supportive cycle, it's not an easy one. You're challenged to dig deeper into your essence and emerge whole and powerful. In the process you discover many gifts, but you also find the debris of guilt and fear that has lain in decay at the core of your being. It's time to eliminate these feelings and move into a more positive use of your personal power. If you have an opportunity to influence change, this is the time to take on the role and enjoy it. You can strengthen your position in your community by working to restore and preserve programs or monuments which inspire and help others. Focus on the vital essence which exists in your relationships and eliminate the responses and interactions which undermine achieving the intimacy and passion you need. Healing can occur on all levels—physically, emotionally and spiritually. Cooperate with this energy so it works to your greatest benefit. You're finally dancing with the dragon; just be sure you know where you're planting your feet!

If you were born from March 18th-21st, you're feeling the energy of Saturn transiting in semi-sextile to your Sun. It's time to take steps to stabilize your life circumstances and balance your burdens. By carefully clearing away the things you no longer need, you can make this a year of positive change and greater security. But you may have to leave behind some attitudes that you've carried for a long time. The fog is lifting, and you can see hopeful circumstances ahead. It's up to you to decide if you want to pursue them.

TOOLS TO MAKE A DIFFERENCE: Spend time this year considering your goals. If you've lived without any particular aims, you'll find that clarifying your path gives you tremendous freedom and confidence. Use your imagination to help you envision the circumstances you want to create through your efforts. Work with techniques like creative visualization, affirmations and neuro-linguistic programming to help you shift your consciousness and allow greater abundance into your life.

To facilitate better health, seek out individuals who can help you work with your physical energy through techniques such as acupuncture, Shiatsu or reflexology. You might also enjoy learning about these techniques, and can benefit from using them to help others. A regular pedicure or foot reflexology treatment can be thoroughly relaxing and physically balancing for you. If you work with crystals, use your stones of amethyst, aquamarine, sugilite and tourmaline to help you bring greater peace and inner calm. Keep your body clear of toxins and maintain a more balanced aura by using these stones in conjunction with visualizations that protect and balance your energy.

Your flower, the water lily, is an excellent focus for a meditational mandala. The roots of this flower reach into the waters and mud below the surface, but the leaves and flower rise above the surface. Focus on these concepts during your meditations and become aware of the effect these images have on your sense of inner peace and calm.

During your visualizations, pay attention to everything you feel. Little by little, let go of the physical sensations and focus only on your breath. Open your mind to the vision of the ocean with the sun shining brightly overhead. See yourself sailing in a beautiful, mystical ship. Your sails are fully open, and you can feel the wind at your back. Ahead, on the horizon, is a mountainous island. Once you reach the shore and drop anchor, you see a paradise before you. A sense of calm and confidence surrounds you as you step onto the shore. Spend some time on this island, and ask to discover a hidden secret or gift. Slowly return to your full waking consciousness, balance your energy and remember your gift. Know that it is a key to help protect and guide you along your journey.

AFFIRMATION FOR THE YEAR: "I believe in the power of love."

ACTION TABLES FOR PISCES

These dates reflect the best (but not the *only*) times for success and ease in these activities according to your Sun Sign.

Change Residence	May 18-June 1
Request a Raise	Feb. 21
Begin a Course of Study	Apr. 21-22; Nov. 13
Visit a Doctor	Jan. 21-Feb. 6; Aug. 10-25
Start a Diet	Jan. 9-10; Feb. 6-7;
	Mar. 5-6; Apr. 1-2, 29-30;
	May 26-27; June 22-23;
	July 19-20; Aug. 16-17;
	Sept. 12-13; Oct. 10-11;
	Nov. 6-7; Dec. 3-4, 30-31
Begin a Romance	July 19-20
Join a Club	Dec. 14-15
Seek Employment	Jan. 1-2; Aug. 10-25;
	Dec. 7-25
Take a Vacation	Jan. 15-16; Feb. 12-13;
	Mar. 11-12; Apr. 7-8;
	May 5-6; June 1-2, 28-29;
	July 26-27; Aug. 22-23;
	Sept. 18-19; Oct. 16-17;
	Nov. 12-13; Dec. 10-11
Change Your Wardrobe	June 2-Aug. 9
End a Relationship	Mar. 8-9
Seek Professional Advice	Jan. 11-12; Feb. 7-8;
	Mar. 7-8; Apr. 3-4;
	May 1-2, 28-29; June 24-25;
	July 21-22; Aug. 18-19;
	Sept. 14-15; Oct. 12-13;
	Nov. 8-9; Dec. 5-6
Have a Makeover	Feb. 21-22
Obtain a Loan	Jan. 13-14; Feb. 9-10;
	Mar. 9-10; Apr. 5-6;
	May 3-4, 30-31; June 26-27;
	July 24-25; Aug. 20-21;
	Sept. 16-17; Oct. 14-15;
	Nov. 10-11; Dec. 7-8

PISCES/JANUARY

PRIMARY FOCUS
Begin the new year with an open mind about the best ways to reach your goals. Balance future hopes with realistic actions.

HEALTH AND FITNESS
Staying active this month is easy, but you can be more careless than usual. Use caution when undertaking high risk activities.

ROMANCE AND RELATIONSHIPS
A surprising change in your love life brings hope and accelerates your feelings of passion near the Full Moon on the 8th. An existing and harmonious relationship can gain momentum. You may feel more open toward actualizing your hopes with a new love. Your ability to attract the object of your desires is strong. Be clear and honest, since you're likely to get what you want! This is a good time to experiment, but you're changing your pattern in expressing your needs and may initially feel uncomfortable with your creation. Stay flexible, and talk about your concerns with a trusted friend.

FINANCE AND CAREER
Your business associates may offer you greater respect early in the month. Changes in the bureaucracy at work can open an avenue of opportunity from the 1st-7th, but you can also take advantage of changes after the 22nd. Working behind the scenes after the New Moon on the 22nd may be less complicated than trying to make connections, but you're still in a good position to nail down an agreement from the 25th-31st.

OPPORTUNITY OF THE MONTH
Use this period of enhanced self-esteem to do things that help you feel better about fulfilling your needs. Be open to astonishing changes on the 7th and 8th.

Rewarding Days: 3, 7, 8, 15, 16, 20, 21, 25, 26, 30, 31
Challenging Days: 5, 6, 11, 12, 13, 14, 18, 19, 24, 28

AFFIRMATION FOR THE MONTH
"I listen to my inner voice."

PISCES/FEBRUARY

PRIMARY FOCUS

Although you're feeling more communicative, an attitude of caution about reaching into unexplored territory prevails. Conservative action may overshadow sweeping changes.

HEALTH AND FITNESS

An undercurrent of nervous energy may result from worry over circumstances you feel unable to change. Channel your thoughts into seeking possibilities, and spend some time in natural surroundings.

ROMANCE AND RELATIONSHIPS

You're making adjustments for the unrealistic expectations that have been present in your love relationship. Romance can flourish now, but you need to focus on the way you feel, and maintain an honest projection of those feelings to your partner. Passion runs high from the 3rd-5th, but you may feel more withdrawn during the Full Moon on the 6th. Hopeful changes occur after the New Moon in Pisces on the 21st, when you may be experiencing greater confidence in your choices and expressions of affection.

FINANCE AND CAREER

Set a limit in your spending before you make large purchases or investments, and pay careful attention to your budgetary needs. A conservative attitude pervades your workplace and may overshadow your ability to gain the recognition you deserve for your efforts. Thorough preparation assures better responses after the 21st. Although communication can be strained after the 10th, you're the one who can translate the confusion into opportunity.

OPPORTUNITY OF THE MONTH

The New Moon on the 21st marks a definitive shift in the action. Proceed with your plans, but be patient while momentum builds.

Rewarding Days: 3, 4, 12, 13, 16, 17, 21, 22, 26
Challenging Days: 1, 2, 6, 8, 9, 14, 15, 28

AFFIRMATION FOR THE MONTH

"I use my resources wisely."

PISCES/MARCH

PRIMARY FOCUS
Keep a close watch on the details of your finances, since changes can produce a period of crisis if you're unprepared.

HEALTH AND FITNESS
The temptation to indulge in treats you don't normally experience can create a feeling of sluggish energy. If you increase your calories, increase your activity level, too!

ROMANCE AND RELATIONSHIPS
You're eager to impress your sweetheart, and may feel more like indulging in your favorite pastimes as part of your romantic repartee. Partnerships gain emphasis during the Full Moon on the 8th, when your more equalitarian attitudes will improve any disputes that have emerged. If you're single, you may be thinking about taking the plunge. But be sure you have a clear sense of your motivations before you act, since your priorities in relationship are shifting. Renewing an existing commitment revitalizes, but may not be enough unless there is significant restorative change.

FINANCE AND CAREER
An unexpected development the week of the 7th may led to dismantling the structure of your current job situation. But it's also a time of completion and can be a period of improvement. Mercury's retrograde in Pisces lasts until the 22nd, giving you a chance to repeat a process or review a situation before you decide to give up. Giving yourself or someone else a second chance can make the difference between success and failure.

OPPORTUNITY OF THE MONTH
Take another look at your finances on the 23rd, and move forward to correct or improve your circumstances on the 30th.

Rewarding Days: 3, 4, 11, 12, 16, 20, 21, 25, 30, 31
Challenging Days: 1, 2, 6, 7, 8, 13, 14, 19, 28, 29

AFFIRMATION FOR THE MONTH
"My life is filled with abundance."

PISCES/APRIL

PRIMARY FOCUS
Initiating a network of individuals who support your aims or efforts has long-term benefit. Watch a tendency to underestimate your worth. Appreciate yourself!

HEALTH AND FITNESS
Your nervous system may be working overtime, making it difficult to rest and relax. Concentrate on stretching and breathing.

ROMANCE AND RELATIONSHIPS
Although you may be questioning the worth of a love relationship, you may actually be undermining your ability to enjoy something truly wonderful. Talk about your feelings, or find a way to share a more intimate aspect of yourself with your sweetheart from the 1st to 14th. Getting in touch with your sensual needs near the Full Moon on the 6th may illuminate some of the reasons for your discontent. But after the 21st you're likely to feel more open and confident about your choices in matters of the heart.

FINANCE AND CAREER
Previous financial blunders seem to keep you under pressure. But creative or artistic endeavors offer substantial rewards. Your solutions may rest in your ability to initiate contact with influential individuals. Schedule important conferences or meetings from the 4th-13th. Follow through on launching new projects or programs after the New Moon on the 21st. New insights into improving your financial situation may emerge on the 19th-20th, but use caution before moving into unexplored territory.

OPPORTUNITY OF THE MONTH
Using your imagination invites options that others fail to consider during periods of crisis and change on the 12th-13th.

Rewarding Days: 7, 8, 12, 13, 17, 18, 22, 26, 27
Challenging Days: 2, 3, 4, 6, 10, 11, 20, 24, 25

AFFIRMATION FOR THE MONTH
"My creativity flows from an endless source."

PISCES/MAY

PRIMARY FOCUS

Cooperative effort requires patience, but avoid taking on another's responsibilities. Use this time toward self-improvement.

HEALTH AND FITNESS

It's easy to push beyond your limits, which can lead to fatigue, muscle strain or other forms of irritation. Make adjustments in your schedule for your health regime.

ROMANCE AND RELATIONSHIPS

Contact with a sibling can be rewarding, but unresolved resentment may surface and can lead to open conflict. Getting in touch with your own feelings offers freedom from the pressure to act in a way that's counterproductive to your needs. Travel or long-distance communication near the Full Moon on the 5th draws forth a sense of deeper understanding of your spiritual needs. By the Solar Eclipse on the 21st, you may want to talk about your experiences in order to better understand them. Be wary of sudden infatuation on the 28th. It's probably just a passing fancy!

FINANCE AND CAREER

Unforeseen changes in your plan of action complicate the outcome of your work. Be wary of the actions of others who may try to undermine your position due to their own jealousy. Ignoring any problems will only lead to a weakening of your position and influence. Keep your spending under control, since financial problems can lead to relationship disputes. Carefully examine investment opportunities before taking any action.

OPPORTUNITY OF THE MONTH

Researching details or probing into problems from the 13th-16th can provide insights which lead to career advancement.

Rewarding Days: 5, 6, 9, 10, 14, 15, 19, 24, 25
Challenging Days: 1, 2, 7, 8, 13, 21, 22, 28, 29

AFFIRMATION FOR THE MONTH

"I listen and respond to the needs of others."

PISCES/JUNE

PRIMARY FOCUS
Scattered involvement can create disappointing results. Keep home and work concerns in their proper perspectives.

HEALTH AND FITNESS
You can be easily agitated during this cycle, and need good outlets for your frustration. Ventilate by staying active. Consider taking mini-vacations to alleviate stress.

ROMANCE AND RELATIONSHIPS
Although home and family obligations require more attention early in the month, you can still enjoy them! The Lunar Eclipse on the 4th marks a powerful time of awareness of your roots and family connections. Children can also play an important role, and may offer a spirit of adventure and strong inspiration. Your love life improves after the New Moon on the 19th, and shows particular promise from the 24th-30th. However, unrealistic expectations can lead to disappointment and conflict on the 25th-26th.

FINANCE AND CAREER
Your support network needs some extra attention, and, if properly developed, can be your best outlet for improved career options. working in concert with others can also prove to be lucrative, but be sure you clear up any power struggles or misunderstandings before you get too involved. Watch for power plays from the 9th-14th. An unexpected change in a group or professional association leads you to try something different after the 16th. But there's a delay from the 23rd-26th that gives you time to reevaluate.

OPPORTUNITY OF THE MONTH
Attend meetings, make presentations or network on the 15th-16th to assure business success.

Rewarding Days: 1, 2, 6, 7, 10, 11, 15, 16, 20, 29
Challenging Days: 3, 4, 9, 13, 18, 19, 24, 25

AFFIRMATION FOR THE MONTH
"My words express harmony and hope."

PISCES/JULY

PRIMARY FOCUS

Relationships become a strong area of concentration, but there may be excessive competition or unusual misunderstandings. Be ready to take an approach you've never tried before.

HEALTH AND FITNESS

With Mars transiting in opposition to your Sun, you may feel a bit on edge. Ease tension by staying active and getting fit.

ROMANCE AND RELATIONSHIPS

Directly address and clarify relationship issues. Recall the special times you've shared, and remember the positive aspects before you emphasize the things about which you're dissatisfied. The energy of the Full Moon on the 3rd stimulates an opening of the heart, but can also open the door to air grievances or to be more honest about your feelings. Take time to consider your needs and make a special effort to reconnect during the New Moon on the 19th. This can signal a period of better success in matters of the heart.

FINANCE AND CAREER

Use caution in your investments, avoiding sudden risks. Political actions can disrupt your plans, but be sure you understand the ramifications of any changes before registering your response. While Mercury retrogrades from the 1st-25th you may also find emotions getting in the way of objective decision-making. This period marks a time when the things from the past seem more beneficial than new ideas. But a new idea is just what's needed from the 18th-31st.

OPPORTUNITY OF THE MONTH

Getting back in touch with former associates can lead to an exciting business opportunity on the 3rd, 4th or 31st.

Rewarding Days: 3, 4, 8, 9, 13, 17, 18, 26, 27, 30, 31
Challenging Days: 1, 2, 7, 15, 16, 21, 22, 23, 28, 29

AFFIRMATION FOR THE MONTH

"I trust my creative inspiration."

PISCES/AUGUST

PRIMARY FOCUS
Attention to the tasks and duties involved in your work takes a high priority. Improving your attitude helps you finish the job more quickly.

HEALTH AND FITNESS
Treating symptoms doesn't seem to satisfy your needs. A holistic look at the underlying causes helps resolve physical distress.

ROMANCE AND RELATIONSHIPS
Abrupt circumstances alter the course of a friendship and can affect your love relationship from the 1st-7th, and you may have a change of heart after the 15th. You're ready for something different, and may create turmoil just to break the monotony. Time spent with children or just allowing your inner child to play will break the tension and create more flexibility. Honor your needs for privacy at the New Moon on the 17th, but allow room for those you hold dear to your heart. Accommodate your increased sensitivity during the Full Moon on the 31st by enjoying something magical.

FINANCE AND CAREER
Your work environment may need to undergo renovation or improvement. At the very least, talk over issues or concerns with your co-workers or those under your supervision. Avoiding difficult situations after the 18th will only lead to complex problems later on. Take direct action in financial matters, but try to avoid increasing your debt load. It's a better time to liquidate and simplify your finances. Seek professional advice on major questions.

OPPORTUNITY OF THE MONTH
A change in the decision-making climate improves your options for creative expression on the 4th-5th.

Rewarding Days: 4, 5, 9, 14, 15, 22, 23, 27, 31
Challenging Days: 3, 11, 12, 13, 18, 19, 24, 25

AFFIRMATION FOR THE MONTH
"I am capable, confident and healthy."

PISCES/SEPTEMBER

PRIMARY FOCUS

Relationships take a front seat. Partnerships need extra care, but your work-oriented contacts are also warming. Accept the support and resources of others.

HEALTH AND FITNESS

Improve your health by getting rid of negative habits. Inner awareness helps you achieve healing of both body and soul.

ROMANCE AND RELATIONSHIPS

The difference between intimacy and interacting becomes painfully clear, since you're feeling a strong urge to merge. Examine your motivations as well as what you're projecting onto others. You may be able to experience a more objective contact during the New Moon on the 15th. Sexual issues emerge midmonth, and may be triggered by the realization that you've been holding back. Sudden infatuation can leave you cold, but openly experimenting with a trusted partner can be the beginning of soul-level bonding.

FINANCE AND CAREER

Money matters can get complicated, and there may be some surprises with taxes or insurance. Double-check your obligations, since mistakes can be costly. However, you can benefit from your partner's good fortune, and may also find this a good time to seek out investors in a new enterprise. A tip from a friend or associate from the 12th–24th may give you the insight you need to take advantage of an auspicious investment or career change. Be cautious with your spending near the Full Moon on the 30th.

OPPORTUNITY OF THE MONTH

Contacts with an influential person open the door to your success on the 28th and 29th. Prepare for change.

Rewarding Days: 1, 2, 5, 6, 10, 11, 18, 19, 23, 28, 29
Challenging Days: 4, 8, 9, 14, 15, 20, 21, 30

AFFIRMATION FOR THE MONTH

"I value the support of others."

PISCES/OCTOBER

PRIMARY FOCUS
The high tide of change brings new hope for a brighter future. Active pursuit of broader horizons leads to success, but you may have to leave behind some old treasures.

HEALTH AND FITNESS
A vacation away from home can be revitalizing. Now's the time to heighten your activity level and directly improve your health.

ROMANCE AND RELATIONSHIPS
A partnership transforms and can become the relationship you've longed for, but you have to be actively involved in the changes to really appreciate them. Share your feelings and thoughts about your spiritual experiences. Traveling can be an excellent way to find a new love or enliven an existing partnership. But watch for misunderstandings about your intentions from the 25th-31st. Be honest about sexual issues during the New Moon on the 15th. Reach out during the Full Moon on the 30th to express your hopes and share your deeper desires with someone you trust.

FINANCE AND CAREER
You can be the beneficiary of another's changing circumstances. Definitive action helps strengthen your career options. Meetings, conferences and negotiations operate to your benefit, but legal entanglements can confuse the issue. Be sure to define your position before Mercury turns retrograde on the 25th. Repeating the same information can give you a chance to take a second look and be sure before you make a final decision.

OPPORTUNITY OF THE MONTH
Imaginative approaches on the 8th lead to the recognition and results you desire by the 25th.

Rewarding Days: 3, 7, 8, 16, 17, 20, 21, 25, 26, 30, 31
Challenging Days: 1, 5, 6, 12, 13, 15, 18, 19, 23

AFFIRMATION FOR THE MONTH
"Every moment is a miracle!"

PISCES/NOVEMBER

PRIMARY FOCUS

Your faith is confirmed by positive responses from your environment. By adding initiative to the window of opportunity, you can experience significant rewards.

HEALTH AND FITNESS

An improved sense of self-worth supports more vibrant health. Stay in the pink by showing gratitude and maintaining hope.

ROMANCE AND RELATIONSHIPS

Traveling or educational pursuits can provide a superb outlet to either improve an existing relationship or to awaken a new love interest. If you're in contact with an old love, pay attention to any unfinished business you need to complete. The Solar Eclipse on the 13th presages a cycle of spiritual awakening which helps you open to a broader perspective of needs. Friction from parents or family can interfere with your love life near the Lunar Eclipse on the 29th. Avoid political or religious discussions unless you're dealing with others of like mind.

FINANCE AND CAREER

The time's right to attend classes or workshops to improve your skills. Double-check all communications or legal agreements, since delays or unexpected circumstances can lead to complications. Your drive to succeed is strong now, and you can easily step on the wrong toes if you're not paying attention. Be sure you know the parameters of your job and the expectations of your superiors. Be watchful of any opposition near the end of the month.

OPPORTUNITY OF THE MONTH

Your attunement to brighter possibilities for the future inspires others while enhancing your own success on the 21st and 22nd.

Rewarding Days: 4, 5, 12, 13, 17, 21, 22, 26
Challenging Days: 1, 2, 8, 9, 11, 14, 15, 29, 30

AFFIRMATION FOR THE MONTH

"My ethical standards are in harmony with Higher Law."

PISCES/DECEMBER

PRIMARY FOCUS
A strong orientation toward your career helps you achieve greater success and recognition for your efforts. But it's easy to alienate the wrong people, so be aware of how others are responding to you.

HEALTH AND FITNESS
Increased stress on the job takes its toll on your psyche and your body. Take time for a massage on the 1st, 2nd, 11th or 28th. Muscles tighten more easily. Remember to stretch before exercising.

ROMANCE AND RELATIONSHIPS
Getting clear about your feelings toward your parents can give you clues to some of the emotional blockages that have impeded your success. Disagreements with family or spouse can become public knowledge, and may spoil your reputation for ease and placidity! Nevertheless, clear communication is important and can illuminate core issues. Let others know how you feel, and avoid wasting time playing guessing games. Your friends are a good source of support near the Full Moon on the 28th.

FINANCE AND CAREER
Although there may be friction in the process, it's a good idea to use this time to advance your career. Patiently working toward your goals pays off by the end of the month, when you can be rewarded for your efforts by advancement or recognition. But the tendency to jump the gun on the New Moon on the 13th can leave you feeling exposed to criticism. Plan to set your project in motion from the 24th-28th.

OPPORTUNITY OF THE MONTH
Fulfilling dreams requires some work and preparation. Choose your mentors wisely, and take the lead yourself on the 29th.

Rewarding Days: 1, 2, 10, 14, 15, 18, 19, 24, 28, 29
Challenging Days: 4, 5, 6, 12, 13, 17, 26, 27

AFFIRMATION FOR THE MONTH
"I deserve success and happiness."

The 1993 Eclipses

Vince Ploscik

Eclipses are New or Full Moons that occur when the Moon is on the plane of the ecliptic (the Sun's apparent path in the heavens). This straight-line alignment of the Earth, Moon and Sun makes eclipses "heightened lunations" of powerful astrological significance.

There are four eclipses in 1993, and they will have the greatest impact upon individuals whose birthdates coincide with the dates of the eclipse, or fall within one day of the eclipse. The birthdate associated with each particular eclipse date will be included in both the "favorable" as well as the "unfavorable" discussion of each eclipse's potential, and it will remain up to the individual to determine if their affected planet(s) is free of affliction (if favorably aspected by an eclipse) or receives mitigating positive aspects (if unfavorably aspected by an eclipse). (Note: Llewellyn offers a complete line of Personalized Astrology Readings if help is needed here.)

Generally speaking, solar eclipses are said to last for a year, while lunar eclipses are said to last for six months. But any eclipse is capable of generating events or changes that may last long beyond these time frames. Since eclipses receive an opening square aspect after about 90 days and an opening trine aspect after about 120 days, their energies are almost certain to be active during the four to five months which follow their occurrence. Hence, this article furnishes possible "trigger dates" for each eclipse through a six-month period. These trigger dates all feature a lunation in aspect to the eclipse, or a transiting planet in aspect to the eclipse along with the transiting moon as a possible catalyst. So all of these trigger dates may at least have the potential to generate hard events, whether positive or negative.

THE SOLAR ECLIPSE OF MAY 21, 1993

The first eclipse in 1993 is a Solar Eclipse at 0° Gemini 32' on May 21st. This Solar Eclipse may be the most problematic for anyone born around 2/19, 5/21, 8/23 or 11/22 (any year). This eclipse may also generate some degree of mental/emotional stress or spark potentially difficult adjustments/adaptations for anyone born around 1/5, 4/5, 7/7, 10/8, 10/23 or 12/22 (any year).

The May 21st Solar Eclipse occurs in a Gemini decanate and in a Gemini dwad of Gemini (every ten degrees of a sign [decanate] has a ruler, and every two and one-half degrees of a sign [dwad] also has a ruler), so individuals born around the unfavorable birthdates cited above may experience concerns/problems related to siblings, neighbors, communications or transportation that may be highly confusing and/or require stressful new initiatives. Transiting Saturn squares this eclipse from Pisces, while transiting Venus semi-squares from Aries, so these eclipse-related concerns may be exacerbated by enormous frustrations, heavy worries/anxieties, erroneous assumptions and information, or mentally and emotionally taxing restrictions and responsibilities. In light of this, the idea is to carefully double-check all facts and figures, to avoid rash/reckless actions and decisions as a result of impatience or impulsiveness, and to use extreme care in the writing/signing of contracts/documents or in the handling of important papers and communications. Involvements with siblings, neighbors, co-workers, parents, older family members and bosses/superiors may encounter setbacks and delays, so it may be important to avoid a negative attitude and to exercise a great deal of patience and understanding. Eclipses in Mutable Signs generally create multifaceted concerns or prompt several problems to occur simultaneously, and as such, they often disrupt personal/professional plans, work schedules, the mail/delivery services, travel/transportation arrangements and time management, so transiting Saturn's square strongly suggests taking extra cautions against carelessness and misunderstandings. Transiting Saturn's square from Pisces may also prompt chronic health problems to flare up, or spark possible accidents/mishaps due to inattentiveness or impatience.

Transiting Jupiter makes a retrograde station (apparent stillness in the sky, moving from direct to retrograde motion) at 14° Libra 42' on January 28, 1993, and this Jupiter station sesquiquadrates the May 21 Solar Eclipse and opposes transiting Venus position on the eclipse date. This may prompt the eclipse to trigger relationship conflicts and emotional misunderstandings dating back to January, 1993, especially in August, 1993, when transiting Jupiter reaches 14° Libra again in direct motion. Also, with transiting Mercury (the ruler of the eclipse) making a sesquiquadrate aspect to transiting Uranus and Neptune in Capricorn on the date of the eclipse, it should be noted that old, longstanding resentments and frustrations or an impulsive desire for freedom/independence may factor heavily into the eclipse's communication problems and exacerbate these possible relationship concerns.

With all the above in mind, watch for the negative potential of this May 21 Solar Eclipse to be possibly triggered around 6/24, 7/3, 7/9, 8/23, 8/26, 9/20, 9/27, 10/1, 10/22, 10/24, 11/8, 11/11, 12/5, 12/22/93; 1/5, 1/7 and 2/1/94. The lengthy duration of this eclipse's influence is due to the fact that transiting Saturn doesn't reach 0° of Pisces (its position on the eclipse date) for the last time until late-January, 1994.

The May 21 Solar Eclipse will make positive aspects for anyone born around 1/20, 3/21, 5/21, 7/23 or 9/23 (any year). Individuals born around these favorable birthdates may enjoy opportunities involving new interests/studies, creative self-expression, communications, travel, children, siblings, neighbors or education. However, since the eclipse squares transiting Saturn and semi-squares transiting Venus, there may be a need to exercise patience and perseverance as well as a need to avoid scattering one's efforts and energies in too many directions at once in order to realize the positive potential of this eclipse. The square from Saturn and the semi-square from Venus may actually help to foster rash or reckless "reactionary" actions and decisions as a result of frustration. With these cautions in mind, individuals born around the favorable dates cited above should watch for the positive potential of the May 21 Solar Eclipse to be possibly triggered around 5/25, 7/5, 7/23, 8/11, 9/12 and 9/23/93, although the 9/23 date (in particular) may require major decisions and/or compromises.

THE LUNAR ECLIPSE OF JUNE 4, 1993

The second eclipse in 1993 is a Lunar Eclipse at 13° Sagittarius 53' on June 4th. This Lunar Eclipse may be the most problematic for anyone born around 3/4, 6/4, 9/6 or 12/5 (any year). This eclipse may also generate some degree of stress or spark potentially difficult adjustments for anyone born around 1/18, 4/18, 5/4, 7/5, 7/21 or 10/22 (any year).

The July 4th Lunar Eclipse is ruled by Jupiter, and on the date of the eclipse, transiting Jupiter in Libra receives a square from transiting Mercury in Cancer. The eclipse occurs in an Aries decanate and in a Taurus dwad, with transiting Mars (the decanate ruler) in Leo semi-squaring transiting Jupiter and inconjuncting transiting Uranus and Neptune in Capricorn. We have an enormously complicated set of aspects here that may prompt individuals born around the unfavorable birthdates cited above to experience highly stressful concerns, problems involving legal matters, in-laws or older family members, matters at a distance, relocation, health concerns or possible disruptive changes in the work environment, all of which may be characterized by much worry, anxiety and stress.

In light of the above, home or real estate, family or relationship concerns dating back to November, 1992 and April, 1993 may factor into these eclipse-related stresses and require major decisions or compromises and concessions. Emotional impulsiveness, volatility or confusion may help to spark reckless actions and decisions as well as communication problems. Hence, between possible accidents, stress-related health concerns, family or partner conflicts, work instability and emotional stress, this is clearly not the year for mental, physical, or financial overextension, and any major decisions that are unavoidable should be based upon objective fact/logic rather than upon assumptions. Again, eclipses in Mutable Signs generally create several problems that occur simultaneously, so the idea is to avoid nervous/emotional over-reactions that may only exacerbate matters.

Watch for the negative potential of this June 4 Lunar Eclipse to be possibly triggered around 6/25, 7/16, 7/19, 7/22, 8/8, 8/18, 8/25, 9/5, 9/12, 9/24, 9/28, 10/2, 10/22, 10/25, 11/5 and 11/8/93. Try to slow down, to use tact/diplomacy, and try to avoid emotional subjectivism.

The June 4th Lunar Eclipse will make positive aspects for anyone born around 2/2, 4/3, 8/6, 10/7 or 12/6 (any year). Individuals born around these favorable dates may enjoy opportunities involving higher education, long-distance travel/relocation, publishing, churches, legal concerns, sports, public speaking, in-laws, or individuals of a different race, religion or culture. However, with the eclipse receiving so many afflicting aspects from the transiting planets, patience and perseverance and thorough preparation may be required along with a willingness to compromise in order to realize the eclipse's positive potential. Mercury-Jupiter square and the sesquiquadrate aspect from Venus may help this eclipse to foster impulsiveness or rash/reckless actions and decisions. With these cautions in mind, individuals born around the favorable birthdates cited above should watch for the positive potential of this eclipse to be possibly triggered around 8/7, 8/24, 8/29, 9/3, 9/19 and 10/6/93. Please note that the September dates may require a much greater willingness to cooperate and meet others half-way.

THE SOLAR ECLIPSE OF NOVEMBER 13, 1993

The third eclipse in 1993 is a Solar Eclipse at 21° Scorpio 32' on November 13th. This Solar Eclipse may be the most problematic for anyone born around 2/10, 5/12, 8/14 or 11/13 (any year). This eclipse may also generate some degree of stress or spark potentially difficult adjustments/adaptations for anyone born around 3/27, 4/11, 6/12, 6/28, 9/29 or 12/28 (any year).

The November 13th Solar Eclipse occurs in a Cancer decanate and dwad of Scorpio, so its energies are likely to focus upon basic, fundamental changes in the emotional, domestic or financial security of the individuals born around the unfavorable birthdates cited above. Transiting Saturn in Aquarius squares the eclipse as well as the direct

station that transiting Pluto makes on August 3rd, 1993, so
this eclipse may generate continued relationship conflicts,
domestic familial changes or emotionally upsetting work
or career changes that may date back to August, 1993, or
even back to November-December, 1991 and August-November, 1992.

With transiting Saturn squaring the eclipse, there may
be continued fallout from the problems of the past two
years, especially with respect to concerns related to real estate, mortgages, taxes, insurances, inheritances, alimony
or child support, disability, pension or retirement funds,
public assistance, debts or joint property or finances.
Placed in the 9th dwad, this eclipse may have the potential
to spark legal problems, or broaden the concerns of the
past two years to include in-laws, property and family at a
distance, or continued changes with respect to relationships and domestic security that may be perceived as
threatening and spark great emotional volatility.

In light of all the above, the basic idea here is to avoid
confrontations and attempts to dominate others, to exercise extreme caution in financial matters and to try to control your own emotional intensity (rather than attempting
to control everything and everyone around you). Eclipses
in Fixed Signs generally create sustained problems that
primarily affect our financial and material security, and
usually there is simply no way under, over or around these
problems. Hence, the challenge is to adapt and/or to
change in accordance with these eclipse-related changes
rather than futilely attempting to resist them. With transiting Mars semi-squaring transiting Uranus and Neptune
on the eclipse date, it may be all the more important to respond to these changes in a controlled and responsible
manner rather than giving in to anger/defiance or unreasonable emotional demands and obstinacy. Fixed Signs
have the greatest difficulty in dealing with change, so individuals born around 2/10, 5/12, 8/14 or 11/13 may be
particularly challenged to "let go" and to move forward.

Watch for the negative potential of this November 13
Solar Eclipse to possibly be triggered around 11/27, 12/1,
12/28, 12/31/93; 1/28, 2/6, 2/10, 2/13, 2/24, 2/27, 3/6,
3/9, 3/27, 3/30, 4/10, 4/13, 4/20, 4/23 and 5/6/94. Generally speaking, the more flexible and cooperative you can

be in your thinking, the easier it will be to work through these eclipse-related changes and concerns.

The November 13th Solar Eclipse will make positive aspects for anyone born around 1/11, 3/12, 7/13, 9/14 or 11/13 (any year). Individuals born around these favorable birthdates may enjoy heightened intuition or financial resources that can be used to make fundamental changes for the better in their domestic situation or their emotional and material security. This eclipse may bring favorable results in legal matters, real estate transactions or concerns involving taxes, insurances, inheritances, pension or retirement funds, alimony or child support or joint finances. Placed in the 9th dwad, this eclipse may also favor religious and philosophical development, self-expression, higher education, publishing or matters at a distance. With transiting Saturn squaring the eclipse, however, the idea here is to exercise patience/perseverance and to set practical, realistic goals. Individuals born around 7/13 and 9/14 may have to cope with stressful adjustments/adaptations as they work toward long-range goals. With these cautions in mind, individuals born around the favorable birthdates cited above should watch for the positive potential of the November 13th Solar Eclipse to be possibly triggered around 12/1/93; 1/11, 1/16, 3/2, 3/12, 3/21 and 4/3/94.

THE LUNAR ECLIPSE OF NOVEMBER 29, 1993

The fourth and final eclipse in 1993 is a Lunar Eclipse at 7° Gemini on November 29th. This Lunar Eclipse may be the most problematical for anyone born around 2/25, 5/28, 8/30 or 11/28 (any year). This eclipse may also generate some degree of mental/emotional stress or spark potentially difficult adjustments/adaptations for anyone born around 1/11, 4/11, 7/14, 10/15, 10/30 or 12/28 (any year).

The November 29th Lunar Eclipse occurs in a Gemini decanate/Leo dwad of Gemini, so like the May 21 Solar Eclipse, once again there may be concerns/problems involving siblings, close family members, neighbors, coworkers, communications or transportation. The November 29th Lunar Eclipse makes a sesquiquadrate aspect to transiting Uranus and Neptune, however, and on the date of the eclipse, transiting Saturn in Aquarius squares transiting Venus' conjunction with transiting Pluto in Scorpio, so this November 29th Lunar Eclipse may generate financial concerns, intense disagreements and or an unwillingness to cooperate. Individuals born around the unfavorable birthdates cited above may also experience stressful setbacks and frustrations involving work/career concerns, real estate/property, older family members, chronic health concerns, joint finances or taxes/insurances that may date back to August, 1993 or even back to November-December, 1991 and August-November, 1992 (which is when transiting Pluto first reaches 21° Scorpio). Hence, it may be important to avoid allowing frustration and emotional subjectivism to interfere with the decisions or compromises that this eclipse may be calling for, while also exercising extreme caution in all financial decisions. Placed in the 3rd dwad, this eclipse may also generate accidents/mishaps due to impatience and impulsiveness, or prompt stress-related health concerns to flare up.

Another factor to consider here involves transiting Jupiter in Libra, which squares the direct station that transiting Uranus and Neptune make in late-September, 1993. Since the eclipse makes a sesquiquadrate aspect to transiting Uranus and Neptune, relationship conflicts, legal concerns and/or financial disputes dating back to September, 1993 may also factor into these eclipse-related stresses. Hence, it may be extremely important to exercise great care in the handling of legal matters, contracts/documents and relationship concerns beginning in September, 1993 as a means of mitigating the communication problems that may follow the November 29th Lunar Eclipse.

With the above in mind, watch for the negative potential of the November 29 Lunar Eclipse to be possibly triggered around 12/9, 12/11/93; 1/8, 1/11, 1/15, 2/11, 2/18, 2/25, 2/28, 3/17, 3/25, 3/31, 4/11, 4/14 and 4/21/94. Transiting Mercury retrogrades in square aspect to the eclipse on February 11th, 1994, so try to avoid major decisions between February 11th through March 25th, 1994. Also, be aware that transiting Saturn squares the eclipse in August, 1994 and then retrogrades, so these eclipse-related concerns may not reach their conclusions until January, 1995, when transiting Saturn reaches 7° Pisces for the last time (note: transiting Jupiter opposes the eclipse position in January, 1995, so guard against impulsiveness and impatience, which may spark a new round of problems out of these old concerns that may last through September, 1995).

The November 29th Lunar Eclipse will make positive aspects for anyone born around 1/26, 3/27, 5/28, 7/29 or 9/29 (any year). Individuals born around these favorable birthdates may enjoy opportunities involving siblings, close family members, neighbors, short trips/travels, studies, communications or self-expression. However, with Saturn squaring Venus and Pluto on the eclipse date, and with the eclipse receiving sesquiquadrate aspects from Uranus and Neptune, once again, there may be a need to emphasize the practical/realistic as well as a need to avoid rash/reckless actions and decisions. With these cautions in mind, individuals born around the favorable birthdates cited above should watch for the positive potential of the November 29th Lunar Eclipse to be possibly triggered around 1/17, 1/27, 1/31, 2/4, 3/13 and 3/27/94. Again, Lunar Eclipses require decisions and/or a willingness to compromise/cooperate, so much may depend upon retaining an objective and responsible attitude in the wake of the afflicting aspects that occur on the date of this eclipse.

The Uranus–Neptune Conjunction

Anthony Louis

One of the major astrological events of the century will occur on February 2, 1993, at 7:47 a.m. EST (calculation based on Pottenger's CCRS90 program), when the outer planets, Uranus and Neptune, meet (conjoin) on the Sun's path for the first time in 171 years. The conjunction occurs at 19 degrees Capricorn 34 minutes. Because of retrograde motion, this conjunction will occur twice more in 1993 around 18 to 19 degrees Capricorn—again on August 20, 1993, and for a final time on Oct. 24, 1993. Capricorn is a sign associated with government, ambition, power, the structure of society, and the material world. We have already felt the effects of this conjunction because these two outer planets have been traveling side by side in Capricorn for the past several years. The close proximity of Uranus and Neptune has coincided with the dissolution of the Berlin Wall, the breakup of the Soviet Union, the re-evaluation of Communism, and the social upheaval of contemporary life.

The conjunction of two slow moving planets always has a major impact on human affairs. Uranus and Neptune have conflicting natures, and their conjunction juxtaposes the needs of the individual with the demands of the collective. Uranus symbolizes the urge for individual freedom and the desire to shatter existing forms and break with established tradition. Neptune is the planet of mysticism, fusion, merging, compassion, dissolution, sacrifice, spirituality, and the collective. Uranus enters our lives like a bolt from the blue. Neptune is more insidious; its influence gradually seeps into our lives like the fog. Uranus was the original Sky-Father god whose son Saturn cut off his genitals and threw them into the ocean (Neptune's domain) in a coup to gain dominion of Mount Olympus. The union of Uranus' genitals and Neptune's sea water produced Venus Aphrodite, the goddess of love. Perhaps the 1993 Uranus/Neptune conjunction will herald a new birth of love throughout humanity at the dawn of the Aquarian age.

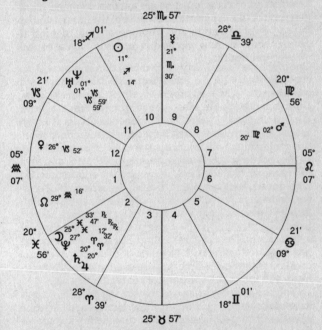

Figure 3
The 1821 Uranus/Neptune Conjunction
WASHINGTON, DC
DEC 3, 1821, 10:54: 0 ZONE 5.00 ST
38N54 77W2
GEOCENTRIC TROPICAL
Porphyry

When Uranus meets Neptune, radical new influences and revolutionary ideals enter human consciousness. People experience major life changes as a result of far-reaching societal forces beyond individual control. There is an emergence of novel methods of creative expression. Intuitive abilities are heightened. People become interested in astrology, mysticism, psychic phenomena, spirituality, and the occult. Some join secret societies or cults to pursue these subjects. Advances in music and art are likely. Altered states of consciousness are another common manifestation of this conjunction. Because of the immense combined power of Uranus and Neptune, any use of mind altering chemicals now can be dangerous to mental as well as physical health.

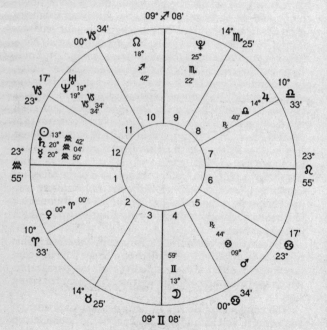

Figure 4
The 1993 Uranus/Neptune Conjunction
WASHINGTON, DC
FEB 2, 1993, 7:47: 0 ZONE 5.00 S T
38N54   77W2
GEOCENTRIC TROPICAL
Porphyry

Because these planets are in Capricorn, their union brings about changes in governments, social structures, and concrete reality. There is a strong impetus to overthrow established routines and break with tradition. Flashes of insight can lead to discoveries in medicine. Astrologer Charles Carter wrote that the last Uranus/Neptune conjunction in 1821 "may well be related to the enormous advance in physical science (Capricorn) and the revolution that took place in our religious ideas."

The last Uranus/Neptune conjunction, also in Capricorn, coincided with the beginning of the Industrial Revolution and the secession of the Latin American countries from Spain and Portugal. The leader of the anti-vivisectionist movement, F. B. Cobbe had a natal Uranus/Neptune conjunction as did the revolutionary biologist Louis Pasteur. The radical religious figure Mary Baker Eddy, who founded Christian Science, was born under the influence of the 1821 Uranus/Neptune conjunction. So was Ulysses S. Grant who led the Union to victory and abolished slavery in the American Civil War. The year 1820 saw the Missouri Compromise in which Missouri entered the Union as a slave state but the rest of the Mississippi valley above latitude 36.5 north was closed to slavery. With prophetic insight John Quincy Adams said of the Missouri Compromise, which was ratified with Uranus closely conjunct Neptune at the end of Sagittarius, "If the Union must be dissolved, slavery is precisely the question upon which it ought to break."

The remainder of this article focuses on the effect of this conjunction in individual horoscopes. To see how this conjunction will affect you personally, read the paragraphs which apply to your own Sun sign and Ascendant or rising sign.

The conjunction occurs in Saturn-ruled Capricorn; if you know it, you should also read about the house Saturn occupies in your natal horoscope. A brief article such as this can only review the highlights of the influence of this conjunction for each sign. For further information you may wish to consult a professional astrologer who can interpret the Uranus/Neptune conjunction in the context of your entire chart.

Uranus brings sudden changes, and Neptune brings

confusion and idealization to whichever house they transit in your personal horoscope. People born within five days of January 10th (any year) or who have 19°+ Capricorn prominent in their horoscopes will certainly feel the effects of this conjunction and are likely to undergo an identity crisis at this time. The same holds true of those whose natal Sun lies 90° or 180° away from the Uranus/Neptune conjunction. Such individuals were born on or within five days of April 9, July 12, or October 13, any year.

If your Sun or Ascendant lies in Aries, the Uranus/Neptune conjunction will take place in your 10th house of career, status, and public reputation. Some of you will change your professions or seek freedom in your vocation under this transit. New career opportunities may unexpectedly present themselves. You may have the chance to try something new or radical in your business life. This transit favors humanitarian work which aims to help the underprivileged or less fortunate. Some individuals will make a career of one of the occult sciences. This is frequently a time of soul searching about how you make your mark upon the world. Some of you will lose or be estranged from a parent, often the mother, under the influence of this transit. The above paragraph also applies if Saturn occupies the 10th house in your natal chart.

If your Sun or Ascendant lies in Taurus, the Uranus/Neptune conjunction will take place in your 9th house of higher education, long-distance travel, dealings with in-laws and foreigners, religion, and legal proceedings. Some of you will develop a strong interest in religion, philosophy, and the spiritual aspects of life. You may experiment with altered states of consciousness, including mystical experiences. A program of meditation can be enriching and gratifying at this time. You are capable of radical and far-reaching insights under this transit. Long-distance travel which broadens your horizons is a distinct possibility. There is some risk of unexpected legal entanglements now. Unexpected problems with in-laws can arise. The above paragraph also applies if Saturn occupies the 9th house in your natal chart.

If your Sun or Ascendant lies in Gemini, the Uranus/Neptune conjunction will take place in your 8th house of joint finances, partnership resources, inheritance, transition, death, sex, the occult, and rebirth. Some of you will develop an interest in the hidden, mysterious dimensions of the human mind. Occult studies and psychic abilities are favored now. Property or money you hold with a partner may be subject to unexpected fluctuations and confusing or deceptive influences. There could be problems with an inheritance. Your partner's income may undergo sudden upsets. Keep all joint financial dealings strictly above board. You are experiencing a major transition; you need to let go of the old to make way for the new. Often such transitions involve the death of a person or close relationship. There is the possibility of an unexpected clandestine love affair. With this conjunction occurring in your 8th house of venereal disease, be especially careful to practice safe sex at this time. The above paragraph also applies if Saturn occupies the 8th house in your natal chart.

If your Sun or Ascendant lies in Cancer, the Uranus/ Neptune conjunction will take place in your 7th house of partnerships, marriage, personal consultants, open enemies, and lawsuits. Some marriages, especially those built on shaky foundations, will break up under this transit. It is not a good time to enter a new committed relationship or partnership because you are not thinking clearly and may be overly idealizing a potential partner. Your mate seeks increased personal freedom under this transit. Deception in partnerships or legal matters is a possibility. Some of you will face opposition from open enemies who may even engage you in a lawsuit. If possible, postpone legal proceedings until several months after this conjunction becomes exact. The above paragraph also applies if Saturn occupies the 7th house in your natal chart.

If your Sun or Ascendant lies in Leo, the Uranus/Neptune conjunction will take place in your 6th house of work, daily routine, subordinates, pets, and illness. You may find yourself working with computers, data processing, electronics, or in some service capacity. Some will find employment in the arts, film, design, music, research, and the field of chemical dependency. You seek a sense of excitement and novelty on the job. Some of you will be working in hospitals or other institutions that care for the unfortunate members of society. If you have been burdened by job related responsibilities, you will want to break free of such restrictions. You may prefer to work alone or in seclusion. Take care to avoid worry, nervous tension, and overstrain; otherwise you are at risk for unexpected or unusual illnesses. You may experience upsets through employees or people who perform a service for you. Your pet may cause quite a stir at this time. The above paragraph also applies if Saturn occupies the 6th house in your natal chart.

If your Sun or Ascendant lies in Virgo, the Uranus/ Neptune conjunction will take place in your 5th house of speculation, gambling, children, creative activity, and love affairs. This is an unfavorable time to engage in risky financial investments. In the area of love and romance you may find yourself seeking an unusual, almost mystical union with a lover. You are more prone than usual to become unrealistically infatuated with a potential sweetheart. Children are a potential source of upset. Your children might also introduce you to novel or spiritual experiences now. A productive way to use the energy of this transit is to engage in a creative, self-expressive project. You can tap into original, inventive, artistic abilities at this time. Recreational drug use and casual, unprotected sex are quite dangerous under this transit. The above paragraph also applies if Saturn occupies the 5th house in your natal chart.

If your Sun or Ascendant lies in Libra, the Uranus/ Neptune conjunction will take place in your 4th house of domestic concerns, residence, real estate, family, parents (often the father), foundations, life structure, and the end of life. You may be going through a time of major difficulties with real estate or domestic issues. Unusual conditions prevail in the home. Some of you will modernize your homes or move to live by the sea. For some this transit will herald a divorce, the illness or death of a parent, a relocation, or a major shakeup of the very foundations of your life. The changes now are fundamental, subtle, and radical. The basic structure of your life is undergoing revision. Some of you will wish to undergo psychotherapy to sort out this period of upheaval. The above paragraph also applies if Saturn occupies the 4th house in your natal chart.

If your Sun or Ascendant lies in Scorpio, the Uranus/ Neptune conjunction will take place in your 3rd house of communications, short trips, neighbors, siblings, and lower education. This is a period of heightened psychic receptivity and artistic expression. The behavior of a sibling may be quite upsetting under this transit. Unexpected messages or correspondence will keep you hopping. You may take up the study of the occult or physical sciences now. Everything new, modern, scientific, and technical as well as mysterious, other-worldly, metaphysical, and occult now appeals to your mind. Some of you will undertake technical training now. Communications occupy center stage. Be alert for confusion, misrepresentation, or misunderstandings in important matters. This is an excellent time for technical or creative writing. If this conjunction is afflicted in your horoscope, you could be subject to accidents or mental difficulties. The above paragraph also applies if Saturn occupies the 3rd house in your natal chart.

If your Sun or Ascendant lies in Sagittarius, the Uranus/Neptune conjunction will take place in your 2nd house of income, resources, values, money, and movable property. Expect radical changes in your source of income, money supply, and value system at this time. You are likely to put material affairs in perspective as you come to appreciate more the spiritual side of reality. This would be a fine time to donate money or time to a charitable cause to help the needy. At the same time be wary of dubious get-rich-quick schemes because you risk losing a lot of money through risky investments. Some of you will find a way to earn income through astrology, psychic talents, or the occult. You might also make money through inventions, creative imagination, intuition, and artistic or musical talent. The above paragraph also applies if Saturn occupies the 2nd house in your natal chart.

If your Sun or Ascendant lies in Capricorn, the Uranus/Neptune conjunction will take place in your 1st house of basic identity, physical body, personality, and appearance. You have been undergoing a major transformation in your sense of identity and are in the process of clearing outmoded situations and relationships from your life. You desire freedom to explore new aspects of your personality and novel modes of self-expression. You are extremely sensitive to your environment and prone to absorb the feelings and moods of others. Excessive use of drugs or alcohol will have deleterious effects on your body. This may be a time of spiritual rebellion. Your current behavior may upset or confuse other people who look at you like you're from outer space. You are likely to espouse the ideal of humanitarian concern and compassion for others. At the same time you need to guard against rescue fantasies and excessive dependency in close relationships. You may find you enjoy taking physical risks as well as pursuing abstract ideas. The above paragraph also applies if Saturn occupies the 1st house in your natal chart.

If your Sun or Ascendant lies in Aquarius, the Uranus/ Neptune conjunction will take place in your 12th house of subconscious influences, karma, the results of past actions, undoing, spirituality, compassion, institutions, hospitals, confinement, and hidden matters. A skeleton may jump out of your closet at this time. Secrets that you thought were buried in the past may come to the surface now. You may discover the power of faith or become aware of psychic abilities. Pay special attention to dreams and intuitions that come to you under this transit. Some of you will become involved with hospitals, prisons, or other institutions of confinement. You may become involved with helping the handicapped. Neptune is at home in the 12th house so this can be a time of spiritual and psychological awakening. An occult master may provide you with spiritual guidance. Now is a time to reflect quietly on the deeper significance of life. If past hang-ups are interfering with your life, this is an excellent time to engage in counseling or psychotherapy to heal old wounds. The above paragraph also applies if Saturn occupies the 12th house in your natal chart.

If your Sun or Ascendant lies in Pisces, the Uranus/ Neptune conjunction will take place in your 11th house of friends, groups, hopes, and wishes. New, exciting and unusual friends may enter your life under this transit. You may become involved in groups or organizations interested in spiritual, occult, or humanitarian causes. You may take up the serious study of astrology at this time. A friend may lead you on the path of spiritual enlightenment. Another friend may bring unexpected disappointment into your life. You will find yourself making a major overhaul of your hopes, wishes, and goals for the future. The above paragraph also applies if Saturn occupies the 11th house in your natal chart.

Chiron in Leo and Virgo in 1993

Sharon L. Harbeck & Scott Hubanks

One of the most exciting developments in astrology happened with the discovery of the "mini-planet" Chiron by Charles Kowal in 1977. Chiron is a planetoid (not quite big enough to be a planet in his own right) which appears to have powerful implications for our budding Aquarian Age. He dances between Saturn (keywords: Old Taskmaster, Father, business as usual, status quo, rigid bureaucracy, old rules, old age, structure, hierarchy/patriarchy) and Uranus (keywords: surprising spontaneity, humanitarianism, egalitarianism, democracy, madcap genius, revolution, friendship, detachment, electromagnetism, charisma), thus leading many astrologers to speculate that Chiron functions as a kind of bridge between the Old Age and the New Age. Many New Age leaders have pointed to Chiron as the likely messenger planet referred to as "The Rainbow Bridge" in Native American legends. Such legends herald a peaceful, healthy, multi-creedal, multi-colored, cooperative world populated with Citizens of the Earth rather than the separatist xenophobes of the past.

Chiron was described mythologically as a Centaur, "the Wounded Healer"—a gifted musician, healer, magician, astrologer, teacher and trainer of warriors. He combined the finest of instinctive subconscious animal traits with the finest spiritual/intellectual/human traits, but his conventional use of poisoned arrows in battle led to his downfall. In one version of this story, Hercules, one of Chiron's students, accidentally shoots Chiron in the knee (an area traditionally ruled by Saturn). In another version, Chiron drops the poisoned arrow on his foot, causing him to suffer terrible agony.

All ended well, however, because Chiron was wise enough to use his agony in a noble manner. Chiron's pain made him particularly sympathetic to the human condition, and to Prometheus' cause to bring fire to mankind. When Chiron offered his own immortality as a sacrifice, in exchange for Zeus' release of Prometheus from the rocky crag to which he was chained, Chiron arranged for both his own and Prometheus' release from suffering. Zeus, impressed with Chiron's self-sacrifice, turned him into the constellation of Sagittarius for his honorable behavior.

Chiron might be interpreted as symbolizing (Prometheus') release from the constraints of the conscious mind. Prometheus unbound could again offer a gift of creative spirit (fire) to others and become an active part of the world. When we block the creative warmth in ourselves and repeat unchallenged habitual slave-like behaviors, we allow ourselves to become entrapped by meaningless, unchosen rituals and the resulting stasis becomes our wounded foot, our impediment.

Chiron interacts with your Sun to sensitize you to the ways in which your central identity can be reformed. By helping you to relinquish thought patterns, beliefs and ideas which are overly rigid, and or which you cherish but may have outgrown, Chiron helps you to transform yourself. But allowing that cherished ideal, person, thing, or emotion to pass out of your life, you become opened up to freedom from the slavery of addiction and rigidity (negative Saturn traits), to the you that is free to chose your path. Having crossed the bridge (Chiron) to Uranus, you can start an exciting, fresh lifestyle, an Aquarian approach to living.

Remember that Chiron was wounded in the more primitive, lower portion of his Centaur's body. That animal portion is the most vulnerable part of humans as well, yet its existence allows humans the capacity for change and transcendence of the spirit. So, in a sense, we are greatly blessed by our addictions, because their hold over us allows us the challenge of breaking free, the exhilaration of being born anew. The nobility in our human spirits lies not in the accomplishment, but in striving against the odds to accomplish; over and over if need be.

In dealing with Chiron, consider your own addictions

to alcohol, drugs, particular people, sex, behaviors and/or food. Use Chiron's creativity in your chart to experiment and try different approaches to deal with whatever you've identified as a problem in your life. Be kind but firm with yourself; that is the balance to strive for between Uranus, which can offer pointless rebellion for the sake of rebellion, and Saturn, which can offer status/security/responsibility/approval at the expense of your individuality and ability to grow creatively. As a harbinger of creative growth processes, I subscribe to the view that Chiron is associated closely with the sign of Virgo, the Healer, although his ultimate linkage to Sagittarius, the Centaur, is equally important to note. Virgo represents human striving toward spiritual/physical perfection; Sagittarius an accomplished manifestation of the same.

CHIRON TRANSITING LEO AND VIRGO

During 1993, Chiron will be traversing the last ten degrees of the sign Leo. This transit has many implications on a general and on a personal level.

Most people gain control of their egos by denying them validity; but with Chiron in Leo, the goal should be to become your ego and express it! This is an excellent time to pick up some form of artistic expression, such as painting, drawing or music. (Some famous people with Chiron in Leo are Paul McCartney, John Lennon, Jimi Hendrix, Warren Beatty and Mick Jagger.) Additionally, Chiron in Leo breaks up old attitudes regarding love affairs and romance. Watch people with "colorful histories" become beset with the urge to settle down (witness the recent marriages of veteran bachelors Beatty and Jagger), while more conservative types enjoy a fresh new approach to the dating and mating game.

Lastly, Chiron in Leo deals with children, especially savants, and the unusual begetting of the same—e.g., artificial insemination, children born to gay parents, *in vitro* births, transferred fertilized ovum, children conceived from frozen sperm, and perhaps even out of the womb gestation. The first test tube baby, Louise Brown, had Chiron on her Ascendent at her time of birth.

Look for unusual art forms, a plethora of creative child prodigies, unusual new approaches to romance on television and in films, the development of erotic films and pornography for women, and strange new forms of recreation to crop up during Chiron in Leo.

In September 1993, Chiron will enter the sign associated with his rulership, Virgo. Virgo is associated with workplaces, healing, holistic medicine, perfectionism, ascetic lifestyles, health, small animals, rituals, haute cuisine, clothing/designing, vegetarianism, and service to others. Chiron's entry will result in a revolutionizing of these forces, and will likely show us new developments in the Catholic Church's stand on celibacy, the development of stronger nursing unions and nurse-run clinics, new regulations for food labeling and perhaps uniform changes in animal use standards for the cosmetic industry. More vehemence by the animal rightists is anticipated.

As we cope with changes wrought by a recessionary economy, more small businesses and cottage industries from home will likely crop up to replace corporate structures. These will help to freshen our approach to work in the 90s. National health care will doubtless be THE major issue this year, with so many just reentering the work force without the benefit of health care plans which their former, larger employers once provided. Discoveries of cheap new hybrid crops that will require much less care and chemical protection will receive a boost from Chiron in Virgo. Perhaps pest-resistent food crops will be part of that development. The development and marketing of cigarette substitutes that do not burn of otherwise foul the environment will be another factor to seek in 1993.

Vast advancements in medicine for nerve regeneration, immune system disorders and brain chemical imbalances will accompany Chiron's advance into Virgo, which continues through 1994. If a cure for AIDS is to be found, the inception will probably come during Chiron in Virgo. Vaccines against autoimune diseases are likely to become available at that time.

CHIRON'S CHALLENGE

We can tackle the likely sore points presented by Chiron's challenges to our Sun signs during the upcoming year, 1993. Some signs will likely have an easier time incorporating Chiron's lessons than others this year, though in my experience the so-called "hard aspects" (conjunctions, squares, quincunxes, oppositions) offer the quickest, most obvious channels for growth—even if they are very sudden and shattering revelations! The easy aspects (trines and sextiles) offer growth of a less distinctive nature, and sometimes allowing the recipients to overlook the opportunity for marvelous changes in spiritual and physical evolutionary developments. Read on to learn how you can identify your personal Sun sign's weaknesses and let Chiron help you heal them in 1993-1994.

ARIES people have been enjoying an easy trine from Chiron since August 1991, when Chiron entered Leo. But because Chiron has put little pressure on Aries to change, the tendency for many has probably been sidestepping issues. With a trine, people have to make a conscious effort to identify traits they want to transform, because it's easier to coast. Aries' weaknesses include: starting projects they won't finish, railroading their ideas instead of seeking compromise, ignoring partnership needs in favor of doing their own things, evading serious marriage or business partnerships altogether and leading others without consulting them for input. Now is an easy time for you Aries to reform such traits, since Chiron is helping you alter them with less loss or pain.

If you have chronic headaches as a result of your type A personality, seek out radical new drug-free therapies and learn management techniques to help you delegate authority better. Otherwise, when Chiron quincunxes your Sun come late 1993-1994, you could find yourself bogged down in a sea of untended details, including hypochondriachal or drug-oriented approaches to health, problems with uncooperative underlings, colleagues and/or pets. Grab your chance to become a healthy, cooperative partner!

Chiron's squaring TAURUS since August 1991 has challenged Taureans' fixed, static nature. Being comfortable ain't what it used to be! Establishing stable routines has become difficult, so what is a stable earth sign to do when his or her feet don't feel like they're touching solid ground?

Let Chiron help you to become a little more impulsive,

and able to keep up with new developments. Give away some of your tired old possessions to friends—Chiron will help you to replace them with better ones, through other avenues. Replace your sugar or other food addictions with a new interest in gourmet nouvelle low-fat cuisines or low-cal Chinese wok cooking (or, supplement an overly-sparse diet with new delicacies and richer flavors, if you've been extreme in the other direction). Cultivate at least one far-out New Age friend, and one more conservative one than you usually have, and introduce them! Everybody can learn from one another. You could also try something fun and new like buying a fortunetelling card deck, taking up painting or a new instrument, and developing your innate psychic sensitivity. Buy or design some wacky jewelry (Taurus rules jewelry) and enjoy people's responses. Be less socially isolated, and don't be bound by a tendency to brooding silence. You have interesting things to say, so say them, rather than being a mere sounding board for others. Remember that people aren't possessions, and neither are you. Enjoy more spirited debates in your life.

Chiron sextiles you GEMINIS in a comfortable way this year; as with Aries, you may be tempted to coast. Instead, try using Chiron's fun, surprising element to turn an ordinary detached friendship into a sizzling, passionate romance (no easy task for generally fickle Geminis). Develop warmer, more intimately personal attachments to highly creative people with fixed goals in mind for both of you. Learn to speak with warmth in your tone, not merely analytical intellectualism. Pick and choose what you say, and how you say it. Work for or with a friend on a creative collaboration of some kind. Fall madly in love and toss your myriad futuristic ideas out the window in favor of a few particular chosen goals. Commit yourself to a social charity group cause, intimacy self-help group or political party. Entertain others on stage solo for a change, getting together your own individualistic "act" rather than casually blending into a small crowd. Plan your future year on a calendar and try to stick to it, without vacillating too much. You'll get a kick out of getting things done and not being overly scattered, while still retaining that delightful Gemini versatility of talents.

CANCER, you need not hide your light under barrels! A Leo transit of Chiron should spark some generosity with your personal resources. Rather than hiding in a shell, share your things, thoughts, feelings and space with the world. You'll be happier for it. Your sweet nurturing qualities can be brought out to help others, and you can take pleasure in caring for a larger circle of friends and acquaintances than in the past. Did you know some of the world's funniest comedians/comediennes are Cancers? Cancer Suns Bill Cosby, Harrison Ford and Robin Williams share your innate comedic style and flair for spontaneous crowd-pleasing.

Personality traits you may want to give a little revision to are: stubbornness, closed mindedness, fear of losing personal security, and clannishness that blocks out new contacts with others. You'll find new avenues for your creative skills and perhaps be given some surprisingly good assessments of your professional self-worth this year. You may become more of a toucher, hugger and touchee, having given a little leeway concerning personal space. You'll find out personal security comes from within as well as without, and that you don't need as much protection as you used to feel was required. All in all, a sunnier, funnier you emerges this year. You'll be protected by your newfound confidence; you needn't worry about losing your reserve entirely—you have reserve in reserve.

LEO, who will recognize you by year's end? You're in the process of ripping down the old worn out wallpaper in your personality, and are becoming ready to tackle a whole new image. Chiron makes you wonder what role you've been playing all this time...you're still regal, but now you'll enjoy sharing power with others more. Your natural affectionate nature shines forth and gleans you new friendships and less of an autocratic attitude, if that's what you've been cultivating. Flexibility presents lovely antidotes to your feeling that you must carry the burdens of leading others all by yourself. Leo may actually wind up enjoying playing second fiddle once in awhile this year. The urge to be always on top of the situation is lessened, be it at work or at home, and your sunny loving warmth is allowed to shine more brightly in relationships. It may be a relief not to be in the spotlight all the time; to enjoy a seat in the audience for a change. For once you've doffed your crown in favor of a new hairstyle and feeling part of the group. You can play "Prince and the Pauper," switching roles and going underground in terms of more anonymity if that's been your style, or getting out and about more often if you've played the palace-bound monarch at home. Chiron helps by giving you more group-identified goals and circumstances.

Leo is becoming more of a citizen of the earth, rather than fighting personal wars to extend personal empires. Chiron helps you go with the flow. Though you may feel pinched to begin with, your pride is wounded only until you realize a radical change of course is going to heal you, and free you from oppressive feelings of total responsibility and rigid role playing. Leo always wanted to be playful and join in the game, anyway, right?

VIRGO, who would have dreamed that you had a romantic, warm "old softie" inside just bursting to get out? Chiron has felt like a ghost sneaking up behind you, a subconscious urge tapping on your shoulder and hinting that there's a lot more fun in life than your shy, proper, conventional, analytical style would betray. You're loosening up a bit on your perfectionism, and are less tied to duty at the cost of spontaneous freedom. Maybe some hidden acting talents begin to show, or you start doing some ad lib instead of doing everything by the book.

Since Virgo tends to think "taking care of business" makes everything right with the world, the big surprise of Chiron is probably the discovery of a cuddly, creative Teddy Bear underneath who enjoys occasionally being center stage, being a clown, admitting to egotism and experiencing joy and passion. You might like lavishing a bit of generosity on others and getting some back, though it might embarrass Virgos to acknowledge these spontaneous whims as part of their natures.

Somehow, doing "all the right things" doesn't cut it this year for Virgos. Patiently picking up after others becomes less appealing. You might begin to openly challenge others when you feel they've done you wrong, of course in your own special civilized manner. You inwardly want to shine, so when you hear the whine you recognize as overly passive in your own voice, you're shocked at the passion beneath your cool surface. Perhaps you could check out a support group (and help lead discussions), lead a group rebellion against unfair practices at your work place, have several new romances with people who become not just sweet lovers, but good friends as well; luxuriate occasionally over junk food and exotic foreign fare with far too many calories, or play hooky from work if you've been buried in too much overtime. Or buy a shocking pink sweater that glows in the dark!

You could wind up accepting a promotion that puts you smack in front of the public eye this year, and you may even like the positive feedback and accept it as your due while returning the favor of praise to those from whom you've accepted it. Creative, romantic and dramatic fantasies can come to light, and your fear of sharing your burdens lessen with Chiron's help to guide you. By next year Virgo can feel like a million dollars, with many new adventures to enjoy, and many new friends to enjoy them with. This year can serve as the seeding process of new fruits on your personal tree of life.

LIBRA, Chiron can help you make up your mind. Your social circle has been broadening, and your devotion to new causes on behalf of the public interest has increased. You're developing powerful new friends and becoming a more public personality, full of ideas regarding a better future for yourself and your community. Choosing which people should remain friends or acquaintances and which people to cultivate as more intimate members of your personal circle is the question Chiron proposes to you. Chiron also opens your heart to both the realms of personal and impersonal love: friendship and passion, creative personal leadership, and democratic group participation. You might want to rethink your former vanity and become less theatrical, more laid back in approach. Or sometimes you might permit others to enjoy the spotlight, and enjoy watching. Although you have always been discriminating in the physical appearance of your friends and lovers, you now can permit a broader vision of what beauty constitutes in others. Love becomes less a set of social rules for you, and more of a warm sharing between partners who are free to challenge each other, get angry now and then, and find solutions to some mutual disagreements without having to share the same viewpoint or compromise on every issue. You can broaden your definition of refinement for both yourself and others this year, and be delighted at the diversity of the universe of new knowledge you discover as a result. You may decide to check out new university coursework, and develop a passion for traditional education of some kind. Sliding by on charm becomes less fun than completing educational milestones.

Libra knows how to lead as well as mediate, be a warrior as well as a go-between peacemaker, create new art forms as well as carry others' ideas out for them. Libra is more of a decisionmaker and has the courage of her convictions, incorporating the fine qualities of Ceres, Athena and Aphrodite in a pleasing, womanly manner, while acknowledging her masculine side as well. Her political skills can develop considerably this year, and she can begin to take interest via Chiron's direction to get politically involved in fair governmental structures. Rather than make excuses for others' bad behavior toward her, Libra can begin to expect that some of her cherished ideals are met. The fun begins when she transforms fluff into substance and admirable strength on not merely a personal plane but in a public forum.

SCORPIO, love may be a many-splendored thing, but not at the expense of either party's freedom of choice. One thing Chiron makes clear this year to you is that self-transformation must supersede your hanging on to subtle powerplays over others. You can be free only when you cease trying to manipulate others from behind the scenes. Passion has to be warm as well as enveloping, sunny as well as deep. You can become less merged with others this year, and emerge as a creative element in your own right as a result. Chiron says that you might take a look at your career and possibly go into business on your own. For guidance, look to your boss, or higher-ups in your social milieu whom you wish to emulate. Control of yourself means the freedom to shake old habits out of you like dust shaken out of an old rug. Chiron's Leo transit brings out playfulness, independence, and theatrical flair. If you wish to benefit most, you might transform the intensity of your nature into warm, care-free passion. Like Leo, feel free to bask in the spotlight. You might find, however, that playing ball with the group for a change will be more rewarding.

You probably will enjoy sitting back and watching others make their own decisions for a change, though in the beginning their willfulness may disturb you. Let the adolescent in you come out, let go of some power, and watch what you let go bloom into fruits you didn't expect. Perhaps you may benefit from ignoring your intuition now and then and simply live for the moment.

SAGITTARIUS, now is the time for you to exhibit those talents over which you have mastery (publicly, of course). Express yourself, and stop apologizing for it! Communicate what you know because in the future it will be very valuable. Chiron will be transiting your solar ninth house this year. Educational friendships will be your strongest asset. Be sure to show off a little. Your friends truly admire you, so just relax when you're feeling conscious of yourself. You may also wish to revive old, forgotten friendships and new ones with foreign ideas. Do so. The lesson of Chiron in Leo means to you that you cultivate friendships that last. Gain some stability via exploration and adventure.

This is also a good year to seek higher plateaus of reality. Pursue a unity with the cosmic forces around you. Listen to your heart, it knows where to go. You may find that gambling is rewarding this year. Do use prudence, however. You'll save yourself trouble if you examine your big ideas before acting on them.

CAPRICORN, know thyself, accept thyself, be thyself, but have some fun while you're doing it. You will be standing on the pinnacle this year. This will make it a good year to take a breather to gather shared resources. It will be good to gather your own as well, but seek productive partnerships. This is, strongly, a year to break through your old rituals. You should seek ventures that enhance your creativity. Perhaps you might wish to involve yourself in local government activities. The significance of this year is: You have reached the highest plateau that you can reach on your own. Your Saturnine resources are at their finest. To go higher, you need someone to help you rappel the vertical rocks on which you will soon find yourself. To scale these alone would be folly.

This is also a good time to clean out your closet. Sort out your reasons for keeping various people as enemies. Find out what *you* may have done first to cause the dispute. Perhaps, then, you could extend the olive branch. It would certainly surprise them for you to do so.

This year will be utilized best if you present the Ben Franklin side of yourself to the world. He wasn't just a politician, you know; he was also an inventor, a writer, a revolutionary. He was, literally, the true father of our country (being rumored to have spawned over a hundred children). Be a little more spontaneous this year and pursue creativity.

AQUARIUS will find this year to be incredibly charged—possibly overwhelming. Take great pains to avoid drug or alcohol use this year, as they could consume you. The way to find those desirable levels of transmutative consciousness is in your relationships. It is okay if they seem consuming to you. Don't resist, surrender. Surrendering is the path to freedom this year.

Indulge yourself in Leonine excesses now and then. The Sun may be blinding, but it is also the location of the Holy Grail. Strap on your wings and fly to it. Just ensure that you're not a drunken (or drugged) flyer. This transit brings an awareness of the need to take a new direction in the forest of life. When the forest becomes too cluttered with brambles, take to the sky.

Try to become more independent this year. This may conflict with your desires to become absorbed into a social group. In reality, there is no conflict. When you become independent and develop your ego, your social experiences will be dramatically improved. When you know who you are and what you're about you can also know clearly what you have to offer to others. The flip side of the coin is that you will be able to develop your individuality best within the context of a one on one relationship. Seek a relationship that allows you to be free to develop yourself.

You may even want to be a little aristocratic this year, setting aside the collective, humanitarian nature. You can always return to it when needed, but exploring different lifestyles can be fun. Indulge yourself in luxuries simply because you want to, not because there is a philosophical reason to do so. Worry less about what is socially correct, do something because you want to.

PISCES is being advised by Chiron to be less timid. Speak your mind, damn the consequences. Don't let people walk over you. This may be a good time to take an extra job so that you can build the house you've been dreaming of. If your job isn't paying you what you'd like, stand up and ask for a raise. You deserve it. Don't tolerate second best, it's not worth your time. Don't sacrifice your own creative projects to help others this year. There is nothing wrong with assertively asking "Could you come back later?" Do things on your time as much as possible, let others do the compromising for a change. This will slow the pace down a little so that you can get more things done.

Since you spend so much time pampering others, why not pamper yourself for a change. Take really good care of yourself this year. Get plenty of rest. You may find that sunbathing is very refreshing. Definitely get plenty of fresh air and sunshine. It works wonders on the health.

It will also be important to connect with whichever force you call God. You may find that camping trips will help you in doing this. When you see nature in its stark nakedness, it is hard not to feel the presence of deity. The more you camp, the closer you'll get to being one with the forces around you. Also, camping provides plenty of the fresh air and sunshine that your body needs. When your body is whole, your spirit follows suit.

The World's Four Great Astrological Traditions

Bruce Scofield

Imagine, if you will, living in a very, very ancient time. You are part of an agricultural community that survives because it knows how to grow and harvest a few crops. When the crops fail, because of weather, pests, or warfare, the community is in trouble and starvation, fear and death is often the result. Life is not easy but a few very intelligent members of your community spend many hours watching the sky for signs that may give them just a little more control over the vagaries of nature. These are first astrologers.

Astrology was born out of a need to stabilize and control human life in an uncertain world. Nomads and hunters have less need for such organization, but agriculturalists thrive on it. After all, doesn't plant growth follow the Sun? When the Sun rises due east, life is bursting forth, seeds are splitting and shoots are rising above the soil. When the Sun rises north of due east, summer sets in and plant life thrives. When the Sun returns to a due east rising point again, the harvest comes and plant life begins to ebb. When the Sun rises south of east, winter, cold, and a life indoors becomes the way. Plant life is dormant, awaiting the time when the Sun rises again in the east.

Agriculture and astrology grew up together. To be more precise, I should say astrology/astronomy/calendrics as all three were intimately linked to each other. This was the first science, the careful measuring of time, designated by a few primary astronomical movements, and the implications of time's distinctions for human life. As we have seen, the careful observation of the Sun's rising or setting point throughout the year will produce a useful body of information about the life cycle of plants. Plant in the spring and harvest in the fall—that's just how it is. Spring comes when the Sun rises at a specific point and this happens every 365 days. So you see, we've got some astronomy here with the Sun watching, some calendrics with the counting of days, and some astrology with the knowledge of the time for planting. The solar year is thus one of the cornerstones of astrology. It designates the yearly vegetation cycle and it marks out the four directions and the seasons.

The alternation of day and night is even more primary than the cycle of the year. This basic astronomical rhythm is our best counting unit. Without it we'd be nowhere. The day is like the year; it has an emerging quality at dawn, a domination of light at noon, a dimming of light at dusk and the domination of dark at midnight. The day literally makes time. How could we define what time is without a rhythmic alteration of at least one astronomical movement, and the day is by far the best candidate for a calendrical cornerstone. There is one other obvious rhythm in the sky, and that is the cycle of the Moon. With its phases it marks off an irregular rhythm, yet one that does correlate with the fertility and birth patterns of wild and domesticated mammals. It relates to the Sun and makes about 12 cycles in one year. How interesting, and what a challenge for the time-keepers of our ancient agricultural community! Measuring and counting time was the first great intellectual challenge for the human animal, and an early step toward mastery of the planet.

In the inhabited world of ancient times, four general regions saw the rise of great agricultural civilizations. These aggregates of humans that lived together produced great art, complex codes of conduct, religions and philosophies to explain the meaning of life and countless labor-saving devices. All of this was made possible by successful agriculture. As would be expected, these centers of culture and civilization had early on developed a sophisticated science of astrology/astronomy/calendrics. Successful agriculture is only possible with this knowledge. In Mesopotamia history records the growth of cities and federations of cities along the Tigris/Euphrates Rivers. In the valley of the Indus River at places like Harappa and Mohenjo-daro, Indian civilization began. The valley of the

Huang Ho (Yellow River) was the place where Chinese civilization took form and along the Gulf of Mexico, near present day Veracruz, Mesoamerica produced its earliest cities and cultural centers.

MESOPOTAMIA

Each of these four regions tackled the challenge of conquering time in its own distinctive way and the astrological traditions that grew out of these earliest of scientific efforts are like wise unique. As Westerners, we are most familiar with the astrological tradition of the West, one which is built on foundations laid in Mesopotamia thousands of years ago. In ancient times, skywatchers on ziggurats carefully observed the risings and settings of Sun, Moon and planets and noted any phenomena occur ring in human lives that correlated with sky changes. They named the patterns of stars that the Sun, Moon and planets moved through and interpreted them in terms of the cycle of life. Although there has been some considerable displacement between the seasons and the constellations over the past 4,000 or so years, the sequence of zodiac signs does seem to be a coded model of the year. The fact that there are 12 signs is probably a result of what is obvious in nature, that the Moon cycles approximately 12 times in one year.

From ancient Mesopotamia comes our 7-day planetary week. In counting time, we have seen that the day itself must be the primary unit. But counting 365 days for the year is unwieldy, so smaller units were necessarily created. Seven days is 1/4 the roughly 28-day cycle of the Moon, and there are 7 visible planets, including the Sun and Moon. Each of the 7 days is named for a planet and is said to be ruled by it. We can see these planetary names in any of the romance languages; English uses the Nordic equivalents of the Roman gods associated with each planet. Each day was divided into 24 hours, 12 for daylight and 12 for night. These weren't equal hours, they varied according to the length of the day which changes during the year. But the system was definitely astrological because the hours were ruled by the 7 planets in a definite order, the order of their average rate of motion against the sky. The 7 planets that rule the hours cycle three times during the entire day and after 21 hours a new cycle begins. Whichever planet rules the first hour of the day, the hour after sunrise, gives its name to that day—hence, the names of the days and the order of the week. What we have here is an astrology that names, and consequently gives meaning to, blocks of time. As we will see, this same concept appeared in ancient China and Mesoamerica and formed the core of their astrological systems.

The astrology of Mesopotamia was an astrology also concerned with sky omens, especially those of the planets. Conjunctions and oppositions were observed in the clear, unobstructed skies of the ancient Near East. Planets on the horizon, just rising or setting, were studied and this emphasis survives as the Ascendant and Descendant points in the modern Western astrological chart. When the Greeks took power in the ancient Near East, they began to geometricize Mesopotamian astrology until it became almost entirely spatial. They added aspects, house divisions, and made the ecliptic based 12-sign zodiac the showpiece of the system. True, much of what they did was built on older ideas, but to them must go the credit for constructing a tight system. By Roman times, astrology was a codified science with a clear cut methodology, described in books and practiced by experts. Today, this tradition is still very much alive and constantly evolving.

INDIA

In ancient India, skywatchers also learned to make calendars and predict where planets would be. The Vedas, the sacred writings of ancient India, reveal a sky-knowledge that dates back to very early times. In 323 BCE Alexander the Great extended his empire into part of India and opened the flood-gates for an exchange of cultures. Greco-Mesopotamian astrology found its way into India and influenced the form that Indian astrology eventually took. By the time the great Indian astrologer Vaharamihira published his masterwork on astrology, the Brihat Jataka, the distinctive elements of Indian astrology, a blend of ancient Vedic and Greco/Mesopotamian astrology, were in place.

The exchange with Western astrology brought in the 12-sign zodiac, but in India its first point became tagged to the constellation Aries, not the vernal equinox as has become the tradition in the West. Today, Indian astronomers practice a sidereal astrology, placing the planets in signs that use the same names as in Western astrology, but are displaced from that zodiac by about 24 degrees. The distance between the two is called the Ayanamsa, a distance that is set officially by the government astrologer in India, though there is still debate among experts who use different figures. The horoscope used in India is very similar to the square charts used by astrologers in Roman and Medieval times. Like Western astrology, Indian astrology became quite spatial and aspects and house positions are fundamental to the system.

Although very wide orbs are used in Indian astrology when interpreting aspects, other techniques are employed that reveal subtle details about the distribution of the planets in the zodiac. Each zodiac sign is divided into thirds, fifths, sixths, sevenths, eighths, ninths, etc. A chart called the Navamsa chart, based on a division of signs into ninths, is commonly used in modern Indian astrology to analyze relationships. Essentially, this chart measures the novile aspects between planets, a minor aspect of 40° that most Western astrologers ignore.

One very unique and probably indigenous element of Indian astrology are the Nakshatras, the 27 lunar mansions or signs of the Moon. These are each 13° 20 minutes in length and begin at the first point of Aries. The Nakshatra in which the Moon at birth is found is the foundation for perhaps the most interesting technique in Indian astrology, the computation of the Dasas. In this forecasting technique, the spatial position of the Moon determines the sequence of time periods that affect the native throughout the course of life. In other words, space is turned into time. But isn't this just what astrology is about and has always done?

CHINA

India was certainly much influenced by Greco-Mesopotamian culture, but China, far more isolated, was less so. In China, astrology took on different forms from any we have seen so far. First of all, the planets, Sun and Moon were not measured against the ecliptic-based zodiac, they were measured against the equator. The pole star that never moves was a point of great importance to the Chinese and it is the celestial equator, not the ecliptic, that relates to this point. Twenty-eight unequal lunar mansions on the equator, called Hsiu, divided the sky and the position of the Moon in each of these zones acquired a meaning. But this is about as far as Chinese positional or spatial astrology went. The real core of the system lies in an interesting interplay of time cycles.

In very ancient times the Ten Celestial Stems, a sequence of ten symbols that are possibly the remnants of a ten-day week, became established as symbolic cycle. Later the Twelve Terrestrial Branches, another cycle of stages, were combined with the ten Stems to create a cycle of 60 days, or 60 years. In a 60-day or 60-year period there are six cycles of the Stems and five cycles of the Branches. Each day or year in the cycle would then have two names, one for the Stem, one for the Branch. This same interplay of ten and twelve, using the same names, was also applied to months and hours. In the case of months, one year will, with fancy adjustments, contain 12 months and so five years will yield 60 months. In terms of hours, five days of 12 hours each gives us the number 60 again. The year, month, day and hour of one's birth, the four pillars of destiny as they are called, are then designated by a pair of names. Associations with the five elements of Chinese astrology (fire, earth, metal, water and wood) and the polarities (yin and yang) further individualize the information about the birth moment. Today, Chinese astrologers still utilize the system and almanacs are regularly published containing tables for determining the astrological qualities of any given day.

A full Chinese astrological reading, however, actually takes into consideration more than just the four pillars of destiny. The 28 lunar constellations are said to rule a day each, such that every four weeks of seven days begins the cycle anew. These constellations indicate the factor of chance and are used not only in interpreting a birth, but also for choosing auspicious days to do things on. Another factor considered in a reading is the animal that rules the year of birth. This is a cycle of 12 years (not to be confused with the Twelve Terrestrial Branches), each named for an animal and beginning with the Chinese New Year in early February. It is this element of Chinese astrology that has become so popular in the Western world, but as we have seen, is in reality only a small portion of a complex system. The influence of the year of birth is said to denote the moral character of the person.

MESOAMERICA

We come now to the fourth, and least known, of the world's great astrological traditions, the time-based astrology of Mesoamerica. Around the time of the ancient Greeks a civilization along the eastern coast of today's Mexico was flourishing. Today known as the Olmecs, these forerunners of the Maya, Toltecs and Aztecs built pyramids, ceremonial centers and created a complex astro-calendrical system that was carried by later cultures right up to the present day. During the Classic period of the Maya, when Europe was in its Dark Ages, this system evolved into one of the world's most sophisticated intellectual constructions. Scholars have long marveled at the precision achieved by the Maya in measuring the year and the cycles of the Moon. The purpose of all this astronomy was, however, to improve their astrology.

The Maya, Toltecs, Aztecs and other pre-Columbian groups of Mesoamerica based their astrological analyses on the interplay of day-counts, not at all unlike the Chinese. They used a cycle of 13 and a cycle of 20 which interfaced every 260 days as the core of their system. Also like the Chinese, they projected this cycle onto a larger frame of reference dividing their creation cycle of 5,125 years into 260 units of 7,200 days called katuns. The present creation cycle is due to end on 12/21/2012, and it is this event that 1987's Harmonic Convergence was heralding. On 4/6/1993 we begin the last, 260th, katun of the series that began in 3113 BCE.

The key concept in Mesoamerican astrology is the notion of time as a sign. As we have already seen the astrology of the West is mostly spatial. The most important yardsticks in that system are the signs of the zodiac, each measuring 30° degrees of space along the ecliptic. A conjunction of planets or an eclipse is interpreted according to the sign it occurs in. In ancient Mexico, astrologers interpreted a conjunction or eclipse according to the 13-day sign it occurred in, as well as other time factors. Perhaps the most carefully watched planet was Venus. The 13-day sign that it began its 584-day cycle in was of utmost importance, yet made predictable using complex tables of its cycle computed by ancient astrologers.

In terms of a horoscope for a birth, Mesoamerican astrology is similar to Chinese astrology. There is no chart, per se, just a list of factors that need to be considered in the analysis of character and destiny. First came the year of birth, one of four signs that were part of a 52-year cycle. Next was the 20- and 13-day periods that the birth fell into. The day-sign, perhaps the most important and personal of the significators, was studied closely. In ancient times it may have been used as a part of a person's name. Each of these signs was linked to one of the four directions that functions in many ways like the four elements in Western astrology. The ruler of the hour of birth and the phases of the Moon and Venus extended the interpretation. Because the Spanish friars did a thorough job in eliminating anything they saw as pagan, we are not completely sure about the elements of a traditional horoscope reading. What we do know of this great tradition is based partly on the works of archaeoastronomers and anthropologists. Also, in remote parts of Mexico and Guatamala, an oral tradition of this ancient astrology has survived and today researchers are recording and documenting pieces of this lost knowledge. Perhaps in the not too distant future, the wealth of knowledge acquired by the great civilizations of ancient America will be available to all.

We have lightly touched on four very different ways of relating the individual to the sky, time and the cosmic environment. In each case, space and time are systematized and used to interpret the life on earth. Did the ancients discover some truly deep secrets about life? It is possible they did since life on this planet evolved within a repetitive cosmic environment. Is it not true that we carry within us today the remnants of earlier forms of life? And is it not possible that these earlier forms utilized the constantly repeating rhythms of the cosmic environment, the alternation of day and night, as "pegs" on which cyclic organic functions are based? If the answer is yes, then we have the sky inside us and the ancient astrologers were pioneers in finding it.

While it is true that there are many differences of opinion among experts in regard to methodology in each of these traditions, the main thrust of each is distinctive. In many respects it is astonishing that these ancient traditions have not only survived thousands of years into the present, but they are still alive and evolving. While modern science seeks to control and dominate nature, astrological science seeks to work with nature and understand man's place within the greater realities of time and heaven. This is a quest well worth pursuing for the sake of all on this planet. It is my sincere hope that those in opposition to this quest (official science, academia, fundamentalist religion, etc.) will experience a change of attitude and acknowledge the need for self-knowledge and timing, the two great contributions of the world's astrologies.

FOR FURTHER READING:

Aveni, Anthony F. *Skywatchers of Ancient Mexico*. Austin: University of Texas Press. 1980.

Braha, James T. *Ancient Hindu Astrology for the Modern Western Astrologer*. Florida: Hermetician Press. 1986.

Dreyer, Ronnie Gale. *Indian Astrology: A Western Approach to the Ancient Hindu Art*. England: The Aquarian Press. 1990.

Gleadow, Rupert. *The Origin of the Zodiac*. New York: Castle Books. 1968.

Kermadec, J. M. H. de. *The Way to Chinese Astrology*. Trs. N. Derek Poulsen. London: Unwin Paperbacks. 1983.

Krupp, Dr. E. C. *Echoes of the Ancient Skies*. New York: Harper and Row. 1983.

Scofield, Bruce. *Day-Signs: Native American Astrology From Ancient Mexico*. Amherst, MA: One Reed Publications. 1991.

Tester, Jim. *A History of Western Astrology*. New York: Ballantine Books. 1987.

Walters, Derek. *Chinese Astrology: Interpreting the Revelations of the Celestial Messengers*. England: The Aquarian Press. 1987.

The Zodiac: Pathway to Power and Peace

Ninah Kessler

Many roads can lead to our destiny. What is important, in the words of Carlos Castenada, is that we choose a path with heart. This means finding the way that is in keeping with our truest nature.

The signs of the zodiac suggest different avenues toward self-realization. They offer various possibilities for connecting with our power and for finding peace. Each sign also has its detours, where we get stuck or sidetracked.

1993 is a special time for all of us, as Uranus, the planet of technology and innovation, conjoins with Neptune, the planet of spirituality. Uranus also represents revolution, and Neptune is associated with an attachment to illusion. Will we use our technology to delude ourselves and destroy our planet? Or will we combine innovation and spirituality to create a better world?

In this article I will explore the characteristic paths and choices of the astrological signs. The focus will be on where the Uranus/Neptune conjunction occurs in the chart, as this is where we have the greatest possibility for the use or misuse of our power in the year ahead.

ARIES
The first sign of the zodiac, Aries always takes the direct route. Like crocuses in the spring, oblivious to the late season frosts, they burst forth with life. They do things for the pure joy of the moment, and can get so involved with activity that they can become "human doings" instead of human beings. To avoid burnout, Aries need to use their heads for more than battering rams. When forethought and insight are combined with enthusiasm, they become

the trailblazers of the zodiac. They dare to go where no one has gone before, pioneering advances in consciousness.

As we are entering a new age, the celestial rams are assuming leadership roles. Many are already positioned among the elite of governments and corporations, in key places to make the changes necessary to safeguard the planet. They have access to world leaders and have the technology necessary to create a balanced global village. Even less well positioned rams are likely to become more influential with their peers. They are likely to become irritable and rebellious if they just try to maintain the status quo. Aries have the power and the capability to make sure that the circles of light are more than just specs in the darkness. They are more likely to succeed if they master the art of networking, accept a little help from their friends, and understand the corporate power structure.

TAURUS

The road that Taurus travels is green, lush, filled with abundance. Like Vulcan, the mythic forger of metals, the bull can make the most of the riches of the earth, The bull also has a definite talent for acquisitions, and his conspicuous consumption can clog his home with possessions and his arteries with cholesterol. When Taurean resourcefulness and perseverance are used more positively, the bull stewards the planet and ensures that each creature can fulfill his basic needs. While Taurus may be slow in getting started on the path, he will achieve his goals. And the bull has the ability to make the most of each step along the way—making a feast from a simple repast and decorating a cottage so it is more comfortable than a castle.

It's time for the bull to aspire to a vision of a better future, and once he knows the direction he will travel he can spread the word to others. Many Tauruses could find themselves involved with teaching at universities, meeting with metaphysicians, or conferring with foreign dignitaries. For those who are unsure of where they want to go, seek a teacher. (Remember that the teacher appears when the student is ready.) You might want to get a doctorate, study in the mystery schools, work with a guru, or learn the ways of the American Indians. Once you have learned what you need to know, you are likely to find a position in a high place where you can share your vision with others.

Achievement is more likely if you can work in cooperation with others.

GEMINI

Gemini rules the roads, and their path is a busy one, filled with dispersing information and interacting with others. While happiest going in several directions at once, the twins are apt to suffer from nervous exhaustion if they don't give themselves adequate breathing room. The way of Gemini is the way of the butterfly—gliding on the wind, spreading beauty and hope. The evolved twins make it look easy, but they have spent time in a cocoon in one lifetime or another. Gemini is the sign of the golden rule—do onto others as you would have others do onto you. It makes sense that the sign that rules siblings and neighbors would teach us about brotherhood.

Now Geminis have the opportunity to decide how they will use their way with words. Will they use double-talk to strengthen their financial empires, or will their eloquence inspire more positive transformation? Even if they started with an agenda to increase their net worth, changes in the economy, the world banking system and corporate finances have made them wonder if they are really on the right path. The twins are in a position to make changes in the power structure that could improve the lives of millions and the health of the earth. They tap into this ability when they realize that greatness comes from service and humility.

CANCER

Crabs move sideways, and while they are active they are seldom direct. They need exoskeletons and camouflage to protect their soft underbellies. Even with all their defenses, they can still be hurt, flooded with negative emotions. Cancers who are traveling in the wrong direction cling to their homes and families, rather than using their connections to support them in new endeavors. Their true path is to nurture the human family and to get there they must grow beyond their preconceived limits. This can be a pretty scary process, as it must be for the crab when he molts. However, when Cancers are able to use their vulnerability positively, then their intuitiveness and imagination can nurture others.

The past few years have not necessarily been kind to Cancers in relationships. Not only have there been ups and downs, but they may have wondered who it was they were relating to. And those who have stayed in relationships for financial security are finding that it was not worth the wait. The cause of all this agony is that Cancers are looking for their soul mates, and these challenging partnerships are constantly reminding them of the work they will still need to do. Once they learn to accept and support without becoming co-dependent, they are on their way to connecting with that special someone.

LEO

Regal lions are the rulers of the jungle, and they rub shoulders with the rich and the famous. When they abuse their power they are pushy, arrogant and conceited. But Leos don't really want to be bullies—they have too much heart for that. They are really just learning how to be themselves. Leos on the path teach us that we are the center of our universe, here to shine, to create and to enjoy ourselves. Leo's season is the height of summer, when the light is the longest, the days are the warmest, and we share our good times with others.

Since many Leos gravitate towards the world of entertainment, and sports, they are particularly at risk for infection, specifically AIDS. Lions may need to learn not to be too attached to fame. Even if they are not in these fields, Leos may be getting sick from all the changes at work. Health and happiness can increase with a return to more goddess-centered values, like the importance of nurturing ourselves, our loved ones, and our planet. Power comes from developing roots and finding work where we are able to be of service to others. While hard lessons come from partners, those who stick with you now are likely to last a lifetime.

VIRGO

Virgo is the sign of the harvest, when we separate the wheat form the chaff and celebrate our abundance. Perhaps the virgin has heightened her discrimination and analytical ability because of all the time she spent looking for the needle in the haystack. Virgos are at risk for overwhelming themselves with useless trivialities, especially an obsession with hygiene. They have a tendency to be overly critical and to settle only for perfection. Perhaps they have such high expectations because of their ties with ancient earth mothers and the Goddesses Eve, Isis, and Mary. They are virgins in the sense of not belonging to anyone, and in the sanctity they create they pursue their ritual observances. Here they nurture the divine, both in themselves and in others.

The Virgin may wish to renew her vows of chastity this year. Love affairs may not have turned out the way she expected them to, and her awareness that the only safe sex is monogamy or celibacy heightens her selectivity. On the more positive side, this is a time of self-expression through creativity and procreation. Virgo's technical mastery could produce masterpieces with crystals, dazzle the world with computer graphics, or use word processing to articulate intellectual innovations. Her power comes from marketing these creative products so that others can access them. This can also be a time of self-expression through participating in the birth process.

LIBRA

Libras are indecisive—at the crossroads not knowing which way to turn. To make this decision they need to cultivate balance and discrimination, represented by the scales of justice. (Thoth used these scales to weigh the sins of the soul against a feather.) Ultimately, this balance entails the harmonizing of opposites—the male and the female, the active and the receptive, the spiritual and the material. While Librans are walking this tightrope, they can use their good looks and social skills to make a good marriage, enjoy the refinements of culture, and get invited to the right parties.

Home is likely to have been on Libra's mind lately. Not just that four-bedroom tudor in the suburbs, but where they came from and where their roots are. This may have been precipitated by all the moving that they've been doing. The lesson is that our true home is the earth, and like all other physical realities, our planet needs to be cared for. Their power comes form stewarding the planet, ensuring that resources are used in an ecologically positive manner. This is facilitated by adapting the most appropriate technology.

SCORPIO

In the time of the Scorpion the forces of the dark overpower those of the light, and the way is within to connect with inner resources. Scorpio is the season of cleansing, of letting go all that is unnecessary. It is the energy of kundalini, curled up at the base of the spine, waiting for cultivation so its power can be used for transformation. Scorpions on the low road are attracted to their desires and attack those in their way. Firebirds are on a higher path, creating intense situations so like the pheonix they can be reborn from their own ashes.

This is Scorpio's time of power, and it comes from letting go of the superficialities and connecting with who they really are. They can become cornerstones of their communities, making sure that there are good schools, health care and social services, a flourishing economy, and a balanced ecosystem. To do this, they need to let go of rigid, self-defeating thought patterns and open to positive innovations. They can succeed if they plant roots, cultivating a life-sustaining ecosystem for themselves, their loved ones, and their families.

SAGITTARIUS

The archers of the zodiac aim for the highest star. Since their goals are often unrealistic, Sagittarians can promise more than they can deliver, disappointing the more earth-bound signs. But since we cannot achieve what we cannot conceive, the Archers also attain far more than other mortals. When Sagittarians choose a path, they want it to be one that covers a lot of ground—whether it be expeditions to distant corners of the globe, forays into universities, or meditations on the meaning of life and death. Their treks are not in vain. The evolved Sagittarian is the teacher, sharing his findings with less adventurous souls and inspiring them to continue on the path.

Many archers are currently discouraged about their present financial situation, experiencing the results of fluctuations in their income levels as well as mad schemes that didn't work out. It is time to discover that they have all of the resources that they really need and to learn the laws of prosperity. Transform financial worries into affirmations, be thankful for what you have, and use your resources in innovative and ecologically sound ways. Meditation, innovation and the humanitarian use of technology can provide the answer to pecuniary difficulties. Rethinking problems with others in your community can make the flow much easier.

CAPRICORN

This sign begins when the light is most scarce and nature is least hospitable. Perhaps this is why the goat thrives on adversity. Capricorns need to watch a tendency to make things too hard for themselves, and may actually need to work at having a good time. But lack of material niceties facilitates travel on the spiritual path. Capricorn is symbolized by the mountain goat, and the mountain represents the challenges that we need to overcome to reach self-realization. In most mythical traditions, those who ascend to the peak do not remain there, but like the bodhisattva, bring the truth back down. An example is Moses and the Ten Commandments at Mount Sinai.

Goats in three-piece suits have climbed to the top of the corporate ladder during the last decade. Now many have lost their liquidity or are finding out that happiness does not come from a BMW or a Gold Card. Capricorns in it for material success alone need to restructure their self-image. Meanwhile, the planet could use their managerial expertise. Their true power comes from working with others of like minds to create an ecologically sound environment.

AQUARIUS

Aquarius is the final air sign, where we explore the farthest reaches of rational investigation. Here information blends with consciousness. As we enter the Age of Aquarius, the way of the water bearer increases in strength. While even the most conservative Aquarian looks toward the future, less evolved natives can get so involved in advanced technology that there is a rift between the mind and intuition. Here we get nuclear nightmares and star wars. On a more personal level, Aquarians can make everyone their friend as a defense against intimate relationships. The more positive path is to use their intelligence and networking skills to inspire others and to create positive change.

Aquarians are powerfully placed in our information age, as they know how to use electronics to access data.

Powerful karmic lessons are coming up in the year ahead. Many are technological experts from previous aeons—some may have been among those who misused personal power in Atlantis. Now there are chances for redemption by following the path of the modern wizard, by using computers, fiber optics, and lasers to serve humanity. When they are on their true path, help is likely to come from those in high places.

PISCES

The symbol of Pisces is two fish swimming in opposite directions—no wonder they are confused. While one fish represents material reality, the other represents the spiritual; Pisces inhabits both worlds. They are most often mislead through the path of glamour. They get hooked on illusion and wind up in addiction and delusion. A more positive path is the infusion of the spiritual into the material, and the recognition that what we consider to be reality is really insubstantial. We are just leaving the Age of Pisces, and the lessons of this sign were well known by Jesus, the master of this age. He advised us not to put our faith into things that could be stolen by thieves or could turn to dust. These words illustrate the primary Piscean lessons of faith and belief.

This year Pisceans may experience changes in what they wish for. They can continue to escape through drugs and addictions, courting serious health problems and sabotaging their lives. Or they can use their imaginations to dream the dreams that others live. The fish can provide the rest of us with the vision we need to create a new world order that respects the rights of all sentient beings. Once they have overcome their inner fears and preconceived limitations, their power comes from the sacred information that they access and share with others.

CONCLUSION

We have all incarnated at a very special time, one in which we will determine the future of the planet. We can create a hostile environment and a foreboding world, filled with noxious chemicals and temperature extremes. Or we can return to the Garden of Eden—lush, beautiful, meeting our needs.

It is said that during the Age of Leo, Atlanteans destroyed their continent through improper use of technology. Now, 10,000 years later, we are entering the Age of Aquarius with the capacity to enhance or destroy the earth. Will we make the same mistakes? Or will we find the path that connects us with our power and enables us to find peace?

Either this...

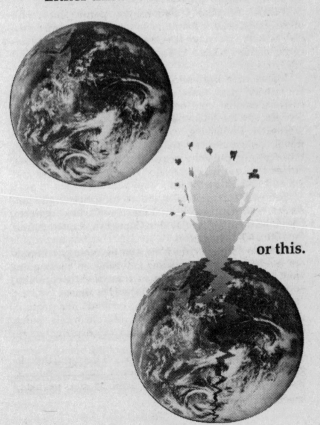

or this.

PLANETARY ASSOCIATIONS

Sun: Authority figures, favors, advancement, health, success, display, drama, promotion, fun, matters related to Leo and the 5th House.

Moon: Short trips, women, children, the public, domestic concerns, emotions, fluids, matters related to Cancer and the 4th House.

Mercury: Communications, correspondence, phone calls, computers, messages, education, students, travel, merchants, editing, writing, advertising, signing contracts, siblings, neighbors, kin, matters related to Gemini, Virgo, and the 3rd and 6th Houses.

Venus: Affection, relationships, partnerships, alliances, grace, beauty, harmony, luxury, love, art, music, social activity, marriage, decorating, cosmetics, gifts, income, matters related to Taurus, Libra, and the 2nd and 7th Houses.

Mars: Strife, aggression, sex, physical energy, muscular activity, guns, tools, metals, cutting, surgery, police, soldiers, combat, confrontation, matters related to Aries, Scorpio, and the 1st and 8th Houses.

Jupiter: Publishing, college education, long-distance travel, foreign interests, religion, philosophy, forecasting, broadcasting, publicity, expansion, luck, growth, sports, horses, the Law, matters related to Sagittarius, Pisces, and 9th and 12th House issues.

Saturn: Structure, reality, the laws of society, limits, obstacles, tests, hard work, endurance, real estate, dentists, bones, teeth, matters related to Capricorn, Aquarius, and the 10th and 11th Houses.

Uranus: Astrology, the New Age, technology, computers, modern gadgets, lecturing, advising, counseling, inventions, reforms, electricity, new methods, originality, matters related to Aquarius and the 11th House.

Neptune: Mysticism, music, creative imagination, dance, illusion, sacrifice, service, oil, chemicals, paint, drugs, anesthesia, sleep, religious experience, matters related to Pisces and the 12th House.

Pluto: Probing, penetration, goods of the dead, investigation, insurance, taxes, others' money, loans, the masses, the underworld, transformation, death, matters related to Scorpio and the 8th House.

Directory
of
Products
and
Services

Finally revealed! Hollywood's best-kept secret!

SYLVESTER STALLONE:
"My Mother's 'Supersuccess' Horoscope Led Me To Worldwide Stardom and Riches!"

Now! Jacqueline Stallone – the world's most accurate astrologer – offers you personal "Supersuccess" Horoscope details absolutely FREE! *(Pay nothing now.)*

Discover here how a new kind of horoscope, Jacqueline Stallone's "Supersuccess" Horoscope, can bring you success and money – even if nothing is going right for you now.

This totally different horoscope has already turned around many lives around the world with spectacular results.

For the surprising reason revealed to you below, details about this "Supersuccess" Horoscope are offered to you completely free (but for a strictly limited time) by the woman who is acclaimed the "World's Most Accurate Astrologer" by the Wallace Book of Records: Jacqueline Stallone. Here — the irresistible free details offer she made to our readers (to you) during a recent interview.

The astonishing confession of Sylvester Stallone

Me, my younger brother, Frank (just nominated for three Grammy Awards), my sister, Toniann (successful author of children's mystery stories) — our lives and careers have been guided by a "Supersuccess" Horoscope prepared by our mother, Jacqueline Stallone.

Thanks to her amazing horoscope, I have always known which route to choose. What I had to do. And when.

The only time I didn't follow the negative instructions of the stars was when I fell in love with Brigitte.

You already know the disastrous results...

EXCLUSIVE INTERVIEW with Jacqueline Stallone

By AMY BLAKE

Question: Can the "Supersuccess" Horoscope solve the money problems of ordinary people who have never been successful — or with urgent financial problems?

Jacqueline Stallone: It is especially these people with money problems whom I would like to help. The fact that some people have to work hard to live but have little money has always made me mad.

Question: Is it true that a "Supersuccess" Horoscope makes it possible to find out if a person will succeed or not? And if they'll be rich or not?

Jacqueline Stallone: As I'm sure you already know, life offers us a choice of many directions to take. One choice can take you to success, money and love. Another direction can take you toward stalemate and failure. The main purpose of the "Supersuccess" Horoscope is to indicate the direction that will take you to success...and money! And if something in your future is negative, your "Supersuccess" Horoscope, prepared especially for you from your date of birth, tells you what to do to make it positive.

Question: Is it true that it was a "Supersuccess" Horoscope which guided the life of your son, Sylvester Stallone, to top-ranked success and money?

Jacqueline Stallone: Yes, it's true. Although I must say that he is also particularly gifted.

For specific details, see page 115 of Jacqueline Stallone's book, "Star Power."

Question: Do you know other people who have succeeded because of this kind of horoscope?

Jacqueline Stallone: Countless numbers. Obviously, professional secrecy does not permit me to reveal their names. Nevertheless, everyone knows that even one of our former presidents ran the White House by a horoscope based on what the stars indicated should be done.

Question: Does a "Supersuccess" Horoscope clearly indicate what to do — and what not to do?

Jacqueline Stallone: A "Supersuccess" Horoscope is like a road sign. It tells you the best route to take to achieve success and money. It also indicates what things or people you have to avoid, and what opportunities and chances you should take. And just as important, it tells you clearly which are the periods during which you should not undertake anything at all. As you'll see, a "Supersuccess" Horoscope contains things that you never would have dreamed could exist in a horoscope.

Question: Can a normal horoscope give the same predictions?

Jacqueline Stallone: A normal horoscope is a general horoscope. It tells you what's going to happen, but it doesn't tell you the best route to take. So you hesitate. Should I do this? Should I do that? A "Supersuccess" Horoscope tells you. The result? You succeed. Words can't express the benefits you get from it. Life will have new meaning for you. You'll do what you want to do instead of having to do things you hate doing.

Question: If a big change is about to happen — like a period of luck, or love — does the "Supersuccess" Horoscope predict it?

Jacqueline Stallone:

A TRUE LOVE STORY

by Irene Hamlen Stephenson

Napoleon and Josephine loved one another very much. They could laugh and have fun together. They loved having people look at them, They needed more attention than average. They were charming, outgoing natural born actors.

Napoleon and Josephine thought alike, They could talk things over. They both were martyr types who could take a lot of abuse. They were drawn toward trouble.

They were alike in the emotional and mental area. Josephine was very confident and sexy. Napoleon was not. Napoleon had wars to prove to the whole world that he was a man. When he was at war he would leave Josephine behind. She would seek company of other men.

Napoleon and Josephine had a to divorce because she did not bear him a son. When they were parted their love grew strong. As long as they were not involved physically they forgot the problems they had in that area and remembered only their love.

Even tho they were not married anymore, Josephine wrote to Napoleon and asked permission to join him in exile at Elba. Before his letter arrived Josephine died.

This MINI Biorhythm Compatibility and Character Analysis show there was much love in their relationship.

- - - - - - - - - - - - - - - - - - - -

IS IT TRUE LOVE?

Is this the love of your life? Is it good enough for marriage? What is missing to keep you from being happy together? I will tell you the vital points of your relationship.

Irene Hamlen Stephenson - BIORHYTHM COMPATIBILITY
P.O. Box 3893-S93, Chatsworth, CA 91313

☐ Enclosed is $20 for an **INDEPTH COMPATIBILITY**
(2 birthdates: month, day, year)

Male or Female   _____   _____   _____
with
Male or Female   _____   _____   _____

You may ask one queston about your relationship with your order. I will answer if I can.

☐ Send your self-addressed stamped envelope for a FREE newsletter on the famous , infamous and non-famous. Irene Hamlen Stephenson is listed in a number of Who's Who books.

Your Name _____

Address _____

City/State/Zip _____

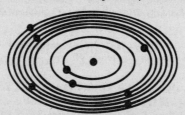

ARE YOU DESTINED FOR TRUE LOVE?
ASK ME ABOUT LOVE SUCCESS MONEY
I CAN TELL YOU WHAT THE FUTURE HOLDS
DISCOVER YOUR SECRET DESTINY!
CALL NOW!
Talk LIVE with America's leading professional Psychics and Astrologers.
1-900-740-2002
Open 24 hours a day. $2.95 per minute. Callers must be 18.
© 1991 Phone Vision, Inc. P.O. Box 307, Mill Valley, CA 94942
For customer service, call 1-800-282-8880

Professional Chart Readings From Llewellyn

Llewellyn is a leading authority in astrological chart readings. Our thirty years of professional experience assures satisfaction and a large selection of special astrological services.

Llewellyn features both computerized chart services and personalized readings. All of our personalized services are done by professional astrologers—whether you need a chart calculated or answers to your questions.

Llewellyn encourages informative letters with each request so that our astrologers can address your specific needs. Be sure to give accurate and complete birth data including: exact time (a.m. or p.m.), date, year, city, county and country of birth. Check your birth certificate for this information. *Accuracy of birth data is important.* We will not be responsible for mistakes made by you. An order form follows for your convenience.

SERVICES AVAILABLE

COMPUTERIZED CHARTS:

APS03-119 Simple Natal Chart: Before you do anything else, order the Simple Natal Chart! This computerized chart print-out is programmed and designed by Matrix. Learn the locations of your midpoints and aspects, elements, and more. Discover your planets and house cusps, retrogrades and other data necessary to make a complete interpretation. **$5.00**

APS03-503 Personality Profile: This is our most popular reading! It makes the perfect gift! This ten-part reading gives you a complete look at your "natal imprint" and how the planets mark your destiny. Examine your emotional needs and inner feelings. Explore your imagination and read about your general characteristics and life patterns. Very reasonable price! **$20.00**

PERSONALIZED SERVICES:

APS03-101 Complete Natal Reading: This is our most complete reading! It not only gives you a computer chart and detailed reading, but also gives you a special interpretation of the trends shown in your chart for the coming year. Learn about your basic nature and personality traits. Discover the natural cycles you will go through in your life. When ordering be sure to include a descriptive letter about the things you would like the astrologer to discuss. **$125.00**

APS03-102 Detailed Natal Reading: Focus on one area in this special reading! With this reading you receive your natal chart plus a specific area of your choice. Whether it be career, love, finance or family, our astrologers will have no problem answering your question. Be sure to specify your focus area. Strictly confidential! **$65.00**

APS03-114 Compatibility Reading: Find out if you really are compatible with your—lover, spouse, friend or business partner! This is a great way of getting an in-depth look at your relationship with another person. Find out each person's approach to the relationship. Do you have the same goals? How well do you deal with arguments? Do you have the same values? This service gives you the two natal charts plus a reading for each and how you interact. Succeed in all of your relationships! **$75.00**

APS03-108 Vocational Guidance Reading: Find your vocational calling! Learn where your career potential is and how you can attain satisfaction in your work. Includes a natal chart plus an interpretation focusing on your career. Give details of work history (résumé) and outline of training and talents. **$50.00**

APS03-132 Lucky Numbers & Dates: Do you play the lotteries? Bet on horses? Make trips to Vegas? This reading will determine the best numbers and dates based on specific planets, degrees and other indicators in your own chart. Learn what numbers are best for you! **$80.00**

APS03-507 Life Progression: Discover what the future has in store for you! This incredible reading covers a year's time and is designed to complement the Personality Profile reading. Progressions are a special system with which astrologers map how the "natal you" develops through specified periods of your present and future life. We are all born into an already existing world and an already existing fabric of personal interaction. Use this report to discover the "now you." **$30.00**

APS03-505 Ultimate Astro-Profile: This report has it all! Receive over 40 pages of fascinating, insightful and uncanny descriptions of your innermost qualities and talents. Read about your burn rate (thirst for change). Explore your personal patterns (inside and outside). Examine the particular pattern of your Houses. The Astro-Profile doesn't repeat what you've already learned from other personality profiles, but considers often neglected natal influence of the lunar nodes plus much more. **$50.00**

APS03-506 Personal Relationship Interpretation: Perhaps you've called it quits on one relationship and know you need to understand more about yourself before you test the waters again. This interpretation will tell you how you approach relationships in general, what kind of people you look for and what kind of people might really rub you the wrong way. **$20.00**

APS03-500 3-Month Transit Report: Know the trends of your life—in advance! Keep abreast of positive trends and challenging periods for one of the three specified timeframes. Transits are the relationships between the planets today and their positions at the moment of your birth. They are an invaluable aid for timing your actions and decisionmaking. The Transit Forecast begins on the first day of the month you indicate. Be sure to specify present residence for all people getting this report! **$15.00**
APS03-501 6-Month Transit Report: See above. **$30.00**
APS03-502 1-Year Transit Report: See above. **$50.00**

APS03-110 Horary Reading: Learn the answer to a personal concern! The Horary Chart answers questions about choices of conscious significance. This reading uses this amazing chart to answer a question that has high emotional impact on you. Be sure to record the exact time and location when asking the question, so our professional astrologer can make an accurate interpretation. **$50.00**

APS03-109 Relocation Reading: Change your luck by moving to a different city! Find out which areas are best for making more money, finding true love or attaining fame. Specify up to three cities at least 100 miles apart and we will analyze their potential for you. If you don't pick three, we will recommend three general areas according to the interests you specify. Your present location may be one of your three choices. **$75.00**

APS03-131 Solar Return Reading: The perfect birthday gift! This is a special predictive reading based on the Sun's return to your exact natal position. Give location where you will be on your birthday (within 72 hours). **$65.00**

APS03-117 Fertility and Family Planning Service: Tune into your personal cycles to anticipate when is the best time to plan a family. This service has been used successfully by thousands of women who either want to have a child and have been unsuccessful using other methods, or for those women who want a more natural form of birth control. **$25.00**

APS03-113 Electional Chart: Choose the best time for all of your ventures. The electional chart involves choosing the date to begin or end a deal. This date is chosen—and usually several alternatives are given—by comparing your natal chart with the transiting planets and the Moon's influences. Know when to: plan your wedding date, sign important papers, start a business, make a major purchase and much more. Be sure to fully describe the event and time you want to schedule. **$50.00**

Astrological Services Order Form

Complete order form with accurate birth data plus your full name for all services.

Service name and number_____

Full name (1st person)_____

Time_____ ☐ a.m. ☐ p.m. Date_____ Year_____

Birthplace (city, county, state, country) _____
_____

Full name (2nd person)_____

Time_____ ☐ a.m. ☐ p.m. Date_____ Year_____

Birthplace (city, county, state, country)_____
_____

Astro knowledge: ☐ Novice ☐ Student ☐ Advanced

Include letter with questions on separate sheet of paper.

Name_____

Address_____

City_____ State_____ Zip_____

Make check or money order payable to Llewellyn Publications, or charge ($15 minimum):
☐ Visa ☐ MasterCard ☐ American Express

Account Number_____ Expiration Date_____

Day Phone_____Signature_____

☐ **Yes!** Send me my **FREE** copy of the *New Times*!

Mail this form and payment to:
Llewellyn's Personal Services, P.O. Box 64383-901
St. Paul, MN 55164-0383. Allow 4-6 weeks for delivery.

Heaven Knows What • Grant Lewi

Easy, fast and amazingly accurate! What better way to begin the study of astrology than to actually do it—while you learn! Draw and interpret your own horoscope, the horoscopes of others, and immediately test astrological principles at work! It's so incredibly simple with this time-tested book.

Heaven Knows What contains everything you need to cast and interpret a complete natal chart without previous experience, training or tricky calculations. Grant Lewi interprets the influence of every natal Sun and Moon combination, and describes the effects of every major planetary aspect in language designed for the modern reader. His readable and witty interpretations are so relevant that anyone will enjoy this easy-to-read book.

Astrology for the Millions • Grant Lewi

It's back! Like its companion volume *Heaven Knows What*, *Astrology for the Millions* enables you to cast a complete, professional horoscope within minutes, without complex mathematical calculations or a computer. But *Astrology for the Millions* goes a step further. It shows you how to apply astrology to your daily life.

With one of the best introductions to transits ever written, this book provides all of the interpretive data necessary to project your chart ten years into the future. Discover major critical times that are to come so you can make the correct decisions. Explore transits that have already occurred and bring new insights into the difficult times of the past. Order *Astrology for Beginners* today, and bring some light into the future!

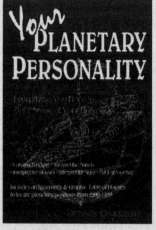

Your Daily Guide to the Heavens

Llewellyn's 1993 Astrological Calendar will guide you through the year with ease.

Forecasting during the year is easy with **Llewellyn's 1993 Astrological Calendar**. This famous full-color calendar is a remarkable reference for astrologers and non-astrologers alike. Each month gives personal horoscopes with rewarding and challenging dates. There are also major daily aspects; important lunar data including the Moon's phase, sign and void-of-course; a handy ephemeris and the best fishing and planting dates.

Llewellyn's 1993 Astrological Calendar also features important articles on vacation and financial planning, lunar gardening, lunar activity, political trends, celestial phenomena for the year and a comprehensive introduction to astrology for the beginner.

Anyone who has the slightest interest in astrology will enjoy this heavenly calendar. It is a must for plotting all yearly zodiacal signs. Order this beautiful calendar today!

**0-87542-902-5 ★ Full-color ★ 10" by 13" ★ $9.95
Please use order form on last page.**

SUPER DISCOUNTS ON LLEWELLYN DATEBOOKS AND CALENDARS!

Llewellyn offers several ways to save money. With a four-year subscription you receive your books as soon as they are published. The price remains the same for four years even if there is a price increase! We pay postage and handling as well. *Buy any 2 subscriptions and take $2 off! Buy 3 and take $3 off! Buy 4 and take an additional $5 off!*

Subscriptions (4 years, 1994-1997)

❑	Astrological Calendar	$39.80
❑	Sun Sign Book	$19.80
❑	Moon Sign Book	$19.80
❑	Daily Planetary Guide	$27.80
❑	Lunar Organic Gardener	$15.80

Order *by the dozen* and save 40%! Sell them to your friends or give them as gifts. Llewellyn pays all postage and handling on quantity orders.

Quantity Orders: 40% OFF
1993 1994

❑	❑	Astrological Calendar	$71.64
❑	❑	Sun Sign Book	$35.64
❑	❑	Moon Sign Book	$35.64
❑	❑	Daily Planetary Guide	$50.04
❑	❑	Magical Almanac	$57.24
❑	❑	Lunar Organic Gardener	$28.44

Include $3.00 for orders under $10.00 and $4.00 for orders over $10.00. We pay postage for all orders over $50.00.

Single copies of Llewellyn's Almanacs and Calendars
1993 1994

❑	❑	Astrological Calendar	$9.95
❑	❑	Sun Sign Book	$4.95
❑	❑	Moon Sign Book	$4.95
❑	❑	Daily Planetary Guide	$6.95
❑	❑	Magical Almanac	$7.95
❑	❑	Lunar Organic Gardener	$3.95
❑		The Goddess Calendar	$9.95

Please use order form on last page.